A HISTORY OF THE OSTROGOTHS

Thomas S. Burns

A HISTORY OF THE OSTROGOTHS

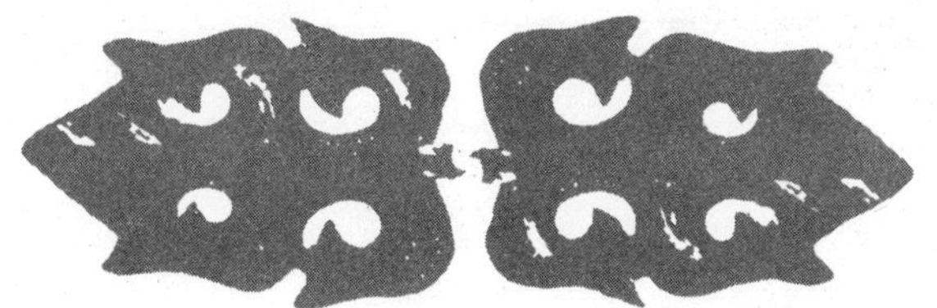

Indiana University Press
Bloomington and Indianapolis

First Midland Book Edition 1991

Copyright © 1984 by Thomas S. Burns

All rights reserved

No part of this book may be reproduced or utilized in any form or by any means, electronic or mechanical, including photocopying and recording, or by any information storage and retrieval system, without permission in writing from the publisher. The Association of American University Presses' Resolution on Permissions constitutes the only exception to this prohibition.

Manufactured in the United States of America

Library of Congress Cataloging in Publication Data

Burns, Thomas S.
A history of the Ostrogoths.

Bibliography: p.
Includes index.
1. Goths—History. I. Title.
D137.B93 1984 909'.07 83-49286
ISBN 0-253-32831-4
ISBN 0-253-20600-6 (pbk.)

2 3 4 5 6 95 94 93 92 91

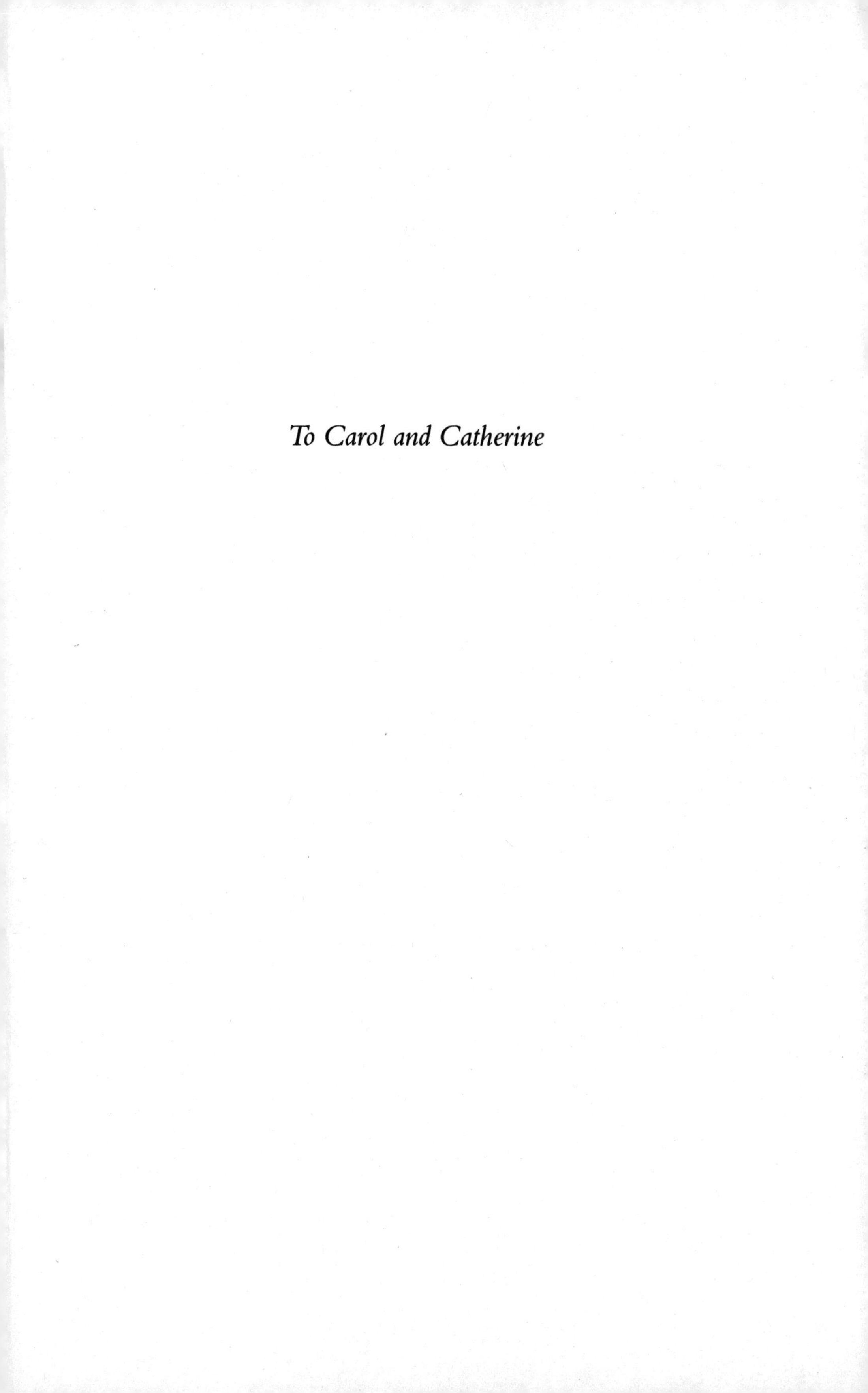

To Carol and Catherine

CONTENTS

ILLUSTRATIONS

Maps

Tables

Drawings

Figures

PREFACE

THE OSTROGOTHS encountered many different languages in their long search for security and prosperity, but, with a little Latin, a German could make his way in the Roman world. The modern academic explorer does not have to confront armed opposition, yet the linguistic barriers may be even more imposing. I have relied extensively upon summaries in Western European languages of Slavic language studies. When that was impossible or inappropriate, I turned to colleagues with both the linguistic skills and the kindness to help me.

During more than a decade of research, the staffs of countless libraries and museums have demonstrated true warmth and professionalism. The Kommission für alte Geschichte und Epigraphik in Munich and the Römisch-Germanische Kommission in Frankfurt, both of the Deutsches Archäologisches Institut, were my hosts during 1982. I thank them. I am especially grateful to George P. Cuttino, Herbert W. Benario, and Bernhard Overbeck for reading the final draft and discussing many aspects of the project. I also thank the Emory University Research Fund for assisting me in 1978 and again in 1982. Patricia Stockbridge's patience, good-naturedness, and expert typing of the manuscript were an anchor of sanity. Finally, I wish to express my gratitude to Sara Ann Lee, whose skillful drawings gave form to Ostrogothic artifacts.

I also wish to acknowledge my debt to several authors and publishers for the use of the following illustrations: Figures 1, 2, 3, and 4 are from John C. Kent, Bernhard Overbeck, and Armin v. Stylow, *Die römische Münze* (Munich: Hirmer Verlag, 1973) and are reproduced with the permission of Bernhard Overbeck. Figure 5 appeared in Kurt Horedt and Dumitru Protase, "Das zweite Fürstengrab von Apahida (Siebenbürgen)," *Germania* 50 (1972): 174–220, and is reproduced with the permission of *Germania*. Figures 6, 14, 15, 16, and 17 are from Volker Bierbrauer, *Die ostgotischen Grab- und Schatzfunde in Italien* (Spoleto, 1975), and are reproduced with the permission of the author. The photographs in figures 7, 10, and 11 are compliments of the Staatliche Münzsammlung in Munich. The photograph in figure 8 is compliments of Bernhard Overbeck and Hirmer Verlag. Figure 9 is reproduced from Max Martin, *Die Schweiz in Frühmittelalter* (Bern,

1975), with the permission of the author. Figures 12 and 13 are from Gyula Lásyló, *The Art of the Migration Period* (Coral Gables: University of Miami Press, 1974), and are reproduced with the permission of the publisher.

INTRODUCTION

The Ostrogoths developed as a people over the course of at least three centuries of direct and indirect contact with the Roman Empire. In essence, Rome nourished Gothic civilization throughout a long life and ultimately destroyed and buried her mature creation. There were others who left imprints on the evolution of the Ostrogoths, but their contributions were subtler and often shortlived. On the other hand, the Roman world was unavoidable and, as far as the barbarian Goths were concerned, truly eternal. The Ostrogoths never developed a refined sense of ethnicity or territoriality despite their history of warfare and prolonged contact with Huns, Sarmatians, Romans, and others across a broad spectrum of time and events. Nevertheless, by the end of the third century, the Greuthingi, the earliest grouping of those peoples destined to constitute the Ostrogoths, were identifiable to Roman authors as a discrete assemblage of Germanic peoples.

During the fourth and fifth centuries, the Ostrogoths emerged as serious rivals to Rome for control of the lower and middle Danubian areas. Their original homelands to the east of the Dniester River gradually became untenable after the arrival of the Huns around A.D. 375. Following the Hunnic defeat of their king Ermanaric, whose efforts were primarily responsible for expanding the Greuthingi into a larger confederacy, the Ostrogothic peoples split. Some sought safety in the Crimea and ultimately served within the allied ranks of the Byzantine Empire. A few fled to Roman soil with a royal prince and his warlords, partly non-Ostrogoths. They played a key role in the decisive battle against the Romans at Adrianople in 378. Most, however, remained behind, on or near their homelands, and became reluctant members of the Hunnic Empire. The exact whereabouts of the Ostrogoths during the late fourth and first half of the fifth centuries is shrouded in darkness. Not a single Roman author reported direct contact with their settlements lying somewhere beyond the Danube. The Romans knew little more than that at least some of their leaders occupied the highest levels of government within the Hunnic world, directly beneath the Hunnic leadership itself. Romans also experienced firsthand Ostrogothic and Hunnic raids into Roman territory. Indeed, thousands of Ostrogoths died alongside Attila at the Catalaunian Fields in the great Roman-Visigothic victory of 451. In 455, the main body of Ostrogoths fled the collapsing and brutal Hunnic dominion, and they were received as settlers on Roman soil in modern Yugoslavia. During the next thirty-four years, the Eastern Empire and the Ostrogoths were entangled in a series of complex attempts to secure the Balkans for Rome and find permanent lands for the Ostrogoths. Moreover, Rome sought to integrate the Ostrogoths into the administrative and military system traditionally used to monitor Roman federates.

By 489 the emperor Zeno and the Ostrogothic king Theodoric the Great were hopelessly at odds, and the Balkan provinces were in chaos. Ultimately Zeno and Theodoric decided that Italy afforded them both an opportunity to achieve their diverse goals. And so the final phase of Ostrogothic history began as a desperate trek to Italy during the late autumn and winter of 489–90. In Italy, Theodoric sought to stabilize his newly established kingdom and to devise a program through which the indigenous Romans and the Ostrogoths could coexist peacefully and productively under the aegis of the Amalian dynasty. His efforts produced the most successful symbiosis of barbarians and Romans in contemporary Europe. Certainly not everyone enjoyed prosperity, nor did all Romans or Goths desire such a relationship; however, there was no viable alternative, as many soon realized. The weaknesses in Theodoric's vision were already painfully apparent even before his death in 526. Gothic and Roman tensions and frustrations mushroomed under his feeble successors until finally the armies of Justinian brought an end to the Ostrogothic Kingdom and the Ostrogoths as a people. The struggle took the better part of two decades before the final Gothic surrender in 554, and by then Italy lay prostrate. Beyond Italy to the east, in lands once disputed between the Byzantines and the Ostrogoths, the Lombards were already restless.

This book attempts to survey the Ostrogoths throughout their eventful history as broadly as the sources permit. Certainly the history of any society should not stop with an accurate political narrative of leaders, migrations, and warfare, yet the standard histories are hardly more than biographies of Theodoric the Great. Despite our efforts, however, the upper ranks of society will always emerge most clearly from the historical panorama. The personalities of noblemen and monarchs alone affected those events recorded by the ancient authors. Yet the lower elements of society experienced equally profound pressures and resolved considerable problems during their various perambulations. Their lives also demand our attention, even if we remain bound by our sources to approximation and must deal with them only as groups rather than as individuals. A synthesis of all our sources, both archaeological and literary, alone offers any hope of evaluating the forces at work upon these men and women. Nevertheless, they continue to appear as if living behind a translucent screen. Against a general background of such conceivably mundane problems as dietary patterns, housing, manners, dress, and even the symbolism of the supernatural, the dilemmas of kings and emperors stand in sharper relief.

Combining archaeological data and the Greco-Roman literary sources can never produce a truly uniform and consistent historical vision. In essence, the physical remains and the traditional documentary records offer solutions to different problems. Nonetheless, all the evidence points to the extraordinary force of the Mediterranean world upon all those to the north. A basic goal of *A History of the Ostrogoths* is to examine the long-term interaction between Rome and her Eastern Germanic neighbors through the study of the Ostrogothic experience. The literary sources provide a slender narrative, essentially of political and military events. Other sources long familiar to historians, such as inscriptions and coins, support the literary evidence but are too rare to create a sturdy fabric for history, especially for the lower classes. Archaeology alone affords opportunities to assess many major transitions and continuities within the period. However, the archaeological data for the *Völkwanderungszeit* simply cannot be forced into the confines of the chronology of political events. That is to say, physical evidence must at times speak to its own questions and thereby illuminate, often obliquely at best, areas traditional to historical inquiry.

The archaeological evidence explored in this book is either definitely Ostrogothic or can be safely assigned to people of Eastern Germanic stock present in areas generally attributed to contemporary Ostrogoths. Occasionally, comparative materials help to clarify significance and interpretation. These instances are clearly noted as comparative and suggestive throughout the text. The ambiguities of the archaeological data are somewhat less onerous after the Ostrogoths established their control of Italy. However, even for the Italian episode, without stamps of manufacture such as were once common on Roman pottery, there can be no certainty. The footnotes should erase any lingering doubts as to the complexity of the problems of ethnicity and dating. Moreover, the notes reveal that others have not hesitated to press Ostrogothic claims to this item or that site. Usually scholarly restraint must and does prevail for all investigators. For example, every historian would surely like to know the locations of Ostrogothic settlements between the defeat of Ermanaric in 375 and the Ostrogoths' relocation on Roman soil in 455. Although the archaeological record clearly reveals the presence of Eastern Germanic peoples at this time in various areas of modern Romania and Hungary, the inquirer can only assume that many of these finds reflect developments among the Eastern Germans under Hunnic domination. Attempts at precise ethnic identification are at best tenuous. Nonetheless, these limitations do not preclude discussing the context of the overall conditions molding Ostrogothic society during these troubled decades. After all, some of their nobles were verifiably members of the Germanic élite ruling for the Hunnic Empire. Thus archaeology can provide a picture of the forces at work among the Ostrogoths even though the specific artifacts in question cannot usually be assigned to any one people. Indeed, we should not be so intent upon traditional tribal associations, since the very identity of the Ostrogoths and their principal rivals, the Gepids, was not rigorously defined.

One final note: this study is a history of the Ostrogoths, not of the Late Roman Empire. Nor is it an archaeological survey; rather, it is a history based on a synthesis of traditional sources and relevant archaeological materials. The emphasis on the Ostrogoths is clear and deliberate. Roman developments set the stage for much of Ostrogothic history, but only in that respect do purely Roman events and personalities enter the narrative. The Ostrogoths merit their own history.

ABBREVIATIONS

Ber. RGK	Bericht der römisch-germanische Kommission des deutschen archäologischen Instituts
CFHB	Corpus Fontium Historicae Byzantinae. Ser. Berolinensis
C.I.L.	Corpus Inscriptionum Latinarum
M.G.H.	Monumenta Germaniae Historica
M.G.H., A.A.	Monumenta Germaniae Historica, Auctores Antiquissimi
P.G.	J. P. Migne, Patrologiae cursus completus, series graeca
P.L.	J. P. Migne, Patrologia Latina
R-E	Realencyclopädie der klassischen Altertumswissenschaft
Settimane di Studio	Settimane di Studio del Centro Italiano di Studi sull'Alto Medioevo

A HISTORY OF THE OSTROGOTHS

1

Rome and the Northern Barbarians

ROME AND THE northern barbarians responded to each other long before the earliest Teutons first glimpsed imperial eagles. The Gallic sack of Rome in 387 B.C., immortalized in Livy's *History*, confirmed earlier Greek accounts of the domination by wild and bellicose Celts of Europe north of the fragile Mediterranean littoral communities. But the principal challengers to Rome for the next three centuries were other urban civilizations in the Mediterranean. Rome fought against Pyrrhus, Carthage, Philip, and Mithridates, until finally Pompey the Great conquered most of the remaining foes of Rome. Even the pirates lurking in bypassed coves were crushed. Thus, when Julius Caesar led his legions into Gaul in 58 B.C., the military outcome was not so surprising, but culturally Rome was far less coercive.

Roman imperialism during the late Republic fed a growing desire among all classes for quick material advancement. Among the senatorial aristocracy, the greed for wealth and, with it, power was insatiable. Pompey was without peer in "investment procedures," although others, like the young Brutus, revealed boundless pecuniary cruelty.[1] In the context of unchallenged military superiority and rampant profiteering, Pompey and his contemporaries preferred client kingdoms to direct rule. Client states paid tribute without the expense of Roman troops or governmental officers. The indigenous customs and systems of government went on undisturbed. Local unrest, even if caused by rapacious Roman agents, was a local matter for the client to solve alone. Obviously, problems arose. As kings toppled or their subjects rebelled, Rome gradually fashioned mechanisms for supervising and supporting clients, at times bringing them into the provincial system with its more direct controls. Just as Rome forged her military organization in the Mediterranean world, so too did she rehearse her governmental responses to new conquests. Caesar and his successors carried both the Republican military system and political attitudes into their dealings with the barbarians, who responded as best they could to such overt challenges to their societies. In reality, barbarian society had already begun to adapt to the influence of the Greco-Roman world long before Julius Caesar.

As Caesar himself pointed out in his memoirs on the Gallic campaigns, Roman wares and diplomatic maneuvering long preceded him.[2] His famous tripartite division of Gaul was a reflection, a mirrored image, of Roman influence still traceable in the archaeological data. The evidence is conclusive: the closer to Rome or its Mediterranean Empire, the more highly developed the socioeconomic stratification. Especially in southern Gaul, just north of Roman territory, the struggle for political power over regionally defined Celtic groups often narrowed to a few families or at times individuals competing for preeminence. Certain *oppida* had emerged as economic foci of regional and extraregional exchanges often involving Roman wares, primarily ceramics, as, for example, Bibracte among the Aedui.[3] In general, however, the Celtic world did not need any particular product obtainable only from Rome. On the other hand, political coordination and stability were almost entirely absent among the Celtic peoples. An alternative to endless feuding was Roman support, hence the title *amicus populi Romani*.[4] Rome, preoccupied with her eastern adventures, was a sleeping tiger. Until Julius Caesar's campaigns, the Celtic communities profited painlessly from Roman power. The pro- and anti-Roman sentiments and factions aroused by Caesar resulted from the intensification of Roman-Celtic interactions when the tiger awoke and turned around.

In the past, Roman support might have consisted of a title and gifts to selected leaders to help them enhance their personal following. There was no threat of Roman intervention or coercion. Now Caesar added Roman arms and thereby destroyed the equilibrium of the Gallic tribes forever, but he did not rush to impose a Roman culture or government upon his clients. That was unthinkable unless all attempts at governing through the control of existing families and customs failed. No Romans flocked to Gaul. There was never a concerted effort to colonize, and as a result Celtic roots continued to grow beneath a civilization that was probably as thoroughly Romanized by the end of the second century A.D. as any beyond Italy. With the sole exception of Dacia, where Rome did sponsor a colonization program, the same pattern of building on existing structures until they broke down was the basic Roman approach to empire from the Black Sea to Caledonia. Celtic and Roman cultures meshed remarkably well as Rome ultimately built provinces upon Celtic *civitas* units and offered the upper classes a chance to participate in a civilization far beyond the horizons of their ancestors. But what were the limits of Roman expansion and symbiosis with the Celtic world?

While Julius Caesar led his legions against Celtic *oppida* as far as the English Channel and even forayed to Britain itself, his mind focused on Rome and his reentry into senatorial politics. He could not remain too long in Gaul, yet he, like all Romans, was accustomed to conceptualizing peoples in discrete geographical and political units—a preconception common and so profound that Livy misunderstood the agonistic strife of Rome's own early centuries.[5] Despite Caesar's firsthand knowledge of the basic similarities of the Belgae and Germani, he always described the former as a Celtic group, whereas the Germans led by Ariovistus were a new people. There had to be an end to the Celtic world; it had to have a fixed geographical demarcation and distinctive cultural qualities. Caesar shared with Cicero and others an essentially moral view of history, with degrees of "hardness and softness" corresponding to qualities of "uncivilized and civilized."[6] Thus, when he composed his accounts, consciously or unconsciously, the Germans formed one pole of a bipolar pattern in which Rome, civilized and at times "soft," competed for Gaul (a discrete territory) with the "hard" Germans. These approaches still colored Tacitus's *Germania*, written a century and a half later.[7]

For whatever reasons, Caesar sought and achieved a coherent picture of his conquests and postulated a rational structure of tribal zones culminating in the Germans. His northern campaigns were complete. Suetonius, not Caesar, revealed the harsh realities of Roman conquest—slaves, desolation, and plunder paraded through the streets of Rome.[8] However tidy Caesar's view of the Germans and Celts, it does not readily agree with the physical remains of those peoples. The Rhine did not constitute a cultural boundary, for artifacts on either side are striking in their similarities rather than their distinctiveness.[9] If anything, the great river probably formed a boundary between various small regionalized groups on both sides of it.

There was a high degree of material and cultural unity across northern Europe. The topography of the great northern plain homogenized peoples; the river merely flowed through Celtic territory. Caesar had not reached a significant ethnographical demarcation.

Varus certainly could not return to Augustus the three legions lost in the Teutoburg Forest in 9 A.D., but it does not necessarily follow that a nightmare-ridden Augustus had to declare an end to Roman expansion to his successor Tiberius. After Rome had regrouped her armies and thereby reconstituted a striking force on the Rhine, she resumed offensive maneuvers but never again reached a stage where a province was planned for transrhenish Germania. Indeed, the Rhine-Danube frontier was imposed by historical accident, not by the rigorous policy of Augustus or his successors. That was especially true in the rugged area of the headwaters of both great rivers. Between modern Mainz and Regensburg, approximately, there were at least five phases of lines of construction before the end of the first century. The provinces of Germania inferior and superior were created circa A.D. 85.[10] Once Domitian and Trajan launched their Dacian wars and Dacia became a province (A.D. 106), the urgency of a better solution to the frontier rekindled Roman vigor. Marcus Aurelius attempted to make his dream of Marcomannia a reality but failed.[11] In fact, the Roman practice of manipulating Celtic chiefs and supervising them with Roman personnel should have worked as far as the Elbe and the Carpathian Mountains, where the evidence suggests that the Celtic world and its influence finally waned and became negligible.[12] Militarily, the mountains of central Europe were more defensible than the Rhine and Danube, but there is no evidence that Rome actively sought defensible lines. The Romans excelled in governing preexisting units and seem to have sought control through governmental supervision and modification more than logistically superior defenses. The great rivers were never the sacred boundary of imperial Rome, not even in a military sense; witness, for example, Constantine I and the transdanubian enterprises in what had been Dacia,[13] or the watchtowers and fortified landing places of Constantius II and Valentinian I.[14] Yet by the middle of the second century a linear frontier did exist, even if it was not sacrosanct. Why?

Perhaps Varus had lost something after all—time. Already in A.D. 9, Augustus felt the weight of provincial government, but for him that meant primarily the efficient conduct of basic operations through a handful of Roman governors with their household staffs. There were many other demands on imperial leadership and military capacity. Claudius added Britain, Thrace, and Mauretania, but Roman armies under Cerialis, Frontinus, and Agricola had to return "Roman peace" to the rebellious isle, and Mauretania remained troublesome for centuries. Domitian and then Trajan fought the Dacians, foes too of Augustus, and elsewhere found their attentions diverted, their energies dissipated. The East could always occupy a restless commander. While Rome looked eastward, the fruits of Romanization ripened in Gaul, Raetia, Noricum, and Pannonia, in fact, everywhere north of the Alps. The proud citizens of such provincial cities and towns as Augusta Vindelicum (Augsburg) in Raetia no longer saw themselves on the front line.[15] They would no longer accept the role of spearhead in a gradually radiating zone of Roman control. Their assets, trade, roads, and, indeed, lives were nurtured by Roman civilization, and they required a realignment of priorities.

Hadrian understood. Once while on one of his countless journeys, an old woman approached, seeking the ear of a tired and perhaps more irritable than usual Hadrian. He shouted her away. "I have no time." She replied, "Then be not a king!" Hadrian paused to listen; there was no relief from the burdens of office.[16] Perhaps the vignette is a rhetorical flourish invented by Cassius Dio, but the story it tells and the emperor it depicts are accurate. Hadrian altered Roman policy toward the barbarians because of new demands within the empire. To that end he manipulated barbarian groups into safe client relationships and actively intervened in their internal affairs, even so far as to support candidates for kingship.[17] His great wall in Britain and that in Germany across the salient between the upper Rhine and Danube were, in final analysis, disasters. In both cases the ramparts cut across feeble ethnic zones and manifested a finality of separation. Whereas before few people lived in the areas beyond the walls, soon the demarcation, with its control points and logistical systems, attracted barbarian groups. Irresistible social and economic interaction as well as the everpresent military threat forced various groups to unite ever more tightly into confederacies.[18] Great walls seem to have accelerated these developments, but everywhere along the newly formalized frontier, the same pattern imposed itself.

The pendulum of change marking the state of German-Roman relations seemed to pause. In fact, what appears as the era of the *pax Romana* was an age of equipoise along the northern periphery of the empire. As the Antonines sought to control the frontier more precisely than before, the distinction between *Romania* and *barbaricum* assumed a sharpened geographic focus parallel to the prevalent literary image of barbarians as cultural assassins. Roman policy reflected, in stone, concrete, and stockade, a deep fear of instability. Stone assuaged the troubled minds of provincials better than wood and turf. Therefore, defenses were upgraded where possible, although the barbarians had not yet mastered wood and turf, and as Tacitus related, they remained ignorant of besieging walls.[19] Roman paranoia culminated in the late fourth century, when walls thick enough to repel Alexander the Great were routinely thrown up against barbarians still admonished to "keep peace with walls" by one of their great chiefs, Fritigern.[20] Rome had once attacked, pursued, and intimidated her Germanic foes, Arminius notwithstanding, and the Germans fled, hopeful that the forest would act as a barrier against the Roman legions. Now, however, Varus and his era had no role in the world of the Antonines. The early brand of Roman peace, "desolation called solitude," was dead. In essence Rome assumed a defensive posture along a well-defined line of fortifications and only occasionally launched short punitive expeditions before returning to her permanent encampments. Nonetheless, the Roman army retained the initiative and would do so for at least two centuries.

Living on the Roman frontier afforded opportunities as well as dangers. Since the traditional Roman aristocracy saw very little to attract them or their investments into the frontier area and increasingly chose to isolate themselves culturally and topographically, the frontier was sustained more than elsewhere by the central government. By the end of the second century, the emperor had to compete with private landowners for scarce labor. The demographic surge in the West supported by Romanization, urbanization, and economic expansion slowed and in the third century was reversed. Disease and marginal agrarian productivity handicapped efforts to sustain tax revenues and military programs. Increasing reference to vacant lands in imperial legislation attests to the continuing problem and the impotence of the government to solve it. Along the frontier, German-Roman relations continued on a course charted by Rome—a troubled and at times pilotless society. Such fragmentation compelled those on the frontier to fend for themselves. Long before Constantine formally instituted the *limitanei*, the frontier had become a way of life.

An umbilical cord of highways, roadhouses, and support facilities connected the units on the *limes* to each other and to the rest of the empire. Solutions to such general problems as labor supply, trade, military recruitment, and communications developed in ways peculiar to the frontier area. This self-reliance was already apparent under the Severans, and, after the shadowy and chaotic fifty years before Probus and Diocletian, the same currents were present in the fourth century. In fact, the house of Constantine institutionalized the status of the frontier as a distinctive and undesirable zone with its policy of segregating the *limitanei* and settling barbarians as *laeti*. Thus when units of the *limitanei* were reemployed in the *comitatensis*, they were called *pseudo-comitatensis*. And so, too, Roman units were usually withdrawn completely when *laeti* took over the defense, and with them went many amenities, such as baths. By the end of the fourth century, the armies of Constantius II and Valentinian were heavily dependent upon Germanic recruits, and numerous Germans, perhaps subchiefs among their own people, rose to high levels of command. Centurions were often Germanic by birth and Roman by choice. Latin was still the language of command, but German or a barbarous blend of Latin and Germanic dialect was more familiar in camp.

As is well known, the Roman army supplied engineers, carpenters, brickmasons, and durable finished items such as tiles and bricks to the civilian communities sprouting nearby. Despite setting the construction standards, however, there were many vital chores the army would not do. Indeed, it was not always eager to repair aqueducts, roads, or even key defenses. The *limitanei* were soon reduced to simple farmer-soldiers, whose usefulness against a concerted attack was limited at best.[21] They were fine for chasing small bands of inquisitive German youths set on demonstrating their prowess, but they were poor engineers and builders. Their ineptitude is revealed clearly in the excavations of transdanubian Dacia and elsewhere. Yet even at the apex of efficiency in the second century, there was always a need for seasonal labor. Certainly by the end of the fourth century, seasonal labor was only a small part of the labor problem. Daily labor for hire was necessary for numerous odd jobs accompanying life on the frontier, for some time had to be set aside for camp duty. These services were employment opportunities for anyone in the area.

The Germans filled the vacancies in the civilian sector just as they volunteered for duty in the Roman army. During times of warfare, infrequent on most segments of the frontier for the two generations following the reestablishment of Roman internal stability under Diocletian and Constantine, the peaceful interchange was suspended. By midcentury, Ammianus reported that almost all barbarians along the Rhine lived in villages within ten miles of the river. They traded at Roman towns and camps, buying everything from jewelry to grain. Doubtless even a black-market weapon or two exchanged hands behind a market stall. German palates liked wheat bread better than the coarse barley of their traditional diet. They wanted to open the frontier and maintain free access to markets.[22] The Germans had learned to live with the frontier and became part of its very fabric—too much a part for emperors like Constantius II, Julian, and Valentinian I, who regarded integration as infiltration. That the imperial view was justified, at least in their eyes, strikes at the heart of the complex set of interrelationships and developments between Rome and her northern neighbors.

Perhaps because the frontier zone was peculiar—not a true image of either parental culture—there were lingering barriers to complete understanding. What did the soldier mean on an inscription he had erected stating: *Francus ego civis, Romanus miles in armis* (*C.I.L.*, III, 3576)? How else could Constantius II interpret the growing political and military power of the Quadi and Alamanni but as a threat to the very vitality of the empire? The Germans too had unresolved problems of interpretation. How could Rome welcome Germans individually on a daily basis and maintain a military system capable of such destruction? Why limit trade with them to specific points, often far distant from barbarian villages, as Constantine and his dynasty did? Who really represented Rome during her civil wars and dynastic divisions, when one side or another might call on her allies for aid? Obviously, in many elementary ways, Rome of the Mediterranean and the Germans of the northern forests always remained far apart, yet in the frontier zone itself, daily concerns merged societies. During the last half of the fourth century, antagonism escalated into violence and the everpresent military rivalry repolarized the frontier. The pendulum reversed. Investigation of the difficult questions just raised must wait.

The fragile sense of security achieved under Constantine the Great against barbarian threats and internal dissension evaporated within a generation. For Jerome, Libanius, and Rutilius Namatianus, the revolt of Magnentius (350–53) and the wanton destruction perpetuated by his defeated supporters and allied barbarians shattered the tranquility anew.[23] Once domestic order was restored, Constantius II launched a campaign against the barbarians. Constantius understood Germanic society well enough to realize the danger of unchecked military and political confederation. Perhaps he feared a time when the Germans would be so tightly organized that they could sustain a coordinated incursion, perhaps even defeat a Roman army in the field. Such foresight would have plagued his dreams far more than visions of Varus ever haunted Augustus. No one has ever claimed clairvoyance for Constantius, but he did strike blows at the Alamanni and Quadi designed to reverse their evolution.[24] Constantius and after him Julian and Valentinian I pursued the barbarians across the river frontiers, attacking and burning villages without warning and putting women and children to the sword. Perhaps the attacks on villages and families worked to accelerate the growing importance of warbands within the Germanic society, since the men were able to escape to the forest and survive. Captured chiefs were paraded like animals in triumphal procession, and men more obedient to Rome replaced them. The client system had to be tied more tightly to Roman policy and the chiefs forced to restrain their youths from trespassing on Roman soil. Such raids posed little military threat but fueled Rome's overwhelming concern for inviolability and security. If the Germans refused, then the lord of Rome himself would set the pace in killing until justice prevailed.[25] Violence and brutality again reigned along the river banks. A savage Roman peace replaced peaceful Romanization.

The German tribal confederations did threaten Rome but were not daggers waiting to be plunged into civilization's back. A heavy paranoia pervaded late Roman society. Constantius II lashed out against his own fear in almost demonic rage, and Valentinian suffered a fatal stroke over the insolence of Quadic ambassadors suing for peace but unable to promise all he demanded. Without whitewashing the German menace, it is still difficult to explain Valentinian's harshness or Jerome's almost apocalyptic warning on the basis of proven facts. The vision of barbarian destruction of Gaul bemoaned in Julian's address to the Athenians in October 363 was self-serving, if not a gross exaggeration.[26] What devastation there was, was largely confined to areas adjacent to the frontiers where brigands and barbarian bands held sway following Magnentius's revolt. The massive walls of even small watchtowers built under Constantius II and Valentinian were designed as much to calm Roman fears as to withstand German assault. If we may believe Ausonius in his *Mosella*, an elusive inner peace returned, at least for a few, as the Diocletianic-Constantinian program took on its ultimate form in a honeycomb of stoutly walled fortifications. The system stretched from modest forts and watchtowers on the frontier to heavily garrisoned towns in the interior with connecting roads, stables, granaries, and hostels. The soldiers of the *limitanei* were to hold on, islands of resistance disrupting enemy communications and supply while protecting their own stores for the inevitable arrival of the field armies. The beauty and security of the daily comings and goings of soldiers and bureaucrats left Ausonius rhapsodic.[27]

The constant interplay of perceptions and misconceptions affected all relationships between Rome and the northern barbarians. As long as Roman power dominated the contact zone, her desires molded the daily realities of frontier life. At times Roman internal problems and aspirations ran counter to the shared interests and opportunities drawing people together in the villages and crossroads of the frontier itself. Such tension between the heartland and its periphery is typical of frontier situations in general, but what is striking here is the fact that many of the troops manning Roman fortifications and in the field armies, although Germans, were willing to march against other Germans. Behind this apparent paradox lies the answer to several of our questions.

The old man whose epitaph troubled us several pages ago was a Frank and a Roman soldier and saw no conflict between these two loyalties, for they were not necessarily competitive. Essentially, being a Frank meant being a member of a family within a web of families, whereas loyalty to Rome was defined by adherence to the laws governing its inhabitants and their institutions. The Frankish warrior focused loyalty and intensified his emotions around the bonds of kindred or the warband, which often competed for his *trustio*. Rome dispersed loyalty through patriotism to an ideological pattern—*romanitas* for the upper classes, men like Ammianus Marcellinus. For the lower classes that could mean as little as a nod to the paymaster. The Roman commanders knew well the limits of German tribal loyalties and usually shifted troops away from their own villages. When they did not, they sometimes encountered an alerted foe or deserted villages. Thus, one of Constantius's attacks against the Alamanni was betrayed by his recruits. However, it should be noted that they urged peace, not ambush. Peace compromised neither the *Francus* nor *Romanus in armis*. Indeed, among the Germans serving in the Roman army as individuals, treasonable conduct was exceedingly rare.[28]

Our anonymous Frankish warrior turned Roman soldier literally came from another world, a world long converging on the highly institutionalized Roman civilization huddled around the Mediterranean Sea. Early Teutons perhaps never haunted the sacred groves of Germania; such primitiveness had nobility for Tacitus and modern romanticists but does not find record in history. Yet the evolution of Germanic groups from small localized units, often fleeting in duration and cohesion, to larger regional conglomerates under warrior nobilities, themselves at the head of ever stronger and more specialized warbands, and then to increasingly permanent confederations with complex ranking and advancing stratification, is the dominant sociopolitical theme among a variety of Germanic peoples. The Alamanni, Quadi, Gepids, Goths, and Lombards all traversed the same paths of social and political development. A similar convergence toward complexity is apparent in craft development, concepts of territory, art, religion, and virtually every aspect of society subject to historical investigation. Roman stimuli were not the sole forces molding Germanic societies, but they were usually the strongest, especially in the areas of institutionalization and social stratification.

Another source of influence was the cultural ganglion of central Asian groups in the area of south-central Russia. The artistic influence of the steppes was most prominent among groups in direct contact with this area, for example, the Ostrogoths in their early period. However widespread the influence, the Germans maintained a core of tradition locked in family structures, lore, and religion that although malleable remained vibrant and distinctive. The old rarely disappeared quickly, and as a result, absolute convergence never occurred with either the peoples of central Asia or those of the Mediterranean.

Despite the gap, or perhaps because of it, the direction of influence was predominantly toward Rome. The Germans were able students, whose modifications could sometimes rival their archetypes in refinement. The essence of the frontier situation with its radiating zones of influence and adaptation prepared the student long before he saw the classroom.[29] The attraction of the frontier was irresistible. The archaeological data support Ammianus's declaration that by the late fourth century most Germans along the Rhine lived within a few miles of the *limes*. Indeed, by the fifth century the barbarians along the upper Rhine, at least, lived in direct proximity to the Roman garrisons and towns across the river.[30] The flow of people and the pattern of growth reflected in the structure and longevity of the communities are beyond doubt. Never city dwellers in a Roman sense, the barbarians along the *limes* abandoned the perambulating village life of contemporary settlements along the Vistula. Once settled in fixed villages and linked in regional alliances through powerful noble families, they were forced to refine their concepts of territoriality. The Alamanni and Burgundians went so far as to delineate their subtribal regions by stone markers, which were also helpful in struggles between the large confederacies.[31] The Goths had words for local and regional land units. Families still lived on the land, but over the simple living units was stretched a thin fabric of political cohesion.[32] Ultimately the early Germanic law codes addressed some of the problems inherent in ownership, possession, usufruct, and seizure, but they did so only after a lengthy exposure to Roman law.

During the fourth century, differences between Germans and Romans on the frontier narrowed and gradually disappeared as the pressure of local recruitment into stationary units of the *limitanei* accelerated the acculturation begun by casual social and economic interaction. One sign of the merging of traditions and values on the frontier was the so-called chip-carved style in personal ornaments such as fibulae and belt buckles.[33] By initially using a lost-wax process, the artisan could produce metal jewelry with a faceted appearance, which when polished would play with sunlight, producing an almost diamondlike sparkle. Pieces produced in this manner became quite fashionable on both banks of the river frontiers and rendered functional items of Roman military dress into beautiful objects valued by the soldiers (mostly Germanic) serving in the Roman army as well as their relations still living on the far banks. Not surprisingly, the chip-carved style was peculiar to the frontier zone from the Black Sea to England, for the inhabitants of the interior, German or Roman, took little interest in this peculiar military dress. The frontier was rapidly becoming a composite civilization with its own tastes. Intermarriage had long ago tied even those families of "foreign origin" to the frontier, where women of Mediterranean stock were few indeed. Studies of language borrowings and personal names suggest that the frontier zone was evolving its own language based on a blending of vulgar Latin and the Germanic tongues with Latin in its purest form preserved in the technical vocabulary associated with the military command and bureaucracy.[34] The brutal wars of the late fourth century disrupted the acculturation process, but nothing could long prevent the continuing emergence of a new and composite civilization.

By the opening of the fifth century, if not shortly before, the struggling new order reached a plateau in the "row-grave civilization." Taking its name from the grid pattern of its graves, all on an east-west axis, with the head to the west, the *Reihengräberzivilization* now appears to have evolved only along the upper Danube and Rhine.[35] After three decades of investigation, the general development of the style and its distinguishing characteristics are clear. The blending of traditions is readily apparent in the custom of burial with weapons and personal ornaments (Germanic) and in stone slab tombs, later often sarcophagi (Roman in origin). Besides such prominent features reflecting both traditions, many more subtle mergings are manifest in the jewelry and clothing styles themselves. In fact, it is the nature of the grave furnishing rather than the systematic orientation that truly reflects the unique characteristics of these people.

The chronology of the row-grave evolution is also instructive. The fusion did not occur until after the Germans had crossed the Rhine and settled in areas where the foundations of rapid acculturation dated back at least to the early fourth century. Here they encountered *laeti*, *coloni*, and resident Germanic military recruits as well as scattered elements of a purer Roman stamp, such as the inhabitants of the surviving *villae*. By the fifth century, the Roman villa culture was in retreat southward, until it had all but disappeared in northern Gaul by the reign of Clovis.[36] In the south, Roman urban and villa life sprouted anew, and from its bastions in Aquitaine and Provence it helped influence the culture of Merovingian Europe.[37] In the north, the row grave became the typical burial style throughout most of the Merovingian era. Christianity reenforced the east-west burial axis, even if it did not originally inspire it, but it discouraged depositing grave goods with the interred. Ultimately a fairly uniform cultural entity extended from the Elbe to the Loire.

Wherever German and Roman elements were cast into the crucible, an alloyed civilization resulted. While the *Reihengräberfeld* peoples transformed life in the comparatively peaceful north, the lower and middle Danube from approximately Vienna southeastward were convulsed in repeated spasms of invasion beginning in the wake of the Battle of Adrianople and extending into the seventh century. Hence, the East Germanic groups—Gepids, Visigoths, Ostrogoths, and minor northern peoples—pursued different solutions to the problems of settlement, government, and defense. They continued politics designed to achieve a balance with the Germanic elements carefully compartmentalized, at least in theory. The *Reihengräber* style of burial emerged among the Gepids and some Visigoths in southeastern Gaul only after a long period of Frankish and Alamannic contact. The Ostrogoths so far as is known never shared in this evolution.

Explosions of violence and hatred occurred, especially in areas where Roman authority had completely collapsed and the barbarian invaders were themselves only loosely united. The Suevic incursions and settlements in Spain documented by Hydatius and the Rugian activities in Noricum preserved in the *Vita Severini* are the best-understood cases in which near anarchy prevailed on both sides.[38] Britain might well be included in this group. Some hardship and occasional bloodshed accompanied the initial settlement period even in the smoothest transitions. Typical of the later type are most of the federate groups established on Roman soil under the rules of *hospitalitas*, in which a legal fiction surrounded the guest-host relationship originally devised for the temporary billeting of troops. The Visigoths and Ostrogoths were such guests. The *hospitalitas* system brought the leadership of both societies together and eventually involved the lower classes in shared problems of agriculture and economic interchange. The Vandals in Africa proved too rapacious for the *hospitalitas* system to withstand, but in southern Gaul and Italy, under Odovacar and then the Ostrogoths, and most harmoniously in the areas settled by the Burgundians in southeastern Gaul and Switzerland, the pairing of barbarian and Roman did facilitate the transition to the barbarian kingdoms.[39] The legal framework of hospitality was a starting point in working out a manageable system of government and settlement that gave each partner the possibility of remaining distinct from the other.

In Visigothic Gaul and, later, Hispania, even ultimately in Vandal North Africa, a few wanted to bridge the cultural gap almost as soon as peace was restored. The majority hesitated; their children hesitated less, and their grandchildren lived in a different world. The variables were complex, differing from one area to another, yet certain factors seem to have been prominent everywhere: among them, the degree of cooperation between nobilities; the religious development of the barbarians; the survival of elements of the Roman army or bureaucracy; the acceptance of Roman models for displaying personal prestige; the willingness of the barbarian lower class to return to their agrarian habits; and the monarchy's effectiveness in controlling and redirecting the nobility and the warbands surrounding them. The list could be extended, and many factors played demonstrable roles in affecting the synthesis of the barbarian successor states, particularly the Ostrogothic Kingdom.

Not all members of any barbarian society responded in the same way to the evolution of Germanic-Romano civilization. As was frequently the case among American Indian groups in contact with Europeans, some Germans clung more tightly to their ancient customs and traditions, while a few, especially the nobility, saw Roman civilization as a cornucopia. The latter quickly adopted Roman ways of dress, symbols of prestige and power, and often intermarried. In part, the nobility was simply responding culturally to the tasks of multiethnic government over the remnants of a highly sophisticated urban civilization unlike anything they had experienced before crossing the frontier. Among the Visigoths at the time of Ataulf, there may have been a conscious attempt on the part of some nobles and the royal line to disassociate themselves from the masses and follow a "pro-Roman policy."[40] Ataulf's talk of reestablishing a *Romania* instead of creating a Gothia may reflect a sharp reorientation of Visigothic policy, so sharp as to lead to his assassination and a new search for balance. After all, Roman emperors still sat in Ravenna and attracted the loyalty of the Orthodoxy in southern Gaul. Regardless of his political motives, Ataulf is typical in his early appreciation of the potential gains from symbiosis and the immense reservoir for assertive leadership preserved in Roman forms.

To the king came the pleas of dispossessed Roman landlords seeking redress and influence. Many Romans were only too happy to lend a hand to the new rulers, who desperately needed a respite from petitions and the demands of cities and merchants to maintain basic security. In many cases the Germanic coalitions led by kings like the Visigoth Ataulf dissolved shortly after the conquests, occasionally during actual campaigns! There was a lingering sense that kingship was unnecessary except for war, especially now that warfare again meant primarily rapine resisted only occasionally by guerrilla operations. And that was the very type of combat favorable to the chief and his warband rather than centralized command. Virtually every king, some having very recently emerged from ducal families, had to redefine kingship and government within the space of a few years, unless there was a sustained Roman resistance and thereby a continuing rationale for confederate cooperation. Many continued to see their positions in terms of familiar federate relationships, which emphasized the royal authority over the competing interests of the independent leaders of the warrior societies, i.e., the nobles and their bands of followers.

Childeric died in 482 and was buried in regal splendor but primarily in the costumes of a late Roman military commander.[41] This early architect of the Frankish monarchy had quickly accepted the fruits of Roman conquest. When compared to the contemporary finds from the *Reihengräber* cemeteries, his suggest a Roman warlord. Childeric held his bands together in confrontations with the surviving elements of the great field army of northern Gaul. Throughout the fifth century, Roman power in Gaul centered on the last Roman army still in operation there. Commanded in succession by Aetius, Count Paul, Aegidius, and Syagrius "king of the Romans," the very presence of a "Roman" force attracted Roman refugees from as far as Britain.[42] The Romans led by Syagrius and his predecessors were as Germanic as Childeric, who may have been as "Roman" in appearance as the "king of the Romans" himself. In 486, Clovis and his allies crushed Syagrius and so ended organized resistance and the military stimulus to kingship. Clovis tied Gaul together with new bonds, including Orthodox Christianity, but kept his sword sharp. The great problem of Frankish Gaul was not Roman subversion but political fragmentation. The Merovingian monarchs supplemented their government of family and personal followers with Roman techniques as well as bits and pieces of Roman statecraft and some Roman garrison troops.[43] However, tradition suggested that familial unity rather than political centralization was the bedrock of leadership—the Merovingian family remained supreme, and, for many, their bitter struggles were unrelated to the unity of the realm. The interplay between Roman concepts and Germanic traditions, formed in the context of the frontier, was relentless.

A sense of urgency permeated every decision made at the barbarian courts. Even if they had had a practice of careful deliberation, time was against them, for confederacies sustained on the march threatened to explode in the success of conquest. People were restless. Many sought a return to agriculture and the settled life of the village. For most Germans the walls of Roman towns held no promises, but few would have attributed their construction to gods and devils as did the Anglo-Saxon chronicle. Many Germans had had contact with Roman towns and fortifications on the frontier and had no fears or superstitions; rather, they sought soils suited to their skills. In the south, especially in southern Gaul and Italy, the *hospitalitas* system offered land, revenues, and labor. The aspiring nobility, initially, at least, dependent on Roman concepts of stratification and conspicuous comportment, could find solace near or in Roman towns with their still-functioning clerical and municipal institutions.[44] Not all nobles sought the heart of Roman culture, but a few even went so far as to have their children educated in the Roman manner. Whereas before their children were hostages, now they became honored guests courted by Roman worthies. Faced with complex problems of settlement, barbarian leaders institutionalized ad hoc decisions and practices. Almost before they could heave a sigh of relief, their kingdoms began to fly apart.

Before the invasions of the fifth century, the Germans reacted to their prolonged contact with Rome by increased political and military cohesion. Yet they remained confederates, not ethnically defined tribal nations. Beneath a political veneer, many aspects of society were still rudimentary and supple to Roman influence. The German conquerors continued to graft Roman vines long after they conquered Roman soil, because in a very real sense the Roman heritage was partly their own. Long accustomed to cultural borrowing, they raised few barriers to Roman civilization beyond an ability to wield a sword. Their hatred was aimed at the Roman army and the agents of the state directing it against them. Once those aspects of Roman society had disintegrated, emotions of hatred faded into oblivion and models of the very government once so despised asserted a renewed influence on Europe. Since Germania had existed only in Roman minds, it could never be revived by the Germanic Kingdoms. Try as he might,

Jordanes, the only German historian, could not write an equal and distinct history for the Goths as a parallel to his *Romana*.

A sustained vitality of German and Roman within a controlled setting, in which each one's strengths were preserved and nourished by the other, was a dream for Cassiodorus and Theodoric the Great. Like all dreams it was fragile, and it dissipated with the dawn of reality. Yet when medieval men with vision dreamed of a better world, the shade of Theodoric and his dream, wrapped in myth, lingered.[45] Through sagas, superstition, and, occasionally, a written word, the Roman legacy and the vitality of the late Roman-Germanic interaction influenced the thoughts of Charlemagne and others throughout the Middle Ages.

2

The Presettlement Phase

THE ENTIRE HISTORY of the Ostrogoths began and ended within the context of Roman-German relations, but much is still unknown, especially the earliest stages of development. The very name Ostrogoth is a product of the late fourth and early fifth centuries, long after profound changes induced by Roman contacts had become accepted as Gothic. As we drift ever deeper into the mist surrounding the origins of the Goths, traditional landmarks, once thought so secure, fade into oblivion. Despite a century of keen historical investigation and archaeological excavation, the cause and nature of the beginning of the *Völkerwanderung* challenge the inquirer as much as ever. Perhaps we have learned more about ourselves and our limitations than about the Goths—so difficult is the task, made no easier by still-active nationalism seeking to claim Gothic glory. If history is limited to its classic attention to war, politics, and intellectual development, then prior to the mid-third century the Goths have no history. Yet they did exist, far from Roman observers, and at least by the end of the first century A.D. a people called Goths lived somewhere in northeastern Europe.

Along the extreme northeastern periphery of the Roman-German world, beyond the Elbe, Roman wares were scarce, and very few Roman traders ever set foot. There people lived a simple life linked with the cycles of the seasons. A sparse population roved from site to site over the generations. Living in small groups of at most a few hundred, they perhaps assembled into larger groups only to invoke the gods.[1] Fairly distinctive patterns still exist in the archaeological record for large regions stretching southward from Pomerania to the Black Sea. The undulating ebb and flow of these regional cultural similarities demonstrates that even at the lowest level of political sophistication, a world of village and lineage, life changed. To say that life changed is almost a tautology, for obviously life itself is change. Yet the observable changes in the cultural zones of northeastern Europe are more significant, because they seem to have directional orientation, a progressive development along a southeasterly axis.

The area between the Baltic Sea and the Carpathian Mountains lying east of the Elbe was influenced by two dissimilar cultures at opposite ends, Scandinavia and the Roman Empire. Even along the Vistula, Roman material culture proved more pervasive than Scandinavian, but each contributed some items of practical value. For example, the peculiar bronze buckets discovered at Pollwitten attest to the Scandinavian influence, whereas the majority of urns and pottery that reveal any "foreign influence" are derivative of products found along the Roman frontier.[2] On the other hand, the Scandinavians followed a life more familiar to peoples of the Vistula than did the Roman garrison populations to the south. The Baltic Sea held the diverse population and linguistic groups in a relatively uniform cultural sphere. The people along the Vistula would have found many aspects of life in Gotland or in Sweden similar to their own—such basic qualities as diet, social development, and probably attitudes toward cult practice, even if not to exactly the same deities.[3] The bonds of family and the basic egalitarian associations within the warbands probably competed with and influenced the evolution of a rising nobility throughout the Baltic area. However, archaeology alone cannot usually penetrate into such conceptual early social developments, since no clear gradations in grave goods had yet occurred, and Roman written sources are almost useless when describing people they hardly knew and could scarcely understand.[4]

Some of the apparent movement southward seen in the changing archaeological record along the great river routes from the Baltic is a result of the growing impact of Roman influence the farther to the south the site was located, but equally important was the actual migration of families. The Roman world drew the small perambulating communities as if they were iron filings attracted to a magnet. Not all the parts of a village, perhaps not even all the members of a family, responded to the lure that reached northward along the great rivers of eastern Europe leading to the Black Sea. No vision of golden treasures sustained them; rather, they responded to simple yearnings for food and, more importantly, perhaps for leadership. What Rome unknowingly may have offered was the opportunity for a few men to acquire and secure the prestige necessary for new lines of leadership. Because of the increasingly militant surroundings, new leadership often developed within the context of the warbands as well as over family units undergoing almost constant regeneration. The royal families, important to the religious life of the people as seen in Tacitus (*Germania* 7), stayed behind. Perhaps they were too intimately associated with ancient cult sites to leave, but at any rate, regal leadership reemerged in the fourth century as a completely new and untested level of cooperation built upon the ducal nobility. The leaders of the scattered groups moving southeastward had unencumbered opportunities for creating new bonds among themselves.

The little known about the early Germans agrees with the anthropological data amassed during the twentieth century from critical and direct observation of primitive societies. The Germans held their groups together through family alliances cemented and extended through marriage, the exchange of gifts, and warrior societies with their own special ceremonies and responsibilities. The latter were enhanced by confrontations with other groups and later the Roman frontier. The Germans of the early migration had a bilateral kinship system with a probable effective range of a few hundred people. Their bilateral structure made possible rapid recovery of lost numbers and greatly abetted acculturation when outsiders were necessarily brought into the family.[5] Within families, the responsibilities were understood but unfortunately rarely written down and hence usually lost. So too the inner workings of the warrior associations remain largely unknown and unknowable. The effective zone of kindred action and response varied according to the circumstance: for example, oath-helpers really had to know the accused and so were limited to his closest kin, whereas a feud could involve the entire kindred.

Leadership in the village or region transcended familial bonds and sought to tie leaders together in special cooperation, often for warfare. Since marriage had finite possibilities at the level of regional alliance, gifts were typically exchanged whereby the leader could bind others to him through his unrivaled generosity, which could be repaid only with allegiance. The *comitatus* of Tacitus is an early example. Gift giving was limited only by the wealth of the giver and not by the physical limits of procreation and could thereby extend familial-like ties beyond the kindred. As such it was a basic bond within the warrior associations. Such alliances were temporary and could be extended only if the leader gave still more gifts and renewed the obligation of reciprocity through allegiance. In numerous societies around the world, the gifts are in effect loans, in which the recipient keeps only a share of the profits and ultimately returns the gift with "interest." Such is typically the case in Indonesia and New Guinea, where the traditional gift of pigs is gradually giving way to money.[6] Regardless of time or place, the object of such exchange is to secure a dependable and favorable response to leadership directives. The archaeological record of finds north of the Danube as far as the lower Bug River suggest that similar "gift giving" was an integral part of life, consciously manipulated by Rome whenever possible but stretching far beyond her borders. When Germanic groups encountered Roman clients and then Rome herself, the ensuing warfare favored the evolution of warbands that fused elements from both the familial and gift-exchange bonds into military units of increasing scope and duration.[7]

The Goths and others moved by families, sometimes individually, generation after generation, and once they had migrated they became newcomers, outsiders to the traditions of the new place. The sparse population could absorb a few, but if an entire kindred entered, they had to keep moving on or accept marginal lands.[8] Their bilateral kinship structure provided the elasticity for the rapid regrowth necessary to replace those remaining at every stop. The relative similarity of culture was a means of social diffusion. The pressure to maintain and rebuild the family combined with the desire for prestige beyond family to push a few southward toward new lands and the Roman world. Such a picture helps explain the flourishing of the Pomeranian-Mazovian culture (see Map 1) in the middle of the second century and its decline in the fourth, when grave fields became widely scattered, with poor grave furnishings.[9] The leaders and with them the most vibrant forces had departed southward.

The primary stimulus for this gradual migration was the Roman frontier, which increasingly offered service in the army and work for pay around the camps. Once Rome had regularized a presence north of the Alps and had pushed her influence across the Rhine and Danube, the peoples living far into the interior had to respond. They could not avoid the Roman world, which henceforth exerted a profound impact on their societies, especially their systems of government. Scandinavia itself responded to Roman goods but remained too distant and poorly organized to challenge Rome or feel the full impact of Roman material culture and institutions. The bits and pieces of

Map 1: East Central Europe

Germanic families left behind at every stage and the few men who put their women, children, and baggage into carts and traveled southeastward saw nothing. They perceived no challenges, especially from Romans they had never seen. Each merely went on living and striving for elusive personal goals, into which Roman concepts and materials progressively intruded.[10]

During the second century A.D., the movement and disruption of peoples gained momentum. No later than the reign of Commodus there was a general agitation and eruption across most of eastern Europe.[11] Along the periphery of the empire, groups such as the Getae and free Dacians pressed against the Roman frontier. Coin hoards buried in the late second century, from the northwestern Ukraine westward in an arc above the Danube through Moldavia and on into Hungary, attest to the widespread fear.[12] Panic routed reason as once-proud peoples buried whatever they could not carry and fled. Rumor fed upon itself until echoes were recorded in the annals of Roman history, but the armageddon was an illusion—the Goths were men after all. Although individually vigorous warriors, the Goths were too poorly organized for sustained warfare and were ready to learn from the people in the south. Two or three generations gave their vitality to the indigenous cultures, absorbing, abandoning, modifying, but not yet ready to lead.

The Goths as they were known in late Roman history were the product of the rapid acculturation taking place as they settled in the areas above the Black Sea. There they encountered civilizations with higher levels of technological sophistication than their own and accustomed to contact with Greco-Roman centers such as Olbia. The Bosporan Kingdom, straddling the straits between the Sea of Azov and the Black Sea, flourished as an entrepôt for trade with various peoples in the Crimea and Ukraine, including the Roxolani, Sarmatians, Scythians, and ultimately the Goths. Dealing in wine, fine jewelry, ceramics, and specialty items such as table services and exquisitely ornamented swords, the Bosporan merchants were important agents for disseminating Sarmatian, Turkish, Roman, and later Germanic goods.[13] Olbia and the communities of the Bosporan Kingdom experienced the violence of the third century in full force. Walls were breached, and repeated incursions threatened life itself, but some trade continued even during the bleakest hours. There was a Roman garrison at Olbia, at least until the end of the third century, after which inadequate repair projects began, using the broken remains of earlier splendor.[14] The same litany of destruction echoed over the cities of the Bosporus, but much of their prosperity returned by the middle of the fourth century, only to be crushed anew in the wake of the Hunnic invasions. By the sixth century, the Ostrogoths remaining in the Crimea figured prominently in the surviving Bosporan trade.[15]

When the Goths first appeared in the Ukraine, they met elements of the Cherniakhov civilization. Since the initial investigations conducted from 1899 to 1906, little concerning the Cherniakhov civilization has remained beyond dispute. The earliest authority believed that the characteristic artifacts began to appear in the second century; other contemporaries disagreed and thought that the third century was more secure.[16] More recently, several prominent Soviet scholars have argued for a pre-Slav early Rus relationship. Others reject the thesis of a Slavic connection and suggest one of a series of peoples culminating with some sort of Gothic overlordship no later than the fourth century.[17] The truth probably lies in the complex multiethnic fusion going on in this area from at least the end of the second century.[18]

What has passed as the Cherniakhov civilization seems best described as a peculiar collection of material items created under the sustained influence upon the indigenous populations of imported wares stemming from the general area of the Black Sea. Because the new groups coming down the rivers flowing southward were inherently inferior to those in the south in crafts and the rudiments of settlement, they readily adopted the standards of the indigenous population and made them their own.[19] Neither the immigrants nor the inhabitants of the small villages, long established along the rivers and bluffs, had much ethnic unity or coherent political organization: the Goths were probably bound together in small raiding bands, whereas the indigenous populations were clustered around their agrarian communities.[20] The Goths and everyone in northeastern Europe traditionally practiced a mixed agrarian-gathering-hunting existence and were ready enough to pause and plow. The climate imposed a certain uniformity of scarcity and plenty upon all and, without the barriers of ethnic perception, allowed the traditional ways to bend to those of zealous newcomers. Each dominant group gave something of itself to Cherniakhov before it too gave way. In short, Cherniakhov was the material legacy of a complex interlocking of traditions, some Roman, others northern, while still others had their roots deep in the rich soils of the Ukraine itself. Out of this crucible emerged numerous groups discernible to Roman eyes as distinct. The greatest among these was the Goths.

Little by little, groups of indigenous peoples throughout the area fell under Gothic influence as the Goths gradually assumed the preeminent role among the legatees of Cherniakhov civilization. In Wallachia, the Gothic imprint stamped itself into the fabric of life throughout the fourth century. As early as the time of Constantine the Great, the Romans could territorialize the peoples there into a *Gothia*.[21] By the middle of the fourth century, the Goths were particularly strong along the Buzan river. Pockets of indigenous culture lingered, but the heterogeneous Germanic groups absorbed most without much strife. In addition to the Buzan area, the Goths were dominant along the Danube itself.[22] The emerging picture is based almost entirely upon the archaeological record and clearly demonstrates the emergence of a Gothic (i.e., East Germanic) culture in which ethnic assimilation played a major role.[23] The Goths matured as a political entity simultaneously with their cultural evolution. They were forced to compete with other groups as soon as they settled in their vicinity. Roman clients and later Rome herself were worthy foes. Fortunately for the Goths, the disruptions along the imperial frontier combined with internal Roman discontent and political upheavals to provide the new Germanic groups a brief respite from coordinated opposition. During the interlude beginning with the succession of Commodus and lasting for almost a century, the Goths struggled to become what Romans had long thought they were—a territorialized political entity.

Once established along the Black Sea, the Goths clashed with Germans already there. Wars flared with the Marcomanni, Quadi, and others, especially the Gepids. The early struggles with the Gepids began a long rivalry, which ended only in the sixth century. Jordanes derived their name from *gepanta*, in Gothic "slow and sluggish," which the Goths used as a reproach. The troubled account in the *Getica* places the wars between the Gepids and Goths before the great mid-third-century invasions and pitted the "ever-alert" Goths under Ostrogotha against the boorish Gepids with Fastida as their king.[24] Ostrogotha is surely eponymous and the structural details anachronistic, but wars with other Germans probably did occur before the Goths ventured into conflict with Rome. Perhaps such confrontation among the Germans stimulated the growth of coalitions of warbands and other Goths as rivalries escalated and genuine animosities replaced traditional ignorance and childish fears. The breakdown of Roman control along the river frontiers and the clashes in the East with the Persians are well known and need no great elucidation. However, the Romans did not face the Goths or a Gothic-led coalition until at least the reign of Decius.

Roman coins perhaps reveal the true nature of the barbarian incursions of the third century as clearly as any other source, especially since so few contemporary accounts are extant after the end of Dio's history (and that preserved by his epitomizer Xiphilinus, writing in the eleventh century). Roman mints commemorated imperial victories over Germans throughout the third century in the traditional manner. Wars against recognized groups were specifically accorded particular recognition, as *Victoria Carpica*, for example. But the situation on the lower Danube was volatile: confederations of various groups shifted as new leaders emerged. Emperors celebrated numerous victories over these loose and temporary Germanic alliances. Such an occasion was customarily denoted on their coinage as *Victoria Germanica*, without giving any specific ethnic attribution to the conquered. Such general slogans were issued by almost every emperor from Pertinax onward. Ill-fated Decius celebrated a victory over the Carpi as well as a general *Victoria Germanica*. Gradually the incidence increased of victories over specific groups, but the first *Victoria Gothii* was not issued until Claudius II Gothicus. Next came an undated series under Aurelian followed by a *Victoria Gothii* under Tacitus. Probus is also represented by an undated *Victoria Gothii*. Constantine, of course, celebrated his Gothic wars with *Victoria Gothica*.[25] Thus the numismatic record suggests that around the middle of the third century, culminating under Claudius and Aurelian, the struggle for hegemony on the lower Danube produced the first lasting Gothic coalitions. Furthermore, the evidence confirms the scanty literary records attesting that an early Carpic-"free" Dacian confederacy, including some Goths, was gradually replaced by an alliance dominated by Goths. How did the great Gothic kings in the *Getica*, Ostrogotha and Cniva, fit into this picture?

The battles, sieges, and, in fact, all the known operational details of the campaigns of Decius, Macrianus, Claudius, and Aurelian took place in an atmosphere of large-scale raids and later invasions of Roman territory without any coherent barbarian strategy. Rome was too involved elsewhere to pursue a lengthy war of retribution in barbarian territory or to mount a concerted counterattack in the Balkans. As a result, the campaigns were usually small operations striking quickly to keep the barbarians off guard and disunited. Eventually Claudius and Aurelian systematically penned and captured starving bands in the valleys of the Rhodope and Haemus mountains. Cniva, traditionally considered as the preeminent Gothic strategist and slayer of Decius, must return to the shades of the half-forgotten heroes of myth. He and Ostrogotha served centuries later as personifications of Gothic greatness and perspicacity. The heroes of the third century were hard-bitten *duces*, who occasionally emerged at the head of one of the marauding bands bent on harvesting the booty of the Balkan countryside.

Although the Goths lived at some distance from the Roman frontier and had only infrequent contact with it, their leaders were important enough to receive annual gifts perhaps as early as 238, when Tullius Menophilus, commander of Moesia, attempted to detach the Goths from the Carpic alliance in separate negotiations with the Goths alone. Philip the Arab reportedly suspended payment, and war followed quickly. If Jordanes (*Getica* 89) is correct, Philip was grossly ignorant of the ramifications of his actions. In Germanic society one simply did not suspend gift exchanges without considerable provocation, for more than honor was at stake. Any realignment in exchange patterns weakened ties of leadership throughout the society and called for swift reprisal. At this stage in Gothic-Roman relations, the annual gift probably constituted only a small fraction of the total exchange network, but nevertheless Philip's cessation was an unnecessary irritant in an already explosive situation.

The Carpi continued to dominate the anti-Roman coalition consisting of themselves, Taifali, Astringi Vandals, Peucini, and Goths until 248, when the Goths assumed the hegemony of the loose coalition. Had Rome been able to concentrate her forces as under Trajan or Marcus Aurelius, she could have brushed the Germanic coalition aside, divided each group through selected recruitment into the army, and thrust loyal leaders into power. Internal chaos beset Rome under Maximinus just when external storms gathered on the frontiers. In the period 248–51, the Goths and other groups ravaged Roman soil, especially Dacia and Moesia. In 248 they besieged Marcianopolis. Philip's assassin and successor Decius (249–51) moved quickly, and with hastily assembled troops entered the Balkans to suppress a potential uprising of troops in favor of elevating Lucius Priscus, governor of Macedonia, to the purple and to crush the still-feeble Gothic incursions.[26]

Decius faced at least four distinct Gothic groups roving the highways in search of easy prey and supplies.[27] Except for Marcianopolis and, two years later, Philippopolis, the Goths avoided confronting Roman towns. The major garrisons at Marcianopolis and Philippopolis required elimination lest they freely disrupt supply efforts and force the Goths to stay together. Thrace was not yet the great granary it was to become in the eighth and ninth centuries after Byzantium lost Egypt and the Near East. In the third century, Thrace and Moesia held a prosperous rural society little changed by Roman contact.[28] The Goths had to disperse in order to find food, but as long as Roman arms controlled the passes in the Rhodope and Haemus ranges, the Goths were effectively penned. By the spring of 251, Decius had achieved several successes against the roving Germanic bands; in fact, both the Milanese and Roman mints commemorated his *Victoria Germanica*. The Goths survived the winter on supplies taken in Philippopolis and the ravaged countryside but were ready to return home. Decius decided to quicken the pace and attacked the consolidated remnants before they could escape. Believing that he was about to administer the final blow, he even stripped the passes of their garrisons. Stung by the death of his son in late 250 near Beroea, Decius hastened after the laborious Gothic wagons bearing their loot northward. In June 251, near the ancient town of Abrittus, Decius and his troops were ambushed in the swamp.[29] The emperor himself lay dead on the battlefield, his army routed, the key passes unguarded. However, the Goths and their numerous allies had had enough of Roman hospitality and continued their retreat, crossing the Danube in the vicinity of Durostorum.[30] Behind them lay a virtually defenseless Balkan peninsula, with Macedonia and Greece ripe for plunder (see Map 2). Eastward, the rich cities of Asia Minor held unknown wealth, if only the Bosporus had not stood as an obstacle.

Map 2: The Danubian Area

The Bosporus proved to be only a minor hindrance, for with the help of ships and sailors pressed into service from towns along the Black Sea, the Goths and others easily crossed the straits and launched repeated raids from 254 to 276.[31] The presence of the Goths released almost satanic violence within Roman society itself. For Gregorius Thaumaturgus, an eyewitness, the invasions turned Roman against Roman, even Christian against Christian. Although Gregory acknowledged the horror of seeing men hanged on the gibbet by the Germans, he saved his sharpest outcries for those Romans who not only guided the invaders but also used the cessation of order and government to cloak preying upon their fellow countrymen. If a Roman taken captive by the Goths somehow managed to escape, he might return to discover his property looted or seized. Some escaped Gothic enslavement only to be put on the auction block in Roman towns instead.[32] The Goths slowly pressed onward in a roughly circular route as they trampled from place to place across most of Anatolia searching for provisions.[33] Like a swarm of locusts, they could not return over the ground they had destroyed. In the Balkans and the cities along the coast of the Black Sea, the candle of civilization itself briefly appeared to be spent, but the flame sputtered and then revived.

In 267 Athens was sacked by the Herulians. P. Herennius Dexippus rallied the citizens and in a valiant effort freed his city and immortalized her resistance in his largely lost works, the *Historia* and the *Scythica*. The intensity of the struggle still strikes the visitor seeing the columns, temple fragments, and bits of statuary piled like cords of wood in the Herulian wall. The Byzantines were fond of a little vignette coming out of the Herulian scourge. The Herulians were about to set the torch to a vast pile of books in the captured city when one stepped forward, urging that "they should leave the Greeks something to occupy themselves in reading so that they would forget to exercise their armies and would be more easily vanquished."[34] The farther north the site, the more intense was the struggle. As barbarian expansion isolated each Roman community, the inhabitants first sought refuge behind their walls, many of them hastily repaired or built for the first time after centuries of neglect. One by one, Roman towns along the Black Sea fell, but, like Athens, many revived and continued on a lesser scale until the great disruptions caused by the Huns. Urban life along the northern and western coast of the Black Sea was weakened but endured.[35] The same pattern emerged further south, where no Roman city faltered, although some, such as Histria in the Dobroudja, were sacked three times before a diminished trading center and refuge was restored under Aurelian.[36]

The client system bordering the Danube and surrounding most of Dacia dissolved. Gallienus tried unsuccessfully to shore it up but could not. Some Germans entered the empire as brigands with the Goths, but others remained behind, seeking a respite from invasion. The Sarmatians, Roxolani, and Carpi ultimately sought and obtained *receptio*, were dispersed throughout the army, and took new homes behind the frontiers as peasant-cultivators.[37] The emperor Probus brought other settlers across the Danube from among the Gepids, Greuthingi, and Vandals—not whole peoples but small groups, displaced and hungry. Aurelian concluded the withdrawal of all Roman forces from Dacia except for a few strongholds along the river and resettled them in a new province on the right bank of the Danube, but only after he had driven the Goths and their allies from Roman soil.[38] As early as the reign of Claudius Gothicus, the Goths moving southward into the Balkans apparently came in search of new homes, piling their families and belongings into wagons. Most of them ended their days in Roman slavery, sold all over the eastern Mediterranean, especially in Asia Minor.[39] The disruptions of war among the Goths went almost unnoticed in Roman histories, yet these pitiful captives attest to its true dimensions.

By 290 at the latest, or, if we accept the narrative in the *Historia Augusta*, a few decades before 270, Gothic political evolution reached a new plateau. For the first time other sources speak of territorialized subunits among the Goths. The Gepids, Taifali, and Herulians, of course, had emerged as distinct members of the Gothic people even before the onset of the crises with Rome, as they and other Gothic peoples struggled for hegemony beyond the Roman frontier, increasingly relegating the Carpi, Sarmatians, and various Celtic groups to supporting roles. The Greuthingi, some of whom were settled in the empire under Probus, and the Tervingi, mentioned in the *Historia Augusta* and *III Panegyricus Maximiano Dictus* (291 A.D.),[40] differed significantly from other Gothic people such as the Herulians, for the Greuthingi and Tervingi were no longer people on the move but had consolidated their hold over particular topographic areas north of the Danube. The Tervingi, perhaps meaning simply "men of the forest," lived in the forest belt stretching from approximately Ploesti in the southwest to Copanca in the northeast. The root of *Greuthingi* seems philologically related to the Anglo-Saxon *greot*, meaning "flat;" hence the Greuthingi were "rulers of the steppes."[41] Concurrent with the emergence of these regionalized groups, the records first noted individual Gothic dukes commanding the large military conglomerates ravaging Roman soil. As the numismatic evidence proves, the Gothic raiders were hardly coordinated, except by hunger and the harassment of Roman troops. But occasionally dukes such as Cannabaudes with his 5,000 followers were paragons of military power.[42]

Between Aurelian's evacuation of Dacia in 275 and the beginning of the fourth century, various Germans, the Carpi and others, fought among themselves for control of the abandoned Roman province. Although the Tervingi and their allies, the mysterious Taifali, controlled the battlefields, they perhaps refrained from entering Dacia until after 300, when the first Gothic artifacts definitely appear in the old province.[43] Throughout the first decades of the fourth century, if not slightly earlier, the Goths expanded gradually toward the south and west, coming into contact with remnants of "free" Dacian populations, east and south of the Carpathian Mountains, and moving westward, where they gained control of the surviving Daco-Romans, still toiling away long after Aurelian's evacuation of the province. They moved into northern and southern Moldavia slightly earlier, in the late third century, but did not occupy the Carpic strongholds of the central area until ca. 300. So too Wallachia slowly entered the Gothic sphere during the late third century, while the penetrations into southern Transylvania were still in progress in the middle of the fourth century.[44] Such was the halting advance of small groups of Goths under ducal leaders, hardly different from the picture of Cannabaudes and his 5,000 followers.

Several factors reenforced Gothic hesitancy to expand westward. First is the likely agreement extracted from them after their defeat in which they probably agreed to an alliance with Aurelian protecting Roman Dacia from invasion. This agreement would have constituted an important aspect of Rome's attempt to reestablish a client system once Roman arms had properly punished the invaders and Rome again turned to diplomacy. Other considerations before Aurelian were the continued presence of Roman civilians even in areas militarily abandoned and the security of Roman troops still stationed in advanced posts on the far banks of the Danube. Aurelian obviously had good reasons for concluding a pact with the Goths, but since they had no single leader, his task was very difficult. No great war leader comparable to Cannabaudes took command after his death in battle. Even had Cannabaudes lived, he was merely one of many dukes, hardly able to speak for his own followers once peace returned, let alone all the Goths. Aurelian continued his campaigns after defeating Cannabaudes and gradually starved or defeated the invaders group by group. Some were taken captive and led in triumphal procession; others returned home to a changed situation. When summoned for the opening of Aurelian's Persian campaign, they duly reported. They then discovered that Aurelian had died at the hand of an assassin and Tacitus was emperor. Loyalty was personal, man to man; to Tacitus they owed nothing, and they revolted.[45]

Nonetheless, succeeding emperors kept the barbarians at bay, confronting their raids and driving them back. Probus tried to defuse the situation by a program of selective *receptio* and recruitment. Among his immigrants were some Greuthingi.[46] These were "rulers of the steppes" in name only, for other families controlled the newly created regional alliance. The process of structuring an amorphous society into local and regional alliances of families and warbands led by a nobility capped by *duces* established new relationships within the ranking system. Some were offended, perhaps so embittered that they sought refuge and recognition within the empire. Thus, until the formation of the Tervingi and other regional enclaves of stable and tested cooperation, at least militarily, the Goths themselves were unable to move into old Roman Dacia. The agreements concluded with Aurelian were maintained because they coincided with Gothic capabilities. Raids into Asia Minor, on the other hand, were short-term, small-scale operations in which the lure of booty reenforced the desire to demonstrate prowess.

Roman internal reconsolidation under the Tetrarchy and Constantine found parallels north of the Danube, where the Goths hammered out a new alliance system built around the regional strongholds of the Tervingi and Greuthingi. These alliances were characterized by rapid ethnic and cultural fusion with the indigenous peoples and their surrounding allies. The scanty evidence on the stages of this restructuring suggests that the fusion occurred at all levels of society but that the upper ranks remained predominantly "Gothic," whereas the humble villages remained essentially non-Gothic but with scattered Goths, some even among the lowest strata of the population.[47] By the end of the fourth century, a rather cohesive group of nobles, some always drawn from allied groups, had emerged and often with the aid of their followers governed the villages within their regions as overlords[48] not always welcomed in their villages.

Rome under Diocletian was content to relieve some of the pressures on the lower Danube through more admissions of barbarians, similar to those under Probus. Most notably the Carpi found a new home in the Dobroudja, while a small Roman presence along the Danube in old Dacia began to harden with a new fortification program. Constantine found little time for the lower Danube until 328, when he spanned the river at Sucidava with a stone bridge and a well-defined road stretching northward. To be sure, minor Gothic incursions in 315 and 323 demanded attention, but troubles elsewhere, particularly with Licinius, had first priority.[49] Constantine, although at first uninterested in the recapture of more Roman territory north of the river, was intent on securing Roman control of her transdanubian footholds and restoring the urban vitality of the cities along the frontier in Moesia, especially in the hard-hit Dobroudja.[50] Impressive monuments to Constantinian vigor, the rebuilt centers at Dinogetia, Capidava, Tomis, Tropaeum Traiani, Sucidava, and Drobeta, entered a new era of prosperity. Until the Hunnic invasions of the late fourth and early fifth centuries, Roman garrisons are attested by tile stamps in at least fourteen sites north of the river.[51] Memories of the last flicker of Roman military and political security still glowed for Procopius (*de Aedif.*, IV, 6), writing almost two centuries after its collapse.

The Goths similarly focused on internal affairs during the reigns of Diocletian and Constantine. As early as 291, the Tervingi were at war with the Vandals, Gepids, and others challenging for supremacy of the recently opened areas but also for the newly won homelands of the Tervingi themselves. The Tervingi and their allies the Taifali drove their foes westward and northward, but as the archaeological record seems to suggest, they may have remained east of Dacia for almost a decade. Further east the Amali line had emerged as a powerful ducal family as the Greuthingi, too, struggled toward an acephalous regional alliance of nobles. The dynastic legends built around Ermanaric, Thiudmir, and Theodoric as recorded in the *Getica* would have us believe that the fourth-century Hunnil, Athal, Achiulf, and Ansila were kings; however, they and others such as Ariaricus and Aoricus, who concluded the first treaties with Constantine, were not kings but dukes fighting for preeminence over a still ill-defined group.[52] Intratribal wars combined with longstanding feuds with the Gepids to occupy the Goths until Constantine earnestly sought to restructure the client system north of the river.

The building of the great stone bridge at Sucidava in 328 symbolized a decisive change in Roman policy, which had begun perhaps as early as 323 and culminated with Constantine's great victories of 332.[53] In the fifty years between Aurelian's final withdrawal of Roman troops from the interior of Dacia and the wars in the last decade of Constantine's reign, a gradually expanding and peaceful exchange of goods had arisen between the Roman strongholds on both banks and the nearby Goths, Taifali, and indigenous groups of Cherniakhov peoples. The Goths had already abandoned much of their ancient material culture in favor of the more refined items and styles of the Roman world as conveyed to them through the Cherniakhov settlements and by merchants striking northward. Once the Goths settled in closer proximity to Rome, the magnitude of the exchange grew but was still limited by the scarcity of Gothic exchange items. Even so, the normal intercourse of the frontier provided numerous avenues of contact. The Gothic incursions of 315 and 323 probably brought a temporary halt to free commerce, but in their way they stimulated a rapid reestablishment of business as usual, since for a short time the Goths had quantities of valuable booty items for exchange. Every community had its own markets frequented by merchants hawking wares to whoever would buy—German, Roman, Sarmatian, it mattered little. Gothic society had no head, no one person or agency capable of centralizing anything. The numerous dukes, safe and powerful in their local settings, wanted access to the prestige of Roman wares and the power that flowed with their newly expanded potential for largess. Nobles probably did seek to acquire favorable positions vis-à-vis the Roman towns, but they would scarcely have plotted to control the trade to the detriment of other families in various villages throughout their sway, for after all, freemen were not slaves and had to have their own access to trade. Petty raids were accepted as a fact of life by all. Safe behind their walls, the Roman population and military centers were immune from small raids, but the incursions of 315 and 323 were on a larger scale and met with quick and appropriate responses.

The situation in 323 was part of a program stretching back to the tetrarchy of playing off barbarians against each other and if necessary striking northward into *barbaricum* against a rebellious ally. After the Carpi were settled in the Dobroudja in 304/05, their lands fell open to exploitation by the neighboring Sarmatians, and in order to control, or at least monitor, their occupation, Rome built a watchpost at Constantia, opposite Margum, at this time.[54] This and other advanced posts could also serve as bridgeheads for invasion when necessary. The Sarmatians were a valuable ingredient in the structure of Roman alliances. After 300 they were also exposed to renewed Gothic pressure and needed assistance. Rome sought to keep her Sarmatian allies even if they were rebellious, as in 310, when Galerius and Constantine took the titles *Sarmaticus Maximus*—Constantine's second and Galerius's fifth such victory.[55] Obviously the emperors took great pains to keep the Sarmatians in line. But in 322 the Sarmatians apparently raided in alliance with the Goths. Thus, Constantine struck northward, probably from Margum-Constantia, against the Sarmatians in 322 and the Goths in 323. However, in both instances he was merely redressing the traditional alliance structure based on a network tying each ally to Rome but prohibiting any alliances without Rome. The rapidly expanding Gothic regional confederations competed with Roman policy, and a major clash loomed as soon as Constantine felt secure elsewhere and so could concentrate his troops. The building of the great bridge at Sucidava in 328 was only a prelude to the launching of a full-scale sweep into German-held lands north of the river. For Constantine the traditional network was long obsolete, and now at last the time was ripe for building a new system.

Constantine took advantage of a Gothic attack in 332 on the Sarmatians in the Banat to unleash his armies under the command of his son Constantine II.[56] The victorious Roman army used the recent clashes among the Germans themselves and the latest incursion of the Sarmatians essentially to abrogate any treaty obligations. Either in the context of the struggles of 332 or probably shortly before in preparation for the Gothic campaigns, the Romans invaded Oltenia and inflicted a severe blow on the Taifali, allies of the Goths since at least 291, and transported many captives to Phrygia. All privileges enjoyed by the Goths as federates under earlier treaties stopped in 332, including the payments of annual subsidies to various chieftains.[57] Constantine clearly sought the return of direct Roman control as far as central Dacia and the destruction of the Tervingi and their allies menacing his flank from Moldavia. Constantine's program was a logical step in the redefinition and reestablishment of client relations along the entire length of the German frontier that had begun in the late third century.

Events following Constantine's death in 337 undermined his efforts and shattered Roman dreams on the lower Danube. Whether the expansion of Roman sovereignty northward from the enclaves on the river itself was militarily prudent became a moot point after resurgent Goths lashed back at Rome in the 340s, culminating in 346–47 with the election of an overall commander, *iudex* or δικαστής, over the Tervingi. Thus the Roman challenge produced the first unified military structure among the Goths, but the new leadership position was still only a temporary expedient and had dissolved with victory before Libanius composed his oration mentioning Constantius and the Goths in late 348 or 349. A brief persecution of Christians, many doubtless Roman captives or merchants, may have accompanied Gothic victories, but a return to the status antedating 332 is undoubted. The subsidies were resumed and the obligations of earlier treaties restored.[58] By 349 a general peace had returned to the Danube with a clearer Germanic presence.

From approximately the middle of the fourth century, the character of the archaeological record changes for the area north of Sucidava. Gradually, inscriptions and coinage disappeared. The well-planned and carefully manicured barracks and officers' homes gave way to smaller houses, perhaps inhabited by squatters or farmer-soldiers and their families. The new isolation was manifest in the decreasing amounts of Roman household and dress items.[59] In their place, the population turned to local wares or items heavily influenced by the Germans, if not indeed manufactured by German hands. The great stone bridge fell into the Danube as the elements or barbarians took control. Little by little, the same fate befell the Roman centers on the northern bank that had befallen the strongholds on the Black Sea in the third century. Isolated from regular contact with the agents of Roman civilization, especially the bureaucracy of trade and the army, the towns turned inward and reached local accommodations with familiar local Germanic chieftains, who had every reason to assure their pathetic survival. Such then were the realities of Libanius's peace "imposed" by Constantius, lauded for his persuasiveness in orations 59 and 89. Behind the facade lurked the grim reality—Rome had abandoned all dreams of territorial expansion forever.

No longer in a position to conquer and hold the lands beyond the river, especially after the bloodletting of Magnentius's revolt (350–53), succeeding emperors tried to keep the barbarians off guard and thwart their progress toward political and military cohesion with preemptive strikes and upgraded defenses.[60] Until the revolt of Procopius in 366, the Goths were *gens amica Romanis, foederibusque longae pacis obstricta.*[61] Why did they break the peace and support a usurper against the house of Valentinian, asked the Roman general Victor prior to the invasions of 367. Because Procopius, asserting his blood relationship with the Constantinian dynasty, asked them "in writing" to live up to their treaty obligations. Thus the Goths had interpreted the treaty in a typically Germanic fashion as an extension of family loyalties to the line of Constantine, not to an abstraction, the state, but to its personification. The Roman general was unimpressed, for his loyalty was to Rome and its "legitimate heads," Valentinian and his brother Valens. The Gothic chiefs (*regibus*) responded to Procopius with the dispatch of 3,000 warriors, not a particularly large force, as a matter of routine.[62] Had they perceived the impending Roman counterstroke, surely they would have elected a *iudex*.

Valens, like his brother Valentinian in the West and Constantius II and Julian before them, attacked. He threw a pontoon bridge across the Danube in classic Roman fashion, rafting ships together and planking a crossway to their gunwales. The Goths fled in panic into the heavily forested mountains of the interior, but many lost their lives en route as Arintheus, commander of the Roman infantry, struck at the wagons encumbered with women and children. The year 368 brought heavy rains, and the swollen Danube prevented an adequate buildup of supplies, so Valens remained in permanent camp near a Carpic village and in the autumn returned to Marcianopolis. The Goths then drew themselves together and for the first time in over two decades elected a *iudex* over them.[63] Even Athanaric, the *iudex*, was powerless to stop Valens in 369, when full-scale operations resumed. Valens drove a wedge through Tervingi lands and pushed his troops deep into Gothia, a term familiar to all Romans, as far as the territory of the Greuthingi.[64] The first direct contact with the ancestors of the Ostrogoths had occurred. Some Greuthingi probably had aided their cousins in their death struggles, but to no avail. Athanaric, reduced to fighting with only his retainers, sued for peace. The war had completely disrupted vital commerce, and the concomitant destruction of Gothic territory had reduced a proud people to the status of suppliants, "because the savages, since commerce was cut off, were so distressed by extreme scarcity of the necessities of life that they often sent suppliant deputations to beg for pardon and peace."[65] Athanaric had sworn an oath never to set foot on Roman soil (hardly a pledge from a determined invader!), and so the treaty was signed in ships rowed from each side to midstream.[66] In the agreement, Rome may have rejected an offer of military assistance and peace in exchange for *receptio* in favor of a recognition of the frontier.[67]

Peace returned, but only briefly—the Huns were moving westward on a collision course. Nevertheless, the struggles with Valens and the ignominious defeat of Gothic warriors, even as far away as the Greuthingi, set a series of complex political events in motion. Athanaric emerged so tarnished that his effective leadership itself was in doubt, especially over such raucous nobles as Alavivus and Fritigern (soon to be the hero of Adrianople) and their followers; further east, Ermanaric used the Roman threat and resulting peace to tighten the assemblage of the Greuthingi and their neighbors into a durable confederacy, known by the opening of the fifth century as the Ostrogoths. Ermanaric remains veiled under layers of myth, which already clouded reality in Jordanes's *Getica*. He took his own life in ca. 375 rather than lead his people into Hunnic slavery, but his suicide was unacceptable to later eras, when Christianity had tempered Germanic society with bonds of a new passion, which was hardly less harsh but which disdained death at one's own hands. Writing in the sixth century, Jordanes recorded a different fate, a heroic death at the hands of irate brothers pursuing vengeance for their lost sister Sundila, whom Ermanaric had had drawn and quartered.[68] Regardless of how he was remembered by future bards, his greatness rested upon the durability of the Ostrogoths as a people.

Ermanaric (Aírmnareiks, reiks = prince) propelled his line to the leadership of the Greuthingi, although his ancestors had suffered at least four generations in eclipse while other more powerful *duces* negotiated with the Romans.[69] Before the Hunnic advance, he had already subdued many long-bitter foes. The Peucini, their savagery still fresh to the poet Claudian, obeyed his summons, as did several groups of Sarmatians, various Celtic peoples long resident along the lower Danube, and numerous groups of Goths. Bordering the Ostrogoths to the east were the Alans; to the west lay the heartlands of the Tervingi (emerging as the Visigothic confederacy) and scattered groups of Gepids, Vandals, and other East Germans.[70] Beneath the Germanic upper strata, the indigenous remnants of cultural forms associated with the Cherniakhov peoples struggled for survival.[71] Ermanaric stood above these competing groups, secured in his position by skillful marriage alliances (perhaps including the ill-fated Sundila), the deft handling of warbands drawn from his diverse allies, and a razor-sharp sword. He was, after all, "the greatest warrior king, dreaded by the neighboring peoples because of his many and varied deeds of valor."[72]

If even just some of our attempts to unravel the ethnicity of the men associated with Ermanaric are correct, then he shared his military command with younger members of his family and incorporated selected leaders from the allied peoples into the top echelons of power. Perhaps Vithimir is also Vinitharius and hence "conqueror of the Vendes," and Videric is Vandalarius, honoring a victory over the "Vandals."[73] According to Ammianus, Vithimir took command and as king continued the resistance against the Alans and some Huns by allying with still other Huns, whom he paid to join his following. He stemmed the advance, but only briefly, before he fell in battle, leaving his son Videric, a minor, to rally a disintegrating people. The bloodline was placed in tutelage as Alatheus and Saphrax, *duces exerciti et firmitate pectorum noti*, took the young heir and a fragment of the people on a slow retreat to the Danube.[74] Alatheus may have been of Sarmatian descent and Saphrax perhaps an Alannic or Hunnic chief commanding the Hunnic contingent brought over so recently by Vithimir.[75]

Regardless of the exact ethnic descent of the regents, their names do not seem Germanic, and their presence at a moment of survival itself attests to the elasticity within the Ostrogothic assemblage and their acephalous opponents, Huns, Alans, and others. Ermanaric built the alliance around his family and secured for them the demonstrations of valor necessary for leadership, but others, Greuthingi and non-Goth alike, were given chances to prove their prowess and leadership within the loose confederacy of the Ostrogoths. *Duces* of various, often traditionally hostile, peoples drew profit from the Amali line, and even after the death of its greatest member, the nexus of loyalty survived the splintering of the confederacy and, except for the small group accompanying Videric and his regents, captivity and suppression under the Huns. After over two centuries of halting migrations, those Goths settling in the steppelands near the Black Sea had finally emerged as a coherent people united under one family but still ready to incorporate others in an almost amoebic fashion. Caught between the hammer and the anvil, the Ostrogoths chose survival and allied with either the Huns or the Roman Empire.

3

Bondage and Struggle

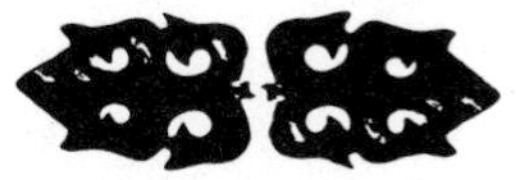

Alatheus and Saphrax, their youthful charge Videric, and scattered remnants of Ermanaric's confederation reached the Danube too late. When the true dimensions of the exodus dawned on the Roman command along the Danube, the fleet blocked the crossings. Ostrogothic envoys sought *receptio* in vain.[1] Lupicinus and Maximus, long rivals for military advancement, each successful and brutal, were trying to restrict the southward flow and effectively to monitor the crossings by checking for weapons and then dispersing the immigrants to various temporary facilities near towns throughout the area. The mechanisms for *receptio* were well established, tested repeatedly over the previous century. Roman frontier policy had hardened under Constantius II and Valentinian I, with rather systematic forays into *barbaricum* keeping the Germans on the defensive, but still *receptio* played an important role in releasing the pressures along the frontier and relieving serious manpower shortages in the civil and military spheres. In fact, the hope of easy recruitment into the army caused Valens to open the frontier to the Visigoths.[2] The Greuthingi were told to wait their turn.

Waiting was difficult. Gothic groups, primarily Tervingi, had ravaged the northern bank for months as they spread out in family groups, scouring the land for supplies.[3] Food supplies were so low on the Roman bank that some parents had sold their children into slavery rather than watch them slowly starve. The slavers offered little. Even a dog was enough recompense for some.[4] The Romans too were in desperate straits. No one anticipated the bursting of the dam; the entire alliance system beyond the river succumbed to the tremors of Hunnic horsemen. But even before the arrival of the Huns, at least as early as the reign of Constantius II, the Romans had resorted to drastic measures to paralyze the evolution of Germanic society. Men such as Maximus and Lupicinus had helped stage brutal raids and occasionally premeditated assassinations of German leaders.[5] As punishment for the Gothic assistance to Procopius during his revolt in 364, Valens had declared a bounty on barbarian heads. Alas, heads are easier to count than identify, and many a Roman ally may have died in the slaughter.

> At the beginning of spring the Emperor quitted Marcianopolis and, proceeding together with the Danube guard, attacked the barbarians. They did not dare to stand and slug it out, but hid themselves in the marshes and from these made secret forays. Valens ordered his soldiers to hold their ground and, having collected as large a throng of sutlers as he could, plus those to whom the custody of the baggage was entrusted, he promised to give a fixed sum of gold for every head of a barbarian they brought in. Straightaway then they all, excited at the prospect of lucre, dashed off to the woods and marshes and throttled every man they came upon. As they produced the heads they were paid the stipulated price. When a multitude had been killed in this fashion the survivors sued the Emperor for peace.[6]

Now these same survivors pleaded for admission into the empire. When the *receptio* system broke down and various groups on the brink of starvation grew restless, Lupicinus sought to defuse the situation by once more disrupting Gothic leadership through assassination. Many Gothic leaders, including the Visigothic confederate leader Alavivus, ate their last dinner at Lupicinus's bloody banquet, but Fritigern and some other nobles were wary and escaped to raise a war cry that culminated at Adrianople in 378.[7] Once the hostilities opened, those Greuthingi with Alatheus and Saphrax were able to cross the Danube secretly and unopposed. Still armed and on their own mounts, they joined their kinsmen in battle. Along with the Greuthingi came small groups of Alans, probably the assemblage brought into the confederacy by Saphrax.[8] Numerically weak in comparison to the host of Goths now rallying to Fritigern's side, the Greuthingi proved their mettle at Adrianople. Starting out of the ravines, where they had fed their horses on the sparse grasses of August, they struck the

Romans assaulting the Gothic laager from behind. In the blinding dust of battle, Romans pressed upon Romans until their compacted mass was surrounded and dispatched.[9] By 380 many of the followers of Alatheus and Saphrax probably found refuge and settlement in Pannonia, but not before they had caused considerable damage.[10] In 379 Gratian had no choice but to allow them to settle in Pannonia Secunda after his commander Vitalianus failed to contain them. By the summer of the same year, Theodosius managed to defeat them, but only after heavy losses. It seems likely that Theodosius split the federates, settling the Greuthingi in Pannonia Prima, the Alans in Valeria. Under his plan, the Hunnic elements were to remain in Pannonia Secunda.[11] Some of the federates in Pannonia assisted Theodosius in 387 against Maximus, but Theodosius also used other troops, including other Greuthingi recently captured on the Danube. In general, the followers of Alatheus and Saphrax were not numerically strong enough to alter decisively the cultural patterns in Pannonia. In fact, after their defeat in 379 and the resulting dispersal, they probably served as miscellaneous replacements recruited into the existing units of the Roman army. As a result, they have not produced a clearly identifiable imprint in the archaeological record.[12] A handful of finds appears related to these Gothic settlers.

The most meaningful and controversial discovery perhaps relating to the followers of Alatheus and Saphrax is the so-called first treasure of Szilágysomlyó. It consists of fourteen medallions from the fourth century and another ten of Valentinian I alone. The medallions were found in a hoard along with a pendant, a standard aureus, eleven gold rings, the end pieces of an armband, and various other items of jewelry. Perhaps even more intriguing than the medallions is the gold necklace with miniature representations of items from daily life.[13] The necklace has considerable religious significance and will demand our attention later. Any speculation as to how the find might relate to structure of the Alatheus-Saphrax group is premature. Surely there were several ranks of chiefs and subchiefs among these Greuthingi, as Olympiodorus reports for the contemporary Visigothic bands of Sarus and Ammianus outlined for the Quadi and Alamanni.[14] However, the interpretation of the Szilágysomlyó finds is clouded by the presence of several barbarian imitations and reworkings of Valens (figs. 1 and 2). They were probably devised by the same hand and are certainly imitations. The reverse die of one (fig. 1) was used again on a clearly non-Roman medallion found in Poland in 1927 (fig. 3). Here two imperial figures face each other in a rather bizarre pose. The legend is absurdly broken, and the Latin is erroneous and virtually

Fig. 1: Barbarian medallion in imitation of Valens (Szilágysomlyó).

Fig. 2: Barbarian medallion of Valens (Szilágysomlyó).

meaningless in a Roman context. Surely only a barbarian making an analogy to his own society would call the two emperors Valens and Valentinian *resis* [*reges*] *Romanorum*.[15] So too the Szilágysomlyó medallion of Maximianus (fig. 4) is reset in a cloisonné wreathlike frame that could date almost anytime from the late fourth through the fifth century. Until further expert evaluation is made in light of new

Fig. 3: Barbarian medallion of Valens and Valentinian found in Poland. Reverse die identical with that of fig. 1.

Fig. 4: Medallion from coin of Maximianus (Szilágysomlyó).

finds and examinations, anything more than dating it to the late fourth or early fifth century and associating it with barbarians (perhaps the Alatheus-Saphrax group) seems unwarranted. Finds from Regölyi and Csákvár are less ambiguous and probably reflect elements of the Alatheus-Saphrax group after their dispersal behind the frontier and gradual integration into the existing military units. They also indicate that assimilation with the indigenous population had begun by the turn of the century.[16]

Perhaps by the end of the fourth century, certainly in the early fifth, the confederates grouped around the Greuthingi were frequently called Ostrogoths. The author of the *Historia Augusta*, writing late in the fourth century, was confused and gave both names in his account of the third century: "Denique Scytharum diversi populi, Peucini, Greuthingi, Austrogothi, Teruingi, Visi, Gepedes, Celtae etiam et Eruli. . . ."[17] The court poet, Claudian, writing under Honorius said: "Ostrogothis colitur mixtisque Gruthingis Phryx ager."[18] The majority of the Ostrogoths were restless allies of the Huns. Prior to the formation of a fairly cohesive political structure among the Huns under Uldin (ca. 400), breaking away was not too difficult, especially for those allies possessing capable leaders.

In 386, thousands of Ostrogoths under *dux* Odotheus hastily cut rafts and attempted to cross the lower Danube into the Dobroudja. Promotus, commander of the infantry in Thrace and the Danubian flotilla, struck them in midstream, filling the river with corpses. Twelve years later Claudian still echoed the victory when the island of Peuce lay heaped with corpses and the blood of the Greuthingi stained the Danube red. The Romans thereby crushed a major exodus of Goths; some had been settled near the river, but other groups were remote and unfamiliar to Romans.[19] Many pitiful survivors escaped the Roman fleet and the bloody river only to die at the hands of soldiers drawn up along the banks. The women and children were carried off, their precious baggage now booty, before Theodosius himself intervened. His compassion (certainly not his most endearing quality, especially at Thessalonika in 390) cloaked a desperate need for troops to confront the rebellion of Maximus.[20] Ultimately some Goths may have ended their days as coloni in distant Phrygia.[21]

Theodosius pursued a consistent policy of playing one Gothic leader and his followers against another in their quest for advancement and honor. For example, late in his reign, Fravitta and Eruilf challenged each other for the favors of the emperor.[22] Awards of titles and wealth in turn enhanced the Gothic leaders' positions within their own society and perhaps especially over their warbands. Many nobles such as Athanaric, an old and sworn foe of Rome, quickly lost much of their animosity in the splendor of Constantinople, Thessalonika, and other cities where they served as allies of the emperor.[23] Except for the events of 386, the Ostrogoths as a people played little role in the turbulent Balkans. Fighting in 391–92 in the rugged areas of Macedonia and Thessaly pitted groups of Visigoths unable to accept their sedentary and restricted lives against the empire, but already in 394 thousands of Visigoths helped defeat the usurper Eugenius at the river Frigidus.[24] Despite numerous skirmishes, some perhaps nearly fatal for Rome and Theodosius himself, the emperor aided by Stilicho managed to walk a thin line between really subjugating the Goths and suffering a Roman defeat.[25] Except for the followers of Alatheus and Saphrax and a few others, including some slaves joining Tribigild's revolt in Asia Minor, most Ostrogoths had to learn to exist within the Hunnic Empire, not the Roman.

The memories of their subjection were bitter long after they had escaped from the Huns following the decisive battle of Nedao in 454. When in 467 a certain Chelchal, a Hun himself, reminded them of their past sufferings, the Ostrogoths rose in anger and slaughtered the Huns among them and terminated a short-lived alliance against Rome:

> These men [the Huns] are heedless of cultivation, and, like wolves, attack and plunder the provisions of the Goths, so that they, continuing in the position of servants, suffer hardships in order to provision the Huns, although the Gothic race has remained for all time without a treaty with them and has been pledged by its ancestors to escape from the alliance with the Huns.[26]

Equally vivid was the fear and trembling that a mere glance from Attila could strike in the leaders of the subject peoples. The Ostrogoths had been fortunate, for Attila had favored the Amali Valamir and his brothers Thiudmir and Vidimir.[27] In fact, it seems that despite occasional hunger and growing animosity, at least the Ostrogothic nobility, and presumably their personal followers, did reasonably well under the Huns. They had little choice once Uldin (ca. 400) consolidated Hunnic leadership. He stifled the independence of such allied leaders as Odotheus and attached them to the leader of the Huns and his family. Indicative of the changed circumstances was the welcoming home of Gainas in 400.

Gainas rose from the ranks to joint command of Theodosius's Germanic troops against Eugenius and was *comes rei militaris* (395–99) and finally *magister militum praesentalis* (399–400).[28] Caught up in the religious and political turmoil of the empire and especially Constantinople, Gainas rebelled and looked toward Asia for plunder but was stopped in a bloody confrontation with other Germanic forces serving Rome led by Fravitta, another Gothic leader. Rebuffed and driven into a sadly ravaged Thrace, Gainas hoped to return home with his men. But Uldin "thought it unsafe to permit a barbarian who had his own army to make his home above the Danube" and joined forces with Rome. In a savage battle, Uldin destroyed Gainas's army and sent his head to the emperor Arcadius.[29] The lesson was repeated in early 406, when Uldin assisted Stilicho and Sarus in crushing Radagaius's invasion of Italy. The court of Honorius drowned its fears amid celebration, but the real victor was the Hunnic alliance. Radagaius in particular may have been an Ostrogoth as the sources suggest, but like Gainas his followers were gathered from numerous peoples. In the future, the Hunnic kings integrated the Germanic nobilities with their warriors into their government and thereby held the Germans, notably the Gepids and Ostrogoths, within the Hunnic alliance. There were no more incursions of large bands of Germans breaking out of the Hun Empire and raiding Roman soil until after the breakup of Attila's kingdom.

Until their settlement in Pannonia in 427, the Huns were usually Roman allies, especially of their ex-hostage, the present Roman commander, Aetius. But once they were inside the empire, relations deteriorated rapidly. By 439 the Huns occupied western Pannonia and with their allies, including some Ostrogoths, were raiding the Balkans. However, the vast majority of Ostrogoths remained somewhere above the Danube, probably still in the area of Moldavia. In 449–50 Attila saw advantage in turning westward, secure as he was with the tribute paid him by Theodosius II. Events in the West turned out contrary to expectations. Perhaps chastened by his defeat at the Catalaunian Fields, upon which the Ostrogoths, the Burgundians, and all the allies left heavy losses, Attila was slowly retracing his route back to Pannonia when he died. Two years later the allies won their freedom at Nedao.[30] Several important finds help illuminate general aspects of Ostrogothic history within the Hunnic federation as they rode the whirlwinds gradually moving westward and leaving destruction and despair. At present, however, exact ethnic attribution to specific East Germanic peoples, such as the Ostrogoths, is hazardous if not impossible. Nevertheless, the general outline of Germanic life under Hunnic overlordship is clear enough.

Once the initial upheavals of the late fourth century had run their course and a Hunnic élite had consolidated its power over German and non-German alike, the Huns built a governmental apparatus in part drawn from Sassanid and Roman models but typically personal and confederate. Just as the Ostrogoths under Ermanaric had established and then expanded their sway through the accretion of allied peoples and leaders, so too did the Huns. But unlike the German confederacies, the Hunnic had far more clearly defined roles for subordinate ethnic groups. Priscus of Panion, recording his embassy to Attila in 448 for Theodosius II, reported the complex interworkings of the Hunnic Empire. At the top stood Attila and his family; next were other primary Hunnic families. Following these in precedence were selected Germanic chiefs (notably Ardaric, king of the Gepids, and the Amali line of the Ostrogoths under Valamir), and finally there was a host of lesser chiefs of conquered peoples.[31] At the base, almost unmentioned in Priscus's account, the masses toiled to provision society. In Pannonia the native Roman population shouldered the burden,[32] but beyond the old *limes* the identity of the laborers is obscure.

The apparent precision of ranks under Attila was the product of earlier manipulation and conflict among and within the allies. The semilegendary Hun Balamber had played one branch of the Amali against another and probably invited non-Amali families to share power as well; only after three campaigns did he finally subdue the Ostrogothic nobility with a compromise allowing for one Goth always to speak for all.[33] As the career of Theodoric Triarius will soon reveal, the Huns probably encouraged certain Ostrogothic nobles in their independence as a check to an Amali-led insurrection. Despite the presence of conflicting loyalties within the empire's alliance structure, the Huns demanded and received absolute allegiance from the Germanic nobilities without which their government of such vast territories was impossible.

The great allied leaders spent long months with Attila's camp, probably supervising the exchange of orders and tribute to remote homelands where the desires of a distant court touched directly the lives of the local inhabitants. Two princely burials discovered in Romania, the Apahida II burial and another from Cluj-Someşeni, doubtless attest to the presence of an East Germanic ruling élite, either Ostrogothic or perhaps Gepidic, serving the Hun Empire about the middle of the fifth century.[34] At Apahida II, the gold sheath and rod (perhaps the remnant of a spear or standard) were apparently part of the symbolic accoutrement of a warrior prince representing the Huns. The spectacular examples of the polychrome style at Apahida II and the only slightly less magnificent items from Someşeni suggest a Gothic provenance. As in the late fourth century, the Goths continued as principal agents for the dissemination of polychrome jewelry. It was still an important item of their dress and among the Ostrogoths was probably restricted to the élites. Already in the fourth century the grave complexes associated with the Cherniakhov civilization show a peculiar distribution of polychrome grave furnishing: it appears only in isolated finds and never in the large necropoleis, thus perhaps indicating the imposition of a ruling group of Goths into the local setting. Other evidence, however, suggests that at least among the Cherniakhov, a general and rapid cultural assimilation between groups took place after a short separation still discernible in the early presence of two distinct burial customs.[35] Under the Huns, on the other hand, the princely burials (here including the somewhat late Cluj-Someşeni burial, probably dating to the period after Nedao) suggest the emergence of an intermediary ruling class of Germanic nobles with their followers, often Ostrogoths or Gepids, above the rest of the indigenous society, including the common elements of their own peoples.[36]

The Goths ruling for the Huns constituted an élite among their own people. The apparently Ostrogothic graves discovered among the twenty-three unearthed at Botoşani-Dealul Cărămidăriei can be tentatively assigned to the period immediately following the Battle of Adrianople (i.e., 380–400).[37] The graves themselves are poor, with no great nobleman buried among them. They seem to represent an early stage of Ostrogothic expansion or resettlement in close proximity to an indigenous settlement at the western edge of the very steppe where they had first coalesced as a people. These Goths had not fled with Odotheus in 386 and therefore were spared the bloodbath on the Danube witnessed by Theodosius. The distribution of artifacts, particularly female jewelry, indicates that here the Eastern Germans, probably Ostrogoths, significantly influenced and interacted with the local inhabitants. Perhaps even an occasional intermarriage was celebrated. The culture of the original population derived ultimately from the Cherniakhov culture of the early fourth century. In the give-and-take of customs and ideas, the Germans had the upper hand. Their world now involved complex tastes and styles circulating within the Hunnic domain and filtering down to even such insignificant settlements. The indigenous culture yielded but did not cease to exist.

The Huns probably elevated certain men from such humble communities and placed them in command. Perhaps they chose the heads of important families or warbands; perhaps they preferred new men whose loyalty was assured. They would have had little difficulty finding such new supporters at this time, since the traditional leadership was in disarray. Odotheus had fled only to be virtually annihilated at the Danube, and remnants of the Amalian line were at odds over loyalty to the Huns.[38] Those Ostrogoths chosen were members of the new élite of the Hunnic Empire. They and their Gepidic and Alanic peers oversaw the workings of government, raising armies and collectively extracting imposts of grain. The nature of their rule dictated that they be dispersed across Hunnic lands from the Hungarian Plain eastward. While the élites grew confident in their positions and displayed power and eminence on their bodies and in the trappings of their horses, the people at Botoşani lived within the narrower confines of the gently rolling hills overlooking the nearby steppe. If that is indeed the case, it would explain the often-isolated locations of finds of princely burials and their wide distribution.[39] Thus, there emerged two levels of Ostrogothic participation in the Hunnic world, thereby stimulating an ever more hierarchically defined nobility. The bulk of the Ostrogoths probably remained in settlements still undiscovered but perhaps much like Botoşani. A few rose to exalted rank in the service of their overlords.

The warrior of Apahida II proudly displayed the symbols of his rank, and the two beautiful polychrome eagles affixed to his saddle boldly glistened in the sun (fig. 5). The eagle was to become very popular among the Gepidic, Visigothic, and Ostrogothic nobilities during their kingdoms, but in the early fifth century this symbol of quick and irresistible power rode with and for the Huns. The lower elements of Ostrogothic society gradually adjusted to their new homes, as they had earlier on the steppes and were to again in Italy by bilateral acculturation. However, there was a considerable reluctance to disperse among the common Ostrogoths. Instead, they lived in clusters or pockets with small settlements of Goths along with similar habitations of indigenous peoples. Within these close centers, cultural contact between two distinct communities was controlled, in the sense that each preserved a cultural refuge while exploring the other's world. For the most part, the Ostrogoths seem to have remained not too distant from their old homelands in this period. Their heaviest concentrations in the early fifth century were probably in the Theiss area, northern Moldavia, and northeastern Muntenia. They may also have gradually spread into the area of Siebenbürgen.[40] It must be emphasized, however, that at the current time we really cannot locate with any real confidence the Ostrogoths vis-à-vis the Gepids and other Eastern Germanic peoples in the area above the Danube. Until the Ostrogoths entered Pannonia in 455, the historical record is simply inadequate. On the other hand, the presence of Eastern Germanic groups is amply demonstrated in the archaeological record of this era. The most one can do is to categorize these Germanic burials, as opposed to indigenous, by grave goods and not hazard precise ethnographic labeling.[41] This categorization reveals extremely interesting and complex patterns of occasionally overlapping styles. Perhaps such fine variations as the presence or absence of combs and the distribution

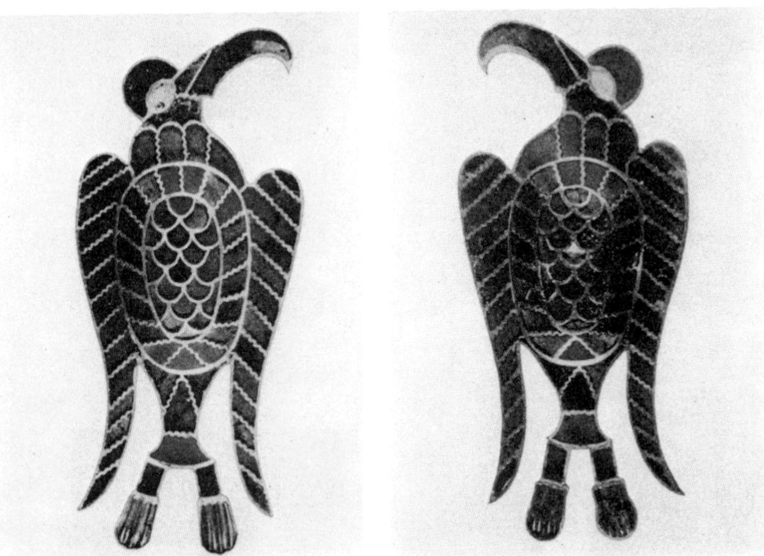

Fig. 5: Saddle ornaments from the second burial at Apahida, Romania.

of peculiar fibulae types, buckles, glass, and so on will ultimately assist the understanding of basic features of Germanic society.

The underlying strengths of Germanic culture were rarely dependent upon the rivalries of the nobilities, yet among the peoples under Hunnic control, the power struggles of the élites alone emerge from our sparse sources. The concept of tribal cohesion doubtless remained an elusive force at best. Under such circumstances, forcing the evidence under ethnic labels probably distorts reality rather than clarifies history. The Huns themselves apparently found temporary homes to the southwest along the Danubian plain, where place names bear witness to their presence. Almost everywhere the indigenous inhabitants survived but changed, supplementing their traditional ways with the new fashions of their Germanic and Hunnic overlords. The archaeological and literary sources strongly suggest that Ostrogoths remained closely associated with Alanic groups in their vicinity as they had since the era of Ermanaric.[42] Many probably remained in the general area of Moldavia until the middle of the fifth century, if not slightly later.

Analogies between the Apahida II finds and the great burial of the Frankish king Childeric are manifest. Like the Romanian finds,

Childeric's grave at Tournai reveals a wide gap between himself and the majority of his people. Indeed, Childeric's burial dress was more closely related to late military Roman styles of the highest rank than to those of his people interred in contemporary *Reihengräberfelden*.[43] Obviously the fifth century witnessed a rapid sharpening of Germanic social divisions in which an élite rejected many traditional customs for more attractive and expensive fashions and symbols closely related to higher centers of authority. Rome exerted an irresistible lure, holding a virtual monopoly of the highest symbols of power, command, and wealth. But for a fleeting half century, especially within the confines of their empire, the Huns were able to add concepts of monarchy and symbols of power (many perhaps borrowed from Sassanid ceremonial) to an essentially Roman stock. The presence of a crownlike ornament or diadem at Apahida II and elsewhere within the area under strong Hunnic influence and the lack of a similar head ornament at Tournai may express a subtle but important distinction in concepts of rule.

The complexity of the conceptual, symbolic, and technical amalgamation occurring north of the Danube during the early fifth century is also revealed in the famous treasure from Pietroasa. The history of the find, its partial demise and restoration, is itself a saga worthy of a mystery novel. Arguments and counterarguments of a century of debate still rage concerning the basic date of burial and provenance among the Goths. Beyond the fact that the treasure was assembled from pieces of various date and origin and that the owner was a Goth of the fourth or fifth century, nothing seems established with certainty. Was the owner a great king or noble? Perhaps the objects were part of a cult center. Was the treasure buried in the late fourth century, and thus associated with the age, if not the person, of Athanaric and the Visigoths? Perhaps Ostrogoths or Gepids wore the beautiful ornaments found at Pietroasa in the fifth century. A date during the first half of the fifth century and an Ostrogothic ownership are possible, perhaps likely. Detailed comparisons to Apahida II, Cluj-Someşeni, and other sites are generally convincing.[44] A most striking feature of the find, however, remains its composite nature, clearly accumulated for half a century or more.

The *patera* dates to the mid-fourth century and was probably produced in the shops of Antioch during Julian's reign.[45] In general, the fibulae demonstrate a rather clear and direct influence from fashions associated with the imperial court and upper echelons of the late-fourth- and early-fifth-century military aristocracy.[46] The eagle-style motif of several items, such as the eagle brooches of Apahida II, probably relates to the role of the Germanic élites in the functioning of the Hunnic Empire, which first gave the eastern stylized bird head an important symbolic place in Germanic dress. The massive collars, particularly the famous gold collar weighing twenty-five ounces and measuring six inches in diameter with a runic inscription, are Gothic and pagan, although the emperor Valens may have worn similar items on his neck and arms.[47] Theodosius knew their importance when he gave such rings to the Gothic leaders in his efforts to bring them into line.[48] The ornamental techniques used to fashion the various pieces representing the polychrome style are also indicative of early-fifth-century Gothic craftsmen.[49] In short, the Pietroasa treasure marvelously illustrates the principal cultural influences at work among the Germanic élites north of the Danube at the end of the fourth and early fifth centuries: Roman, Hunnic, and rapidly evolving Germanic components.

How the Ostrogothic élites reacted to the death of Attila remains unclear. The Ostrogoths played little part in the battle of Nedao in 454. They could have thanked, but did not, Ardaric and his Gepids for raising revolt rather than merely watching as Attila's sons cast lots for control of the allied kings and peoples.[50] Some Ostrogothic nobles refused to follow the Amali line and struck out on their own, allying themselves with Rome or perhaps merely staying where they were when most of the Ostrogoths were settled in Pannonia.[51] Most notoriously independent were Theodoric Strabo, son of Triarius, later to war against the Amali on behalf of Byzantium, and Bessas, who was heralded by Procopius as an important Byzantine ally during the War of Justinian. Some Ostrogoths found employment in Majorian's army, which was raised to subdue the Vandals in late 458.[52] No one could have expected the entire Ostrogothic nobility to rally around the Amali line, for, in part at least, they owed their elevation directly to the Huns, although their functioning in office was under the supervision of the Hunnic court, where Amali influence was paramount. That the bulk of the Ostrogoths clearly looked for leadership to Valamir and his brothers is a lasting testament to the effectiveness of their sway under Hunnic domination and the fear of a Hunnic rebirth.

Even after the breakup of their empire, the Huns continued to harass the Ostrogoths and threatened to undo the Balkan alliance structure at any moment. The salient fact of 455 was not the settlement of the Ostrogoths in Pannonia under the Amali brothers but the Vandal sack of Rome and the near severance of seaborne contact between Constantinople and the West. Against images of fire and looting in Rome, the events in the Balkans stand in sharper focus. The

Western emperor Majorian, eulogized by Sidonius with quavering excitement as a savior, and his Eastern colleagues Marcian and Leo pursued a policy designed to reestablish a semblance of tranquility in the Balkans and thereby free troops for a campaign against the Vandals. The campaign met with disaster off the coast of Gaul in 459, but the loss did not erase the dreams of reconquest. The settlements in Pannonia probably extended from north to south, with Valamir in the north, then probably the Sadagis separating his lands from those of Thiudmir, and still farther to the south the territory assigned to Vidimir. There were clearly numerous problems with the initial allocations, not the least of which were the previous occupants, who included numerous Germanic and Roman elements, even perhaps the descendants of Alatheus and Saphrax. Valamir took an early opportunity to attack the Sadagi. This attack and subsequent skirmishes against Suevi, Rugians, Sarmatians, and everyone else in the Pannonian area had more to do with the restructuring of warbands than with territorial acquisition. Valamir had little choice but to lead his restless followers in search of occasions for valor and booty.[53] So too Thiudmir and his son Theodoric were to reorganize groups of followers in the 470s. The old system imposed by Hunnic persuasion had to make way for new men outside the ken of history. The process of realignment among all the once-allied groups was ongoing, but it was probably particularly intense in the years immediately after Nedao.

The Huns struck into Pannonia to restore their control but were repelled before Thiudmir and Vidimir even received news of the invasion.[54] The Huns were probably living in nearby Dacia Ripensis and launched their attack soon after the settlement in 455.[55] This episode may have produced the legendary "Battle between the Goths and Huns" recorded in Nordic and English poetry.[56] By 461, Valamir could no longer hold his bands in check. Angered by the Roman favoritism shown to Theodoric Strabo, son of Triarius, and the delay of the annual imperial gifts due to them according to the settlement agreement, Valamir and the Ostrogoths rebelled. A new treaty with three hundred pounds of gold per year pacified them, but Thiudmir in return, and with reluctance, had to send his son Theodoric, then seven, to Constantinople as a hostage. Only Valamir could convince Thiudmir to release him.[57] The three hundred pounds of gold enabled Valamir to reward his followers according to their rank and to maintain the peace, but within a few years his eager bands attacked the Sadagis and thereby broke the *foedus* with Rome and invited a final attack from the Huns. The Huns comprised only a remnant of their former strength, for only four groups now rallied to battle. The Goths routed them and drove them from the field.[58] One of the Hunnic groups, the Bittugures, joined the Ostrogoths and eventually migrated to Italy with them in 488–89. In fact, Ragnaris, the leader of the Gothic holdouts at Campsa in 553, was not "Gothic" but a Bittuguric Hun and was still distinguished as such.[59] The Ostrogoths relived their old fears and hatreds against the Huns only once more. In 466–67 the Huns recrossed the Danube, and Rome was forced to deal with another uprising of her Balkan allies. The Roman generals Anagestes, Basiliscus, and Ostryis (except for Basiliscus obviously Germanic and probably Gothic) had little difficulty penning the Goths in the mountainous valleys, where starvation won submission of both the Goths and the numerous Huns among them. The Romans demanded that they split into groups corresponding to the subdivisions of the Roman army to facilitate their feeding and ultimate dispersal to lands for settlement. To the leaders of one of these groups of Goths, Chelchal delivered his fateful reminder of their bondage with which we began our discussion.

Freed from the accursed attacks of the Huns, the Ostrogoths spent a decade warring and cattle rustling. First the Suevi under Hunimund crossed the Danube and drove off some cattle grazing in the plains there. By this time Gothic herdsmen had wandered into Dalmatia from their original settlement areas in Pannonia. Thiudmir launched a swift night attack near Lake Pelso and captured Hunimund and many others. Some were enslaved to the Goths, but Thiudmir showed great mercy to Hunimund and his personal followers. In a gesture stemming from the heart of a long tradition of blending the traditions of kin and follower, Thiudmir adopted Hunimund as his son and, freeing him, sent him back across the Danube with his men. The episode demonstrates the continuation of basically family-oriented solutions to problems among the Germans, whereas they dealt with Rome through treaties and legally defined mutual obligations. Unfortunately, Hunimund and the Suevi proved themselves as feckless as Sundila and the Rosomonni had been to Ermanaric. Hunimund allied with the Sciri, an Alanic people previously on peaceful terms with the Goths, and attacked. Valamir died while encouraging his men from horseback sometime around 471. The Sciri suffered full vengeance but refused to return peacefully to Moesia, where they were living at the time.[60]

Thiudmir took the banner of kingship from his fallen brother and pursued the war against the remnants of the Sciri, under Edeca and Hunuulf. Meanwhile, the Suevi brought in some Sarmatians as allies.[61] At this time the Eastern emperor Leo overruled his *magister militum* Aspar's neutrality and aided the Sciri.[62] Both Leo and Aspar knew the situation well. Leo had served as a military tribune in Dacia Ripensis and commanded the garrison of Selymbria on the southern coast of Thrace. Aspar had ruled the East in all but title since 434 and was himself a Goth. His marriage to the aunt of Theodoric Triarius and his command of numerous Gothic contingents kept him particularly well informed of events in the Balkans. Possibly Leo hoped to prevent the Amali-led Ostrogoths from solidifying their power in fear that they would then drift under the influence of Aspar and the Gothic faction at court and thereby further unbalance the delicate military and political situation. Although the motivations of Leo and Aspar are unclear, their hatred toward each other still illuminates the records.[63] Leo owed his elevation to Aspar, who had been commander of Thrace when Leo served at Selymbria, and was determined to free himself of his warlord's tutelage. Their animosity and mistrust explain why Leo chose his incompetent brother-in-law Basiliscus rather than Aspar to head the great expedition of 468 against the Vandals in Africa. Rivalries at court spun a web of intrigue involving the future emperor Zeno and the control of the Isaurian troops in Constantinople, the last weight on the balance to offset Aspar and the Gothic faction. In 471, probably the same year as the decision to aid the Sciri, Aspar fell victim to assassination by the palace eunuchs.[64] The Germanic troops rampaged through the city and into the palace but were stopped short and forced to flee. Under Count Ostrys, escaping Goths fled to Thrace and joined Theodoric Triarius and the Ostrogoths serving there as federates. Triarius now demanded the legacy of Aspar. Leo immediately saw his new foe as a continuation of Germanic domination and set about neutralizing his claim to the leadership of the Gothic faction—he sent Theodoric, son of Thiudmir, home.[65]

A treasure from the vicinity of Cluj-Someşeni probably dates from the period after the disintegration of the Hunnic Empire but before the end of the century and adds several dimensions to the era. The polychrome style is similar to that at Apahida II, but the symbols of Hunnic sway are absent, replaced by designs derived from the Eastern Empire, especially polychromed finger rings and pendants in the shape of a cross, implying a Christian influence.[66] The collars and rings of pagan power still held their allure but were already locked in a competition with Christian/Roman concepts that was to last throughout Ostrogothic history. Alas, the similarities to the finds from Reggio Emilia in Italy are not striking enough to establish securely the ethnicity as Ostrogothic; a Gepidic origin is also possible.[67]

However, the buckle is quite similar (but not identical) to finds from Slovakia and the western Carpathians, particularly at Gyulavári.[68] Some of these in turn are closely linked stylistically to late-fifth- and sixth-century items found among the Ostrogoths who remained in the Crimea. In fact, the treasure from Cluj-Someşeni, especially its Christian influences, is quite comparable to Ostrogothic artifacts from the Crimea, where there is no question of Gepidic advance.[69]

The odds then seem to favor an Ostrogothic identity for Cluj-Someşeni and perhaps for several finds from the Hungarian area, particularly at Gáva, Kosino (Barabás), Tiszalök, Kiskunfiligyhaza, and Gyulavári.[70] That is the area traditionally regarded as under Gepidic control. Such finds may indicate a lingering of Ostrogothic bands scattered across the area of the former Hunnic Empire for several decades before most, but not all, joined Theodoric in his march to Italy. Culturally, the Ostrogoths were locked in the web spun outward from Byzantium more completely than ever before. But unlike the Ostrogoths in the Crimea who became faithful allies of the empire and orthodox Christians,[71] those under Thiudmir and his son drifted virtually out of the Byzantine military and political system.

When Theodoric at the age of eighteen returned to his father in 471, he found him at war with those Sarmatians allied with the Sciri. Bands of Sarmatians had crossed the Danube, and Singidunum was in their hands. Theodoric now accepted his manhood as an Amali prince and assembled a large following of retainers, including several trusted warriors from his father. With these he crossed the Danube to strike at the Sarmatian villages, whose riches were his booty, and turned to free Singidunum. In short order the old Roman city was "safe," but it was an imperial city and as such should have been returned, at least nominally, to Leo. Theodoric kept the city for himself.[72] There is no reason to doubt Jordanes on the treatment of Singidunum, especially since it parallels some of the actions of the Rugian kings Feletheus and Flaccitheus in Noricum.[73] However, Leo must have regarded Theodoric as a traitor. In fact, Leo may well have encouraged Theodoric to attack the Sarmatians as part of a reversal of policy designed to appease the Amali at the expense of the decimated Sciri and their allies. But already his fragile juggling of Ostrogothic factions, in order to control both Theodorics, was in jeopardy.

By 473, famine—a grim reality rarely absent among all barbarians—forced Thiudmir to drift southward, while his brother Vidimir departed for the west, ultimately joining the Visigoths in Gaul.[74] Thiudmir's assault on Naissus in search of food aroused imperial concern if not compassion. Leo offered lands in Macedonia near Pella where they could find supplies and settle. Ulpiana and Stobi opened their gates and probably provided supplies as ordered by Leo. The plan was carefully supervised by the patrician Hilarianus from his garrison at Thessalonika, doubtless according to the dictates of *hospitalitas* as generally spelled out in the Theodosian Code (VII, 8). After some minor skirmishes, the Goths took up their grants around Cyrrus (Cerru), Pella (Pellas), Europus (Europa, northeast of Pella), Methone (Mediana), Pydna (Petina), Beroea (Bereu), and Dium (Sium).[75] Presumably *comites* such as Astat and Invilia, important commanders loyal to Thiudmir and Theodoric, were paired with local magnates in each of these areas under the supervision of Thiudmir and Hilarianus. Similar billeting and/or settlement procedures were later used in Italy and are much better documented. Neither Leo nor Thiudmir lived to witness the complex struggles and alliances their settlement produced. Thiudmir died soon afterward, having appointed his son as successor, and Leo was probably already dead, replaced by Zeno.

Unfortunately, the Goths under Theodoric Triarius already lived in Thrace as *foederati*.[76] The juxtaposition of two rival lines within the narrow confines of the Macedonian plain produced immediate friction. Theodoric Triarius pressed his claims against the empire in an effort to secure the inheritance of Aspar and enhance his position vis-à-vis all the Goths in the area through Roman support. Zeno initially planned to use Theodoric Thiudmir and some of his followers to strengthen the inner defenses of the Danubian *limes* by stationing them near Marcianopolis, but the majority of the Amali-led Ostrogoths remained in their settlement areas around Pella, where some may have cast their lots with Triarius. By this time Zeno and Triarius were traditional enemies dating well back into the reign of Leo, when Rome found in Zeno and the Isaurians an effective counter to Aspar and the Goths. Their hatred intensified when Theodoric Triarius gained control of Aspar's soldiers.[77] Zeno at once stopped tribute payments made since 473–74, when Leo had also made Theodoric Thiudmir *magister militum praesentalis*, and issued an ultimatum for Triarius to renounce the leadership of the Goths and send his son to Constantinople. If he did so, Zeno would allow him to retire to his personal estates.[78] Such generosity earned a quick response—Theodoric Triarius assembled his people for war.

Triarius and his allied commanders, including Basiliscus, returning from his ignominious defeat at the hands of Gaiseric and the Vandals, drove Zeno from the capital. For over a year and a half (475–76), Basiliscus ruled in Constantinople while Zeno launched a coordinated attack upon Triarius in Macedonia. Theodoric Thiudmir was to march south from Marcianopolis and join forces with the *magister per Thraciam* and 2,000 cavalry in the Haemus range. Together they would then continue to Adrianople, where they would join the garrisons of the various Thracian cities, numbering 20,000 foot and 6,000 horse.[79] Events still went against Zeno. The garrisons of Thrace and even the cavalry attached to the commander disappeared, leaving the rival Theodorics face to face near Sondis. Since Theodoric, son of Thiudmir, had taken only some of his forces to Marcianopolis, he was badly outnumbered. Still worse, Theodoric Triarius held the high ground. After a few exchanges of booty—especially cattle rustling—the leaders taunted each other, each insulting his opponent's leadership. After Triarius won command of the field in verbal combat, Theodoric Thiudmir had no choice but to listen to his own people. He saw them back away and refuse to die against other Goths. They had suffered too much to waste their lives settling an old personal rivalry. Their stomachs and their families demanded food and land.[80]

Theodoric Thiudmir had lived up to his commitments to the empire, and his failure and humiliation were laid at Zeno's feet. He demanded a new settlement, for returning to the recent establishments near Pella was unthinkable.[81] The emperor now had every reason to court Triarius rather than to accede to the humiliated Amal's desires. In Constantinople, Basiliscus was proving as incompetent as emperor as he had been as admiral and soon alienated Triarius by bestowing high positions on a young kinsman, Armatus, the lover of his wife, the empress Zenonis.[82] Zeno decided to secure the Balkans under Triarius. He rejected Theodoric Thiudmir's demand for new lands and declared war, offering Triarius Theodoric Thiudmir's command in return for his leading a picked force of 13,000 Goths at imperial expense.[83] After complex intrigues and defections, Zeno returned to a capital partially ruined. A great fire had swept the city while he was away. His travail had only begun.

Theodoric Thiudmir, enraged at his betrayal but powerless against the forces arrayed against him, lashed out in a brief and bloody reprisal against the communities in the Rhodope Mountains. His bands carried off livestock and slaughtered peasants.[84] Quickly, however, sanity overcame his tantrum, and he led his people westward in retreat. At Thessalonika the people overthrew the military government and placed the city in the hands of the bishop, who promptly concluded an agreement with Theodoric. Alas, hunger knows no law, and the Goths spilled over the town and countryside in desperate foraging for supplies.[85] Marching along the arterial highway of the Balkans, the Ostrogoths sacked and burned Stobi in Macedonia.[86] At Heraclea, supplies from the archbishop enabled Theodoric to move on without laying waste the countryside.[87] Only after such plundering did Zeno finally offer a settlement—near Pautalia, a town in the province of Dacia Mediterranea (see Map 3). There the prefect would pay them two hundred pounds of gold to buy the provisions necessary for survival until their crops were harvested.[88] Theodoric refused.

Although the city of Pautalia exhibited vestiges of Roman town life, the surrounding territory was still basically Thracian, and the scattered Roman villas had already been in ruins for a half century, probably victims of Visigothic wrath following the battle of Adrianople.[89] The Ostrogoths knew that better lands for settlement were open farther west along the coast. After all, many of them had first proven their prowess in raids in Illyricum, toward which they again turned their wagons. West of Heraclea, the terrain fractures into mountainous boulder heaps cut by small streams, ideal for ambush, especially where the Via Egnatia sliced through narrow passes. Steadfast defense could have quickly reduced the Goths to starvation, but the Byzantine garrisons fled with most of the inhabitants of the towns. Only the town of Lychnidus held out, but to no avail. Once past Scampa, whose residents fled at the sound of Gothic wagons, the Via Egnatia descended to the flat coastal strip south of Dyrrachium.[90] The Ostrogoths, tired and hungry, sought a place to stop and settle, preferably centered in a "walled city" where they could find refuge and supplies.[91]

Theodoric sent one of his followers, Sidimund, ahead to Epidaurum. Sidimund knew the town and its inhabitants, since he himself had lived there, and had little difficulty scaring the citizens out. Theodoric split his forces, leaving the baggage and most of the army behind, and dashed ahead with his cavalry to secure the abandoned city. Negotiations with Zeno had resumed and were entering a final phase of working out the details for a settlement in "fertile and uninhabited" Dardania.[92] Theodoric had no reason to fear for his people left behind under his most able commanders, *dux* Soas and Theodoric's brother Theodimund—or did he?

Zeno had regained control at Constantinople and was apparently ready to reattempt his juggling act with the Theodorics. What is more, he feared that Theodoric Thiudmir was about to set sail for Italy, thereby complicating any efforts to influence events there and leaving Triarius without peer in the Balkans. So it was perhaps with nightmares of Aspar clouding his vision that he scuttled the negotiations just when they promised success. Theodoric Thiudmir had agreed to surrender his mother and sister as hostages, provide 6,000

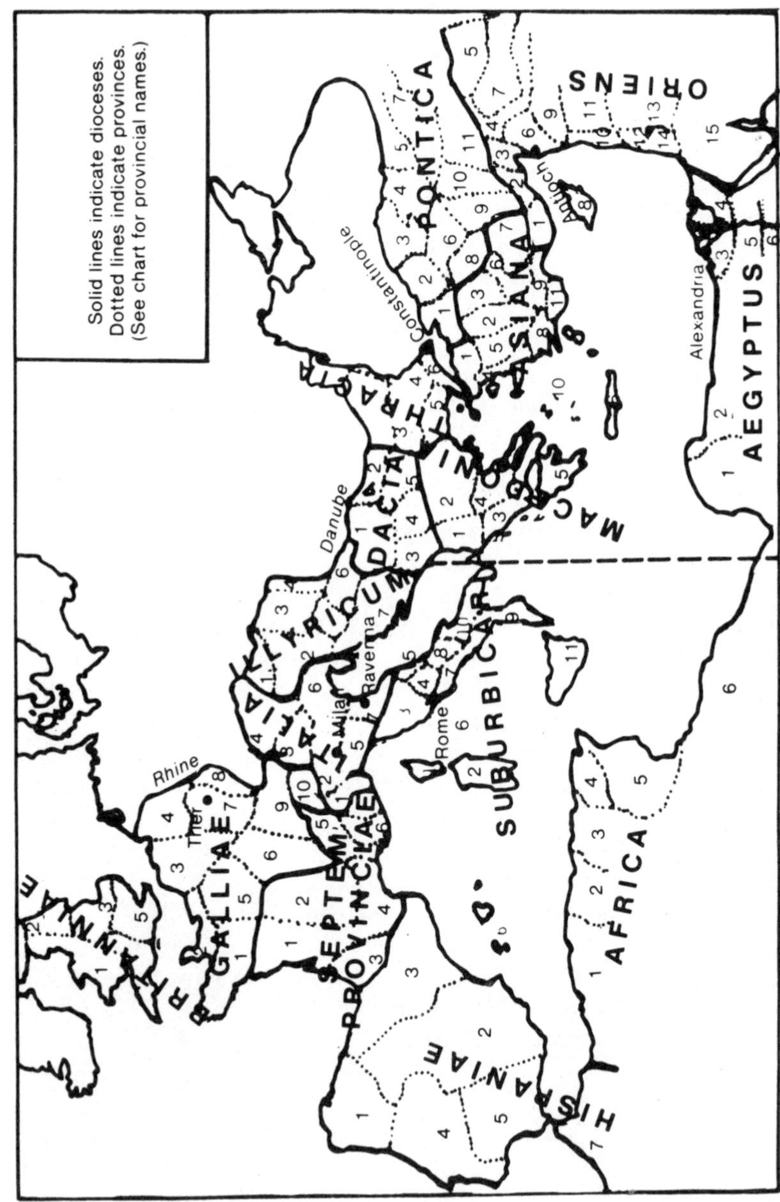

Map 3: Dioceses and Provinces of the Roman Empire in the Fourth and Fifth Centuries A.D.

Key to Map 3
DIOCESES AND PROVINCES
Western Division

Britanniae
1. Valentia
2. Britannia II
3. Flavia Caesariensis
4. Britannia
5. Maxima Caesariensis

Galliae
1. Ludgunensis III
2. Ludgunensis II
3. Belgica II
4. Germania II
5. Ludgunensis Senonia
6. Ludgunensis I
7. Belgica I
8. Germania I
9. Maxima Sequanorum
10. Alpes Poeninae

Septem Provinciae
1. Aquitanica II
2. Aquitanica I
3. Novem Populi
4. Narbonensis I
5. Viennensis
6. Narbonensis II
7. Alpes Maritimae

Hispaniae
1. Gallaecia
2. Carthaginiensis
3. Tarraconensis
4. Lusitania
5. Baetica
6. Insulae Balearum
7. Tingitania

Africa
1. Mauretania Caesariensis
2. Mauretania Sitifensis
3. Numidia
4. Africa
5. Byzacena
6. Tripolitania

Italia
1. Alpes Cottiae
2. Aemilia
3. Raetia I
4. Raetia II
5. Liguria
6. Venetia et Histria
7. Flaminia et Picenum

Suburbicaria
1. Corsica
2. Sardinia
3. Tuscia et Umbria
4. Valeria
5. Picenum Suburbicarium
6. Roma
7. Campania
8. Samnium
9. Bruttii et Lucania
10. Apulia et Calabria
11. Sicilia

Illyricum
1. Noricum Ripense
2. Noricum Mediterraneum
3. Pannonia I
4. Valeria
5. Savia
6. Pannonia II
7. Dalmatia

Key to Map 3 (*continued*)

DIOCESES AND PROVINCES

Eastern Division

Dacia

1. Moesia I
2. Dacia Ripensis
3. Praevalitana
4. Dardania
5. Dacia Mediterranea

Macedonia

1. Epirus Nova
2. Macedonia
3. Epirus Vetus
4. Thessalia
5. Achaea
6. Creta

Thracia

1. Moesia II
2. Scythia
3. Thracia
4. Haemimontus
5. Rhodope
6. Europa

Asiana

1. Hellespontus
2. Phrygia Pacatiana
3. Phrygia Salutaris
4. Asia
5. Lydia
6. Pisidia
7. Lycaonia
8. Caria
9. Pamphylia
10. Insulae
11. Lycia

Pontica

1. Bithynia
2. Honorias
3. Paphlagonia
4. Helenopontus
5. Pontus Polemoniacus
6. Galatia
7. Armenia I
8. Galatia Salutaris
9. Cappadocia II
10. Cappadocia I
11. Armenia II

Oriens

1. Isauria
2. Cilicia I
3. Cilicia II
4. Euphratensis
5. Mesopotamia
6. Syria
7. Osrhoene
8. Cyprus
9. Syria Salutaris
10. Phoenice
11. Phoenice Libanensis
12. Palaestina II
13. Arabia
14. Palaestina I
15. Palaestina Salutaris

Aegyptus

1. Libya Superior
2. Libya Inferior
3. Aegyptus
4. Augustamnica
5. Arcadia
6. Thebais

men against Triarius and the Goths in Thrace, again in revolt, or even to restore Nepos in the West. For that he demanded to be made *strategos* in Triarius's place and to be welcomed as a Roman citizen in Constantinople.[93] Zeno was in no mood to trade one German overlord for another. Citizenship for a Germanic *strategos* in Thrace resurrected visions of Gainas in 400 and more recently Aspar and Triarius, images of emperors resisting tutelage from their barbarian condottieri. The actual restoration of Nepos was, perhaps, no longer desirable, for by continuing to accept Odovacar tacitly, Zeno could exert more influence on Odovacar's brother Onoulph, an important but restless and virtually independent commander in Illyricum. Furthermore, Odovacar acknowledged both Zeno and Nepos until the latter's death in 480. Thus, while negotiations were still going on between Theodoric and the Byzantine envoy Adamantius, Roman troops assembled at Lychnidus and attacked the Gothic wagons under Theodimund. At Epidaurum, Theodoric knew nothing until it was too late. Even Soas and the bulk of the army were too far ahead to save the situation. At Candavia, the Byzantines under the *magister militum* for Thrace, Sabinianus, and some troops dispatched by Onoulph, *magister militum per Illyricum* and brother to Odovacar, captured 2,000 wagons and over 5,000 Goths. Theodimund and his mother barely managed to escape by literally burning the bridges behind them. So many wagons were captured that Sabinianus canceled his requisitions from the cities for transport and still had to burn many lest they fall back into Gothic hands.[94]

Sabinianus was content not to press the attack against the forces under Theodoric, and until Zeno ordered his death in 482, he was able to contain Theodoric and his followers in Epirus Nova. Denied freedom of action to the east, Ostrogothic bands roamed northwestward, even perhaps as far as Noricum, where they apparently raided the pitiful cities along the *limes*. Gothic raids were one more disaster to those communities seeking to tread a path between subjugation to the Rugians and absolute annihilation at the hands of numerous uncontrolled groups of warriors. In desperation, many towns turned to Saint Severinus, sought to restore contact with the Roman army, and ultimately had to surrender their freedom to Rugian kings or obey the summons from Odovacar to abandon Noricum and flee to Italy.[95] The Ostrogoths found themselves naturally against Odovacar, the Sciric lord and son of Edica, brother of Onoulph, and traditional enemy of the Ostrogoths. The luckless Zeno meanwhile (ca. 477–82) faced the rebellions of Illus and Marcian.[96] Triarius died in battle in 481, in his final effort to save Zeno, but prior to his death he reestablished links with the Goths in Epirus Nova.[97] In seeking the alliance of his old rival, Triarius perhaps planned to follow the crushing of Marcian with a concerted drive to harness Zeno with a Germanic dependence. If so, his death intervened. But in 482, Theodoric Thiudmir (henceforth simply Theodoric), no longer restrained by Sabinianus, left Epirus Nova, raided Greece, and sacked Larissa.[98] The final act of the long struggle in the Balkans was reaching a climax.

The rebellions at home, the death of Triarius, and the foolish slaying of Sabinianus left Zeno with none to whom he could turn but Theodoric, who was probably moving eastward anyway. To clear the way for an alliance with Theodoric, Zeno ordered the execution of Triarius's son Recitach.[99] This act ultimately enabled Theodoric to unite under his command almost all of the Ostrogoths in the Balkans. Zeno, however, was still reluctant to pit Theodoric directly against Illus, perhaps fearing their alliance against him. So he withheld the Gothic troops, already at Nicomedia, and sent some Rugians under Ermenaric, son of Aspar.[100] By then it was too late for a decisive campaign. Illus bargained for an eastern command and spent the next six years in Antioch and Isauria, where he was captured and beheaded in 488.[101] Zeno then had to placate Theodoric and moved a step closer to reviving the German tutelage that had lapsed since Aspar's death. In 483 Theodoric became *magister militum praesentalis* and consul designate for 484; as such he commanded the Danubian provinces of Dacia Ripensis and Moesia Inferior and the adjacent areas.[102]

Theodoric established his main camp at Novae. In 486 the Ostrogoths pillaged Thrace. In 487 Melentia and many other cities in Moesia and Thrace were attacked.[103] Most rapidly recovered from these raids and, in fact, achieved a return of prosperity in the sixth century. The Bulgarian invasions and settlements ultimately destroyed the antique urban centers in the area.[104] Novae itself was only slightly damaged, since it was the seat of Ostrogothic power during these troubled years.[105]

Meanwhile, Odovacar decided to press his advantage and threatened to invade the western Balkans, now freed as he was from his old rival Theodoric and cut off by circumstances from any Byzantine intervention. Zeno dispatched the Rugians, by now bitter foes of Odovacar after his campaigns in Noricum, but they were ill-matched and easily routed. Their king and his followers sought refuge with Theodoric at Novae.[106] Next Zeno made one last attempt to secure Theodoric's support by returning his sister, perhaps a hostage for almost a decade.[107]

The gravity of the situation during the last half of the fifth century is reflected in the apparent demise of the Danubian fleet. The Romans maintained their fleet even during the difficult reign of Theodosius the Great.[108] Theodosius II in 412 reemphasized the fleet, whose effectiveness is confirmed by Vegetius.[109] As late as 443, units were stationed at Viminacium, Aegeta, Ratiaria, Transmarisca, and Noviodunum.[110] Then there is silence in our rather ample sources until reference in Theophanes Simocatta to movements in the early and again in the late sixth century.[111] Thus in the late fifth century, not only was land contact with the West lost, but so too was the river artery. No wonder the cities of Noricum felt isolated, with barge traffic irregular and often virtually at a halt, with food and oil sometimes scarce.[112] Crisis was at hand.

The Ostrogoths were running out of supplies and patience—their dreams of settlement and for many a return to a routine of farming, herding, and petty raiding were still unfulfilled. Zeno, enmeshed in eastern problems, was desperately trying to strengthen the defenses of the Haemus and Rhodope ranges lest Constantinople itself come under attack.[113] The departure of the Ostrogoths for Italy in 488 was mutually advantageous, so much so that the sources give both men credit for the idea.[114] Neither could have anticipated the future successful coexistence of barbarian and Roman under the Ostrogothic Kingdom in Italy. Theodoric and his followers, now including many of the Triarian group and other recalcitrant nobles, but not all, turned back toward their longtime foe and the hardships of migration.[115] By now Roman control had so slipped that few established markets could be expected. Human vultures had picked the countryside bare, and at least one winter still loomed between them and the fertile Po Valley, to say nothing of Odovacar and his allies. Zeno could allow himself only a half smile, knowing too well that the departure of the Ostrogoths was in a way a defeat. He was free from a powerful German warlord, but for how long? The Romans were still too weak to reestablish a strong presence in the Balkans. The road to revitalization took many turns before Justinian could restore Roman control.

News of the Ostrogoths on the march far outdistanced their wagons. Cities along the route either closed their gates or could not provide a market capable of sustaining perhaps 40,000 hungry people.[116] Sirmium might have, but it was probably under Gepidic domination and dared not befriend the Ostrogoths. By the time the Ostrogoths reached the Ulca River, actually a swamp draining into the Danube near Cibalae, famine had begun its relentless summoning of the weak.[117] At the Ulca, the Gepids defied Theodoric, yelling insults across the swampy stream. There was no turning back, for to empty stomachs this battle was a final one. The struggle raged until nightfall, when Theodoric's men broke through and seized the Gepidic wagons laden with the harvest. With these supplies they pushed on, up the Drava River (modern Drau) through the winter of 488–89.[118] By spring the leading elements were descending the Julian Alps and awaiting the stragglers at the staging area east of the Isonzo River. The last wagons did not appear until late summer, affording Odovacar ample time to fortify the fords and gather his forces.[119] Once again food was scarce and battle imminent, but this time Italy and visions of a cornucopia were within sight.

4

Theodoric's Kingdom Surveyed

THE VISION

PERHAPS THEODORIC found time while awaiting his scattered people on the eastern bank of the Isonzo River to reflect and ponder what lay before him.[1] Certainly his immediate thoughts centered on Odovacar and war, but his confidence in victory doubtless grew as the army assembled. Of course, he would rout an accursed Sciric prince just as his father and uncles had a generation before. Beyond the final reckoning with his traditional foe, Theodoric anticipated the settlement of his people on the lands of Italy and his own triumphal entries into Ravenna, Milan, and, most especially, Rome herself—the very heart of his conceptual world. Rome had begun to mold his thoughts and the lives of his followers long ago. Forget that Milan had for generations usurped much of the economic and military leadership of Italy and that Roman emperors had abandoned Rome as indefensible, seeking refuge behind the swamps surrounding Ravenna. There they felt safe from the barbarians, if not from the mosquitos. To the barbarians, Rome was still the mistress of the world.

Zacharias of Mytilene compiled a description of the city during the early sixth century.

> Now the description of the decorations of the city, given shortly, is as follows, with respect to the wealth of its inhabitants, and their great and pre-eminent prosperity, and their grand and glorious objects of luxury and pleasure, as in a great city of wonderful beauty.
>
> Now its pre-eminent decorations are as follows, not to speak of the splendour inside the houses and the beautiful formation of the columns in their halls and of their colonnades (?) and of their staircases, and their lofty height, as in the city of wonderful beauty.
>
> It contains 24 churches of the blessed apostles, Catholic churches. It contains 2 great *basilicae*, where the king sits and the senators are assembled before him every day. It contains 324 great spacious streets. It contains 2 great capitols. It contains 80 golden gods. It contains 64 ivory gods. It contains 46,603 dwelling-houses. It contains 1797 houses of magnates. It contains 1352 reservoirs pouring forth water. It contains 274 bakers, who are constantly making and distributing *annonae* to the inhabitants of the city, besides those who make and sell in the city. It contains 5000 cemeteries, where they lay out and bury. It contains 31 great marble pedestals. It contains 3785 bronze statues of kings and magistrates. It contains, moreover, 25 bronze statues of Abraham, Sarah, and Hagar, and of the kings of the house of David, which Vespasian the king brought up when he sacked Jerusalem, and the gates of Jerusalem and other bronze objects.[2]

Thus even to an easterner, Rome inspired awe. To a barbarian, she was truly beyond words. Theodoric was one of only a handful of rulers to see both Rome and Constantinople in late antiquity. In the West, Rome was incomparable. Once-prosperous Trier remained, engulfed but still Roman, as an enclave in Francia, but Rome and Italy still vibrated with all the sights and sounds of late Roman life. The Ostrogoths, unlike any other barbarian group, entered the living heart of the Western Empire. Here alone the currents of civilization still flowed in unison.

During his life, and for decades thereafter, Romans saw in Theodoric the best and worst qualities of Valentinian I. Ennodius, praising him in panegyric in early 507, repeatedly drew from Quintus Aurelius Symmachus on Valentinian I.[3] So too the popular *Gesta de Xysti purgatione* cast Theodoric during the Symmachian Schism as a demented Valentinian.[4] An anonymous source written in Byzantine-controlled Ravenna in the 540s went so far as to claim that Theodoric deliberately modeled his rule on Valentinian's reign.[5] Consciously or unconsciously, Theodoric did emulate the great warrior-emperor of the fourth century, for their worlds were similar in many ways. An important feature of both reigns was the obstinate, often frustrating, but nonetheless crucial, presence of the Roman senatorial aristocracy. Many of the great Roman clans in sixth-century Italy traced their family's rise to prominence directly to the late fourth century.[6] Ties of *amicitia* still penetrated deeply into the fabric of religion and politics. Cleavages within Christendom had replaced the celebrated last stands of paganism, but the exchange of literary anecdotes and tediously arcane letters flourished still.

The parallels between Valentinian and Theodoric went far beyond mimicry and reveal the great debt Theodoric and many other barbarian kings owed to syntheses produced within Roman society during its Indian summer from Julian through Theodosius the Great. That was true for several reasons, and foremost among them were the needs for an effective and vigorous military command, renewed participation in the government by the upper classes, and a more efficient bureaucracy. As a result of the continuance of these demands, never of course realized, the role of the senatorial élite had not changed appreciably, particularly the importance of the great propertied families in and around Rome. Following time-honored patterns, the holding of public honors leading to the urban and praetorian prefectures punctuated periods of stately leisure.[7] When in office, the pace of the élite's political lives quickened. Old friends turned to them for assistance, and substantive issues more frequently entered their letters of *amicitia*. Out of office, their concerns remained essentially the same, focused perhaps even more intently on the world of their estates and the cultural envelope gradually blending *Romanitas* and *Christianitas* that clearly defined their class. Of course, to secure their diminished but still-impressive lifestyles, they, in their turn, looked to the centers of power—Ravenna, Rome, and Constantinople. Expressions of friendship addressed to them at leisure reverted to the vacuous effusions typical of the day.[8] As self-centered and shortsighted as this élite remained, the government of Italy, and, after 509, of Provence, found it indispensable. Men like Boethius, Ennodius, Faustus, Festus, and Symmachus provided a sustaining ruling class intimately concerned with the swirl of events affecting their estates and the centers of culture. Their frequent interactions as a group in and around Rome converged on the senate, particularly the area around Trajan's forum where many may have studied as youths, and where their own protégés now labored over the fine points of Latin. Another center had emerged at Saint Peter's, accompanying the papal entourage. The import of their discussions was conveyed to Theodoric formally, informally, and even surreptitiously by the still-menacing *agentes in rebus*, by his own men, especially the *saiones* and *defensores civitatis*, and by the senators themselves.[9]

The almost overwhelming Roman presence forced Theodoric to

devote his reign to crafting a special place for his people and his dynasty. In a letter written for Theodoric by Cassiodorus (ca. 508) to the emperor Anastasius, not surprisingly the first letter of the *Variae*, Theodoric said, "Our kingship is an imitation of yours, styled on your good purpose, a copy of the real empire; and in so far as we follow you do we surpass other nations."[10] But in reality his vision of rule matured significantly beyond mere imitation, for as king of the Ostrogoths he felt a duty to provide his people with a system of government in which they could preserve their own strengths and traditions within the overall harmony of the Roman world. Moreover, the Goths living along the frontiers had long been a part of that world. Now they confronted Rome herself. Although they had to conquer Italy from Odovacar, officially they still came onto Roman soil as immigrants. Roman law once again guided their settlement, and the Roman bureaucracy continued to serve the state almost everywhere they turned. The Ostrogoths were similar to many other immigrants in their struggles to adapt to their new homes without losing their identity. What singles them out is their king, Theodoric. He alone was able to articulate and had the power and finesse to initiate a program of controlled assimilation of Germans into Roman society. The royal family was to take the lead, followed much later by the nobility and the rest of society. Theodoric had his daughter and grandson tutored in Latin letters and paid the salaries of professors at Rome, but he forbade Goths to attend Roman schools.[11] Perhaps we can best gain an overall glimpse of his program, followed to some extent by all of his successors, in the outlines presented in Ostrogothic coinage.

Symbolically, Theodoric minted gold coins scarcely distinguishable from the issues of the East. Indeed, the Ostrogothic kings, like Odovacar before them, never questioned the basic structure of the Roman monetary system. The thought probably did not even occur to them. They took for granted the imperial prerogative to control the striking of gold, which for Goth and Roman alike secured and guaranteed the psychological acceptance of the entire coinage. Silver and bronze coins were subspecies used for regular exchange, and their symbolism varied substantially, especially on the Ostrogothic bronze issues, without ever affecting the monetary structure as a whole. Theodoric again led the way, introducing several new series in bronze and fixing new rates of exchange for the three metals.[12] Yet despite these technical and stylistic innovations, the Goths actually parted from Roman traditions very gradually. Thus also in coinage Theodoric and his successors carefully explored ways to express Gothic diversity and independence within overall Roman unity.

Although many aspects of his government in Italy evolved out of his conception of the office of *magister militum* and his experiences as a federate commander, by 489/90 Theodoric was already clearly different from either Aspar or Triarius. He had spent fifteen years in the Balkans, usually as the acknowledged leader of 30,000 to 40,000 men, women, and children with a gradually tightening concept of group identity. Furthermore, he was a veteran of settlement and resettlement. Indeed, the settlement near Pella in 474, made under his father, had occurred in accordance with the same Roman law of *hospitalitas* that applied in Italy. In the Balkans, Theodoric had revealed his conviction that any durable settlement had to be conducted by Roman officials and properly recorded.[13] However, his past experience with settlements and his duty as king doubtless made Theodoric pause before going ahead, but he had little choice. Compromises and risks had to be dared. He doubtless knew that some of the Gothic nobility would almost certainly seek their own gain at the crown's expense. Many had abandoned their homes along the middle Danube to follow Theodoric on his journeys, and now he realized that they would try to reestablish their own enclaves in Italy.[14] Nor had he forgotten their perfidy after the settlements around Pella, when he had taken some soldiers to Marcianopolis in fulfillment of his treaty commitments only to discover some of those he had left behind drifting into alliance with his rival Triarius. Italy was too big to govern without delegating much of his power to regional lords, and he did so anticipating many problems.

Because of his inevitable insecurity, Theodoric, like Alaric and a host of other kings of his era, searched for greater authority over his own people by invoking the conceptual hierarchy of Christian Rome with its titular elevations and ranks delineated in dress and court ceremonial. He was quick to perceive the potential for dynastic continuity in associating himself with Roman tradition and the special role of the monarchy in Christendom.[15] In part that explains Theodoric's desire for such Roman denotations of power as the praenomen Flavius, the title Patrician, the consulship, the rank of *magister militum praesentalis*, and his efforts to have his regal position in Italy recognized in Constantinople.

Faced with complex problems of loyalty from both his aristocracies, Theodoric sought to create unity within diversity, to give Roman aristocrats a sense of purpose while controlling his own Gothic nobility's desire for leadership and independence. Italy was to be a divided society in which Roman and Goth were to remain separate but complementary. Under these trying circumstances, Theodoric became more than a king but less than an emperor. We may credit him with the most complex vision of society and government since Constantine. However, having chosen to stand at the apex of both the Roman and the Gothic hierarchies, his footing could never be fully secure. In the end, Theodoric's program fell victim to the same obstacle that has frustrated countless others: the fact that no culture is ever entirely successful in picking and choosing which aspects of another culture to welcome and which to reject. Assimilation proceeded at its own pace. Certainly by 489, it was too late for anyone, even a Theodoric, to hold Goths and Romans apart culturally while in fact throwing them together in so many other areas of life. Culturally, as we have seen and will further explore, some Goths were already heavily Romanized, and virtually all were changed from their remote ancestors. From their religion, a centerpiece of communal life, to the fibulae adorning their personal dress, they unwittingly manifested Roman influence. The momentum of Romanization among the Ostrogoths was irreversible and irrepressible. The bits and pieces of Roman life were inextricably intertwined, and to accept one was to risk accepting all. The tasks of governing and defending left no choice for Theodoric but to associate Goths with Romans and take the gamble that he could control their relationships.

THE STRUGGLE

Late in 489, the Ostrogoths crossed the Isonzo but were able to inflict only a temporary defeat on Odovacar, who yielded the fords grudgingly before falling back to Verona to protect the Po Valley (see Map 4). Between 27 and 30 September, Theodoric drove Odovacar out of Verona as far as Como, where in 490 Odovacar unsuccessfully made a stand at the Addua River. From Como, Odovacar broke southward through Milan and then, absorbing his garrisons and their families along the Po, proceeded to Ravenna. Ravenna proved beyond Theodoric's reach, for without a fleet he was unable to prevent resupply by sea. Bowing to necessity, Theodoric briefly accepted Odovacar as coruler, but in 493 he terminated joint rule by hewing Odovacar in two with his own hands, boasting in almost epic fashion that his suspicions were at last confirmed—Odovacar had no *backbone*.[16] In fact, however, their lifelong opponent bequeathed to the Ostrogoths many enduring legacies upon which to base their rule.

If anything, Odovacar was more vulnerable than any other ruler in the fifth century and, unless we include Theodoric, more successful. Odovacar rose to power at the hands of Orestes's rebellious troops

Map 4: Italy and Its Environs

and over his body. The troops rose in revolt in 476, after their demands for settlement were denied, and elevated Odovacar in order to achieve these aims. Their loyalty was bound to him by the oaths of warriors, but he lacked the security of blood ties and marriage networks. After all, his own people, the Sciri, were in large part destroyed in their wars with Thiudmir and the Ostrogoths. Their most famous leader was Odovacar, but they were too few to augment his military following significantly. Without a secure ethnic base among the Germanic troops, who regarded him as merely *primus inter pares*, although hailing him as king, Odovacar had no alternative but to turn to the Roman authorities for legitimacy and support.[17] The deposition of Orestes's son, Romulus Augustulus, in 476 was far from disagreeable to the Romans, since for many, especially Zeno, Nepos was the sole legitimate authority over Orestes, not his child. In fact, the return of the imperial insignia in 476 could be seen as a bizarre twist in the restoration of traditional government. Nepos was in Dalmatia in refuge from Orestes and his troops. Odovacar held no title giving him control over both the civilian and military governments, and so he asked Zeno to accept him as patrician and at the same time returned the insignia of imperial office to Constantinople. Romulus Augustulus was allowed to live on blissfully in Campania, where he died a natural death sometime after 507, apparently still secure with his pension of 6,000 *solidi* per annum.[18] Zeno accepted Odovacar as patrician but urged him to seek recognition from the legitimate ruler of the West, Nepos. Odovacar duly celebrated Nepos or Nepos and Zeno jointly, on his coins until Nepos fell to assassination on 9 May 480.[19]

Under Odovacar, the senate and its membership continued to play an active role in politics and government, just as they had throughout most of the fifth century, when the emperors were ephemeral and secluded at Ravenna. Great families like the Fausti, Probi, Flavii, and Symmachi illuminated the life of the city, their names carefully inscribed around the Colosseum and elsewhere, attesting to their philanthropy and influence.[20] They were at least nominally Christian, and as leading families they appeared in various conclaves of the church and were prominent in papal and episcopal affairs. Always conscious of titles and prestige, they were amiable to Odovacar's programs and supported his rule. In return, their world of office holding and the complex hierarchy of interrelated titles and dignities was preserved. Coinage in gold, silver, and bronze was struck at Rome, Ravenna, Milan, and Arles.[21] The gold series were especially sensitive to the delicate symbolic and political relationship with the East and so bore the traditional head of emperor without modification. On the other hand, on the silver and bronze coinage, Odovacar not only used traditional portraits and symbols, most frequently the cross, but also minted in his own likeness and displayed his personal monograms.[22] Here too he followed fifth-century Roman practice; the earliest such monogram dates from Theodosius II (408–50).[23] The relative importance of circulated coins in the economy remained constant during his reign, and the collection of taxes functioned in a typically late Roman manner, with appropriate response to abuses and relief for areas stricken by natural disaster or invasion.[24]

At the top of the bureaucracy stood the *magister officiorum* and the praetorian prefect. The daily operation of government, the maintenance of the post, road repair, and the like, primarily remained the preserve of the *magister officiorum*, to whom the notorious *agentes in rebus* also made their nefarious reports.[25] The praetorian prefect, and in the city the urban prefect, supervised the primary logistical tasks of government and were ultimately in charge of the fiscal system with its complicated system of collection, tallying, storage, and distribution. Odovacar entrusted routine administration to the traditional bureaucratic structure, but in keeping with the importance of the *magister utriusque militiae* during the fifth century, he turned to the special cadre attached to this highest military command, the *comitiaci*, for especially sensitive problems whenever and wherever they arose.[26] Indeed, the jurisdiction of the *magister officiorum* may have been particularly affected by the encroachments of the corps of *comitiaci*. Although Odovacar ruled as *rex*, Zeno refused to acknowledge him as such and thereby confined his *de jure* jurisdiction to that of a military commander, subordinate to the imperial authorities. Moreover, since he had no "people" of his own but, in fact, relied upon Roman support for his precarious role as *primus*, he had little choice but to rule through the sanctioned channels of military procedure, recently ratified by the Roman senate and ultimately Zeno and Nepos in their bestowal of the honor *patricius*. The centralized officialdom under Odovacar proved efficient, expeditious, and at least by contemporary standards accountable. Good government generally stabilized the Italian economy and restored the confidence of the upper classes.[27]

Since the settlement of the troops was the principal reason for both his elevation and the assassination of Orestes, Odovacar lost little time in setting the *hospitalitas* system into motion as outlined in the Theodosian Code (7. 8. 5):

> 5.[8] Emperors Arcadius and Honorius Augustuses to Hosius, Master of Offices.
>
> In any city in which We Ourselves may be or in which those persons who perform imperial service of Us may sojourn, We remove all injustice both on the part of Our quartering offices and of the persons quartered. One third of a house shall be assigned to a quartered person, and the owner shall possess two thirds of his house as his own in full confidence and security, to the extent that when the house has been thus divided into three parts, the owner shall have the first opportunity to choose his portion, and the person quartered shall obtain whichever part he wishes second, while the third part shall be left for the owner. For it is the full measure of equity and justice that the person who enjoys possession by right of succession or who had the good fortune to have purchased or built his home should have the portion of his own particular choice and also the remaining third portion.

> 1. Workshops that are assigned to trade shall not be subjected to the annoyance of the aforesaid division but shall be undisturbed, free, and protected from every annoyance of compulsory quartering. They shall be devoted to the use of their owners and lessees only. But if there should be no stable for a military man in his third of the house, as sometime happens, stable room shall be assigned in the workshops, unless the owner should provide for it by some means, in accordance with the number of the animals and the nature of the house.
>
> 2. We decree that to Illustrious persons not one third of a house but half a house shall be assigned by the right of compulsory quartering, under this condition only, that one of them, the owner or the Illustrious person, whoever may prefer, shall divide the house by an equitable decision, and the other shall have the privilege of choosing.[28]

There were extraordinary difficulties lying beneath the edict of Arcadius and Honorius when applied to permanent occupation rather than temporary billeting, as we shall witness with the coming of the Ostrogoths. Odovacar's was the first major settlement of barbarians in Italy, although foreign garrisons had put down roots in various areas, such as Pavia, as early as the fourth century.[29] As the first it was doubtless the most difficult, and it paved the way for the Ostrogoths, who took over these earlier divisions and expanded the network.[30]

Odovacar's primary task was probably the assurance of revenues to his various nobles and their followers, principally warriors. In many cases, the warriors associated with the great nobles were themselves probably ranked within the complex world of the specialized warbands, which made up at least a significant part of the troops under Orestes's and later Odovacar's command. Nevertheless, some doubtless sought physical occupation of functioning estates. The mixture of familial groups and warbands pledged to various members of the nobility was much more complex under the Ostrogoths. After all, they were not merely warriors united under a *primus* but an entire people with a multitude of factors binding them together and establishing a peculiar social and political equilibrium. In that sense, neither the provisions outlined in the Code nor the actions of Odovacar were adequate precedents, although they certainly were helpful.

So successful were Odovacar's settlement programs and his relations with the Roman population that he was able to concentrate his military adventures in the borderlands. Together with his brother Onoulph, he sought to stabilize the disintegration of Noricum and Pannonia and to tie the remaining Roman enclaves there to his Italian-based kingdom. The two brothers, sons of Edeco, the Hunnic prince of the Sciri, shared in victory and defeat. In fact, Onoulph died seeking asylum in a church shortly after Theodoric slew Odovacar in 493. Prior to the arrival of the Ostrogoths, Onoulph managed to resurrect the family fortunes following the defeat of the Sciri by Thiudmir. He found refuge and service at Constantinople, and there rose to *comes* and *magister militum per Illyricum*.[31] As *magister* he joined forces with Sabinianus, commander of the Thracian army, in the Byzantine attack on Theodoric's rearguard on the march to Epirus Nova.[32] Thus until 482, Onoulph was the physical link between Odovacar and Zeno, but in that year Zeno reversed his policy. Since the brothers had supported Illus in his rebellion, once Zeno reemerged in control he launched the Rugians against Odovacar. The difficult situation on the frontiers began to disintegrate rapidly.

In 482, Noricum Ripensis still struggled for life. Isolated strongholds, once bolstered by the personal vigor and charisma of Saint Severinus, faced survival without their holy protector. The chaos of disrupted trade and communication was heightened after Odovacar and Onoulph defeated the Rugians in 487. Many Rugians followed their king Feletheus to Theodoric at Novae and henceforth were part of the amalgamation of peoples making up the Ostrogoths.[33] Their bitterness toward Italy revealed itself in full when, left in temporary charge of Pavia, they proceeded to plunder and pillage. Feletheus and his father Flaccitheus before him had based an uneasy truce with the Romans of Noricum Ripensis on a common need to control the numerous undisciplined bands of barbarians raiding the countryside and beyond anyone's control.[34] The events of 487—the defeat and flight of the Rugians—unleashed the hounds of war anew, but this time the situation was hopeless. Finally, in 488 Odovacar, once a friend of Saint Severinus and his followers, ordered Onoulph to evacuate the surviving independent Romans to Italy.[35] Many had long since abandoned their freedom for Germanic protection and could not flee.[36] At Faviana, Saint Severinus—his body marvelously well-preserved—was crated in a special sarcophagus to his final resting place outside Naples.[37] Odovacar held Noricum Mediterraneum until his death transferred it to Theodoric.

The year 482 was portentous for other reasons as well. As part of his policy to unify the East after a period of rebellion and schism, Zeno announced his resolution of the Christological controversies, the Henotikon or Edict of Union. Theologically crafty, too crafty to win universal respect, the decree immediately became a principal feature of political and diplomatic life in Italy. The Chalcedonian formula of 451 agreed, after long harangues, on the wording advanced by Pope Leo I, the famous *una persona, duae naturae*. The monophysite churches of Jerusalem, Antioch, and Alexandria resented the political encroachment of Constantinople into the theology of Chalcedon, regarding the essential ambiguity of the language of the Henotikon (suggested by the Patriarch Acacius of Constantinople) as a further dilution of the Godhead.[38] In the West, the pope and the majority of the nobility—spiritual and temporal—rejected the formula entirely, claiming the obvious: that it avoided the whole problem of the nature of Christ through circumlocutions and thus went against Chalcedon. More stridently offensive was the concept of theology as the word of pharaoh implicit in the Edict. For the first time the emperor overruled the bishops *in cathedra* instead of following Constantine and confining the imperial role to *ex cathedra* concerns. During the fifth century, the Pope had grown accustomed to the Constantinian understanding and, if anything, had acted as a principal spokesman of the civil authority within the city and beyond, while the emperors sulked in the shadows of their *magistri*.

The Acacian Schism, as it is called, was the first official disruption of communion within Christendom and contributed immeasurably to the stability of Odovacar's regime and the flowering of a symbiosis of Goth and Roman under Theodoric. Like Odovacar, Theodoric tried to find a workable coexistence for Romans and Germans within the late Roman cultural world now radiating primarily from Constantinople. The peculiar balance could endure only if and as long as the composite lure of Rome toward its legitimate ruler—the emperor—and its religious heart—the eastern Mediterranean—were somehow divorced from the pervasive and irresistible cultural focus conveyed in mental images, dress, and the very concept of civilization itself accompanying the emperorship. The Henotikon split these forces and gave Theodoric time to attempt to redirect Roman culture back to Italy and Rome and also to define a special role for the Ostrogoths. However, the forces arrayed against him were very powerful. The magnificent grave goods of Cluj-Someşeni, with their Byzantine inspiration, clearly manifested the strength of the East well beyond its frontiers, when as early as the last quarter of the fifth century, Byzantine influence was reestablished and the peoples there began again to bend their knees to late Roman civilization in its Christian/Byzantine form.[39] Almost all the ingredients of the successful Ostrogothic Kingdom were already present under Odovacar, all, that is, except the Ostrogoths and Theodoric.

The brutal slaying of Odovacar and Onoulph betrays a side of Theodoric's character difficult to perceive in such sycophantic writings as those of Ennodius or the official, carefully edited, and tedious works of Cassiodorus. Yet behind the subtlety of his political and cultural programs or his deft handling of the Roman aristocracy lurked a man of ferocious wrath, and all those around him knew it. Even Ennodius, whose panegyric ennobled the king, was careful to guide his friends around the jagged rocks in Theodoric's temperament.[40] Perhaps all men, especially great leaders, harbor certain basic convictions that add contour and personality to their politics. A very few, and Theodoric was one, can harness their emotions and frustrations, especially when their will is thwarted and their trust betrayed, and convince people that the imperfections of their character are really endearing eccentricities. In an age of violence and abrupt ends, Theodoric's inner harshness was respected and accepted as part of his charisma. For Theodoric himself, violence was in the final analysis an aspect of justice. Justice listened and weighed and even bent, but ultimately acted. Among the first Romans to feel Theodoric's justice and witness his wrath were the citizens of Pavia.

After the victory over Odovacar at Verona in 489, the Ostrogoths followed him westward toward Como, but they were in poor condition themselves and so turned south through Milan and took up quarters in Pavia. Here they camped in large clusters of families, razing whole sections of the city to make room for the encampments and to provide fill for the hasty repair of the walls.[41] Ennodius in his *Vita S. Epifani* has left a marvelous picture of overcrowding and quarreling as Romans and Goths made the best of forced circumstances. Such uncomfortable quarters were imposed by Theodoric because he feared the consequences of a major redefection of some of Odovacar's troops under a certain Tufa.[42] Tufa had just recently deserted to Theodoric but decided to return to his old chief Odovacar. The last thing Theodoric wanted was a winter raid against an exposed camp, desperate for supplies, so he brought everybody within the walls. Enraged over Tufa's betrayal and constantly bombarded by aggrieved claimants seeking redress for the endless series of petty thefts and assaults, Theodoric announced that all Romans not supporting him would lose their rights to testament and the sale of property.[43]

Most Romans were content with neutrality, since they perceived little gain in a change of masters. Doubtless they anticipated a new settlement through *hospitalitas* if Theodoric vanquished Odovacar, but Theodoric's outburst foreshadowed not structured sharing under law but outright confiscation. They all realized that without the right to sell property, the mechanisms of settlement would be hopelessly hamstrung, producing a situation where confiscation of entire areas would surely result. Without testamentary rights, the Roman way of life would cease within a generation as property acquired over decades and often centuries fell to the whims of the barbarians. With property went *dignitas* and the social order. The Romans trembled. Fortunately, Theodoric listened as well as raged, and little by little the Romans, acting through their chief spokesman, Bishop Epiphanius, persuaded him to restrict his ire to the active supporters of Odovacar—by now a very small group indeed. Theodoric turned the matter over to a certain Urbicus, *vir inlustris* and a trusted adviser, to put his decision into official Roman legal terminology.[44] This act is one of the earliest indications that Theodoric would expand his core of advisers, his *comitatus*, through the creation of a regular court staffed with traditional offices and structured in late Roman hierarchic fashion. Urbicus, in fact, was acting as *quaestor sacri palatii*, a long-hallowed position at the imperial courts.[45] At last the Romans could relax. They had seen reason overcome anger and justice transcend violence. So too the Goths themselves had held their breaths during Theodoric's outbursts following their refusal to fight Triarius near Sondis some twenty years before.[46]

With Odovacar dead and his troops purged, Theodoric faced the exceedingly complex problems of settlement. Cassiodorus, writing some years later (ca. 507–511), reminded the Roman senate of the joys of sharing. One cannot help but wonder how many smiles and quiet stirrings of incredulity arose as he praised Liberius, charged with the division, in his letter drafted for Theodoric, elevating Venantius, son of Liberius, to the senate:

> We especially like to remember how in the assignment of the Thirds he joined both the possessions and the hearts of Goths and Romans alike. For whereas men desire to come into collision on account of their being neighbors, with these men the common holding of their farms proved in practice a reason for concord. Thus it has happened that while the two nations have been living in common they have concurred in the same desires. A new fact, and one wholly laudable. The friendship of the lords (*gratia dominorum*) has been joined with the division of the soil; amity has grown out of the loss of the Provincials, and by the land a defender has been gained whose occupation of part guarantees the quiet enjoyment of the whole. One law includes them: one equal administration rules them: for it is necessary that sweet affection should grow between those who always keep the boundaries which have been allotted them.[47]

Perhaps a decade or more had clouded some memories, but behind the stilted prose was a series of terribly tense negotiations, still hinted at in our sources. The process was far more complex than Procopius seemed to recall when he wrote that the Ostrogoths simply took over the allotments made under Odovacar.[48] Surely Theodoric did not dispossess most of the followers of Odovacar. In fact, it seems that he incorporated them into the Ostrogothic tribe and bound them directly to him through a special ceremony of kingship, his third, as he further augmented and solidified Amalian leadership.[49] But men like Tufa and other diehard supporters were proscribed. Building on Odovacar's foundations was just a beginning.

Liberius paired each senator with a Gothic nobleman as the first step in the *hospitalitas* system. Yet the simple division and selection as outlined in the Code would have destroyed the productivity of the estates, and that neither side desired. The Code also avoided the crucial matter of labor supply. The villa economy depended upon its ability to utilize the various types of soils and products within it. Each estate needed woodland, pastures, and arable land and the manpower (slaves or coloni) to work it. The Gothic noble had somehow to provide further for the families under his care and the warriors attached to his person. Dividing an estate into thirds, without careful consideration of land types and the distribution of labor, was unthinkable for the Ostrogoths as well as Germans elsewhere.[50] In a great many cases, the only solution was sale or revenue sharing.[51] Theodoric, moreover, could not disperse his approximately 40,000 tribesmen all over the Italian peninsula without surrendering any hope of maintaining their ethnic cohesion and loyalty to the Amali line.[52]

As a result of these manifold considerations, the physical settlement of the Ostrogoths occurred in three areas: around Pavia, the area of Ravenna, and Picenum.[53] Garrisons were established in key towns throughout Italy and along the frontier areas in the north and northeast.[54] Small units were also stationed along principal roads.[55] In 509, the settlement and garrison pattern was extended into Provence in an effort to stabilize the area in the wake of the disintegration of the Burgundian Kingdom and the pressure of the increasingly hostile and aggressive Franks.[56] Wherever the Ostrogoths concentrated their settlements, many returned to agriculture. In order to maintain agrarian continuity, there must have been a great amount of sale and purchase as great Gothic lords sought to round out their lands and senators sought to save what they could or leave with as much cash as possible. Unless a senator had estates in a multiple of three, sale was the only solution short of fragmenting the agrarian system. The Gothic nobleman could exercise many options concerning the fate of the laborers, but he probably kept most of them himself, since he personally, and also the specialized warriors in his following, had no desire to revert to being plowmen but demanded productive sources of revenue. At least in the north, probably around Pavia in particular, where the Po Valley allowed more effective use of the land in small units, the Goths apparently subdivided their shares into family farming units called *condamae*.[57] The close associations of warriors that made up a part of those dependent upon the nobility could have been provided with lands or more probably revenues according to their rank once the basic agrarian concerns of the family units were attained. The latter were the chief concerns of Theodoric and his people in the Balkans and remained so in Italy.

A nobleman was entitled to half the estate under paragraph 2 of the law of hospitality. We have an echo of such a division preserved in the papyri from Ravenna. Dated 4 April 553, at Ravenna, a rich woman named Ranilo, *sublimis femina*, made a gift to the church and confirmed an earlier bequest of her father, Aderit, *vir gloriosus*, made several years before. Since Ravenna passed out of Gothic control in 540, there is no assurance that Aderit was an Ostrogoth, despite his clearly Germanic name. Nevertheless, his gift corresponds almost exactly with what a Goth of his rank might have received as a share in the settlement under Roman law.

> . . . my deceased father Aderit, formerly *vir gloriosus*, namely 50 pounds of silver; in income 100 solidi and indeed 6/12 of the Massa land with dwelling house Firmidiana, in the vicinity of Urbino, and of the Massa . . . liana 6/12, in the vicinity of Lucca, that is half the property of the indicated Massae with all the documented equipment and appurtenances, whatever belongs to them, including the contiguous farmhouses and their surrounding lands, with their boundaries and boundary stones, and those there bound in servitude, and the slaves, who actually are on the properties in question, and further those who can be found there still, since they have been able to run away during time of barbarity.[58]

The reference to runaways and barbarous times relates to the recent unrest following Narses's victories over Totila and the end of Ostrogothic rule. Obviously the labor force was as important as ever, and the grant involved both land and revenues.

The *Edictum Theodorici*, traditionally attributed to Theodoric the Great but perhaps issued by Theodoric II at Toulouse (458–59), and the *Leges Visigothorum antiquiores* set moratoria of thirty and fifty years respectively for appeals arising from settlement claims.[59] In Italy, the courts were swamped with appeals. The correspondence of Ennodius, writing as deacon at Milan, reveals the pressures exerted by influential Romans through their friends at court. When Lupicinus, his nephew, begged his assistance in ameliorating the settlement, pairing him with a certain Torisa, Ennodius explored the matter fully. First he wrote to the local *comes Gothorum*, Tancila, who had obviously represented the Goths settled in the area when Liberius implemented *hospitalitas*. Tancila refered Ennodius to Theodoric.[60] Theodoric had reserved all cases involving redistribution and claims for himself and the central legal apparatus of the praetorian prefect, at the time Faustus, a close friend of Ennodius. Faustus soon received a letter from Ennodius on behalf of Lupicinus.[61]

Other friends and relatives, particularly around Arles following the Ostrogothic settlement there in 509 (also under Liberius's supervision), also wrote to Ennodius. Occasionally he corresponded directly with Liberius, perhaps trying to avert ratification of preliminary pairings and divisions.[62] But little by little a pattern emerged. Theodoric was extremely reluctant to reverse the settlement grants once the decisions involved the Ostrogothic nobility. Rather than arouse their wrath by uprooting them and their people, Theodoric preferred to redress the wrong by awarding the claimant lands elsewhere.[63] That was not always welcomed, but certainly a man like Lupicinus could hardly have regretted an opportunity to leave his "guest"—a guest who may have sorely abused Lupicinus and his family. On the other hand, Theodoric attempted to stop the most flagrant violations of the law, but even he was unable to control the forced sale and "liberation" of Roman land by Gothic warlords and powerful Romans.[64] Indeed, the problem continued throughout his reign and grew under his weak successors. The Gothic nobles were as avaricious toward the lands of other Goths as those of their Roman hosts.[65]

The settlement would have created considerable, if only temporary, economic disruptions in times of peace, but Italy, especially the Po Valley and the area around Ravenna, had suffered terribly during the wars against Odovacar. The battles and blockades diverted Theodoric from the tasks of routine government, with a resulting general breakdown in law and order throughout Italy. Even within the alliance network of the Ostrogoths themselves, the Rugians were free to pillage Pavia after Theodoric departed in pursuit of Odovacar despite the understanding reached through Epiphanius. Disease hit the destitute in the wake of the collapse of transport and the requisitions of war. Once started, sickness and famine took a frightful toll. Pope Gelasius, writing in 494, sanctioned the immediate elevation of laymen to the priesthood. So many clergy had fallen to war and pestilence that mass went uncelebrated in many churches.[66] As if times were not difficult enough, the Burgundians raided Liguria and carried off numerous captives, leaving harvests to rot. Theodoric himself dispatched an embassy to them under Epiphanius, bishop of Pavia, with his pledge to ransom personally up to 6,000 captives.[67] Yet if one were rich enough or had influence at court, these calamities could seem as distant as a thunderstorm fading on the edge of the horizon. The key was influence at the centers of power—Ravenna and Rome. But even if one had influence at the highest levels, the legal machinery was overwhelmed and painfully slow, as again the letters of Ennodius reveal.

Ennodius was one of many people in the sixth century, as throughout antiquity and the Middle Ages, suffering from perennial eye ailments. His depression and restless search for relief at holy shrines and with the best doctors of his age still resound all through his tortuous style with intense pain.[68] When the doctors in Milan recommended the cleaner air of the countryside, Ennodius sought to lease a villa from his friend Faustus, the praetorian prefect. Despite their lofty ranks and positions, the simple and uncontested case of lease and transfer took years to resolve. In fact, no fewer than five letters from Ennodius and unknown intercessions by Faustus were required. The matter was settled only after the intervention of Triwilla, a *saio* of Theodoric.[69] Perhaps priority was still accorded to the cases deriving from the settlement and the tax relief granted to some areas in the wake of the war with Odovacar over a decade before. Hidden considerations may have also clouded the issue, for Faustus was only one avenue to Theodoric.

Flavius Anicius Probus Faustus is himself a demonstration of the continuity of life among the members of the late Roman aristocracy under Odovacar and then Theodoric. His name appears twice on the seats of the Flavian Colosseum in Rome, indicating his rising fortunes (ca. 476–83).[70] Consul in the West in 490, by 492 *magister officiorum* under Theodoric, Faustus rose rapidly as *quaestor palatii* (503–506) and finally praetorian prefect (509–512).[71] Ennodius eulogized his cultural attainments, literary poise, and support of papal policy during the turmoil of the Symmachian Schism, which raged from 498 to 506 and had lingering effects throughout Theodoric's reign.[72] He was made *patricius* shortly after his quaestorship, and as his title Flavius indicates, he was among the very highest ranks of the Roman nobility.[73] He apparently fell from favor while praetorian prefect, perhaps in 511 when Cassiodorus, writing for Theodoric, instructed *saio* Triwilla to investigate a charge leveled by one Castorius against Faustus for illegal seizure of property.[74] Behind the charge lurked a probable change in the balance at court. Castorius and a youth, Florus, owed their education and rising fortunes to Faustus. Florus was *advocatus* at Ravenna from 508 to 510.[75] Forgetful of their mentor and benefactor, Castorius and Florus apparently struck out for higher rewards. Neither was successful in his clawing for the top, but shortly after their attack, Faustus faded out of the close circle of Romans active around Theodoric.

Throughout most of these years, Flavius Rufius Postumus Festus actively vied with Faustus. Behind these two were arrayed many of the most prominent families of Roman Italy, all carefully entwined through marriage and allied by blood and political convenience. Festus began his political career a generation before Faustus. He was consul in 472 and by 490 was the senior member of the senate (*caput senati*, the oldest living *consul ordinarius*).[76] In the Symmachian Schism he sided with the rival candidate Laurentius and lost to Pope Symmachus and his chief supporter, Faustus. Festus died sometime after 513 and was succeeded in the senate by Quintus Aurelius Memmius Symmachus, the great-grandson of the homonymous famous defender of the Altar of Victory under Valentinian. Symmachus generally sided with Festus, but the Symmachian Schism saw him supporting Faustus and Pope Symmachus, although the two Symmachi were apparently unrelated. Q. Aurelius Symmachus married his daughter to Anicius Manlius Severinus Boethius, the great scholar and politician. Symmachus followed his son-in-law to the executioner's hall in 525 after allegedly plotting treason against Theodoric.[77]

Until late in his reign, Theodoric allowed the senatorial factions to play their games. Despite intense pressure upon him to decide between them, he saw nothing to gain in rejecting one group in favor of another. Until his last years, Theodoric was concerned with faithful service to the state and was willing to look beyond the machinations of a Faustus or a Festus so long as their loyalty to him was not suspect. We will never know for certain what occurred to bring down Faustus, but a reasonable hypothesis seems to be a last and successful political alliance organized by a vengeful Festus still bitter over the loss of face in the Symmachian affair.

The most visible victor of factional strife was Cassiodorus Senator, who during these struggles managed to climb from the obscurity of the middling southern Italian aristocracy with traditions of serving in relatively minor posts. He was *magister officiorum* under Theodoric and held the praetorian prefecture (533–37/8) under Athalaric and then briefly under Theodahad. He did little under Witigis during his final year in office except to draft the official announcement of the accession.[78] Cassiodorus Senator apparently took quiet advantage of the fluid situation at court to rise through the ranks, but his rise was gradual and closely attached to the Gothic court, whereas men like Festus and Symmachus looked toward Constantinople for acknowledgment of their virtues and for models in literature and life.

In order to find a haven for a Gothia within Romania, Theodoric worked with all families, new and old, to achieve internal harmony. In this regard he was extremely dexterous. In 490 he sent Festus to Constantinople in an attempt to gain further recognition of his position from Zeno. But Zeno had little interest or enthusiasm for affairs in the West and chose to ignore the request for official approval of the title *rex*, at least until the problems of the Henotikon and the resulting Acacian Schism were settled to his liking. Zeno died before the issues were resolved.[79] In 493, shortly before Pope Gelasius's temper terminated discussion, Faustus, then *magister officiorum*, took up the challenge on Theodoric's behalf, but against a rising tide of personal animosity to the new pope, Faustus too failed.[80]

After the pope's death, Theodoric renewed his efforts to gain official acknowledgment of the title *rex*, which he, like Odovacar, had simply used without imperial approval, and in 497 he designated Festus to head another embassy to Constantinople.[81] The new pope, Anastasius II (see Table 1), seemed quite willing to reopen negotiations over the schism and manifested a clear desire to return to the Constantinian compromise, temporarily lost sight of in the fiery outbursts of Gelasius. He saw Christendom and the papacy as rightfully under the political aegis of the emperor, with both pope and emperor as special unto God. Acacius was damned, but since the patriarch was dead, even condemnation seemed an acceptable starting point for negotiation. The pope was willing to accept all of Acacius's sacramental acts, and was even ready to discuss exonerating him completely. No mention was made of the Henotikon itself.[82] This time Festus was successful: "Peace was concluded with the Emperor Anastasius concerning Theodoric's assumption of rule, and Anastasius sent back all the palatine ornaments, which Odovacar had transferred to Constantinople."[83] The emperor Anastasius asked only that Pope Anastasius publicly accept the Henotikon. Festus returned thinking that he could gain papal support, but unfortunately the pope had died while he was away. Festus turned to his friends among the Roman aristocracy.[84]

Some of the oldest and noblest families in Roman Italy could trace their ancestors far back into the early empire, and many who could not tried nonetheless. Their dress, their speech, and even their

Table 1: List of Popes

Gelasius I	492–496	Boniface II	530–532
Anastasius II	496–498	John II	533–535
Symmachus	498–514	Agapitus I	535–536
Hormisdas	514–523	Silverius	536–537
John I	523–526	Vigilius	537–555
Felix IV	526–530	Pelagius I	555–561

basic vision of mankind flowed out of the imperial environment despite the recent dearth of *noble* Romans on the throne. Zeno himself was actually an Isaurian named Tarasis.[85] The education of a Roman aristocrat was increasingly literary and completely Greco-Roman. Boethius's love of Aristotle and Greek literature is legendary, but many shared his love without his brilliance. Greek scholars and theologians found encouragement in senatorial homes, and some, like the religious refugee Dioscorus, rose to prominence in Catholic Italy.[86] Dionysius Exiguus, a Scythian monk at Rome and probably the most important scholar of the day, provided the first really complete collection of canons in the West, his *Codex Canonum Ecclesiasticorum.*[87] They all looked to Constantinople for cultural leadership, not to Rome and the papacy and especially not to Ravenna and the Ostrogoths. Foremost among them stood Festus. Already *consul ordinarius* in 472, Festus owed nothing to either the present crop of barbarian claimants or to popes. He now was determined to add religious unity to the political unity offered in the recognition of Theodoric and the return of the symbols of imperial rule.

Neither Festus nor Theodoric saw religious reunification as treason directed against the Ostrogothic Kingdom. Indeed, Theodoric, unlike the Orthodox Roman aristocracy, was not alienated by the Henotikon; it was after all irrelevant to an Arian. His coinage continued to bear witness to his willingness to maintain a discreet independence within the imperial orb.[88] If anything, the ending of the Acacian Schism was viewed as a welcomed step toward simplifying diplomatic relations with the East and as a necessary step in securing the final recognition of an independent Gothic Kingdom of Italy within the Imperium Romanum. Theodoric anticipated that Zeno would symbolize his acceptance by the official recognition of his position as *rex*. Thus Theodoric and all those around him, including Festus and Faustus, failed to perceive the extraordinary anomaly of the barbarian overlordship under the Amali in terms of cultural continuity. Instead, they saw a chance for titular and legal clarification and took the risk. Theodoric lived to regret his lack of foresight.

At this early date, 498, there was probably very little in the way of an organized Gothic faction at the papal court or among the lay aristocracy. Everyone was "pro-Gothic" and still holding their breaths while the settlement proceeded and regular government returned. The competition between Faustus and Festus was within the rules of the game of courtly politics. Indeed, the basic factions had changed little since the days of Honorius.[89] Once Theodoric recanted at Pavia from his uncompromising stance toward Odovacar's supporters and began to operate through a familiar court structure and within the context of Roman law, there was nothing about Ostrogothic rule to crystalize an opposition. In fact, it was readily apparent, at least to men like Ennodius and Cassiodorus, that a new era of prosperity had dawned. Ennodius went so far as to suggest that Theodoric was "heaven sent."[90] In short, Theodoric's deft handling of the transition, only occasionally manifesting weariness and resulting apathy, effectively encompassed all elements of late Roman Italy. When Festus returned from the East to find Anastasius dead, the deceptive tranquility began to disintegrate, but very slowly. Festus apparently committed his personal honor in the negotiations with the emperor, pledging that the pontiff could be convinced to accept even the Henotikon. Perhaps Pope Anastasius would have accepted the formula, but he was dead. Symmachus, elected in holy synod as his successor, at Rome was unsympathetic.[91] Festus rallied the aristocracy behind his candidate, Laurentius. Faustus, of course, backed Symmachus, as did the powerful Symmachi (no apparent relationship to the pope), but the majority of the aristocracy favored Laurentius and a return to religious unity under the emperor as outlined in the Henotikon.[92]

The Roman aristocracy had other equally compelling reasons for supporting Laurentius. They had probably already identified Pope Symmachus as a follower of Gelasius and no friend of the aristocracy. Like his predecessor, he was adamantly opposed to their attempts to include in their secular *dignitas* the control of the lands of Saint Peter. Gelasius had come down hard on all attempts at the "reappropriation" of church land by the original grantors. His characteristic decisiveness could only check the merging of secular and temporal, but in regard to property his views prevailed. The senatorial aristocracy as a class confronted an impossible predicament. Their lifestyles demanded displays of political extravagance, sumptuous villas, and occasional outbursts of religious and social largess. During the fourth century, many in the West, fewer in the East, retired to their favorite villas, and there they were supported by a truly international network of land holdings and business interests extending throughout the Roman world. We can still see echoes in their correspondence of their keen interest in the exploitation of their vast holdings. Living in such a style demanded the systematic collection of the limited revenues from all over the empire. But the West had turned sour following the loss of area after area to the barbarians.

Even when a peaceful settlement limited losses, the net result was disastrous to those on the edge. All across Europe, church councils held firm—land given to the church was held in perpetuity for God. And everywhere the survivors of the Roman nobility refused to accept defeat and struggled to regain their bequests in order to maintain the traditional accoutrements of their class. Obviously, as the conciliar *acta* attest, isolated battles were won by the nobility. If their own kinsman were bishop, their chances were much improved, and well into the sixth century that was typically the case. But in conclave, whether at Orléans in 549 or Paris in 557 or remote Braga in Spain in 563, the bishops followed Gelasius and Symmachus against the repatriation of lands. In parts of Italy, while the number of large holdings grew at the expense of the small *possessores*, the actual wealth of the average member of the aristocracy declined steadily throughout the fifth and sixth centuries. Some simply could not maintain themselves after the loss of so much of their transalpine possessions and were already groveling in the fifth century. Doubtless Theodoric's settlement and the requisitions during the struggle with Odovacar nudged still others over the precipice. These rallied to Festus and Laurentius in desperation.[93]

Support for Laurentius took time to mobilize and exert pressure within the city. In the meantime, Theodoric decided to visit Rome, meet the new pope Symmachus, and in general celebrate the restoration of Roman government inaugurated by the return of the insignia from the East. He also wanted to elevate his kingship by participating as the acknowledged representative of imperial power in the ceremonies of office. The Anonymus Valesianus text is marvelously succinct:

> At that same time a dispute arose in the city of Rome between Symmachus and Laurentius; for both had been consecrated. But through God's ordinance Symmachus, who also deserved it, got the upper hand. After peace was made in the city of the Church, King Theodoric went to Rome and met Saint Peter with as much reverence as if he himself were a Catholic. The Pope Symmachus, and the entire senate and people of Rome amid general rejoicing met him outside the city. Then coming to Rome and entering it, he appeared in the senate, and addressed the people at The Palm, promising that with God's help he would keep inviolate whatever the former Roman emperors had decreed.

> In celebration of his *tricennalia* [read *decennalia*] he entered the Palace in a triumphal procession for the entertainment of the people, and exhibited games in the Circus for the Romans. To the Roman people and to the poor of the city he gave each year a hundred and twenty thousand measures of grain, and for the restoration of the Palace and the rebuilding of the walls of the city he ordered two hundred pounds to be given each year from the chest that contained the tax on wine.[94]

Beneath the reverence for the outward manifestations of Roman rule, the lavish rebuilding of Rome, and the careful attention to the sacred *populus Romanus* lies a deep conviction that Rome, not Constantinople, was still the capital. Theodoric hoped to restore her grandeur and refocus the eyes of his Roman aristocracy upon Rome herself. Perhaps he chose to commemorate his entry into Rome by issuing his triple-solidus medallion in the spirit of imperial tradition (see fig. 6). But this medallion was no barbaric imitation like those of Szilágysomlyó, for Theodoric himself graced the obverse as Pius Princeps Invictus Semper, thus proclaiming his own peculiar vision of rule. Although properly issued from the Roman mint, the medallion asserted no claim against the emperors in the East with whom Theodoric stood in official accord. He supported schools and scholarship at Rome, and throughout his reign Rome moved closer to regaining her lost eminence.[95] But Rome without the emperor's presence was beyond revival. The senate ceased to meet sometime after 603, and the secular shrines of Roman glory crumbled into ruins.[96] Theodoric failed to revitalize Rome and so to redirect the loyalties attached to the emperor back through Rome to him.

Surely Theodoric knew all was not well with the election of Symmachus before his visit in 500, but by avoiding personal intervention he kept the door open for a return of the Laurentian faction. Finally, when it was clear that the split was widening, he ordered a synod to meet in 502 to decide the matter. The conclave duly met and confirmed the validity of the Symmachian election.[97] Theodoric said nothing and, characteristically, showed complete impartiality toward the rival factions. Both had supporters elevated to the consulship during the next four years and participated in other aspects of government.[98] Unfortunately the Roman aristocracy had visions of Valentinian swirling in their heads, and they would settle for nothing short of a definitive legal pronouncement.[99]

Finally in 506, Pope Symmachus's adviser Dioscorus, the refugee scholar, convinced Theodoric to intervene. Theodoric confirmed his unqualified support of the Synod of 502 and ordered Festus to aban-

Fig. 6: Triple-solidus medallion of Theodoric the Great: Rex Theodericus Pius Princ(eps) I(nvictus) S(emper).

don his hold over any churches in his hands.[100] By now the majority of the churches in the city had followed the senior clergy into the Laurentian camp. The elder churchmen had natural and, indeed, close familial ties to the aristocracy. Before his death in 514, Pope Symmachus managed to retaliate. By carefully filling clerical positions, he installed his supporters all over Rome.[101] His appointments stamped papal politics and Italian affairs for four generations of popes. His successors Hormisdas, Felix IV, and Agapitus all owed him their diaconates, the entry point to high office. His scholar-adviser Dioscorus was also elected pope, but by 530 the climate had changed completely.

Theodoric gained very little by the settlement of the Symmachian Schism. Its parent, the Acacian Schism, still festered as an open wound, now unfortunately bearing his reluctant imprint. The Symmachian purge and resulting monopoly of papal elections alienated some of the most venerable elements of the aristocracy. They increasingly regarded the new men in Rome as favorites at Ravenna, and thus a "pro-Gothic" faction emerged almost as a self-fulfilled prophecy of the Roman aristocracy itself. There is no evidence whatever that Theodoric sought a "pro-Gothic" group or gave support to its creation or development. In fact, to the extent that it ever existed, the pro-Gothic faction was the result of a divorce within Roman society and quickly took on the complex customs of class tension and courtly intrigue.

In 509, riots erupted in the circus in Rome, where the Greens and

Blues rallied behind their respective champions, Theodon (a barbarian) and Helladius (a Greek). Theodoric moved expeditiously and nominated as patrons to the then-patronless Greens two brothers, whose other brothers were open supporters of the Blues faction. Behind the games, the aristocracy was perhaps again trying to regain control over the lands their families had given the church. At the least, Theodoric could not allow such lawless conduct to continue among the senatorial class. Nor could he risk having their petty rivalries become involved in deeper issues—animosities aroused in the Symmachian Schism, papal control over church lands, or unrest at the Ostrogothic hegemony. Apparently Theodoric's ploy of divided patronage was enough to stop the riots from escalating into class warfare, and the circus returned to its usual contained roar throughout his reign.[102]

The Acacian Schism lingered as a barrier to the cultural and religious reunification of the Roman world, but the balance in Italy had decisively swung to the Symmachian side. Few were ready to surrender when Emperor Anastasius tried one last time in 515 to dictate the terms of a reunion. His death at age eighty-eight in July 518 ushered in the new dynasty of Justin and his nephew Justinian. Rigorous Chalcedonians, almost at once they asked Pope Hormisdas (514–23) to send an embassy to restore union. In March 519, after just three days of discussion, the schism ended with the absolute condemnation of Acacius and even of the emperors Zeno and Anastasius. Justin and Hormisdas acted with the full knowledge of Theodoric, whom they kept well informed at every stage.[103] The new dynasty wanted and obtained a tabula rasa; the papacy basked in the role of defender of the faith. It seemed that the Constantinian balance of church and state had returned. Theodoric had cause to rejoice in the reestablished propriety of unity. The single most sensitive focus of strife among his Roman subjects was gone, and with it an obvious kernel for rebellion.

To mark the political accord and recognize the balance of Gothic independence within Roman unity and give both the stamp of destiny, Theodoric nominated his blood relative and son-in-law Eutharic to hold the consulship with Emperor Justin.[104] Eutharic was the presumptive heir to Theodoric and the father of Athalaric and Matasuentha. An Amali, the son of Veteric, he had lived his life in Spain among the Visigoths, to whom his father had fled from the Huns (ca. 450).[105] His marriage to Amalasuintha and elevation to the consulship brought together the many facets of Theodoric's vision. Joy filled all ranks of society. Cassiodorus, who had already risen to high office from modest beginnings, celebrated it with the publication of his

Chronicon and praised Theodoric's vision in panegyric.[106] Theodoric saw the event as another step in his program of supporting the best qualities of Roman society with the strengths and leadership of the Ostrogoths. Probably at this time the mint in Rome struck three new bronze issues dramatizing the concert of Romans and Goths. On all three obverses the eagle, long a symbol of Gothic nobility and power, was juxtaposed with more traditional Roman symbols. The reverse of the forty-nummi and twenty-nummi pieces held the bust and legend of *Invicta Roma*. A lone eagle stood on the obverse of the forty-nummi piece, with its wings spread for flight (fig. 7a).[107] The twenty-nummi coin displayed a pair of eagles on either side of a palm tree (fig. 7b),[108] perhaps thereby recalling Theodoric's address at the Palm, with the Ostrogothic support of Roman traditions here symbolized by the eagles. Finally, on the ten-nummi piece a solitary eagle, frontal with head to its right, was joined by a star to either side. The reverse of the ten-nummi coin is the bust and legend of *Felix Ravenna*, itself an Ostrogothic innovation but otherwise here quite traditional (fig. 7c).[109] The pairing of the eagles with *Invicta Roma* and *Felix Ravenna* accorded well with Theodoric's vision of separate but complementary roles for the two peoples of Italy.

Although the year 519 was the highwater mark of the Ostrogothic Kingdom, Eutharic also manifested some of the problems besetting the fragile balance. Among these was his reputation as an anti-Catholic, an appropriate quality in Spain but not in Italy.[110] Fortunately he predeceased Theodoric and so was unable to carry out a religious program. Eutharic's selection as husband for Theodoric's eldest and most cultivated daughter was but a part of an overall plan to draw all the royal Germanic families of the barbarian kingdoms into a network around the Amali line, and thereby to extend Theodoric's peculiar brand of leadership throughout much of the territory of the Western Empire. A necessary step was the reunification of Amali blood scattered during the early migrations, and Eutharic was heir to the only other line surviving from the great Ermanaric. Issue from his loins with a daughter of Theodoric would indeed be heir to greatness and legend across Germanic Europe.[111]

The union between Eutharic and Amalasuintha produced the weak and rash Athalaric (526–34), hardly a worthy successor to Theodoric, and Matasuentha, whose hand gave legitimacy to the warrior king Witigis (536–40) and comfort to Justinian's nephew Germanus (see Table 2). Between the reigns of Athalaric and Witigis, Amalasuintha tried unsuccessfully to associate herself with her violent and reclusive cousin Theodahad (535–36). Theodahad quickly rewarded

Fig. 7: Bronze issues of Theodoric bearing eagles. (a) forty-nummi. (b) twenty-nummi. (c) ten-nummi.

her with exile and openly celebrated her death in the bath, even (see Table 3) while pleading his honorable intentions to Justinian.[112] Nevertheless, at the time the marriage of Eutharic was to consummate Theodoric's vision of the Amalian dynasty and secure its place in the political fabric of the Imperium Romanum. The dynastic network stretched far beyond Eutharic. He was merely the apex of a long series of political marriages.

Within a decade of his victories over Odovacar, Theodoric himself married Audefleda, daughter of Childeric, king of the Franks, and ca. 500 matched his widowed sister Amalafrida with Thrasamund, king of the Vandals.[113] The next generation provided the wives of three kings (Thuringians, Burgundians, and Visigoths) as well as a wife for Eutharic. Shortly after 510, this generation of alliances began to break down; Amalaberga returned to Ravenna from Thuringia, after her husband Herminifrid's death in 532. Perhaps she had counseled him to fratricide against his two brothers and tempted him into an alliance with the Frankish king Theodoric.[114] Thus Theodoric himself married a probable granddaughter of Theodoric the Great through the Burgundian king Sigismund. When Theodoric the Frank smashed the alliance and invaded Thuringia, adding it to the expand-

Table 2: Ostrogothic Kings in Italy

Theodoric	490–526	Hildibadus	540–541
Athalaric	526–534	Eraric	541
Amalasuintha	534–535	Totila	541–552
Theodahad	534–536	Teias	552
Witigis	536–540		

ing Frankish kingdom, Herminifrid died and Amalaberga, no longer protected by the umbrella of reverence and fear of her uncle, fled to Italy.[115] After Ravenna fell to Belisarius in 540, she and her son accompanied the Gothic captives to Constantinople. There the young Amalafrid rose to *magister militum* under Justinian.[116] These events were set in motion in close proximity to Theodoric's death in 526. The assassination of the first royal Thuringian brother, Berthachar, took place perhaps as early as 525, followed by civil war and the slaying of the second brother, Baderic. Finally the royal family concluded a dangerous external alliance with the Frankish Theodoric (ca. 527) in a desperate attempt to control the spreading rebellion. The primary result of all this bloodshed and intrigue was that the Frankish invasion speedily triumphed over a badly weakened kingdom.[117] In North Africa, Thrasamund died in 523, leaving Theodoric's sister Amalafrida isolated and a potential threat to the new Vandal king, Hilderic, who wanted nothing of the old alliance structure and was moving closer to his ancient rival, the Eastern Empire. Amalafrida fled toward Byzacena but was captured and imprisoned. She died, perhaps murdered in cold blood shortly after her brother's death.[118]

The marriages of Theodoric's two daughters born in Moesia to his first wife fared only slightly better. His eldest daughter, Areagni, married Sigismund, son of Gundobad, the king of the Burgundians, as a part of the complex diplomacy directed at stabilizing the Rhone valley, particularly the area around Arles and along the Durance River, against the rising power of the Franks. By 509 the Ostrogoths were moving into the area in settlement strength in alliance with the Burgundians.[119] Sigismund died in 523; his wife had apparently predeceased him (ca. 520). He left a daughter, Suavegotho (?), by Areagni and two sons by his second wife, whose jealousy prompted Sigismund to murder his son Sigiric, one of Theodoric the Great's three grandsons, in 522.[120] Suavegotho, in a hint of a swing in the balance of power, married Theodoric, son of Clovis by a concubine, and king of the Franks (511–34). The same Theodoric drove Amalaberga from Thuringia in ca. 532, with complete disregard for the Amali blood she and his wife held in common.

Table 3: The Amali Descended from Thiudmir

3a: *The Family of Amalafrida*

Thiudmir—Ereliva (mistress)

(1) d. ca. 500 m. *Amalafrida*
(2) Thrasamund m.
(K. of Vandals d. 523)

Daughter

Theodimund

Theodoric (the Great)

Herminifrid m. Amalaberga (returned to Italy shortly after husband's death. After fall of Ravenna in 540, she went to Constantinople.)
(K. of Thuringians d. 532)

Theodahad m. Gudeliva
(K. of Ostrog. 535–536)

Amalafridas

Rodelinda m. Audoin
(K. of Lombards)

Theudegisclus

Theodenantha m. Ebrimuth

3b: *The Family of Theodoric the Great*

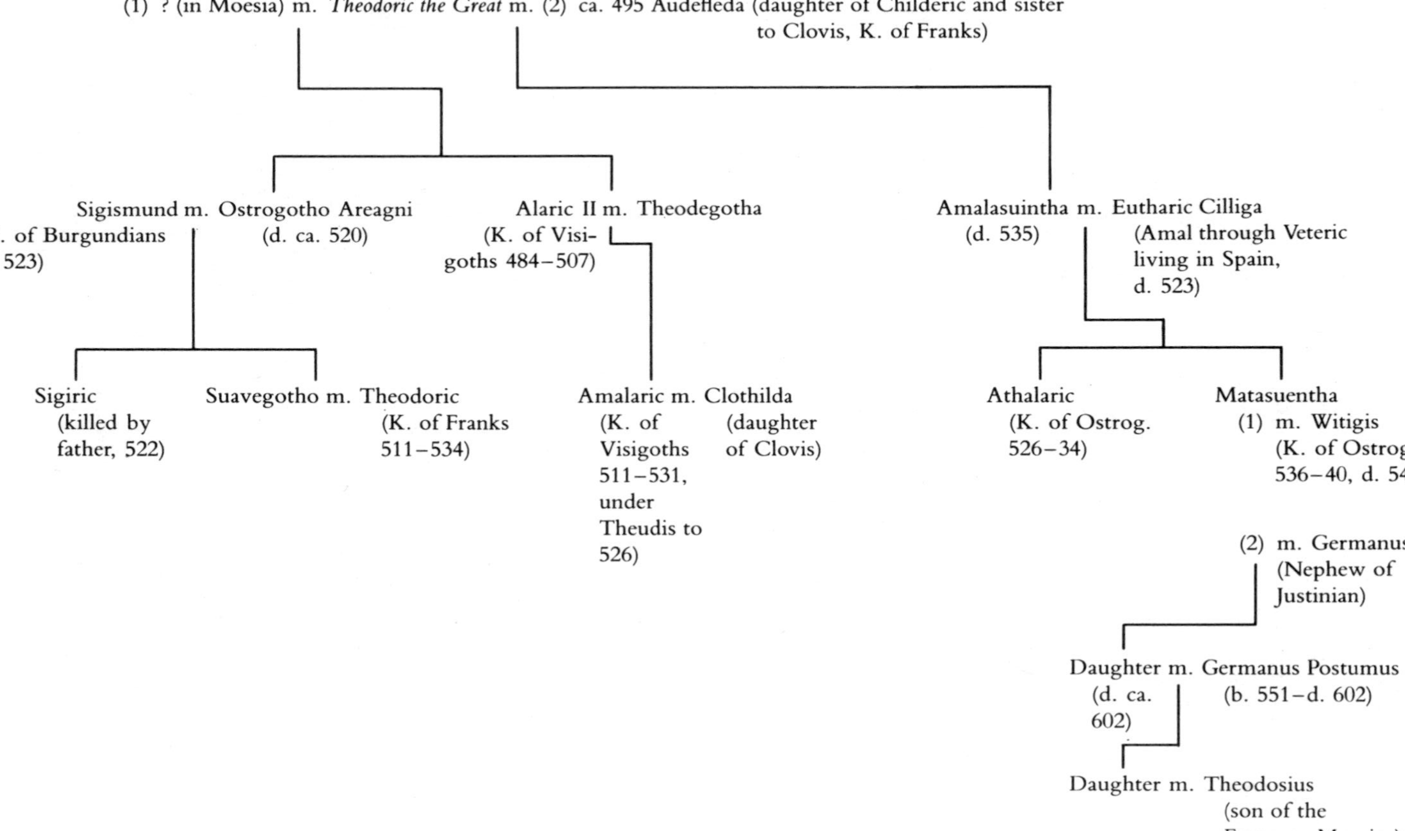

Meanwhile, another marriage was giving the aging Theodoric the Great still more concern. His second daughter, Theodegotha, married Alaric II, son of Euric, and king of the Visigoths (484–507). Alaric managed to sire a son shortly before his death in battle at Vouillé (near Poitiers) against the Franks. His son, Amalaric, was only a child in 507 and had to await the overthrow of his half-brother in 511 before he was declared king.[121] Yet even then he was a mere youth and was put in tutelage to his grandfather Theodoric the Great. There he remained until Theodoric's death in 526.[122] Theodoric took his duty very seriously, in part because of the opportunity to merit and enhance his position of leadership in the Germanic world but also with an eye toward the Rhone and the growing power of the Franks. In fact, the regency for Amalaric was the only instance in which the Ostrogoths and their king directly "profited" from the numerous marriage alliances of Amali blood. Theodoric dispatched a certain Theudis from his personal bodyguard to rule the Visigothic kingdom for him and his ward.[123] The careers of Theudis and Amalaric cast into relief some of the distinctive features of the Ostrogoths and their Visigothic cousins and illustrate the frontierlike independence enjoyed by Ostrogoths ruling far from home.

Once in Spain, Theudis ruled as king, an office he held outright from the slaying of Amalaric in 531 until his own assassination in 548. Such violent ends disguised a rather quiet interlude for the Visigothic Kingdom. The little surviving evidence suggests that peaceful coexistence between Romans and Goths ripened with greater attention devoted to its legal apparatus and the extension of a typically Ostrogothic tolerance of Catholicism. The Franks lost a few of the gains made following their victory at Vouillé when the Ostrogoths sustained an offensive in the Rhone valley and Gaul from 511 onward.[124] As military commander and guardian in distant Spain, Theudis was expected to function independently of Ravenna. However, in a fashion characteristic of many Ostrogothic noblemen, he married a wealthy Roman lady and supported a retinue of 2,000 from her estates while many of his men found wives among the Visigoths.[125] So independent was Theudis that he alone of all Gothic nobles is recorded as refusing an invitation to hail Theodoric in Ravenna. Theodoric swallowed his pride and urged him on in the wars with the Franks, all the while gratefully accepting the annual *tributum* shipped from Spain.[126]

In a now-classic manner, Theodoric divided the administration between Roman and Gothic administrators and collected as a royal right the *tributum* from Spain just as from Italy. Out of these coffers he paid the Goths in Spain their annual donatives. He was particularly concerned late in his reign (ca. 523–26) that the Spanish granaries offset the shortfall in supplies traditionally set aside for Rome. To remedy the diversion of grain by the shippers to lucrative markets in Africa, he ordered his *comes* Liuverit and the Roman nobleman Ampelius to investigate the entire marketing network, restore fair weights and equitable collection, and fine the guilty merchants a total of 1,038 solidi for their illegal profits (280 s. for the sale and 758 s. for the fares of passengers taken along).[127]

Amalaric showed little of his grandfather's capacity for rule and died in 531, universally hated, most violently by his wife, the Frankish princess Clothilda, a daughter of Clovis. Their marriage probably occurred after Theodoric's death and was an attempt by Amalaric to reassert his independence. Life was difficult enough for women of political marriages, even when their husbands were fairminded and able. These women assisted at court functions, tended the royal household (no mean task), reared the next generation, and slept knowing that their material welfare was secured in their dowry. But they did so in a foreign environment filled with court personalities vying for power and ready to use them in their intrigues at every turn. Often the intense hatreds at court left them friendless and despised. In this era the queen frequently acted as missionary to her husband and the royal entourage; however, if converting Amalaric to Catholicism was part of Clothilda's bridal chest, she was badly mistaken. Amalaric, like his distant kinsman Eutharic, was an Arian fanatic with his own dreams of conversion—enrolling his wife in the true faith of Arius.[128]

Poor Clothilda found herself in a nightmare from which there was no awakening. Amalaric was ill-advised to take her hand in the first place, for since her religion was anathema at his court, she could never function as a queen, only as a concubine, uniquely able to produce full-blooded noble heirs. His religious fervor blinded him to the inevitable severance of relations with her family when he persisted in forcing his brand of tribal Christianity upon her. Finally, Amalaric, having had enough of her obstinacy, carefully stationed his men along her path to church. As she passed, they showered her with dung. According to Gregory of Tours, she was even beaten for her faith and sent a bloodied handkerchief to her family.[129] Gregory, of course, had a keen eye for martyrs, but this one was soon rescued by her brother, Childebert, in a quick sortie into Septimania, the Gallic province of the Visigothic Kingdom. Amalaric fled from Narbonne to Barcelona, and there his own troops, perhaps urged on by Theudis, put an end to his reign. Amalaric had few lasting achievements, but he was successful in negotiating with Theodoric's successor Athalaric the recognition of his independence and stopping the drain of tribute to Italy. He also recovered the Visigothic royal treasury, previously in the hands of his Ostrogothic regents, and won the right for those intermarried Visigoths and Ostrogoths to choose their nationality.[130]

Theudis succeeded to the throne outright and set about ordering affairs, legislating a limit to acceptable payments made to judges by claimants in 546, and stabilizing the frontiers of Septimania against the Franks.[131] But within two years of his accession, a new force stirred even the remote plateaus of Spain—Belisarius. Theudis entered into negotiations with Gelimer, king of the Vandals, and in 533 perhaps offered Gelimer a hope of asylum if the struggle in Africa continued to worsen. He may even have agreed to garrison Centa on the opposite side of the Straits of Gibraltar as a gesture of support and, if need be, a first line of defense for Spain.[132] So powerful was his image to the Goths in Italy that his nephew, Hildibadus, was elected king of the Ostrogoths in 540, over his richer rival, Uraias. The Ostrogoths hoped in vain that Theudis would aid them in their own war with the Byzantines.[133] The Frankish invasion of 541 dispelled any thoughts he may have had of sending troops to his kinsmen in Italy. A palace uprising in 548 killed Theudis, and within months his death was followed by that of his principal military commander and shortlived successor, Theudigisel.[134] Thus ended forty-one years of Ostrogothic rule over the Visigothic Kingdom. The real cause of their deaths was probably the growing animosity among the Visigoths, especially in the army, over the hoarding of power by a ruling élite, foreign even if Gothic.

Thus the seven years left to Theodoric after the glorious hopes of Eutharic's consulship in 519 were everywhere filled with sorrow and visions gone awry. His sister wasted in prison, and a new and haughty Vandal king ruled North Africa. The Franks had destroyed the balance in the north. Amalaberga and Herminifrid were hard pressed in Thuringia. Theodoric's eldest daughter, Areagni, was dead in Burgundia, replaced by a Frankish princess. In Hispania, Amalaric was obviously not in the Amali image and likeness, even though he was of his blood. Theudis was efficient but arrogant. At home Eutharic died in 523, leaving Athalaric, a minor of limited capacity, as heir. Still more disturbing was the emergence of an ever-stronger yearning among the upper stratum of the Roman aristocracy to forge closer political links with Constantinople. Perhaps even his hold on the Ostrogothic nobility was slipping. Thus when Boethius flaunted Theodoric in 523, he aroused frustration and anger rarely seen since those early days in Pavia.

Boethius took to heart Plato's call for philosophers to serve the state. Reared in the opulent halls and gardens of the Symmachi after the early death of his father, Boethius could have remained cloistered with his books in the cocoon of late Roman erudition. Instead he chose the active life. Before he became consul in 510, Boethius translated into Latin many Greek works, including writings from Pythagorus, Ptolemy, Nicomachus, Euclid, Plato, and Aristotle. His translations won the highest praise from Theodoric himself,[135] who doubtless saw in them the fruits of his own labors at raising the Latin world, centered on Rome, to heights equal to those of Constantinople. In 522, Theodoric and Justin nominated Boethius's two sons, Boethius and Symmachus, as joint-consuls, a truly exceptional mark of distinction usually reserved for the imperial family.[136] Boethius remembered the event from captivity as the crowning achievement of his life. In appreciation, he delivered an oration in praise of Theodoric before the senate with both sons presiding.[137] In 523, Boethius became *magister officiorum* for Theodoric. Thus did the king express his deep admiration for one of the last great minds of antiquity. Boethius in his turn wholeheartedly supported his king. If in *The Consolation of Philosophy* Boethius remained somewhat incredulous as to the events surrounding his fall, we can be certain that he saw no treason in his actions or in those of his codefendants.[138] They had, after all, exchanged correspondence with the emperor on religious policy openly for decades, yet somehow their present correspondence precipitated accusations of treason, trials, confiscations, and imprisonment. Boethius saw his life as a defense of the Catholic faith and the freedom of the Roman senate.[139] What had changed, and changed very rapidly, was Theodoric's perception of the links between Orthodox religion and imperial politics among his Roman subjects. Even worse, their machinations had tarnished his vision for the Goths themselves.

The consulship of Eutharic in 519 celebrated the end of the Acacian Schism, among other things, but true to form, Justinian was still not wholy content. Many of his eastern subjects rejected a return to what they regarded as the essential ambiguity of Chalcedon. When a group of Scythian monks offered *unus ex trinitate passus carne* as an emendation to the Chalcedonian formula, they rekindled the emperor's passion for complete union within Christendom and domestic peace in the East.[140] In July 520, led by John Maxentius, the monks departed for Rome armed with their doctrine of Theopaschism to convince Pope Hormisdas. The pope reacted defiantly and already in August was calling them "despisers of ancient authorities, seekers after novelty." In the spring of 521, the Scythians, bitter over their rejection and claiming foul play, left for Constantinople. Hormisdas promptly denounced Theopaschism in his official reply to Justinian.[141]

The Theopaschian affair brought new elements of the pro-Eastern faction to light, including many old opponents of the Laurentian candidacy in 502–06. Perhaps even the aged Faustus entered the lists for one last hurrah.[142] Boethius and Dionysius Exiguus stood at the head of the intellectual reawakening in Rome that sought to push Italy into the mainstream of Greek education and philosophy. Since only a handful of Romans were still bilingual, the necessary first step was the translation of the basic texts of the eastern program into Latin.

Boethius died while translating and commenting upon the Aristotelian corpus. Hormisdas's successor, John, backed the intellectual movement and was himself eager to restore closer communion within Christendom.[143] Symmachus, Albinus, and many other senators were deeply troubled by the Theopaschian dilemma and rallied their supporters behind the debates. Boethius and Dionysius soon turned their pens to the religious crisis. Boethius wrote tracts deeply influenced by Theopaschian doctrines and used by John Maxentius in his defense of the new formula. Dionysius helped the monks translate several works by Cyril of Alexandria written in the fifth century against Nestorius and in defense of Christ's divinity—the root of the entire Christological debate.[144] The changing nature of Christ in Theopaschian theology allowed him to suffer on the cross as a human *in passing*, thus protecting the key of salvation, while reaffirming his essential divinity within the Godhead.

Theodoric remained aloof. Doubtless aware of the brisk exchange of letters between Rome and Constantinople and informed of the occasional embassy, he apparently still thought that union would profit all concerned, including the Goths. The singular honor of joint-consulships for the sons of Boethius in 522 attests to his forbearance with the participants in the religious controversy. But the events of 523 caused him concern and sorrow. Deaths in his family, the imprisonment of his sister in North Africa, and the rising oppression of Arians in the Eastern Empire all contributed to a sense of desperation at Ravenna. Although it will never be known precisely what inspired Theodoric to entertain charges against the ex-consul Albinus, it is known that a letter was apparently intercepted in which

Albinus betrayed his political sympathies for the imperial rule and against the reign of Theodoric. Cyprianus, *referendarius* at the royal court, drew up the charges and presented the case before the court, then at Verona. Boethius, *magister officiorum* and as such a member of the consistory, rushed to defend his friend, saying that "the charge of Cyprianus is false, but if Albinus did that, so also have I and the whole senate with one accord done it; it is false, my lord King."[145]

Theodoric was in no mood to suffer such arrogance and ordered the charges expanded to include Boethius and apparently referred the matter to the senate, or more likely to the proper subcommittee, the *iudicium quinquevirale*.[146] When the royal entourage was in residence at Pavia, he summoned Eusebius, prefect of Rome, to communicate the senate's judgment. He rendered sentence upon the guilty without further ado, probably stripping Boethius of his wealth and honors and sending him to the distant estate of Calventia.[147] That was in 523, and Boethius had not yet begun the *Philosophiae Consolatio*. Theodoric ordered Pope John to Constantinople to settle the problem of the persecution of Arians and to restore those lapsed into Orthodoxy. Justinian agreed to stop any persecutions but would not force converts back to Arianism. For Theodoric, John and his mission of Orthodox bishops—Ecclesius of Ravenna, Eusebius of Fanum Fortunae, and Sabinus of Campania—and "pro-Eastern" senators—Theodorus, Importunus, and Agapitus—failed.[148] Perhaps they had not tried hard enough; perhaps their pro-Eastern sympathies had gained the upper hand over loyalty to him. A weak and elderly John quickly succumbed to death in Theodoric's prison and was immediately hailed as a martyr by "the senate and people" of Rome.[149] *The Consolation of Philosophy* would never reach conclusion, for now convinced of widespread culpability, Theodoric ordered Boethius and Symmachus executed. According to tradition, their deaths haunted him throughout the few remaining days of his life. Struggling with visions of their tortured heads, he died of dysentery. Of course, our orthodox sources saw heavenly justice when the champion of Arianism died, just as had the founder of his accursed heresy.[150]

All the events so far associated with the fall of Boethius reflect only Roman characters and Roman plots. Theodoric never saw events as simply Roman. No, indeed: his rage was so complete that only a mortal wound can account for it. When Theodoric ordered Boethius imprisoned, the spirit of the warrior and *magister* returned. Ultimately Boethius was supposedly tortured with a cord twisted about his head until his eyes began to crack. Only then did his executioners dispatch him with a club.[151] Boethius himself gives us a hint at the causes of such deep despair and outrage, although he went to his grave refusing to accept his conduct as treasonable.

In addition to Cyprianus, Boethius denounced his other accusers with utter disdain:

> But by whose accusations did I receive this blow? By theirs who, long since having put Basilius out of the King's service, compelled him now to accuse me, by the necessity which he was driven to by debt. Opilio likewise and likewise Gaudentius being banished. . . .[152]

They were hardly so despicable a lot. Cyprianus, who was just doing his job, was promoted to *comes sacrarum largitionum* in 524 and *magister officiorum* in 527 under Athanaric. Cyprianus is praised by Cassiodorus for being able to read Gothic.[153] Opilio followed his brother Cyprianus as *comes sac. larg.* (527–28) and in 534 was addressed by Pope John II as *vir inlustris et magnificus*. Opilio accompanied Liberius to Constantinople later in 534 to explain the intentions of Theodahad toward Amalasuintha. And unlike Liberius, who apparently defected, Opilio defended his king loyally. Opilio was related through his wife to the great Basilian family.[154] Gaudentius was *consularis Flaminiae* in 517/518 (perhaps 502/03).[155] What is more important is that these men were associated by Boethius with the Goths Cunigast, in 527 addressed by Cassiodorus (writing for Athanaric) as *vir inlustris* and delegated a difficult case of land seizure, and Triwilla, *praepositus cubiculi* at Ravenna (520–23).[156] Earlier Triwilla was the *saio* ordered to supervise Faustus's return of some illegally seized property. He also helped Ennodius ultimately to purchase a villa.[157] Of course, Boethius claimed that he had protected the poor against their collective avarice.[158] Except for Boethius's bitter allegations, there is scarcely a hint of impropriety in any of his accusers or the Goths he associated with them.[159] Nor did Boethius portray them as a pro-Gothic faction, but for most Roman aristocrats they clearly were.[160]

Boethius's call from his splendid isolation at Calventia had little to do with Theodoric's order of execution, which in fact resulted from Theodoric's own investigations. On the one hand, that the correspondence of the Roman pro-Eastern faction probably evinced their straightforward hierarchy of political loyalty without reference to Theodoric was very disappointing but hardly unpredictable. On the other hand, Theodoric witnessed the unabashed emergence of a pro-

Gothic party including some of the most trusted Romans and Goths. That too was probably acceptable for the Romans, even if unsought. However, the Gothic nobility had immersed itself so deeply into aristocratic Roman life that it could not resist playing factional politics, with all its jealousies, hatreds, and betrayals, and that went against the very heart of Theodoric's program of separation and cooperation. The very presence of Goths so closely associated with important Roman aristocrats belied any attempt to claim that the correspondence in question was purely religious and cultural, for the Goths were Arians unconcerned with the subtleties within the orthodoxy. The entire exchange of letters stretching between Rome and Constantinople was now suspect. The basic ethos of Theodoric's kingdom was destroyed. All around him Goths were merging into Italian society with all its imperfections. Only their Arianism singled them out, and even here Theodoric had in part failed as a protector. The Romans had betrayed his trust. He despaired for the future and began to prepare Italy for invasion.

Shortly before his death, Theodoric instructed his praetorian prefect, Abundantius, to initiate the building of a fleet of 1,000 light ships and gave orders for levying sailors. Shippers and fishermen were exempt, and even slaves would be paid (two or three solidi) for their special service. His concerns went beyond the traditional worrying over supplies and communications, for now he warned of a potential need to oppose invasion.[161] There was only one capable navy—the Byzantine. The Vandals were in disarray at home, and their fleet was probably only marginally effective after years of neglect.[162] But whatever the eventual strength of the Ostrogothic navy, it played little part in the struggle against Justinian some ten years later.

Thus during the final years of his reign, Theodoric despaired as, one after another, aspects of his dream were washed away. In his sorrow, in his final rage and nightmares, uncontrolled and grotesque, one can still grasp a glimpse of the most complex vision of society since Constantine. The hope of controlling the merging of Goth and Roman now appeared unattainable. Standing at the summit of power, Theodoric oversimplified both the Romans and the Goths. On the one hand, he interpreted Roman dissatisfaction with the East as support for his program, apparently never realizing that ultimately many Romans, especially Justinian, were bound to regard his program as a cancer. On the other hand, the Ostrogoths were far more complex than he realized. The ancient yearnings of the leading Goths for independence and power, long muffled by his charisma but never erased, poised anew around his dynasty, now destined to struggle under the carefully tutored Amalasuintha and the weak Athalaric. Ultimately the nobility rejected much of Theodoric's vision and thrust to power Witigis, holding him aloft on a shield amid a ceremony of circled swords.[163] Witigis was a warrior without the tutored culture of *Romanitas*, but he too clung to the legend of Theodoric by marrying his granddaughter Matasuentha. There is even a hint that their marriage was celebrated in traditional Roman panegyric.[164] Although Cassiodorus, like Theodoric, saw the events of 519 as the culmination of history, he lived to dream again and again until finally the birth of Germanus Posthumous gave him a final glimmer of hope for harmony between Goth and Roman. Like all others, this hope too was false, for Germanus showed no interest in Goths and died in the intrigues surrounding the accession of Phocas in 602.[165]

The revolution which Procopius, writing after 542, claimed as the cause of the downfall of Boethius and Symmachus was, in reality, still far from men's minds in 525. Theodoric alone perceived the destiny of the Ostrogothic Kingdom when he said: "One who has gold and a demon cannot hide the demon. Also, a poor Roman plays the Goth, a rich Goth the Roman."[166] As we shall see, the Gothic nobility was becoming too deeply enmeshed in money and Roman society, while the poor Gothic soldier-farmers were gradually merging into the lower ranks. By the time Procopius drafted his chapters, a revolution of Roman aristocrats was in full progress.[167] Yet not even the screams of battle during the long wars with Justinian extinguished all hopes. As late as Totila, the basic aspirations of Gothic rule as developed under Theodoric survived at least as a distant goal. Until the very end of the kingdom (ca. 554), the conception of a balanced society of Goth and Roman, discrete aspects of a united Italy, echoed through the courtyards of Ravenna and later at Pavia. The balance is clear on the coins of almost every Gothic king after Theodoric. In part, they reproduced his themes, indeed his likeness, and even his monograms, in order to rest part of their burden upon his shoulders. But also, I believe, Theodoric's successors came to share his view that if Gothic kingship were to prevail over *Roma*, there was no alternative to an accommodation which recognized the strengths of both Roman and Gothic cultures.

Beneath the labyrinth of diplomacy linking the Amali to virtually every house in the Germanic West and the endless streams of legal actions, the vast majority of Ostrogoths gradually learned to live in their new homeland. The ethereal balance of Roman and Goth at the top of society provided the stability necessary for their own simple adaptations. Their lot seldom interested men like Cassiodorus, Ennodius, and Boethius, the office holders in government and the literary giants of their day, and so remains largely hidden. Nevertheless, the history of the Ostrogoths is also their story.

5

The Metamorphosis of Ostrogothic Society

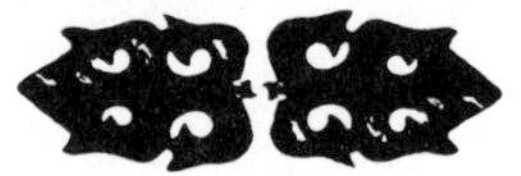

WE CANNOT RECOVER much of the basic fabric of existence for the Ostrogoths, especially before they entered the empire in the middle of the fifth century. Only an occasional point of reference protrudes above a clouded landscape. The Ostrogoths were never a very cohesive people, and they were always ready to accommodate new allies into the confederation. The farther back in time we search, the less complex was their organization and the more difficult is our task. Acculturation went hand in hand with their simple surroundings. It is really not until the fourth century that we can confidently speak of a "Gothic style" in personal ornament. Even then, however, it is often best to include within our classification the Gepids and other East Germanic stocks. The archaeological record mirrors the life of the East Germanic peoples in many ways, not the least of which is the elastic boundaries between developing politicosocial groups, traditionally called "tribes." Ethnographic precision is especially difficult for the Gepids and Ostrogoths, since they developed quite similarly throughout much of their history in adjacent or at times overlapping areas. The boundaries between them were in reality extensions of the rivalries between and among their nobilities and the associated warbands. This friction was heightened when both élites were conquered by the Huns and enrolled in their empire. The Huns from at least the time of Uldis profited from the rivalries between Gepids and Ostrogoths. The result was mistrust so deep among the Ostrogoths that they held back from joining the Gepid king Ardasic at Nedao despite the fact that his cause of freedom was also theirs. The apparent ethnic inconsistencies in the material record are thus a lasting reflection of the realities of life among the barbarians. They were primarily confederates and competitors; the concepts "Gothic" or "Gepidic" were notions of only occasional importance even in the fourth and fifth centuries.

The evolution of a warrior nobility during the third and fourth centuries was primarily a response to growing military necessity. The availability of Roman goods, some like the armbands produced mainly for trade with the barbarians, encouraged the development of increasingly hierarchic definitions of rank within the societies and especially among the warbands surrounding their chiefs. The *comitatus* of Tacitus with its reciprocal obligations and essentially egalitarian membership beneath the great warrior was transformed by the end of the fourth century into a system of complex ranking and stratifications. And as we have seen in the previous chapters, once established, the emerging nobilities dominated the remaining history of the Ostrogoths. The Hunnic overlordship sparked a realignment among the Ostrogothic nobility and helped secure the supremacy of the Amalian line. Our exploration of the physical and spiritual environment accompanying these social and political changes must often resort to comparative analysis from better-documented cases among similar peoples, particularly the Visigoths. Moreover, even with this caveat, the exceedingly limited and often contradictory evidence will not usually permit more than a sketch.

Not even the Goths on the steppes were true nomads. So far as our exceedingly limited data go, the small groups of Eastern Germanic peoples coming into the area north of the Black Sea during the early third century were semimigratory farmers and herdsmen. Once in contact with the Bosporan Kingdom and the Cherniakhov people, the Goths immediately began to modify much of their material culture. Their traditional handmade pottery gave way rather rapidly to the finer styles produced on the potter's wheel. The designs and coloration also changed.[1] It appears that their diet began a lengthy shift toward the tastes of the Mediterranean, specifically to more wheat products. The availability and use of metal, especially iron for weapons and special domestic items, dramatically increased as the Goths came into the trade orbit of the Black Sea and Bosporan Kingdom. Technically advanced Roman-type plowshares, iron hooks, sickles, and other basic farming implements of iron became common and widespread. Scattered among the numerous finds of pottery are also fine examples of Roman glass.[2] For those Greco-Roman cities on the northern littoral surviving the great disruptions of the third century, as most did on a reduced scale, the new trade spawned a brief period of commercial prosperity. Now as before, traders from centers like Olbia interacted with the peoples along the rivers to the north.[3]

The combination of animal husbandry and crop raising sustained life in the small unwalled villages and hamlets. Although the Goths were primarily farmers, cattle were always very dear. Their herds virtually meant life itself during many difficult moments. In the Balkans, when the Goths were unable to purchase grain or grow their own, cattle were their primary source of food. Cattle rustling was a "native sport" still practiced in Italy. The descendants of some of Theodosius's Gothic settlers still remained in Moesia in the sixth century. Of them Jordanes reports that "they are a numerous people, but poor and unwarlike, rich in nothing save flocks of various kinds and pasture lands for cattle and forests for wood." These people produced little wheat or other grains and knew wine only as an import. They preferred milk.[4]

In addition to cattle, the early Goths raised sheep, horses, swine, and poultry. Wheat, oats, and hops were grown. Their combs, knife handles, jewelry, and delicate woodworking tools were made from the bones of deer and elk. Rabbit too was a staple fare. The ubiquitous spindle whorls attest to the long hours spent weaving clothing, blankets, and the like. Housing itself had changed from the large (two or three rooms plus stalls) houses of the Baltic, whence at least some of their ancestors derived. Typical of the south were small single-room houses in widely dispersed hamlets along the slopes of the rivers. Such areas were best suited for farming.[5] The houses were similar to the more extensively explored and somewhat more elaborate contemporary Carpic homes along the Prut River in Moldavia.[6] But unlike the Carpic settlements, in which Roman trade items were rare, finds in the Gothic areas manifest an eager receptivity. In general, however, the Goths adapted to new circumstances without completely abandoning their own traditions.

Most of the published archaeological data on the fourth-century Goths derive from the areas of Roman Dacia and as such reflect developments of the Tervingi and their allies more directly than the distant Greuthingi east of the Dniester River. Great care must be taken here. Dacia was never a uniformly Romanized area. Much like Gaul of the *Bellum Gallicum*, post-Aurelianic Dacia fell into three divisions: the area along the river, usually under some type of Roman administration even if in a highly barbarized form; the zone beyond this area, from which Roman military personnel had withdrawn, leaving a sizable population behind that was heavily Romanized; and finally what is now the northern parts of Moldavia, Crişana, and Maramures. This final area was always peripheral to the Roman province, not militarily occupied but nonetheless controlled by Rome and part of the Roman provincial economic sphere.[7] Here lived the various peoples, including the Carpi, often called "free Dacians." The Goths, either the Tervingi or Greuthingi, never settled all Dacia. The first lands taken over by the Tervingi Goths were in Moldavia, and only during the fourth century did they move in strength down to the Danubian plain. The Ostrogoths were still more isolated, as we shall see, but even the Visigoths preferred to live among their own kind. As a result, the Goths settled in pockets. Finally, although Roman towns continued on a reduced level, there is no question as to their survival in the middle and southern zones of Dacia. When the progenitors of the Tervingi moved onto Roman soil in northeastern Dacia around 300, they did so against the opposition of the Carpi and other free Dacians. Once victorious, they were challenged by the remnants of Roman control. Some of the partially Romanized population remained and carried on under the Goths. In many ways the picture we have of the complex cultural and economic interactions at Olbia from the pen of exiled Dio Chrysostom in the first century is chronologically extended by later archaeological evidence from the late third, fourth, and on into the fifth century.[8] The Black Sea centers projected a continuous influence upon the Germans and the traditional population. Indeed, in many respects the Bosporan Kingdom and the other commercial centers were able to promote a freer and more extensive exchange than were the carefully established trading centers along the Danubian *limes*. Thus, the direction and magnitude of acculturation with the Mediterranean world were probably as strong among the Greuthingi as among their western cousins.

Yet, for most of those who were to become Ostrogothic, primary contact with Romans and their civilization had to await the disintegration of the Hunnic Empire. By then they were quite well prepared. Even before the arrival of the Huns, they had had at least a century of experience gained from contacts along the northern coast of the Black Sea. Pressures from the north and east forced them to begin to consolidate as Greuthingi long before the arrival of the Huns. Such peoples as the Alans, Sarmatians, Antes, and others pressed upon them. Ultimately, of course, Ermanaric built a kingdom including many of the great families of these rival groups. Saphrax, an Alan, and Alatheus, perhaps a Sarmatian, were among the most notable leaders in his confederacy.[9] It remains unclear in what ways these various groups interacted and how specifically they influenced Ostrogothic domestic life. There were probably few differences among them and hence no great influence in either direction. Within a few years of the death of Ermanaric, the Ostrogoths fell under the domination of the Huns. By 380–400 some had apparently moved westward as far as Botoşani. Some also seem to have settled in the area of the Theiss River, northern Moldavia, and northeastern Muntenia. Later, perhaps around 420–50, they may have expanded southward to include the Siebenbürgen region, but their precise location is still unclear.[10] Roman influence came to these various East Germanic peoples through the remnants of the Romanized customs of the indigenous population, continued contacts with Roman trade items, distribution of Roman tribute to the Huns, and the increasingly visible presence of Christians.[11]

Subtle changes in diet, metal crafts, carpentry, and trade habits often veil the early stages of more decisive developments. Among the Ostrogoths, we can only say that conditions were propitious for significant change by the mid-fourth century. Elsewhere, however, the process is clearer, and the mechanisms are better understood. The Romans had long known the political values of controlling military gifts to the Germans. Tacitus speaks of such gifts made to German commanders of Roman *auxilia*. These commanders were, in effect, the heads of warrior societies in Roman employment, but they related to their men as warriors, just as they had beyond the frontier. During the third century, specific types of military decoration derived principally from Roman uniforms served to denote membership in the warrior societies themselves. Armbands made of gold were particularly symbolic of belonging to a warrior group. By the late fifth century, the golden armbands were symbols reserved for the highest authorities.[12] We might include in this category bands such as those from the tomb of Childeric, the noble burial of Apahida II, and the great band with runic engraving from Pietroasa. The last two examples were perhaps actually worn by Ostrogoths. Their symbolic significance was not lost on the Romans, even among themselves. Saint Ambrose rebuked the emperor Valens for wearing them, because of their pagan connotations.[13] Such was the symbolic power of these bands that those of gold were restricted to the "regal families." Others wore less spectacular bands of baser metals. Theodosius the Great carefully selected the Germanic recipients of his gifts, specifically including armbands, in order to coincide with his policy of playing one Gothic leader against another.[14] Through such handling, rather than decisive campaigning, he established and maintained the Goths as federates.

The point is perhaps obvious. Once the Goths and others incorporated Roman items into the basic fabric of their society, they risked dependence and manipulation. Arm rings are probably the easiest items in the trade network to explore but are probably less significant than other aspects of exchange in the total process of acculturation. Trade in weapons was repeatedly decried in imperial legislation to no avail, but arms production was also the highest state of the smith's art among the barbarians. Certainly they produced their own weapons; nor were barbarian swords technologically inferior. The problem was supply. The availability of sufficient quantities of weapons was a limiting factor in any major campaign. There seemed never to be enough swords and spears to go around. Of course, after they had been disarmed crossing the Danube in 376, the Visigoths had no choice but to scavenge weapons from the fallen enemy.[15] Yet almost twenty years later, Alaric still boasted of forcing the Roman towns under his sway to forge weapons for him.[16] Under ordinary circumstances, each warrior came with his own weapons. Only rarely do we find more than one sword in a Germanic grave. Goths rarely interred weapons, for unknown religious reasons, and this practice may have helped maintain their basic supply. During battle, swords were broken or damaged and had to be repaired or replaced. Protracted conflicts like those under Alaric produced scarcities difficult to overcome.

Dietary changes toward Roman tastes are manifest. Wine and wheat bread were very popular. Germanic dress, especially among the élite, paralleled Roman military garb.[17] Although the Gothic suppliants on the base of Theodosius's obelisk (fig. 8) wore the traditional pelted coats meeting at the collar their long flowing hair, which distinguished the Germanic nobility across much of Europe for centuries, the Goths had also adopted certain features of Roman dress.[18] By the end of the fourth century, they knew the Roman custom of wearing shoulder torques and had been introduced to the chip-carved style of the frontier. As usual the Goths integrated these styles into their own traditional fashions. The nobility continued to prefer cloisonné fibulae throughout the century and, indeed, still wore them with pride until the end of the Ostrogothic Kingdom in Italy. The Ostrogoths became truly fond of the chip-carved style only after their settlement in Pannonia (ca. 455) and then continued to refine its use throughout their history. By the opening of the sixth century, several

Fig. 8: Obelisk base of Theodosius the Great (erected in the hippodrome in Constantinople, ca. 390).

designs and techniques of working chip-carved pieces distinguished Ostrogothic Italy.[19]

We must be exceedingly circumspect when discussing style. When an isolated object of Roman manufacture was worn beyond the frontiers, nothing need be said about stylistic influence. On the other hand, if numerous pieces of certain types occurred and if their use conformed to Roman practice, then we have a rather clear example of stylistic borrowing. Certain types of torques and Roman medallions fall into this category. The first treasure of Szilágysomlyó, with its blend of authentic and imitative medallions, is a spectacular example.[20] The bracteates of Scandinavia are perhaps the most famous barbarian imitations. They typically bore only a remote resemblance to Roman coins and medallions. More common, however, were local workshops and craftsmen working in familiar motifs within the broad norms of local fashion. Their products reflected a complex intertwining of the artistic creativity of the jeweler and the demands of the wearer, for the recipient of the piece had to have something appropriate to his own rank and use. Borrowing scarcely describes the process.

Along the *limes*, a multitude of elements was present at all times: Roman, Greek, and, less significant overall but still viable, elements from the Near East merged with other traditions originating among the Germans themselves or the Celts and steppe nomads. These elements could serve as artistic stimuli, but they did so only within prescribed contexts and were themselves constantly changing. Forcing artifacts produced under fluid circumstances into ethnographic categories is not merely difficult, it is usually counterproductive. The same is true of the techniques of manufacture, although here we are often on firmer ground in assessing chronology. Nonetheless, a few styles became so common among specific groups that their presence is a strong indication of the ethnic and at times tribal status of the wearer. For example, in the fifth century the five-digited bow fibulae with diamond-shaped lower sections were characteristically Ostrogothic, whereas contemporary eagle-headed belt buckles occurred more often among the Gepids.[21] The selection of metal and variations in detail, such as employing semiprecious stones or cut glass and garnets to add brilliance, were typical devices through which the artist manifested his originality even within the bounds of so-called national styles. Once in a great while we can see that a truly magnificent piece, doubtless worn by a great nobleman, was so extraordinarily beautiful that it became a model and style in itself. The famous "masked fibula of Hegykö" is a case in point. Probably produced just prior to 568 and therefore early Lombardic, it has design variations deriving from the Ostrogothic period in Italy and was truly archetypical for several generations of Lombards.[22] Moreover, the symbolic worlds of the Eastern Germans were quite similar, and pieces from one center were attractive over broad distances.

The Eastern Germanic peoples, furthermore, wore their basic ornaments in ways distinct from the northern Germans. For example, the Ostrogoths and Visigoths wore their clothing in such a way as to enable them to gather the garment at the shoulders, where it was anchored with fibulae. Men usually wore a fibula on their right shoulder, whereas women wore them on both shoulders (Drawings no. 1 and no. 2). Alamannic and Frankish women, on the other hand, typically used two or more fibulae and pins to secure the frontal closing of their garments (Drawing no. 5, p. 157). Thus, many Ostrogothic fibulae discovered beyond the Alps were worn in the north Germanic style. For example, the Alammanic grave no. 126 from Basel-Kleinhüningen (fig. 9) in northern Switzerland reveals an assortment of personal ornament, including distinctive Ostrogothic fibulae, all worn in the northern style.[23] Only rarely do we find Ostrogothic

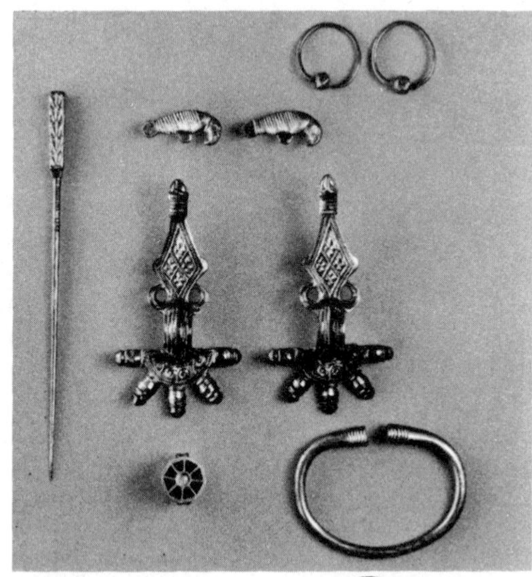

Fig. 9: Jewelry from Basel-Kleinhünigen.

Drawings 1 and 2: *Left:* Ostrogothic female fashion. *Right:* North Germanic style with Ostrogothic types of jewelry. Based on finds from Basel-Kleinhüningen.

jewelry worn in East Germanic (i.e., shoulder position) fashion. Then we must ponder a real presence of at least a few Ostrogoths in the territories far beyond Italy.[24]

Before the Visigoths crossed the Danube, they had developed numerous craft specialists, and a few locations were producing more than was necessary for purely local consumption, e.g., at Vales Seacă-Bîrlad and Fedaşti Şuletia.[25] Along with the emergence of a powerful nobility and a permanent confederate leadership with their expanded household staffs and retainers came a need for some planned accumulation and storage of supplies from the villages surrounding the residences of the chiefs. The resultant demands from the aristocracy also probably expanded and regularized local trade networks. The study of words in the Gothic Bible reveals the existence of a wide variety of crafts and artisans. The village market was a center for the exchange of merchandise and a public forum for the discussion of daily events and matters of community concern: *market* (*maþl*) meant discourse in public (*maþleins*), profit or gain (*gawaurki*). In fact, the language is well stocked with terms implying a rather sophisticated knowledge of business transactions: several words derive from *dulgis* (debt), including *dulgiskula* (debtor) and the reverse *dulgahaitia* (creditor). The words for debt are often linked with guarantees (*wadi*) and related terms for securing the transaction. Workers in metal were *aiya-smiþa*, and their tools had Gothic names. Many other products were likewise commonly known, particularly woolens and leather goods. Slaves existed as war captives but apparently were not very important in production. Most, but not all, were sold to the Romans. Goths did acknowledge freemen (*fralets*), but their role in the economy is unknown.

The Gothic language further reveals a world of kindreds, villages (*weihs*), and small regions (*garvi*). Towns (*baurg*) were probably the remains of Roman cities and fortlets. *Kuni* meant kin, tribe, and generation; *sibja* defined a more general relationship of family, including adopted sons. *Unsibja* meant lawless, impious, godless, or as a noun a transgressor. *Garvi* was the equivalent of the Latin *pagus* and within it ties between neighbors (*garazna*) and kin-organized life. But not everyone fit into this picture. There were also terms for outcasts such as brigands, thieves, and harlots. Although unwanted, they nevertheless had families and therefore kindred, but neither the outcasts nor the craftsmen were readily contained within the normative structures of agrarian society.[26]

The Visigoths themselves had made considerable advances in economic specialization and had begun to integrate Roman products and ideas into their society by the time of Ulfila (ca. 370). They were able to do so quite rapidly, in part because they were close to the advanced outposts of Roman civilization. Some Visigoths may have moved into the areas in northern Dacia as early as 291, but long-term confrontations and adjustments began in earnest during the reign of Constantine the Great. At this time the Roman garrisons north of the river exposed many barbarian groups to Roman material culture and the functioning of the empire. These same troops secured the landing points for Constantine's campaigns of 313–22, but by the middle of the century the Constantinian bridgehead began to crumble and change. Gradually, inscriptions and coinage disappeared to the north of Sucidava, where the great stone bridge built for the Gothic campaigns succumbed either to the elements or to the barbarians.[27] Typically barbarian housing of small single-room dwellings replaced the barracks and stately quarters built for officers. The local pottery of the surviving inhabitants became mixed with Germanic material, and the peculiar blending dominated the late strata.[28] Whether these people were, in fact, still recognized as part of the Roman army is unclear. Finally, by midcentury the Goths were living on the northern shore of the Danube under an agreement with Rome that provided limited access to Roman towns and garrisons along the Danube, still the main economic artery of the Balkan Peninsula.

Ammianus Marcellinus remarked that in some areas along the Rhine, the inhabited zone extended only ten miles eastward before the forest began.[29] Virtually the same could have been said about the areas under the Visigoths, for they too were attracted to the *limes*. As Ammianus also well knew, the barbarians in the interior were usually less sophisticated than those along the frontier.[30] The archaeological evidence along much of the Rhine and part of the Danube generally confirms his assessment and reveals that Roman trade goods decreased significantly with increased distance from the rivers and the exchange points. By the last century of the empire in the West, if not before, barbarian settlements were often directly across the river boundaries, sometimes quite close to Roman advanced posts and landing areas on the far bank. Future excavation may establish this pattern as truly normative.[31] Already in the fourth century, Goths and others definitely and frequently found refuge and shelter in abandoned or partially abandoned Roman defenses of transdanubian Dacia. Their lives never returned to the rustic conditions of their ancestors.

Throughout the fourth century, the Goths and other barbarians along the river frontiers of the Roman Empire lived in sight of and sometimes within the Roman camps and towns on the *limes*. The Roman army itself became increasingly Germanic and *sui generis*, especially the *limitanei* of the forward areas.[32] Commands were still issued in military Latin, but in the evening Germanic tongues joked and talked idly around the camp fires. Many Goths found service in the Roman armies.[33] In most places a strong voice could easily carry across the river to understanding ears on the other side. The Danube flowed through a military district and gave both banks a focus for life. Trading centers were established and regularized under Constantine and his family in order to control the barbarians. But as far as the Goths were concerned, they wanted open access to markets everywhere. As has so often been the case along frontiers, the more advanced society tried to manipulate the other politically through restricted economic intercourse. A major disruption or cessation occurred in the wake of Valens's strikes into *barbaricum* (ca. 367) and brought considerable suffering to the Goths.[34]

Rome constantly rebuilt and modified the entire *limes* system. In some areas along both the Danube and the Rhine, Rome built new watchtowers and fortifications; in others, old legionary and auxiliary camps were repaired. Mobile field armies became permanent and were linked to the frontline fortifications with roads and supply depots. Additional hostels and stables also greatly improved transportation and communications along the major highways. Sometimes new arms factories were built preceding particular campaigns.[35] The military buildup gave economic manipulation and traditional diplomacy a chance to create a complex alliance network to further peace and limit brigandry and raiding to acceptable levels. The old alliance system of the principate had vanished in the third-century crisis and had to be restructured, but the incredible costs of such a massive military and diplomatic program bore heavily upon Rome's resources. To lessen costs and meet the demands for maintenance and repair, the empire had little recourse but to utilize better the existing manpower along the *limes*.[36] Land transport was, as always, extremely expensive for bulk goods, and that unquestionably had been a factor in the original deployment of the system along rivers centuries before. Any food the *limitanei* produced near the frontier found a ready market. The Roman district commanders, the *duces*, might well have declared labor shortage as their greatest concern. Their men, however, had a different and more traditional concern: women. Women were always in short supply around military camps with their high concentrations of young men. Just across the river were men for hire (in Gothic, *asneis*) and women for companionship (*kalkjo*) and marriage.[37]

Willing hands found much to do. Barbarians here as elsewhere were easily parted from their earnings by Roman wares. Some of them were buried with their treasures of Roman glass and jewelry. In central Dacia, where the pagan funereal practices continued among the indigenous population throughout the fourth century, they often held a sacred meal over the grave and tossed Roman coins into the hearth.[38] The Goths were typical in their relationship to the frontier except that they were probably somewhat slower than others elsewhere to accept the essentially peaceful interchange as normal. After all, Constantine's campaigns and those of his children, particularly Constantius, took decades to stabilize the military situation, and even then probably not to Rome's satisfaction. In fact, the struggles continued until the early 340s, when the Goths rallied around a temporary *iudex*, the confederate leader (*thiudans* in Gothic). During these wars the commercial exchange was doubtless suspended.[39] However, from the forties until Valens's expedition in 367, the peace held firm. The Goths were *gens amica Romanis, foederibusque longae pacis.*[40]

Within a decade of the Gothic selection of a *iudex*, much of the West erupted in violence that did not directly concern the Goths until the revolt of Procopius in 364. Constantius II crushed Maxentius's revolt, only to face wholesale pillage and rapine from his defeated followers and their barbarian allies. The already severe tenor of life along much of the *limes* and in the settlements in the interior of many provinces seems to have worsened after the midcentury disorders.[41] Something had to be done to restore security and the relaxed environment it brings or appears to bring. As Julian saw firsthand in Gaul, the transalpine provinces needed a respite. Rome took the initiative. Constantius II, Julian, and Valentinian strengthened fortifications and launched punitive attacks against the Alamanni, Quadi, and others. They sought to disrupt and prevent the process of confederation, but events ran counter to their wishes. The raids into *barbaricum* were savage, cutting down men, women, and children and putting whole villages to the torch. Leaders were captured and paraded through the streets of the capitals. Rome left weaker claimants in power. The disruptions of village life may have severely altered basic social and economic patterns. The villages, the centers of agriculture and family life, were immobile and vulnerable. The warbands, on the other hand, retreated into the forested interior.[42] To make matters worse, the victorious Romans often requisitioned food and labor for their garrisons and fortifications from barbarian stores already reduced by war.[43] The resulting hatred and deprivation strengthened anti-Roman resolve and tribal cohesion, the very thing Rome sought to curb. From time to time Rome would grant dutifully submissive groups *receptio* and disperse them into the lands behind and along the frontiers, but always in groups small enough for rapid assimilation.

The Goths from 364 until as late as Alaric's revolt in 395 were entangled in aspects of this coercive policy or its successor, the federate system. Valens executed a punitive raid, similar to those of Constantius II and Valentinian, against the Goths who had backed the ill-fated rebel Procopius, but he was somewhat restricted when he lost a whole season because of high water. Nevertheless, he was able to disrupt village life severely. He launched plundering expeditions and captured as many fleeing Goths as was possible before they found refuge in the forests and mountains.[44] At least he did not place a bounty on their heads, as Valentinian did against the Quadi, but for this gesture he received no plaudits from the Goths. The barbarians would not, of course, tolerate punitive raids into their territory. Nevertheless, the Goths and others were subject to the same relentless political and economic forces, regardless of outbursts of warfare. Once peace returned, their leaders with their warriors were recruited into the army and often pitted against each other for imperial favor. The markets in the Roman towns attracted curious and needy barbarians as usual. If anything, the economic interaction intensified in the last half of the fourth century. In general, this progressive adaptation is also apparent in their language.

The Goths were, as we have seen, familiar with the basic crafts, and their own artisans had a long tradition of producing handsome products. The existence of Gothic words for so many items and specialities manifests a gradual modification and development. After the late third century, however, the Goths were in ever more intimate association with the advanced structures of the Roman world. To deal with Romans, they had to understand terms for a wide variety of technical functions previously unnecessary. An early stage in the process is reflected by their direct transplanting of many terms from Latin and Greek into Gothic. Another technique was to borrow and only slightly modify Latin suffixes (particularly, Latin *tudo*, Gothic *dupi*, and Latin *arius*, Gothic *areis*) and append them to Gothic common nouns so as to make a term for the specialist responsible for the product: e.g. *mota* (toll), *motareis* (toll collector); *boka* (book), *bokareis* (scribe). Thus, the Goths had a substantial familiarity with a wide variety of Roman objects and concepts; toll and book were obviously Roman in origin, and long had had Gothic terms to express them. However, increased contact with Romans forced them to conceptualize the much more refined division of labor that lay behind such items as tools. Subtle occupational divisions and the underlying hierarchical infrastructure of Roman society were beyond the simple descriptive capabilities of the Gothic language, which had to resort to borrowing forms of classification from Latin. The terms and concepts most demonstrably affected derived from contact with the Roman army, particularly its command structure and procedures. Similar analysis reveals two other areas of strong interaction: the ecclesiastical structure of Christianity and the bureaucracy, particularly those aspects involved in trade.[45] Implicit in this argument is that the Goths were simultaneously learning to take Roman wares for granted as just another routine feature of their own lives.

When the Ostrogoths first migrated into the northern parts of Dacia under pressure from the Huns, they encountered only those vestiges of Rome preserved among the indigenous population of the peripheral zone. The Hunnic settlements on the Danubian plain to the south effectively blocked most contact between the Ostrogothic groups perhaps settled in the Theiss area and elsewhere in northern Dacia and the Roman towns along the Danube. Thus, the Hunnic episode for most Ostrogoths was a continuation and probably only modest intensification of their encounter with the Greco-Roman world via the Black Sea trade. The Roman tribute paid the Huns was perhaps redistributed, in part, to their allies, including the Ostrogoths. The pattern of gold coins formed in the Baltic area and traced by types and die identities to the Ostrogoths slightly later, specifically from Pannonia and Italy, appears to begin during the Hunnic episode.[46] Most coins given in tribute were destined for trade along the Danube, where exchange continued between the Huns and certain Roman towns, but apparently much of the gold passed into Hunnic hands as ingots and ultimately found its way into jewelry, as did the Baltic coins. A few such ingots have turned up in Transylvania and might reflect this practice.[47] To be sure, those Ostrogoths moving into Dacia were the first to live side by side with partially Romanized farmers, but that was hardly a great leap into another civilization. Their strongest recollections once within the empire were of the requisitions they had struggled to meet for their overlords, the Germanic élites and the Huns. The same pattern of adaptive response to Rome that we have outlined for the Visigoths seems applicable to the Ostrogoths as well, although their prolonged stay north of the Danube seems to have slowed the process and ultimately perhaps thereby made it easier to undergo direct contact after they once settled inside the frontier.

The Pannonia of 455 was still a land of towns, villas, fortifications, and roads, but most were in a state of disrepair. The shock of repeated invasion and Hunnic occupation had destroyed the network. Numerous villas were abandoned, and townsmen huddled within their reduced and more defensible walls.[48] Nevertheless, these pitiful fragments of a once-vibrant province were probably more impressive than anything the Ostrogoths had seen before, except perhaps when they had accompanied Attila on his great sweeps into Gaul and Italy. Details of life among the Ostrogoths in Pannonia from 455–71 are lacking, despite our growing awareness of their settlement areas. There were many other barbarian peoples already present and serving as federates. The settlement of the Ostrogoths was one of the last attempts to control the key areas in northeastern Pannonia along and just behind the river through federates. Conditions were poor. Failure of Roman plans to reestablish control over the land and river routes connecting East and West seemed inevitable. Huns, Sciri, Gepids, Sadagis, and others competed for lands and imperial favor. Cattle rustling was rampant.[49] Culturally and economically, northeastern Pannonia was still linked to the world of the Roman *limes*. The surviving dress ornaments reveal a fascination and experimentation with styles traditional to the frontier. Specifically, they began to adapt the chip-carving techniques to their own tastes in fibulae and buckles.[50] Barge traffic flowed, although intermittently, on the Danube as far north as Lauriacum and Batavis. There Saint Severinus rallied the Romans and their allies for one more struggle. Undisciplined bands of barbarians were raiding their livestock and carrying off anyone found in the open; even those working within sight of the walls of their own city were sometimes unsafe.[51] The presence of the Ostrogoths and their highly competitive bands did nothing to further stability. On the contrary, their raids may have carried them as far as Noricum Ripensis. The Rugians shared their wrath. Like the Rugians and later the Lombards, the Ostrogoths probably settled in the countryside near Roman towns, where trade still offered some variety even in necessities. For the period 455–71 we can be certain of little.

We are no better informed as to life in the settlements around Pella (474) or Novae (ca. 487). The literature merely attests to their continuing search for supplies and a longing of many for a permanent return to farming.[52] The Ostrogoths and their leaders, the two Theodorics until 481, were aware of the plight of the poor local farmers with whom their people sympathized.[53] These were lean years. Theodoric Triarius once upbraided his rival, saying:

> Why do you destroy my kin, you villain? Why have you widowed so many women? Where are their husbands? How has the wealth, which everyone had when they set out with you from home on this campaign, been wasted? Each of them had a pair or three horses, but now they advance horseless and on foot, following you through Thrace like slaves, though they are free men of no mean race. Since coming, have they shared a single medimus of gold?[54]

In contrast, Italy was an oasis. Anyone but a barbarian would have pointed to the undisguised destruction caused as long ago as Alaric's campaigns at the turn of the century and the Vandal sack of Rome in 455. The estate system in Italy was not what it once was. Restrictions on commerce and freedom of movement had isolated some members of the senatorial aristocracy from distant parts of their holdings. Those who had invested heavily in areas now lost or shared under *hospitalitas* were especially depressed.[55] In the area around Veii, just outside Rome, intensive field surveys and excavations have revealed a continuous contraction in the number of villas and a growth in the average size of each. The frequency of shortlived squatter's occupations also was on the rise.[56] The lands of the church, based upon generations of pious bequests, offered a tempting target for some. But successive popes and councils effectively banned the reclamation of churchland by the descendants of the original grantors. Thus the plight of the middling Roman aristocracy was often desperate. They saw themselves on a precipice of financial ruin. The truly great were politically sensitive to these problems and possibilities, but their lifestyles were safe. The *adventus Ostrogothorum* in 489–93 kindled a variety of emotions on both sides.

The settlement of the Ostrogoths created the essential physical environment for the rest of their existence as a people. The main features were a return to farming within the context of the late Roman estate system for many, direct participation in the economic system as both producers and consumers, the gradual redirection and integration of the warrior associations into settled life (never completed), and finally the gradual adaptation of life to Roman legal and governmental systems. However, at no time did the common Goths simply abandon their own heritage. Except for a decade or two in the Balkans, the Goths had never experienced the fruits of settlement. The initial joy and relief must have overwhelmed the faint-hearted. Alas, our records labor to describe the process and the impact upon the Roman aristocracy. The lowly settlers are passed over in silence. Yet the visible fabric often allows us to imagine some of the missing details and thereby gives credence and coherence to the few traces of daily life among the Goths.

Once their leaders had fixed the division or "sharing" under *hospitalitas*, the next step was to restore fragmented estates in those areas physically occupied. Presumably Theodoric and his principals had previously discussed and selected the areas for actual settlement. Liberius, for one, would have known the full range of problems and possibilities in each region. Theodoric and his *comitatus* were equally concerned with the political and military realities of governing a newly occupied land. Despite the fact that Zeno had invited Theodoric to go to Italy, the wars with Odovacar had revealed several potential problems, especially the need to control the road network. The economic, political, and military considerations combined with a strong social and cultural tradition, dating back centuries, of clustered groups of Goths settling in restricted areas and thereby preserving something of their own customs. The result was a concentration of Ostrogoths in Liguria, Picenum-Samnium, and the lower Po Valley centered on Ravenna. Within each locality, the first task was the sale or exchange of the fragments of those estates not divisible into thirds without yielding destruction. This "rounding-out" was absolutely necessary whenever and wherever a division of revenue was unacceptable.

The Goths in Italy clearly wanted certain lands and were not always evenhanded in their techniques of acquisition. The Roman landowners were perplexed. Several letters in the Ennodian corpus relate to their attempts to obtain redress at the court in Ravenna for the misdeeds of the Ostrogothic nobility.[57] The near contemporary Paulinus Pellaeus, writing of events in southeastern Gaul under his guests, the Visigoths, had a more sanguine attitude. For him and his family, the right guest could be a great boon—a vigorous protector against further predation. He was in desperate straits in Marseilles when as from heaven news came that a Goth was interested in buying the remnants of some of his wife's property, long abandoned in their retreat southward. The Goth offered a fair price. Even Pellaeus thought it quite good.[58]

A very simple recognition lay behind these events. The productive strength of Roman agriculture was the villa-estate and the carefully balanced agrarian system focused on it. Without a balance of arable fields for vines and grain, meadow and forest, the unit could not function. That was a primary fact of life for every settler, every farmer. And that is where the legal structures of *hospitalitas* had to yield to reality. Yet even here, the Goths at least forced the inherent guidelines of Roman testamentary law to serve their needs. As far as the records allow us to look, we see Gothic nobles buying and selling in the traditional and often archaic Roman legal forms, including calculating in *As* units of twelve, which dated far back into the Republic.[59] These were considerations beyond the ken of the common Goths eagerly awaiting their shares. But it was just such practical necessity of dealing with complex Roman traditions to overcome the limits of *hospitalitas* that illuminates the early gradients of Romanization among the Goths. Every Gothic noble had to concern himself with these problems immediately. They were not, nor could they have been, problems solely for the royal court.

Land without labor was as useless as land without meadow or forest. In Liguria, at least, the nobles subdivided the blocks of land units awarded them into *condamae*. These were apparently family farming units, impossible to define in detail but perhaps comprised of families linked into a specific *fara*.[60] Even in Liguria, however, labor for the central estate and other specific functions associated with seasonal and occupational differentiation demanded additional labor and equipment. The *Edictum Theodorici* offers us a splendid picture of the initial problems facing the monarch of Gothic federates becoming governors and farmers. Because of the continuing dispute over its authorship—either Theodoric II at Toulouse or Theodoric the Great—this extraordinary document can be used with confidence only to create a comparative perspective. There is nothing in the Ostrogothic materials that contradicts the resultant images, but there is also a scarcity of corroborative data. The same can be said of the early Visigoths, but with the addendum that they at least have left copious examples of their legal tradition, at the beginning of which the *Edictum* might well be placed. Despite these limits imposed on precise ethnographic identification, the *Edictum* offers a vision completely consistent with the tribulations surrounding the early arrivals of the Goths both in southern Gaul and later in Italy.[61]

The disruptions caused by the confederate Gothic peoples with their sometimes unruly allies—Alans among the Visigoths and the Rugians and others with the Ostrogoths—were disastrous for many of the indigenous poor. The vicissitudes of life were often harsh for those at the bottom—too much rain or too little, insects and rodents feasting while they faced starvation. To these woes, the wars of occupation waged against Odovacar added a human pestilence, as roving armies and bands of warriors unleashed their demands and frustrations. The *Edictum* reached out to the poor in a curious way. They were to be allowed to buy back their children at the price for which they were sold into slavery.[62] The law still distinguished the *honestiores* from the *humiliores* among the Romans. Dependence between rich and poor was as old as Rome herself, doubtless older, and behind the legalisms existed complex gradations among and between them.[63] Great landowners, facing an acute labor shortage, pooled workers from several areas and transferred others from domestic duties in town to agricultural labor (obviously an unpopular move among the tenants).[64] The lords were also trying to reconstitute their laboring populations, sometimes so unscrupulously that the king ordered an immediate restoration of coloni and slaves to their original owners unless all purchase agreements with dealers had already been concluded.[65] The lords even shared such basic equipment as oxen and plows. Heavy fines punished anyone overworking the slaves or oxen of another.[66] Great care went into the peaceful transition to agrarian settlement. The *Edictum* specified the types of land essential to the villa economics, especially arable fields (*seges*) and forest (*arbor*).[67]

The monarch was equally concerned with the quick restoration of other aspects of economic life, including fair marketing conditions and the rebuilding of essential structures destroyed during the wars.[68] The Goths and other barbarians too came under the *Edictum*. Those serving in the army received under the traditional provision of Roman law the right to make testaments.[69] The king admonished both Romans and Goths against the illegal seizure of property.[70] Cattle rustling had become a major problem needing redress.[71] There was much shifting of boundary markers, and that was to stop.[72] Perhaps both sides found such a simple mechanism irresistible during the settlement. Certainly, if true, these violations attest to the Gothic concern for real land divisions in many areas and not mere revenue sharing. In an effort to control the violent warbands of certain nobles, the king bemoaned that armed men were carrying off property, beating people with clubs or stoning them, and setting fires. Such offenses were henceforth seditious and subject to the harshest penalties.[73] As if to underscore the essential progress of peaceful coexistence, the *epilogus* of the *Edictum* left no doubt that the rule of law extended over all, Goth and Roman, Arians, Orthodox and Jews. The restoration of order and prosperity was everyone's responsibility, and to this goal the Gothic government was committed. No other extant source is so clear.

Even without the *Edictum*, certain facts are clear. Theodoric himself agreed to ransom captives from Burgundian raiders during his first year in Italy.[74] He reserved the right, rather the onus, of hearing all appeals flowing from settlement cases.[75] The net result was a successful transition from life around the campfires of migration to evenings spent before the hearths in Italy. And this transition was accomplished with a minimum of disruption and hardship. Even the Roman aristocracy, although struck another blow, often was able to recover and prosper. The general economy stabilized and probably grew gradually until the outbreak of the War of Justinian. Signs of peace and ordered life were all around. Cities along the Adriatic Sea and the great highways not only survived, but a few prospered. The pages of the Anonymous Geographer of Ravenna, writing ca. 700, probably reflected the condition of urban centers under the Ostrogoths.[76] He could record over a score of cities in Dalmatia alone and along the highways of northern Pannonia and the area around Aquileia. But that is hardly surprising, for the Ostrogoths had long ago grown accustomed to towns. In fact, at Epidaurum in Dalmatia in the late 470s, they deliberately plotted to scare the inhabitants out so that they could move into the vacated houses and find safety within the walls; while at Novae, before their departure from the Balkans for Italy, they apparently moved in without much disruption of city life. And we have previously examined in some detail their early experiences in Pavia as seen through the eyes of Saint Epiphanius and Ennodius. Theodoric and his successors in Italy repaired roads and kept the Tiber open to barge traffic. The *cursus publicus* ran its routes, probably with fewer flagrant abuses of the system. Wherever the Goths did not settle, their third, *tertia*, soon merged as a part of the *tributum*, or general tax, which fell primarily on Romans.[77] Any new lands purchased, acquired through marriage to a Roman, or otherwise acquired by a Goth were subject to the appropriate tax.[78] The original shares of the settlement, here as elsewhere, were apparently free from taxation. Within a generation or two, most Gothic nobles would have held lands subject to taxation. Whether they paid is a different matter. Under Theodoric, at least, they probably did. The mere idea of Goths paying taxes to their king had been unknown before their march west into Italy.

Part of the taxes paid to the central government returned to the ordinary Goths as donatives paid each year, either formally at Ravenna or more typically through the *millenarii* in each locality.[79] The donatives must have helped many Gothic farmers to avoid slipping into the pit of dependence along with the Roman *humiliores* when their crops failed. In Italy, of course, they had unrestricted accesses to markets. The new Gothic coins circulated along with Roman issues, and by the end of the kingdom the exchange rates fixed under Theodoric for Ostrogothic coinage had carried the field so completely that they were maintained in Byzantine Italy.[80] In a world in which barter and monetary exchange always coexisted, the Ostrogoths did much to stabilize and energize the latter.[81]

With money in their pockets and traffic on the roads and sea lanes, the Ostrogoths lived in a different world from that of their ancestors of even a generation before. Romans and their cities were everywhere. Many Goths must have felt threatened and uncomfortable in these new surroundings. Goths living in the towns often lived in a definable quarter, where their Arian church rose to dominate the landscape. At other places they built their churches just outside the walls of the cities. Ravenna was special, since it was the capital and was surrounded by a Gothic settlement area. There the Goths had a large community with at least three churches: Saint Theodor (the Arian episcopal church), San Apollinare Nuovo (Theodoric's palatial church at the time dedicated to Christ the Redeemer), and congregational churches like San Andrea dei Gothi.[82]

The presence of the court with its high-ranking nobles promoted the exchange and symbiosis of Gothic and Roman traditions in many ways, most obviously in the personal interaction of important Goths and Romans but also in craft specialization. Ravenna seems to have been the center for Ostrogothic goldsmiths, some of whose splendid products found their way over the Alps and into the hands of Franks, Alamanni, and others. The concentration of wealth at Ravenna provided a sustaining market. Especially beautiful and popular were the gilded bow fibulae made for women and the exquisite spangenhelmets that adorned many princely heads among the north Germans as well as the Ostrogothic king Theodahad (fig. 10). These and other works probably derived from workshops near Ravenna.[83] Around Ravenna, construction and decoration techniques combined elements of late Roman, Byzantine, Christian, and Gothic into harmonious symbols of power and authority that reached far beyond the Ostrogothic Kingdom. Jewelry, helmets, and Ostrogothic coins radiated northward, some ending their trek only in the Baltic islands and in Scandinavia.[84] Reverse influences seem to have been less powerful but were nonetheless present. Whatever the economic value of the transalpine trade, it probably played a great diplomatic role, especially under Theodoric.[85] Although relatively few Ostrogoths were involved or affected, the materials themselves beautifully illustrate one rather subtle way in which the syntheses produced in Italy were conveyed to a receptive Europe as a whole.

The forces at work among the Ostrogoths were not in concert, indeed the society survived as a result of the countervailing forces. Economically, as politically and socially, the Goths fell into essentially two groups, with numerous variations within each. At the top the great nobles competed for power and influence at court and ruled unchallenged at home. Even in such common aspects of their lives as table service, they sought, and by the end of their sway had often obtained, a merging with noble Roman practice. Tableware is a marvelous illustration of Ostrogothic nobles' emulating the best in Ro-

Fig. 10: Bronze forty-nummi piece of Theodahad wearing spangenhelmet.

man fashion. Among the great finds at Desana in Italy are several beautifully engraved silver spoons. The recessed and slanted attachment of the bowl to the handle clearly places the spoons in the last phase of late Roman design. Such spoons were common features of noble Roman households during the fifth and sixth centuries. The church alone used them after the opening of the seventh century in the liturgy. There they became a recognized part of the Christian service throughout the Middle Ages, but during late antiquity such spoons were a part of Roman secular society into which the Ostrogothic élites were merging. At Golognano in Italy, another find of silver tableware may provide some of the last testaments to an Ostrogothic presence as late as the end of the sixth and early seventh century. Chalice no. 3 bears the inscription *Hunc calice pusuet Himnigilda Acclisie Galluniani*, and the plate (20.3 cm) *Swegerna pro animam suam fecit*. Both personal names were apparently East Germanic, probably Gothic, and attest to the quiet merging of Goths into the fabric of Italian lay and religious life shortly after the military demise of their kingdom in 554.[86]

In order to propel themselves ever higher in the social hierarchy, the Ostrogothic nobility needed wealth, both to look like noblemen and, if need be, to lead their followers into battle. Land was the safest, most prestigious acquisition and provided direct access to local and perhaps ultimately national power. Noblemen in general took every opportunity to acquire wealth and land. Already under Theodoric we find reference (507–11) to *pignoratio* in southern Italy.[87] Protection for hire and the illegal seizure of property as security in a law suit, *pignoratio*, are symptomatic of continuing pressures placed by the aristocracy, both Goth and Roman, upon the underclasses. An old Gothic soldier gone blind petitioned (523–26) Theodoric for protection. Two fellow Goths, Gudila and Oppas, were trying to enslave him. The local *comes Gothorum*, Pythius, was unable or unwilling to help. So too *dux* Gudui was charged with enslaving his fellow Goth.[88] The situation worsened after the death of Theodoric. An edict of Athalaric (ca. 527) portrayed a general breakdown in order as officials turned against the towns and *curiales*.[89] The situation was bleak. Provincial *iudices* charged with routine justice were incapable of settling disputes between nobles.[90] In 533–35 Athalaric denounced the return to lawlessness, the appropriation of land by the powerful, forced donations to the rich, the personal abuse of those under special royal protection (*tuitio*), the local editing of his decrees, and a disruption of morality.[91] The same king also rescinded the payment of tribute from Amalaric in Spain.

The legislation of Theudis in faraway Spain in 546 was directed at scaling the payments made to the *iudices* for rendering justice. We might be tempted to call it an attempt to define bribery legally, but the payment for services rendered or anticipated was an accepted aspect of justice. Indeed, Theudis as an Ostrogoth and ex-regent for Amalaric used the Ostrogothic practice as a model. In Italy, before the collapse of effective royal authority under Athalaric, the ordinary Ostrogoth may have routinely used some of his donative to push legal claims, as in the case of the old blind soldier. Without the donative, his access to justice would have been increasingly that of a Roman *humilior* trying to resist a powerful *honestior*—in other words, none at all. Theudis moved against abuses at a critical juncture of the political, economic, and social fabric. Obviously, similar action was appropriate but either untried or ineffective at home. If there were no limit to the fees payable for justice, then justice belonged to the rich. Athalaric was unable to exert royal authority to control the nobility, and disintegration followed. Belisarius and the long struggle for Italy revitalized the Ostrogoths as a people, but with defeat and pacification came a return to local affairs in the earlier manner.

Occasionally Procopius provides a rare glimpse of the Ostrogoths during the war. They were farmers and warriors, nobles dressed in fine armor and humble soldiers fighting to protect their loved ones on the farms and in the towns of Liguria and Picenum. The nobility vied for social eminence and tried to dress the part. After the jealous wives of *duces* Hildibadus, once commander of Verona and now king, and Uraias, his closest comrade, met at a bath, the queen confronted her husband with a great social affront. Uraias's wife not only had better clothes, she had ignored her queen's presence! Surely a plot was brewing, she alleged.[92] Dress and titles, the foremost symbols of social and political power, were grave issues even at critical times during the war.[93]

A few papryi preserved at Ravenna from the brief period following Narses's victories and before the Lombard invasion of 568 evoke a final picture of life among the Goths of the kingdom. On the one hand is the case of Guderit, a poor freedman who died intestate sometime shortly before his master in 564. The document is from the *Exarchate*, but it reveals relative material differences between rich and poor probably applicable to the Ostrogothic period. Several of the names are clearly Germanic, perhaps Ostrogothic. Germana, the widow of Collictus, had employed the priest Gratianus as the legal guardian of her son Stephen. The priest's fee was a third of the son's inheritance, including cash, revenue from land, a house, several slaves, and the property of a freedman, Guderit, whose possessions had reverted to his former master when he died intestate. Gratianus received thirty-six gold solidi as his share of the monetary wealth, the proceeds from the sale of slaves (*mercedes*), and the value of the domestic slave (*ancilla*) Ranihilda and the oxen, neither of which was apparently sold. The household items of one manor house and the possessions of the deceased Guderit were sold and their prices listed. The total amount received from the sale of property and paid to Gratianus was forty-five gold solidi, twenty-three gold siliquae, and sixty gold nummi:

THE DOMUS IN RAVENNA[94]

No. of Items	*Description*	*Value (when recorded)*
7	spoons (*cocliares*) soup ladles?	2 pounds silver (items 7 spoons through 12 molds)
1	large bow (*scotella*)	
1	clasp (*fibula*) for an apron	
1	clasp for a garter	
12	molds	
2	woven colored tapestries	1 solidus and 1 tremissis
1	embroidered cover	1 solidus
1	old basket [*pliction*?]	4 gold siliquae
1	shirt of silk and cotton in scarlet and leek-green (*camisia tramosirica in cocci et prasino*)—green	3 ½ solidi
1	variegate leek-green garment	1 ½ solidi
1	locked trunk with key	2 siliquae
1	mixed silk shirt (short sleeves)	2 gold siliquae
1	linen pair of trousers	1 gold siliqua

No. of Items	*Description*	*Value (when recorded)*
1	pillow	½ solidus
1	large copper barrel (?)	
1	small cooking pot	12 pounds iron scrap (for the small cooking pot, small copper pitcher, and copper lamp together)
1	small copper pitcher	
1	copper lamp with attached chain	
1	vat for vinegar	1 tremissis
1	small vat	2 ½ siliquae 40 nummi
1	barrel for grain	2 ½ gold siliquae 40 nummi
1	small grain box with iron binding	2 gold siliquae
1	harvesting sickle	1 gold siliqua
4	1 barrel, 1 hoe, 2 oil barrels	1 ½ silver siliquae
1	cabinet	4 gold siliquae
2	twisted ropes	6 gold siliquae
1	chair with a seat of woven iron	1 semis
1	chair with woven wooden seat	40 gold nummi
1	table and flat (cuttingboard?)	1 gold siliqua
2	stone mortars	1 gold siliqua
1	wooden trough	40 gold nummi
1	pack saddle	1 gold asprio
1	lambskin blanket	2 gold siliquae
1	slave named Projectus	

The possessions of Guderit

No. of Items	*Description*	*Value (when recorded)*
1	closed trunk (iron binding, key)	2 gold siliquae
1	other trunk in poor condition	1 siliqua and ½ asprio
1	used wine vat	1 asprio-siliqua
1	old cooking pot with iron handle (weighing 1½ lbs.)	
1	broken kettle (1 lb.)	
1	iron cooking chain (2½ lbs.)	
1	seeding tool (*satario*)	1 asprio-siliqua
1	sharpening stone (whetstone) with the oil to moisten it	2 asprio-siliquae
1	kneading-trough, broken	
1	small box	80 nummi
1	small earthen jug	80 nummi
1	broken earthen pot (*olla* = *estea*)	
1	bar (*talea*)	1 asprio
1	tub (*albio*)	80 nummi
1	grain basket (*rapo*)	1 asprio
1	measure (*modio*)	1 asprio

No. of Items	*Description*	*Value (when recorded)*
1	grain jug (*butticella granaria*)	1 asprio-siliqua
1	old colored (dyed) shirt (*sareca*)	3 gold siliquae
1	decorated shirt (*camisia ornata*)	6 gold siliquae
1	cloth (*mappa* in Souter = linen book)	1 asprio-siliqua
1	old coat	
1	old *sagello*—a short, thick cloak worn by the Germans (Tac. *G.* 17) (*sagum*) usually a military cloak in Cic., now Tjäder suggests a traveling cloak, a *Reisemantel* in German.	

The household items for the domus as listed represent the total articles in the house. Gratianus then received a third of their sale value. He also received a percentage of the revenues from the various other estates throughout the Romagna. His total income was a third of Stephen's inheritance, but he did not receive a third of the revenue from each estate. In several cases he did receive 4/12 of the revenue, but in others 2/12, 3/12, and even ½ an *uncia*. One explanation of the fractions is that Stephen himself had not inherited the entire estate in which less than a third was given to Gratianus.

The similarities are striking. The domus had finer kitchen utensils, two colored tapestries, a green and red shirt made of silk and cotton, two chairs, and a few other items of exceptional value. Guderit too owned a dyed shirt, and one with ornate decorations, but his dyed shirt was old, and the decorated one brought only 6 gold siliquae, whereas the best shirt in the domus was valued at 3½ solidi. The domus was not Stephen's only holding, but the list gives a detailed account of what wealth entailed—more and slightly better items, but generally the same as those of a freedman. Other estates had other houses, but they were probably similar. Historians tend to overemphasize material differences between rich and poor. The case of Stephen and Guderit suggests that the real differences were not so much material as social. Stephen was neither very rich nor very important, but even if he were a high official, his domestic surroundings might not have differed greatly. To be sure, some exceptional senatorial estates continued to have private baths and elaborate plumbing.

Guderit was a German, as his name and *sagello* (a short, thick cloak) indicate. So too perhaps was the domestic slave Ranihilda. They may have been Goths sold into slavery following a battle or for any number of reasons. Guderit possessed a wide assortment of items familiar to Gothic farmers for generations, the iron-handled pot, the iron cooking chain, and the like, but he also had two shirts probably manufactured in nearby shops and purchased by him or given by his old master when he was manumitted. The ordinary Goth shared in the world of Guderit more than in that of his nobility. They were no longer conquerors, just men.

Another papyrus gives us a view from the top and probably reveals the continuing power struggles of the Ostrogothic nobility after they had returned to their estates. The papyrus fragment, dated 6 December 557, from the *Acta* of the city of Rieti located along the *via Salaria*, an area of heavy Ostrogothic settlement, is revealing.[95] Gundihild, the widow of Gudahals, asked the curia of Rieti to appoint a special guardian for her two sons Lendarit and Landerit in order to pursue legal action against Aderid, *vir inlustris*, Rosemund, also called Taffo, and Gunderit, *vir magnificus*. These men had seized property belonging to Gundihild's sons, who, as minors, could not defend themselves in court and were incapable of physically expelling the accused. Every participant has a very Germanic (Ostrogothic?) name. Aderid and Gunderit were nobles bearing important Roman titles. Rieti was in an area of known Ostrogothic settlement. The probability is high that the case was the result of the breakdown of order within Ostrogothic society after the victories of Narses. Less than five years had elapsed since Ragnaris surrendered. Narses sent many of the recalcitrant rebels at Campsas to Constantinople but did not drive all the Ostrogoths out of Italy. Instead, following Belisarius's precedent, he returned them to their homes in peace. It seems likely that Aderid, the highest in rank, expanded his control in alliance with Gunderit, a lesser noble, and that Taffo was a member of Aderid's following. Thus we also have a rare glimpse into one of the surviving Gothic warbands that doubtless comprised much of the following of many nobles throughout their history.

In response to Gundihild's appeal, the council of Rieti appointed a certain Flavianus so that "right can be established and the boundaries can be correctly determined." Gundihild was an *inlustris femina* and knew how to use Roman legal processes to protect her rights. Since the record is dated after the fall of the kingdom, perhaps Felix Dahn was correct in his belief that two bodies of law coexisted in Italy. However, it should be emphasized that less than five years after the defeat of Totila, people of obvious Germanic descent eagerly and effectively sought Roman justice. Others clung to their heritage and were trying to live under Gothic laws and customs even under the Lombards.[96]

During the equipoise of traditions and powers marking the reign of Theodoric, the Ostrogoths produced some of their finest artistic triumphs and explored various opportunities to trade with their Germanic cousins beyond the Alps. During the late fifth and early sixth century, the imitative styles of fibulae and personal ornament evolved into the final precursors of the famous animal style known to archaeologists as Salin Style I. The chip-carving of the Roman frontier was transformed into ever more complex forms and designs. Motifs already apparent among the Ostrogoths on the middle Danube matured still further and established a clear stylistic evolution, for example, the mask fibulae of Acquasanta.[97] The elaborate cloisonné fibulae, pins, and earrings became even more colorful with almandine and colored glass. Sometimes the craftsman subtly curved each facet so as to enhance the filigree and accent the curves of the piece itself, for example, the great bow fibula from Desana and the magnificent gold eagle fibulae found near Domagnano (part of San Marino today).[98] Thus within their own settlements, garrisons, and quarters, the Ostrogoths remained true to their own customs of dress as these had already evolved in the context of the Roman frontier. The balance of Ostrogothic independence within Roman unity was apparent here as in their coinage and the concepts of rule developed by Theodoric and his successors.

Characteristic products of Ostrogothic workshops have turned up in excavations as far away as Brabant. Closer to home, numerous pieces found their way into Raetia, where the *ducatus Raetiarum* provided a frontline defense of Italy. Raetia Prima was briefly under Ostrogothic administration but broke away about the time of Theodoric's death in 526. The Thuringians had an Amalian queen, Amalaberga, niece to Theodoric. Archaeological finds support Cassiodorus's testimony that the relationship between the Ostrogoths and Thuringians was particularly close in the early sixth century (ca. 507–11) while Theodoric negotiated the marriage alliance with King Herminifrid.[99] So too the Alamanni, Burgundians, and others elsewhere in the transalpine areas valued Ostrogothic materials highly. Surely most of the finds being discovered were not the property of actual Ostrogoths. Rather, the Ostrogoths under Theodoric assumed a leading role among the barbarians to the north, much as had Rome in the centuries before or as Merovingian Gaul was to influence England later. Theodoric and his people were revered for their cultural and artistic stature as well as for their diplomatic and political power and leadership. The Ostrogoths also played an important but as yet indeterminate role in trade with the lands bordering the Baltic Sea. They seem to have begun serving as southern agents in some sort of exchange system extending northward as early as the Hunnic Empire, when large amounts of Roman gold entered the Baltic area. Later the presence of imperial coinage from Ostrogothic mints in Pannonia and Italy and the evidence of die identities suggest that the flow of coins was the result of trade contacts. The islands of Öland (pre-476) and Gotland (post-476) served as Baltic entrepôts. Disbursements radiated from these commercial centers into outlying areas, where they were customarily converted into jewelry.[100] What went south in return is unknown.

Throughout the fifth and sixth centuries, the majority of Ostrogoths were simple farmers. Instead of living in huts similar to those depicted on Roman coins such as those issued during the reigns of Constans and Constantinus II for *receptio* on the Rhine (fig. 11), they were now more likely to occupy abandoned or evacuated Roman housing, often near the great estates. This pattern emerges most clearly from excavation in Pannonia. There throughout the fourth through sixth centuries, walled villae often became islands in which Roman life styles continued, changed but surviving. The Germanic peoples moving into the area settled round about and mixed with the indigenous populations from the fourth century onward, right through the period of Hunnic domination.[101]

Fenékpuszta was such a site, and it extends our chronology into the Ostrogothic period and beyond. The site lies along one of the principal road arteries in north Pannonia and is just one reflection of Ostrogothic concern in the area. We have already discussed the more general interest in the roads and towns leading to Italy in Pannonia with the help of the lists in the Anonymous Geographer of Ravenna. Originally, Fenékpuszta seems to have been an imperial latifundium and was inhabited until the ninth century. In the course of the fourth century, the urban complex was surrounded by a rectangular wall and tower system characteristic of late Roman military architecture. Recent excavations have demonstrated the presence of two extramural cemeteries of different periods. The exact relationship between the two remains unclear, but it seems that the burial sites were used in the late Roman period and again in the ninth century. In addition, the 1959 excavations of the basilica unearthed sixteen graves of another cemetery within the city. Diggings in 1966 raised the number of graves to thirty-one. These graves, the Fenékpuszta-*Horreum* burials, raise a great many questions about the sixth and seventh centuries: e.g., the survival of the Roman population, the establishment of various barbarian groups, and their precise identity.[102]

The *Horreum* burial is clearly Germanic. To be sure, there are late Roman precedents for disk fibulae and the other jewelry found in

Fig. 11: "Hut-type" coin of Constans.

the *horreum*, but the aggregate grave goods are very similar to fifth-century burials in Hungary and elsewhere, where there is no question of Roman survivals. Several graves contain curious reminders of the Roman-Christian background shared by the barbarians. For example, grave no. 9, the final resting place of a rich woman, contains numerous earrings of gold and silver, a gold head band, hairnet ornaments, assorted glass beads of various colors, and a silver ring with a gilded Byzantine cross and a circular shield. The otherwise poor and simple grave no. 31 contains a small bronze coin of Valens.[103]

The *horreum* is divided according to wealth along a north-south axis. The rich graves, such as no. 9, are located in the north, the poorer in the south. Since the indigenous population was buried outside the wall in the late Roman cemetery and even the poor graves in the *horreum* are undoubtedly Germanic, the evidence of grave goods demonstrates some stratification of the ruling group based upon wealth. The rich were buried close to the basilica or within it, perhaps implying a belief that eternal prestige followed in accordance with earthly success. The poor interments were not survivals of the autochthonous population, buried elsewhere, but were subordinate members of the ruling group.

It is possible to offer more than random guesswork regarding the ethnic identity of the group buried in the *horreum*. By comparing the chemical composition of human bones from fifteen sixth-century sites in the Pannonian area, using the fully excavated Lombard site of Szentendre as a standard, it has been possible to establish certain norms in blood type ratios, decomposition rates, and sex/mortality functions. According to these studies, Fenékpuszta-*Horreum* dates from 500–525 and is clearly neither Lombardic nor Avaric.[104] Almost all the Germanic grave goods from the *horreum* can be connected to similar styles and developments in Ostrogothic Italy: gold earrings with small basket-pendants, disc brooches, the Bellerophon portrayal, and others.[105] However, excavation has yet to unearth any purely Ostrogothic materials, such as characteristic fibulae. The nature of the *horreum* material does not suggest a uniform ethnic group; it suggests rather a group essentially different from either Lombard or Avar, yet heterogeneous. The early sixth-century date, the distinctive bone-analysis patterns, and the geographic location of Fenékpuszta along the road network connecting Italy and the central Balkans all point to a strong Ostrogothic interest and presence. Yet if the scattered Ostrogothic materials here and from such sites as Rifnik and Dravlje are any indication,[106] the Ostrogothic domination of the Sava-Drava area was an ethnically diffuse hegemony incorporating other Germanic groups as well as elements of the surviving Roman population.

The Ostrogoths in Italy lived with other Germans in their midsts. Rugians, Bittuguric Huns, Gepids, and others are all attested in the sources. These lingering subgroups of the Ostrogothic confederacy from the Balkan episode kept some of their own customs and dress even within Ostrogothic-dominated Italy—pockets inside pockets, if you will. Eagle-headed buckles were long popular among the Gepids and Ostrogoths and were rare but not unknown in Italy.[107] Other examples of Gepidic artifacts in Italy and Ostrogothic influences among the Gepids are rather common. Some may have been war booty from the battle before Cybale in 488/89 or the Sirmium War, but we know for a fact that later Theodoric transferred some Gepids to the Gallic frontier in 523–26 in order to support that theater. They passed through Venetia and Liguria en route and were supplied by the Goths living along their path.[108] There was a demonstrable interplay between their artistic development in fibula styles, and both may have spoken a Gothic tongue. Thus even among old Germanic rivals, the concepts of ethnic identity remained weak and their life styles similar and interrelated with familiar warrior élites presiding over thousands of followers content to plow and raise livestock alongside their Roman peers.

In conclusion, let us return to examine in detail the splendid golden charm necklace from the first treasure of Szilágysomlyó (Drawing 3 and figs. 12 and 13). There are, of course, many problems associated with this find. However, regardless of whether it derives from the Alatheus-Saphrax group settled in Pannonia in the late fourth century or some other Germanic group, the necklace marvelously illustrates the real world of the barbarians and Romans alike, a world of simple but often arduous tasks and spiritual powers be-

Drawing 3: Golden necklace from Szilágysomlyó.

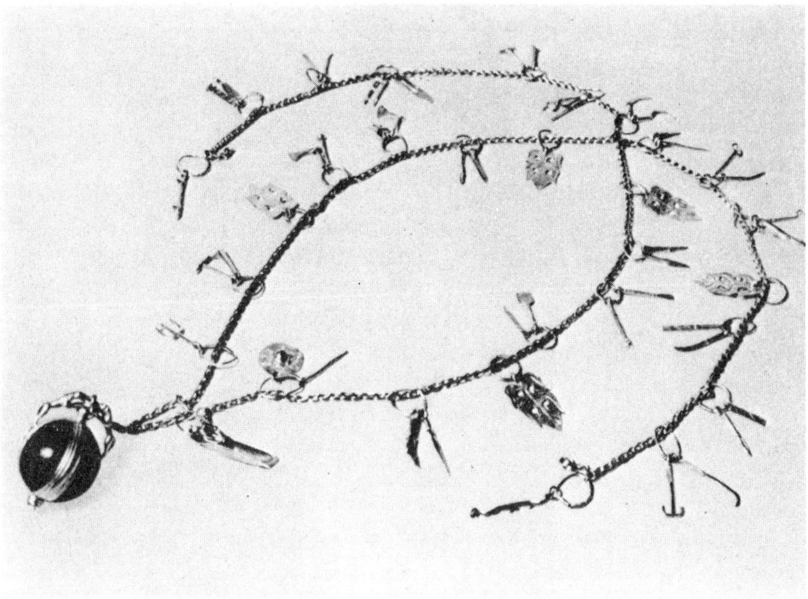

Fig. 12: Golden charm necklace from Szilágysomlyó.

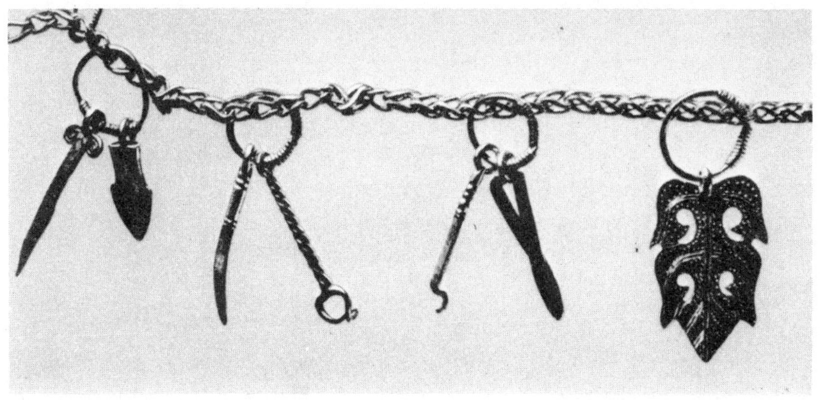

Fig. 13: Detail of golden charm necklace from Szilágysomlyó.

yond our recognition. From the bottom hangs a smoked-topaz globe surrounded on each side by panthers drinking from a vase on the top. Next up, with both chains passing through its ring, is a boat or dugout with a bald man holding a rudder in his left hand. Scattered about the chain are five well-defined vine leaves and forty-five model objects: (1) yoke, (2) anchor, (3) sickle, (4) vine framing shears, (5) decorated peg (?), (6) pruning saw, (7) file, (8) *vine leaf,* (9) hook, (10) hinged pruning shears, (11) forklike tool (?), (12) knife, (13) plow, (14) plow brake, (15) *vine leaf,* (16) spear, (17) arrowhead, (18) club with head specially faceted in squares and triangles, (19) chisel, (20) peg (?), (21) spade, (22) *vine leaf,* (23) dagger or sword, (24) model hand, (25) narrow spoon, (26) shield with central boss, (27) trident, (28) hammer, (29) anvil, (30) *vine leaf,* (31) axe, (32) club, perhaps especially for slaughtering animals, (33) round currying comb, (34) mattock or hammer with hollowed blade, (35) sled runner, (36) pouring spoon with ringed handle, (37) *vine leaf,* (38) serrated sickle, (39) vintager's knife, (40) blacksmith's chisel for horse hooves, (41) tongs, (42) hammer, (43) anvil, (44) sheep shears, (45) ladder, (46) and (47) cobbler tools, (48) hook on the end of a decorated plate, (49) decorated wheelwright's tool, (50) wagon brake or another yoke.[109]

The necklace contains objects familiar to agrarian life in the village and intersperses them with vine leaves, perhaps symbolizing life, and life leading inevitably to death, the old man in the boat. We can almost recapture the pruning of the vines, the plowing and sowing, the slaughtering of animals, the shearing of sheep for clothing. But the villagers also knew the world of the craftsmen in their presence, the wheelwright, the cobbler, and twice on the necklace the blacksmith. War and killing played their part in life, too, but to these villagers a modest role indeed—perhaps a diversion from their daily rounds. Life and death, work and war are depicted here in miniature. The effect inspires a sense of the deep religiosity surrounding the routine aspects of life.

6

Religion

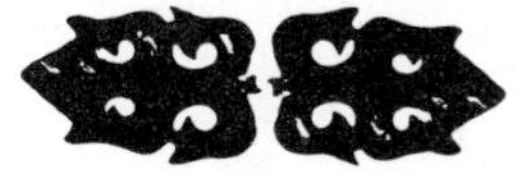

THE PERSONAL RELIGIOUS beliefs of the Ostrogoths lie beyond our grasp. To be sure, we can piece together a considerable amount of data, but to penetrate very far into the world of Germanic paganism is impossible. We tend to think of primitive peoples personifying the forces of nature in their gods, perhaps thereby hoping to gain some control over them as over their human friends and enemies. However, the spiritual powers invoked by mysterious cult practices cannot be understood as basically simple personifications and hence rationalizations of hidden powers. Whenever we accept a listing of Germanic gods and goddesses as descriptive of religion, we are self-serving at best. Lists and names allow us to avoid confessing our perpetual ignorance. Even Tacitus recoiled from trying to see behind Germanic cult practices into a world content with belief, powerful and direct. The gods seem to have evoked an expectation of virtually immediate response to cult worship without any recourse from the worshippers to rational systems of cause and effect or the niceties of personified powers linked into a hierarchy. The Greco-Roman world had abandoned such a humbling vision of man long, long ago. Yet, in a sense, Christianity had revived such a vision. No less a scholar than Saint Augustine wrestled throughout his life to contain the elemental powers of the Christian God within the boundaries of faith and reason. Deep within the *City of God* lurks an indescribable, uncontrollable divinity. For Augustine, and indeed for others, for example, Franz Kafka in *The Castle*, the pathways of reason must retreat again and again, ever approaching and thus creating a vision of the boundaries of faith without once narrowing the majesty they describe. The Goths had no need of an Augustine; for them the powers of their gods were simply there.

Germanic religion did not lure followers away from the religions of the Mediterranean world. Indeed, it did not even attract Germans; it held them as a basic force in their environment. The tenacity of the religious patterns stemming from paganism is apparent throughout the history of the Ostrogoths, despite their conversion to Arian Christianity. The evidence for Gothic religious beliefs, pagan or later Arian, is far from reliable. Moreover, the twentieth century is so far removed from the Goths, indeed from Arius, Athanasius, and Augustine, that any survey can only hope to touch upon the truth as if by chance.[1]

Tacitus depicted the early Goths as obedient to their priests, "acting in accordance with god, the inspirer of warriors." The priests alone punished, sometimes by flogging or imprisonment, or even reprimanded the warriors; neither the commanders (*duces*) nor the kings (*reges*) had the right.[2] The structure of the Gothic tribes seems to have mirrored that of its cults. The noblest families were deeply involved in cult practice. The kings came from their ranks and held their people together through elusive rites. Germanic cults stressed group participation rather than the importance of the individual worshipper. In the cult of Nerthus, the sacred wagon carried the cult object across the fields to restore fertility to the earth. Neither Nerthus nor the related Freyr bore weapons, perhaps attesting to a belief that the shedding of blood destroyed fecundity. A peculiar grave feature of the Goths throughout their history was the rarity of weapons in burials. And that was probably a further statement of agrarian cult rites.[3] So, too, family genealogies and myth preserved the special religious functions of the noble lines, most notably for the Amali themselves but doubtless also for the other great families following Theodoric to Italy. These cult traditions and sagas of ancestral lore formed an enduring set of subtribal bonds and associations at the heart of Gothic society.[4] As a part of the basic structure of the Gothic people, these were slow to change. Certainly Christianity had only just begun to penetrate this network when Byzantine armies destroyed their independence.

The Ostrogoths as a people, not yet distinct or united, thus began as many others did beyond the *limes*. Their daily concerns for food and security pulled them together around certain cults and the families perhaps associated with holy sites. The various groups were primarily religious cult communities in which, according to Tacitus, the Gothic peoples were unusually obsequious before their kings.[5] Perhaps these royal families were in fact so closely associated with particular sites that they remained behind while other families slowly sought new opportunities through migration. At any rate, the old *reges* are no longer apparent among the Goths in the south. However, the outlines of religious life remained the same. The protection of Wodan, the inspiring force of warriors, was often beseeched on arm-rings. The great gold ring of Pietroasa measured six inches in diameter and weighed twenty-five ounces. On it is a Runic inscription honoring Wodan, but the text is broken, and there is no agreement on its meaning except as a religious invocation. Recent arguments advance a date in the early fifth century; the runes are Gothic.[6] There is no need to hedge on the specifics of Ostrogothic religion during the third and fourth centuries, for the darkness is total. On the other hand, religious developments among their western cousins, the Visigoths, are particularly interesting and enlightening. The Ostrogoths were converted about a half century after the Visigoths and perhaps by them, but nonetheless, the Visigothic experience seems quite relevant to understanding the forces at work among the Ostrogoths.

Despite an eagerness to exploit political divisions among the barbarians, Rome only slowly, and never fully, grasped the power of converting the barbarians. The apparently elaborate church organization in Roman Scythia during the fourth and fifth centuries may have been involved in some sort of missionary activity toward the barbarians, but if so it has escaped the literary sources.[7] Once the barbarians crossed the frontiers, however, conversion was expected as a significant step in pacification.[8] Perhaps the apparent religious buildup in Scythia Minor was in anticipation of a *receptio* rather than a precursor for an external missionary endeavor. Whatever its exact nature, Valens reportedly considered the area of great value as a buffer area to the Gothic tribes. His efforts to force the inhabitants away from the Nicene Trinity, however, were rebuffed.[9] That the Goths were converted to Arianism demonstrates how little effect the Christians in Scythia Minor had on the barbarians on the far bank. In general, moreover, the Roman emperors ignored the possibilities of converting the external barbarians, and it was not until the sixth-century Irish monks that we encounter true missionaries. Ulfila was, however, instrumental in furthering the cause of Christianity, but primarily through his translation of the Bible. His small group of followers found *receptio* in Moesia under Constantius II and, as Jordanes reports, stayed in their settlement area for generations.[10] Valens turned to Ulfila after political events in *barbaricum* had finally linked religion and politics in Roman eyes. That occurred only after a political split had weakened the power of Athanaric and raised Fritigern and others to prominence. Roman policy since at least the time of Constantius II had exploited every opportunity to achieve exactly such internal divisions. Thus, Valens's campaigns of 367–68 had gone quite according to plan. He now moved quickly to widen the fissures among the Gothic nobility. Valens may have offered direct military support to Fritigern from the Thracian army, and in return Fritigern perhaps offered to accept Arianism, the religion of Ulfila and Valens. Then at last Valens began to see some profit in supporting Ulfila and Christianity among his enemies.[11]

Athanaric and his nobles launched a political counterattack to drive the opposition out and into Roman territory. The result was the famous persecution of Christians (369–72) recorded in Roman ecclesiastical authorities with all the condemnation of the self-righteous. Athanaric ordered a purge of Christians, which took the form of a cleansing of the soil. At least, that appears to be a likely explanation of his order that a *ζόανον*, a cult statue of some type, be carried about the land.[12] Surely the ancient cult of Nerthus carried in the wagon to purify and fructify was used in this way centuries before—to purify but not in a political purge. This specific rite and test was apparently limited to the areas under the personal control of Athanaric as the head of one of the great families. The nobles reacted variously. Only the priests of the *φυλαί* could have carried the sacred cult objects, and they were not everywhere present in carrying out the persecution.[13] The martyrdom of Saint Saba reveals much about the Goths, cult practice, the evolving nature of warbands, and the religious climate then current above the Danube.

Saint Saba was martyred at his own insistence. A simple man of little means, Saba had won many friends in his village and perhaps not a few converts. He was probably an Orthodox captive or a descendant of captives. Since he had nothing of value and was therefore politically unimportant, Atharid had little zeal to bother with him. Atharid came at the head of his band of followers from outside the village. He acted in accordance with a decision made by the leaders, *megistanes*, among whom sat his father Rothesteus, *βασιλίσκος* (*reiks* in Gothic). The *reiks'* power over the villagers was not challengeable, at least not directly, and so the villagers resorted to devious means.

The villagers met and without much ado decided to shelter the Christians in the community. Furthermore, they knew well that although Atharid and his men were not eager to slaughter lowly farmers, they still would have to report the cleansing of the village to the *megistanes*. True to their customs, if not to their gods, the villagers held a cult feast associated with purification. Saba refused to share in the common meal. Nevertheless, Atharid's men passed on, and with them the first wave of persecution. Returning sometime later, Atharid's men again asked the village to hand over any Christians. Had the inquisitor's suspicions been aroused elsewhere, or had there been an informer? The villagers swore there were no Christians present. Again Saba openly declared his faith; other Christians remained silent. A crisis was at hand. Either Saba had to leave or the villagers and especially the other Christians would face the wrath of the *megistanes*. Twice the villagers had invoked their gods to shield the Christians, but in their actions Atharid would surely see treachery. Saba departed. Once the persecutors had gone, Saba returned, only to face still a third inquiry, and this time was placed under guard by Atharid's men. His hour had still not come. An old woman risked herself to free him during the night. Ultimately the warriors recaptured Saba and tortured him. He and his friend and fellow Christian Sansala adamantly refused to eat meat consecrated to pagan gods (meat was probably a common sacrifice). Atharid had sent it as a test. Nonetheless, Sansala was released, and Saba could have joined him. Only when Saba demanded that his captors do their duty did they kill him. His reward was martyrdom.[14] No cult object called a *ζόανον* was present at any time, but the operative rituals had the same effect. Had not Saba repeatedly stepped forward to champion his God, the persecution would have passed. For Saba, martyrdom came on 12 April 372. Elsewhere the persecution yielded more important figures.[15]

Another great noble of the same rank as Rothesteus, Winguric by name, martyred twenty-six in his lands. The widow of one of his nobles was an Arian named Gaatha. Gaatha managed to save only the charred bodies of the martyred.[16] Other Gothic Arians died, too, specifically Wereka and Batwin. Fritigern is not mentioned during the actual persecution, and this fact is difficult to reconcile with his apparent offer to accept Arianism. He was a *reiks* like Winguric and Rothesteus and could have played some part in the decision to drive out the Christians. Admittedly our sources are thin and random, but the Gothic Calendar, 23 October, specifically recognized him as a *reiks* (*Friþareiks*) and honored his death along with those of many Gothic martyrs, *Gutþiudai mangize marytre.*[17] He clearly did not join in the persecution, and Athanaric was unable to do anything about it. The arrival of the Huns reordered priorities completely.

Athanaric was not impotent in any sinister sense. He was a great warrior and as events were to prove a tenacious opponent. Only the priests of the *φυλαί* are reported to have carried the cult statues across the Danube as the Goths fled the Huns. To order a nationwide cult ceremony of the ancient rite of purification was beyond the power of the *iudex*, the confederate commander. Tradition empowered the *megistanes* (*optimates* in Latin) to protect the cults of their own group (*φυλή*), but as yet there was no Gothic religious unity. After all, the Roman military and political challenge had just recently produced the *iudex* as a permanent confederate leader. Religious practice changed much more slowly. Athanaric resented Fritigern's challenge and pro-Roman machinations and struck at the "foreign elements" in Gothic society in an attempt to strengthen the hands of his supporters over their own lands and people. Fritigern could be dealt with militarily later and under more auspicious conditions once the local lords had removed any seditious followers at home. Athanaric and his nobles may also have sincerely wished to cleanse their lands of spiritual disturbance and thereby raise their yields. Athanaric had pleaded to no avail that commerce across the Danube be freely opened so that prosperity could be restored after the raids of 367–68. Our ecclesiastical sources would never have accepted the efficacy of such a pagan ritual as the carrying of cult statues and would have omitted it entirely in favor of discussing the presentations and martyrdoms of the saints. Obviously our understanding of the events surrounding the persecution remains inconclusive. Politically, at least, it seems clear that the persecution was only a preliminary skirmish to a battle that quickly lost significance. The specter of Hunnic captivity confronted the participants with questions of survival itself.

Unlike the Burgundians, who had a true king, Hendinos, responsible for fortunes in war and good harvests, as well as a permanent and irremovable tribal priest,[18] the Goths of the fourth century were religiously and politically diffuse. The subtleties of Christian theology went unnoticed. Both the Orthodox Saba and the Arian Wereka and Batwin suffered death for their God. Apparently, no one asked about the Trinity or the lack of one. Moreover, Christianity as a simple faith exerted a powerful force at two distinct levels. While at the top some noblemen saw Christianity as another dimension to their own political resistance to centralization and rather quickly adopted it, at the base of society the lower classes were only very slowly accepting the new faith. Christianity crossed the Danube as early as the raids during the third century, when some of the captives brought Christ to Gothic lands.[19] Christian cells survived within *barbaricum* for over a century. Ulfila himself was a product of their influence, but he and his followers had to seek refuge in Moesia. The letters of John Chrysotom attested to the presence of Christian enclaves along the northern coast of the Black Sea in the early fifth century. These were in closer contact with the Ostrogoths than were the Christians along the Danube. There remains but one major event left to explore.

The Roman raids against Gothic villages (367–69) as far as the Greuthingi greatly disrupted the tenor of life far into the interior. The Goths probably did not see the raids as a demonstration of the power of the Christian God, but rather the violence and destruction weakened their faith in the old gods to such a point that villagers could shelter Christian friends even while their leaders were rebuking Christianity for disrupting heaven and earth. Religion was as important as ever, but there was a new willingness to listen among the lower classes. The acceptance of Saba, indeed the "conversion to Christianity," was the beginning of a gradual replacement of pagan beliefs by Christian parallels.[20] Among the Ostrogoths, the process was incomplete even when Narses brought an end to their political independence. Sheltering Christians was only a first step for the Visigoths and probably the Ostrogoths later on. Ultimately, Christianity provided a necessary commonality for prolonged assimilation among the lower classes, but this process took centuries.

The nobility, on the other hand, viewed Christianity in essentially political terms. Fritigern may have volunteered to become a Christian as a straightforward exchange for Roman military support in his struggle with Athanaric. Indeed, throughout the period of conversion, political considerations were paramount for many barbarian nobles regardless of nationality: the Gepids, Franks, and the Visigoths in Spain experienced similar forces. Where there was no central pagan religious authority vested in a priest or king, the developing monarchies were especially quick to see the advantages. Fritigern, Alaric, Clovis, and Theodoric the Great greatly enhanced their political power by modeling aspects of their rule upon the role of the emperor within Christendom. The Constantinian Compromise may not have satisfied the emperors Zeno and Justinian, but barbarian kings facing limited religious authority like Athanaric's found it extraordinarily attractive. In fact, the tribal traditions flowing out of paganism, regardless of their scope, and the legacies of Constantine combined to produce a very potent force in both religion and politics during the Middle Ages. Kings were thereby better able to restrain their recalcitrant nobilities, endear themselves to the people, and rally the support of the priesthood. But for the present, the Visigoths only vaguely perceived these potentialities in terms of opportunities for rebellion—exactly as Rome wished.

When the Huns settled along the Danubian plain in the southern part of old Roman Dacia, they in effect blocked direct contact between the Ostrogoths and the Christian centers to the south, which they repeatedly attacked.[21] There may have been a few Christian stragglers in northeastern Dacia from earlier times, but these were insignificant. However, there is no doubt that the Ostrogothic leaders were Arian Christians before they crossed into Pannonia in 455. When and how were they converted? There is no answer, only guesswork. The Ostrogoths in Italy used Ulfila's Gothic Bible; indeed, the extant manuscripts are Ostrogothic. Furthermore, at least some of the nobility seem to have moved westward into the area of the Hungarian plain about the time the Huns took over Pannonia. Thus the earliest opportunity for direct contact with sizable Christian populations was ca. 420–27. Perhaps the Goths remaining in the area of Pannonia or Moesia brought their Bible and Christianity to the Ostrogoths at this time. In Pannonia only a very few Ostrogothic settlements, if any at all, could have survived intact so long after the settlement of Alatheus and Saphrax, whereas in Moesia, as Jordanes points out, the poor descendants of those Goths who had settled with Ulfila almost a century before lived on. The conversion to Christianity was also a statement of political independence on the part of the Ostrogothic elites. The Huns rejected Christianity completely.

Christianity did not suddenly make the Ostrogoths a new people. The years in the Balkans witnessed the protracted struggle between the Theodorics and desertions from one camp to another. Theodoric the Great really began to build on imperial/Christian traditions of kingship only after the settlement in Italy. Ceremonies traditional to his people and their great warlords marked the early stages in the growth of his power.[22] And despite his attempts and those of his grandson Athalaric and Theodoric's daughter Amalasuintha to incorporate the dress and ceremonies of the eastern imperial court into the Ostrogothic kingship, the raising of Witigis on a shield amid a circle of raised swords demonstrates how little progress had been made. Nevertheless, some permanent, if modest, changes were apparent. When Cassiodorus wrote an introduction for Witigis announcing his kingship to the Goths, he did so in a manner similar to letters proclaiming new emperors to the army. The same Roman military theme and modeling are apparent in Cassiodorus's *laudes* for the wedding of Witigis and Matasuentha, but here the courtly culture of Constantinople and Rome come more to the fore.[23]

Theodoric tried to blend the powers of a traditional Gothic king, a noble warrior of the Amalian line, and *magister militum* with the majesty of the imperial court and the powers radiating to the rulers of Christendom from God. His efforts were readily acceptable to his Roman subjects, long accustomed to similar claims. Ennodius in his panegyric praised Theodoric for his noble birth, his honorable conduct, and his justice. Theodoric wore the purple cloth of royalty, decorated with multicolored precious stones. The richness of his garments contrasted with the simple fairness of his skin and the height of his body. Ennodius went on to declare that he had no need for a diadem (a standard part of imperial dress), for God had given Theodoric as great a majesty through nature (an oblique reference perhaps to his long hair). What other rulers signified with the diadem was Theodoric's gift from God. Thus Ennodius celebrated Theodoric as a ruler who had brought two different peoples and traditions into harmony before God.[24] The same linkage and sense of balance between the human and the divine surrounded the worshippers in Theodoric's palatial church, San Apollinare Nuovo, originally dedicated to Christ the Redeemer and altered along with its mosaic to its present form and name in two stages. Shortly after their reconquest of Ravenna, the Byzantines renamed the church for Saint Martin, after the famous Gallic warrior against heresy. Finally Pope Agnellus rededicated it to Saint Apollinaris in the mid-ninth century.[25] At the west end of the nave, Theodoric emerged from his palace, flanked on either side by his aides. King and court were juxtaposed with Christ enthroned and surrounded by angels at the east end. Long processions of saints and martyrs on both sides were seen actively binding the rulers of earth and heaven. A similar contrasting placement of a mosaic of Ravenna across from Theodoric and the Virgin opposite Christ further stressed that earthly prosperity and joy (Felix Ravenna was an Ostrogothic innovation seen also on coinage) flowed jointly from the celestial Christ and their tireless king, Theodoric. Surely this imagery was not lost on the Ostrogoths worshipping there.

The lofty symbols of Christian rulership in San Apollinare stood high above the worshippers both figuratively and literally. What information we have concerning popular religion, and it is not much, reveals that the basic beliefs in the forces governing their lives had changed, but only slightly. On a beautiful gilded helmet found near Montepagano in Italy is a series of drawings and symbols, including a cross with the A and ω suspended from each arm. (Drawing 4, fig. 14.)

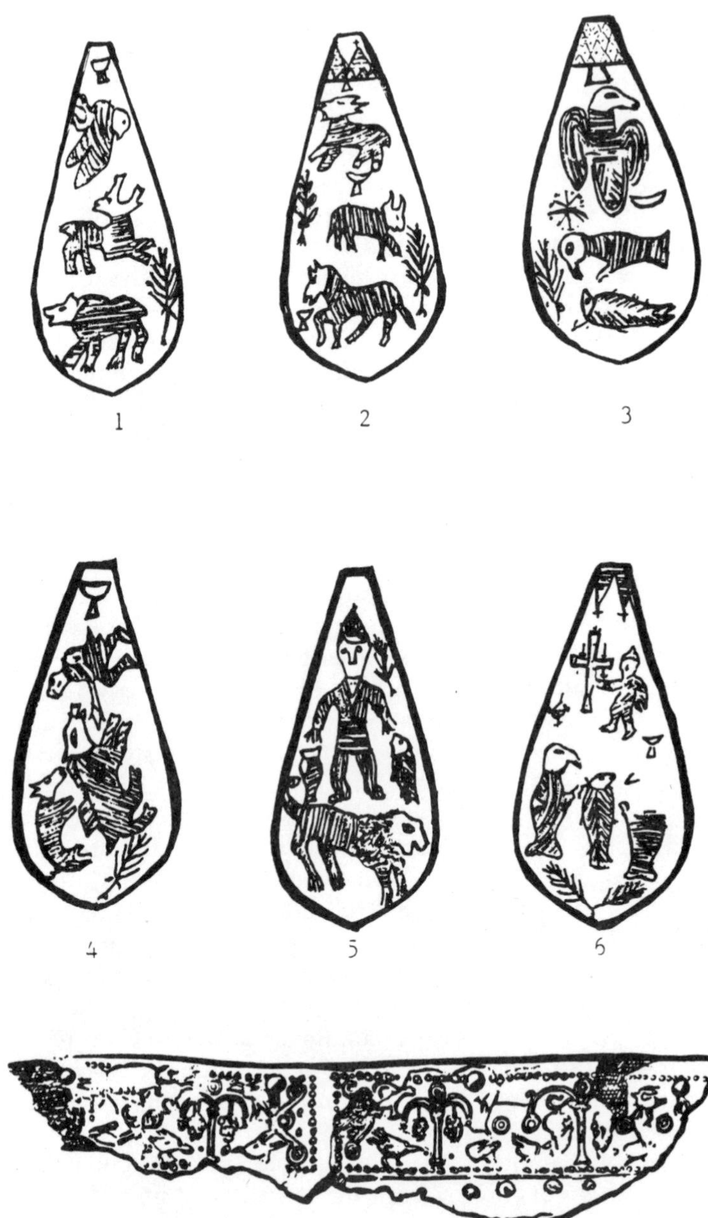

Drawing 4: Designs from the spangenhelmet found at Montepagano.

Fig. 14: Spangenhelmet from Montepagano, Italy.

Although only fragments remain, the scenes on these extant pieces are clearly defined. In a sense, the composite effect is the same as the village life portrayed on the charm necklace from Szilágysomlyó. The familiar late Roman/Christian scene of vines bearing their fruit surrounded the helmet. Some birds are eating the fruit fallen to the ground. A similar view of vines and birds was carved on one of the marble pillars surrounding Theodoric's tomb in Ravenna. Further examples are abundant on grave stelae from all over the empire.[26] Above the headband, the helmet was formed by six bands (*Spangen*) with six pear-shaped lobes or panels, each with engravings. All the panels contain at least one possible symbol of sacrifice. A shallow ceremonial goblet appears on four. Also on each is at least one branch, probably a tree, since in all but one case the roots are clearly visible. Like the birds and grapes, the tree, usually interpreted as the "tree of life," was a popular Christian symbol and along with the birds probably stood for paradise. Fish were also commonly associated with these as holy symbols on funeral monuments, and altogether they formed a part of the basic repertory for inscriptions and the spangenhelmets.[27] The first panel apparently depicts a common domestic scene, with what looks like a dog barking at a hawk or eagle, perhaps to protect the pig standing below. The second panel is also a domestic scene, with a horse, perhaps about to drink from a goblet, and above an ox or cow (?) and a goat with another goblet between them. Two trees link the elements into a unit. The third lobe is more difficult: an eagle with wings flared over an eight-pointed star or sun and a crescent, probably symbolizing the moon. Below, another eagle is about to pick up a fish. A tree is at their side. On the fourth panel a hunter with his dog (?) spears a boar; a goblet is at the top and a tree below. Next, on the fifth panel, a man carries a vase and a fish, perhaps as an offering, while a lion stands in the foreground. The familiar tree is to the right of the man's head and shoulder. Finally, the most complex panel, number six, depicts a man in procession carrying a cross with A and ω between two smaller objects. The one on the right is another ceremonial goblet, the left a goblet of a different type or perhaps a censor. Below the procession, two eagles grasp a fish. A double-branched tree takes up the bottom.

Positive identification and interpretation of several specific depictions are impossible. Nevertheless, the general theme seems clear enough. The aristocratic warrior wearing this helmet invoked the Christian God to protect his livelihood, farming and animal husbandry. Artistically, the trees served the same unifying purpose as the grape arbor on the headband and the leaves on the necklace from

Fig. 15: Eagle fibula from Domagnano, San Marino.

Szilágysomlyó—an agrarian image of renewal, figuratively the "tree of life." The panels depicted life as a carefully observed round of sacrifice and observance culminating, perhaps, in a processional in which the cross was carried. Perhaps this picture was a crude illustration of a Christian processional to ready the ground for the sowing of seeds, a common practice in the Middle Ages. The processional also might represent a simple votive offering customary for a great many occasions in village life throughout antiquity and beyond. The eagle was a standard symbol among the Ostrogoths and other Germanic peoples, usually denoting nobility and power. As such it occurred frequently. The eagles on the Ostrogothic bronze coins issued by Theodoric ca. 519–22 were in this tradition. So too were the great cloisonnéd eagle fibulae, among the finest works of Gothic art (fig. 15). They were very rare. Indeed, their cost and symbolism limited them to the wealthiest and most powerful members of the Visigothic and Ostrogothic nobilities. The lion had significance for both late Christian

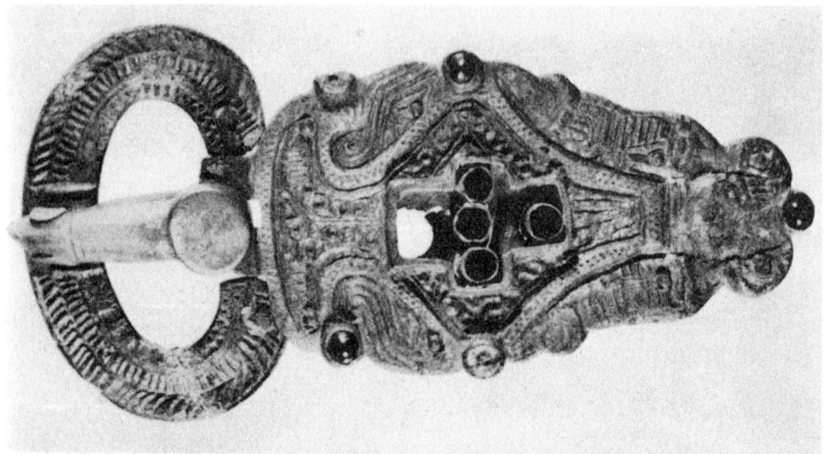

Fig. 16: Belt buckle from Vecchiazzano, Italy.

and Gothic art.[28] Thus, the helmet from Montepagano evinces a curious blend of late Roman/Christian and pagan Ostrogothic symbolism. It and many of the other examples of contemporary spangenhelmets derived from Ostrogothic goldsmiths or possibly Roman craftsmen working for the Goths, probably working near Ravenna with its strong late Roman and early Christian traditions. These same craftsmen probably also produced the splendid bow fibulae found in contemporary burials across northern Europe.

A picture emerges of a substantial cultural and economic exchange between Ostrogothic Italy and her Germanic neighbors to the north, many of whom were also involved in Theodoric's diplomatic initiatives. But as the distribution of coins, especially silver, reveals, the economic interaction continued throughout the entire history of the kingdom. Even the brief reign of King Teja is represented in the finds.[29] The spangenhelmets were among the rarest and most esteemed items in the exchange. More typical, however, were small pins in the shape of grasshoppers, familiar images since the fourth century, and demonic animals. Often the animals have attenuated shapes, for example, the animals on the chip-carved belt buckle from Vecchiazzano (fig. 16). Four other demonic faces appear on a disc fibula found near Udine in northeastern Italy.[30] Similar faces and forms strike out at the observer from the tongues on two buckles at Acquasanta (Drawing 5, fig. 17), matched with two pagan-style "masks" on the buckles themselves.[31] All across barbarian Europe,

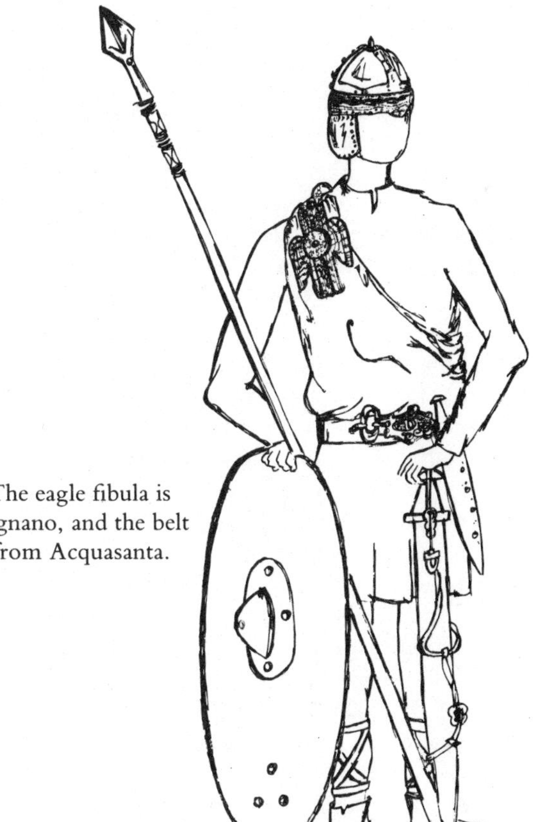

Drawing 5: Male figure: The eagle fibula is similar to that from Domagnano, and the belt buckle is modeled on one from Acquasanta.

Fig. 17: Belt buckle from Acquasanta (near Ascoli), Italy.

belt fittings and strap ends frequently took the form of demons. Such demons and masks were probably apotropaic devices to ward off evil spirits.

In general, a pattern seems present in the evolution of the animal styles and the decorations on personal ornament that corroborates, at least in part, the more detailed picture of conversion preserved later in sagas and other sources.[32] The Icelandic sagas from the period of conversion are of particular importance to our understanding, for in Iceland, writing followed soon upon the coming of Christianity and was able to record many of the early songs. Over the centuries, the Christian world penetrated to the heart of Germanic paganism, as little by little Christian and Biblical stories fused with the legends of the old sagas. Saints and martyrs went along on epic voyages, and Christian interpretations took over the explication of the pagan symbols. Certain Romano-Burgundian belt buckles help illustrate the transition. Samson, replete with long hair, was a natural hero for the masculine story-tellers and is depicted destroying the temple. The longhaired Germanic warriors might well have seen themselves in his place. Daniel facing the lions demonstrated to man and God his courage.[33] Indeed, the Old Testament provided many similar stories of heroism for God and of warriors struggling in battle. No wonder then that the Old Testament was so popular throughout the early Middle Ages. The path from the animal styles to Romanesque art and medieval bestiaries took many centuries to traverse. Some Ostrogoths made a beginning; the warrior at Montepagano took several steps. Still others, perhaps most, remained essentially pagan. Despite the Arian churches that marked their quarters in and around the cities, most Ostrogoths were farmers and were doubtless unwilling to abandon the traditions of their ancestry.

Theology, specifically the Arian denial of the Trinity, mattered little to most Goths. Perhaps the owner of the Montepagano helmet was an exception. His helmet may have portrayed his Arianism by not using the more common Christogram replete with the P for Christ as well as the cross. The helmet used a simple cross. Yet just as the persecutors under Athanaric struck at Christians in general, so too the average Ostrogoth probably saw Christianity as a single religious force. Theodoric, on the other hand, apparently enjoyed hearing theological disputes at court.[34] His own mother, Hereleuwa, converted to Orthodoxy. A Roman teacher, the lady Barbara, was Catholic and, nevertheless, it seems tutored Theodoric's daughter, Amalasuintha, in Latin letters. Others also converted to Orthodoxy.[35] At the same time, the Catholic bishops had to remind their flocks not to listen to

Arians.[36] Again an important difference in religious attitudes is apparent. Theodoric and the nobility essentially viewed religion as a part of politics. Theodoric's vaunted statement to the Jews that "we cannot impose religion, and no one can be made to believe in spite of himself" extended toleration in exchange for political loyalty.[37] He showed a similar perspicacity toward the pope and Catholicism. The great struggle for survival during the third century that gave rise to the Dominate also formed an essential background to late Christian paranoia for the universality of belief. The Ostrogoths came from a more diffuse background, religiously and politically, and under the politically astute tolerance of Theodoric were able to live with religious variations. The Visigoths and Burgundians also showed a marked tolerance for the Orthodoxy of the Romans. The Visigothic king Euric alone actively restricted Orthodox worship, but he seems to have limited his efforts to forbidding the filling of vacant Orthodox sees—hardly a persecution of the Lactantian type.[38] Other kings maintained the rights of the Orthodox church. When finally in 589, at the Third Council of Toledo, King Reccared decided on an end to Arianism and a public acceptance of Catholicism, the Visigoths, many of whose nobles were present, had little difficulty accepting his decision.[39] No one ever suggested a return to paganism. Only the Vandals aggressively took the offensive against the Orthodox, seizing churches and property and forbidding the Catholic mass in areas assigned to the Vandals.[40] Huneric went so far as to place guards at the doorways of Catholic churches to intercept anyone dressed in Vandal attire, especially those wearing a special Vandalic hair ornament.[41] The Catholics suffered persecution until after the death of Thrasamund in 523, when King Hilderic repudiated many aspects of the previous reign, including Theodoric's sister Amalafrida.[42] The contrast to the enlightened religious toleration under the Ostrogoths could not be sharper.

The Ostrogoths as a people clung to Arianism for political and social, not theological, reasons. Theodoric championed Arianism in the Eastern Empire as an extension of his role in Italy, where he set about to control the process of assimilation. He envisioned distinct spheres for the Ostrogoth and the Roman, despite the fact that government and settlement increasingly threw them together. One viable center of Ostrogothic society was their Arian faith, which set them apart from the Orthodox majority. The same can be said of long hair and distinctive dress, particularly their jewelry, for both identified their rank and ethnic heritage. Arianism allowed Theodoric to extend toleration to Catholics and Jews in exchange for their political support. He waited patiently while the Roman factions bristled with resentment at his apparent ambivalence in the early months of the Symmachian-Laurentian Schism. So too, he and his nobility were supposed to be disinterested in the theological rapprochement with the East.

Arianism was their national religion, and as such it was an institutional force acting in concert with the monarchy to preserve a special and distinctive place for the Ostrogoths in Italy. Yet had it not been for the protracted war with Justinian, the Ostrogoths probably would have joined their Visigothic cousins and accepted Orthodoxy. Once the political and social reasons for group solidarity and exclusivity had lessened, there would undoubtedly have been little resistance to conversion. Indeed, until the tragic events surrounding the fall of Boethius, the Ostrogoths and Romans were moving steadfastly toward a harmonious symbiosis politically. Political Arianism would in all likelihood have succumbed early, since its theological roots were so shallow. Even during the war, individual Goths continued to convert.[43]

After the war, most Goths rapidly accepted their new status under the Byzantines. They quietly intermarried and, in general, lived within the social and legal structures of reconquered Italy.[44] Conversion to Orthodoxy continued and probably swiftly accelerated. Goths even served as priests, deacons, scribes, and lesser clerks in the sixth-century Orthodox church. The *Documentum Neapolitanum* lists: "Optarit et Vitalianus praesb(yteri), Suniefridus diac(onus), Petrus subdiac(onus), Uuiliarit et Paulus clerici nec non et Minnulus et Danihel, Theudila Mirica et Sindila spodei, Costila, Gudelivus, Guderit, Hosbut et Benenatus ustiarii, Viliarit et Amalatheus idem spodei. . . ."[45] The Gothic names Angelfrid, Alamoda, and Gudilebus appear in the *Documentum Aretinum*. Offices such as *spodei* occur only in these documents and may represent a brief incorporation of Gothic (i.e., Arian) nomenclature during the period immediately after the dissolution of the Ostrogothic Kingdom.[46]

In conclusion, although many aspects of the Ostrogoths' religion remain unclear, their religious beliefs sustained their lives and defined much of their world throughout their history. The fast pace of politics exposed the nobility to a variety of influences. For some nobles, their conversion to Arian Christianity was a convenient political statement made at crucial times. The nobility did not give up their pagan beliefs any more than did the commoners. The fine masks, one with long hair flowing into the design, from Acquasanta, the gilded silver buckle from Vecchiazzano with the demonic animal, all belonged to the nobility. Such pieces were among the finest examples of the goldsmith's art and were beyond the reach of ordinary men. The nobility may have grafted Arianism into their pagan beliefs for political reasons, but as the themes on the helmet from Montepagano demonstrate, Christianity reached out toward the heart of the agrarian world as well. Sowing and stock raising were basic features of peasant life, whereas hunting and warfare concerned primarily the nobility. The poor Goths shared with the Roman lower classes a simple belief in demons, evil spirits, and Christ. Both peoples were still learning to accept Christianity into their lives. A comparable situation was reported by Eugippius in his *Vita S. Severini* for the Rugians and Romans along the upper Danube. There, too, the Orthodox holy men drew a distinction between Arian-barbarian and Orthodox-Roman, but all shared the superstitions surrounding illness, relics, and natural phenomena. The barbarians respected Severinus no less than did the Roman townsmen. Even to Saint Augustine, writing from Hippo in North Africa, demons stalked the Earthly City. Of course, his demons were a part of an intellectual vision of the Christian universe shared by few, none of them Goths.

Arianism was understandably slow to penetrate the elemental world of pagan cult practice, long so much a part of agrarian life. However, Arianism was something more than Germanic paganism ever was or could have been. The Arian church with its bishops, priests, even a few scholars commenting on the scriptures, provided an institutional focus and shelter for the Ostrogoths as a people.[47] Immigrants to a strange land, they naturally tried to preserve something of their past. They settled together and around the cities often lived in the shadows of their churches. Ostrogothic Arianism allowed them to be Christians and hence part of the larger world of *Christianitas* and *Romanitas* without asking them to forsake either Gothic pride or their ancestors. That is why it is necessary to understand their Arianism as a tribal religion and not as some lingering form of an Alexandrian heresy. Nor was it merely a political statement in opposition to Catholic imperial authorities. Only their own institutionalized faith could have sustained the peculiar combination of pagan beliefs and Christian teachings in the heartland of the Roman church. The Arian church assured the essential elements of continuity in the Gothic experience and abetted the gradual transference of Roman culture. As elsewhere, the church relentlessly sustained a common message of Christianity, regardless of its theological orientation, generation after generation. As a body of beliefs acting over centuries, Christianity gradually replaced or incorporated aspects of the pagan world. The Ostrogoths and their contemporaries across barbarian Europe took a few hesitant steps along this common path. In essence, initially the Ostrogoths broke up Christianity into tiny facets and then over generations fit them into what was at the outset a basically pagan structure. Only later and only among a very few was the sustained clerical influence of the Catholic religious structure able to fuse these aspects into a coherent Christian faith. Nonetheless, unless the Goths were totally ignorant of, or repulsed by, their surroundings and the iconography within their own churches, such as San Apollinare Nuovo, they were made constantly aware of the basic tenets of Christianity from an early date. Adapting these sometimes lofty concepts to their daily lives took generations of piecemeal accretion. Time ran out before enough generations had come and gone for the complete penetration of Roman Christianity.

7

Leadership and Government

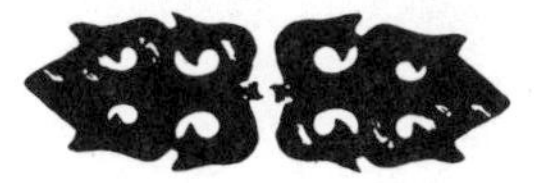

THE TRANSITION FROM personal leadership to institutionalized government was never fully completed among the Ostrogoths. Today good government often tries to instill human qualities in its offices and bureaus. Nevertheless, we usually think of leadership within institutions or over them with only a few high officials or private individuals claiming to lead the people. In this respect we stand far closer to the late Romans than to the Ostrogoths. The Ostrogoths and other barbarians had difficulty grasping the essential qualities of institutions in general. Even in Italy most Goths dealt with their own leaders on a personal or familial level rather than in accordance with titles and prescribed procedures. Decisions made at Ravenna and passed down through the *comites Gothorum* and various other officials were making headway. Yet at the base of their acquiescence in the system of government was the faith that the king would personally remember them or their family and set things aright. At least that was true under Theodoric, when the loyalty produced during the struggles in the Balkans was still fresh.

A Goth could never see himself primarily in relation to public offices and written laws transcending his own lifetime. The concept of Gothia itself remained elusive. It always lacked territoriality and ethnic precision. Theodoric's theme of Gothic independence within

Roman unity perceived "Gothia" as a people, but the very process of building a confederacy and securing the monarchy left "the people" only vaguely defined. Thus it is hardly surprising that even before Justinian destroyed Ostrogothic Italy, the Gothic nobility was able to reestablish itself between the limited governmental structures of the monarchy and the common Ostrogoths. Moreover, since the development of regional nobilities and the monarchy up to the conquest of Italy has frequently entered into our chronological presentation, we need only review its evolution and refine certain features before exploring the structure in Italy through which the Ostrogoths governed themselves.

The stress and confusion of the early migrations southward toward the Black Sea must have created opportunities for new men to lead, as families and individuals decided whether to move or stay, generation after generation. The Gothic world of Tacitus provides a starting point for analysis, but the fragmentary Roman records for the third-century invasions make it clear that much had changed. The royal family charged with the maintenance of the cult sites apparently remained behind and disappeared. The third-century invasions witnessed the emergence of powerful *duces* leading increasingly sophisticated bands of at most a few thousand warriors. By the end of the century, some Goths brought their families along in the marauding caravans scouring Moesia and Thrace. The *duces* were the supreme war leaders, as they had been in Tacitus's *Germania*. The creation of a noble class is apparent in the distribution of grave goods and Roman artifacts into an increasingly stratified pattern through the late third and fourth centuries. Roman items, such as distinctive armbands, once distributed primarily to auxiliary commanders inside the Roman army, became important indicators of membership and status within the warbands all along the *limes*.

Thus society itself was shaped in a largely unrecorded and probably rarely perceived competition for loyalty between the warbands, ultimately based on the ancient *comitatus* and the familial life centered in the villages and hamlets. Warfare and raidings were important to the expansion and perpetuation of the warbands. And the constant irritant of violence permitted the *duces* and their followers to impose control over the villagers within the area. There is ample evidence for this assertion among the Visigoths in the late-fourth-century *Passio S. Sabae* and the extant writing of Eunapius of Sardis.

The *φυλαί* as described by Eunapius were basic organizations among the Goths. The Greek term *φυλή* usually referred to a group united by blood and living in the same area. Each *φυλή* had its own cult objects and holy men to care for and carry them.[1] The *φυλαί* formed temporary confederations for specific purposes. Their leaders conducted affairs in councils, but the exact makeup of these varied. In some assemblies, the *optimates*, probably consisting of the *dux* and principal members of the nobility, made the decisions and enforced them. In other areas, the council of elders decided action and dominated the younger men.[2] The apparent distinction between *optimates* and elders was in reality blurred, since many nobles were themselves elders of important families. Nonetheless, the great ducal families, it would seem, were not everywhere able to control the *φυλαί* in their area. In such cases the elders probably represented the various villages within the *φυλή*. The *φυλαί* were not territorially but religiously defined. Their political unity became more cohesive during the fourth century. The Gothic word *garvi* does not seem to have described areas as large as those inhabited by the *φυλαί* but rather was a term used to denote the Latin *pagus*, the rural area around towns and villages.[3] Even in a *φυλή* where one family clearly controlled the actions of *optimates* and villages alike, there were ways to manifest the traditional independence of the village as a unit within the regional federation.

Generally, our Greek sources referred to the head of a *φυλή* as *ἄρχων* or *ἡγεμών*; in Latin he was usually called *regulus*, *ducator*, or *dux*. The Gothic texts used *reiks* to describe these men.[4] The *Passio* recorded that the greater leader was Rothesteus, the *βασιλίσκος* (*Passio* 4), and Atharid was his son. The task of driving out Christians in Saba's area fell to Atharid and his band, which went from village to village in its search. Resistance to the leadership of the nobility over the *φυλαί* took the form of subterfuge rather than open defiance. Indeed, after the failure of the pagan feast and oath taking to convince the persecutors, or more specifically Saba to stay out of sight, the villagers handed him over. Except for twice branding the chief persecutor simply as such, *ὁ διώκτης* (the persecutor), the *Passio* used terms to describe outsiders, in the sense that *unsibja* in Gothic could mean lawless, those without family, an outsider.[5] The Greek *Passio* used the more restrictive Greek *ἄνομος* (218. 14), *ἄνομοι* (219. 3), and *ἀνομίας* to translate what probably came from a Gothic witness as *unsibja* or *unsibjis*. Thus, *ὑπηρέται τῆς ἀνομίας* (220. 17) becomes simply the "servants of the outsiders," or specifically the henchmen of the *megistanes*, who were beyond the village and not tied to it by bonds of family. As such, Atharid and his band could not penetrate the solidarity of Saba's fellow villagers after the latter had decided to shelter the Christians. The villagers easily deceived the "foreigners" twice. The nobles controlled the *φυλή* with the assistance of their warriors and were themselves under Rothesteus, but the struggle smoldered between their leadership, enforced with arms, and the agrarian world of kindred and marketplace.[6] And, as we have seen, the *Passio* also revealed the limits of their religious authority.

Rothesteus was clearly chief, but the *optimates* (*megistanes*) surrounding him were not a single egalitarian mass. This fact is further demonstrated in the case of Sarus, Alaric's rival. Sarus's following of two hundred to three hundred was made up of freemen, some of whom were nobles.[7] Athanaric included in his following free warriors, kin, and nobles with their own men. The same was true of the Ostrogothic Radagaius, who raided Italy in 405–06.[8] Even on campaign, these leaders were constrained to heed the advice of their various supporters. The ducal leaders in turn cooperated only with the *iudex*, in Gothic *thuidans*, in response to the military challenge of Valens and later the Huns.

The election of a temporary tribal leader, *iudex* or *thiudans*, over the Tervingi in 346–47 was a military reaction to Roman pressures. Athanaric was the first permanent leader of the confederacy built around the Tervingi, probably in the wake of Valens's campaign of 367–68. Athanaric was doubtless *thiudans*, perhaps meaning "leader of the whole people." The Gothic Calendar called Constantine *Kustanteinus þiudanis*. The greek βασιλέυς was similarly translated into Gothic *þiudans* in the Gothic Bible (Mat. 5:35).[9] Nevertheless, his position was hardly imperial. He was unable to deal effectively with Fritigern after the latter opened negotiations with Valens. Once Fritigern succeeded to power following the demise of his chief Alavivus, himself probably *thiudans* during the crossings of 376, Fritigern too was unable to control his various nobles. They were apparently free to lead their followers—the warriors of their bands as well as the uprooted villagers—anywhere they wished in search of food and booty. The bands of Colias and Sueridus ineffectively besieged the fortifications of Adrianople until Fritigern reminded them that it was best to "keep peace with walls." Meanwhile, a major battle raged north of the Haemus near the town of Salices without Fritigern's being present.[10]

The heads of the φυλαί simply acted autonomously until a grave danger, such as Valens's march from Constantinople in 378, compelled them to accept a central direction. In 377, Farnobius, an optimate of the Goths, felt free to conclude his own treaty with the Taifali. Theodosius took advantage of this freedom of the heads of φυλαί to conclude separate treaties. He neutralized some Gothic power and resolve by playing one ἡγεμών against another, for example, Fravitta and Eriulf. There is no question that the φυλαί continued as the basic political and military units long after their settlements in the empire.[11] The same can be said for similar groups among the Ostrogoths, although the evidence dates to the later period.

Various records for barbarians settled in Gaul, especially the Burgundians, and in Pannonia and Italy, notably the Lombards, reveal that the basic subdivision of these Germanic peoples was the *fara*. The *Liber Constitutionum sive Lex Gundobada* gave the *faramanni* responsibility for the just division of the actual property of the senatorial host in accordance with the rule outlined in the *lex* itself. Again the basic procedure was *hospitalitas* as delineated in the *Codex Theodosianus*, but with the Burgundians in most cases taking two-thirds instead of half of the senatorial estate. These *faramanni* were the heads of the *farae*. The Lombards settled Pannonia by *farae*, and probably the Gepids did so as well after the collapse of Ostrogothic control post-534.[12] Sometime before their settlement in Italy in 568, the Lombardic *farae* had been partly superseded by powerful warrior associations with dukes as military leaders. Thus when *dux* Gisulf settled the area around Forum Julium, he asked for his choice of *farae*.[13] It would seem thus that the *duces* had not yet established their control over specific *farae*, but this control developed rapidly enough after the settlement. These Burgundian and Lombardic *farae* were comprised of blood kin, servants, and the personal followers of the leaders. They were basic units of kindred relationships and military units.[14]

The *fara* was structurally and functionally the same as the φυλή among the Goths. There are three, perhaps four, Ostrogothic *farae* known from various sources. First, however, we must accept that the suffix *fara* attached to personal names indicated the personal prestige surrounding the heads of the Ostrogothic *farae*. This practice was true among the Lombards and was probably a general custom among various Germanic peoples. The name Senefara appears on an inscription from Dertona dated A.D. 541.[15] Theudafara is also attested.[16] Wilifara was important around Centum Cellae (now Civitavecchia) and was recorded on an inscription there dated A.D. 557.[17] To these examples we might add Stafara from the wedding ring found at Reggio Emilia.[18] The Ostrogothic *farae* and their heads may well have played a role similar to that of their Burgundian and Lombard counterparts. Moreover, Jordanes, a major Gothic source for the settlement period, was at great pains to record "tribal names" in the *Getica*.[19] One possible reason to mention these ancestral peoples was to recognize the lineages still important in his own day, i.e., the mid-sixth century. These, too, may have been related to the surviving *farae*.[20]

Governing Ostrogoths was a constant struggle to pull the forces of villages and kindreds, nobles and their followers, *farae* and allied peoples into line behind the will of the monarch. Tradition strengthened the hands of the nobility, prolonged crisis those of the royalty. Under such circumstances, Rome usually held the initiative and the Goths reacted as best they could. Consistent and long-term policy was virtually impossible. Even on campaigns, the king was rarely able to control his own people except *in extremis*. Fritigern before the Battle of Adrianople, Videric and his guardians Alatheus and Saphrax, Valamir in Pannonia, even Theodoric himself when at Marcianopolis, were not truly able to control the Goths under them. Often the best for which they could hope was to place themselves in the lead and then deflect popular actions toward some higher goal. Even that was often impossible. Ermanaric created the Ostrogothic confederacy as a military structure to establish a broad regional control over the numerous groups in the area and then led it against the Huns. And in this way he endeared himself to generation after generation. Ultimately medieval bards transformed his resolve and suicide into the makings of legend.[21] The Hunnic episode raised an élite far above the masses. The Amalian line profited from Hunnic favor, but the basic problems of leadership remained. Indeed, the great Ostrogothic noblemen ruling for the Huns may well have been even more prone to independence, although they were usually thwarted by the Amalian line and the Hunnic royal family. Certainly the somewhat later case of Bessas demonstrates a profound self-assertion. Bessas refused to follow Theodoric to Italy and remained in Pannonia, where he eventually sided with the Byzantines. During the Justinianic War, Bessas vigorously fought his cousins in Italy until forced from Rome and reassigned to the East.[22] Theodoric suffered few Bessas types. When Odoin rebelled, he was summarily executed.[23] Yet Theodoric more than any other monarch was able to go beyond his personal charisma. Against the centrifugal forces of society, he held up a vision of peaceful coexistence and prosperity fostered through government working on a daily routine.

Once the Ostrogoths took over Italy from Odovacar, Theodoric faced the difficult task of government and set about it with his customary vigor. In terms of government there was, of course, but one alternative—the late Roman imperial system. As a king of an allied people and as *magister militum praesentalis*, consul for 484, patrician, and Flavius, Theodoric saw his task as essentially the establishment of an adequate system of government over the Goths to refocus gradually their personal loyalty from him onto his agents and officers. Insofar as possible, he allowed the Roman bureaucratic state and its many departments to function as usual. The two aspects of the government, Gothic and Roman, were then centered in his *comitatus*, itself patterned after late imperial tradition. The *Variae* of Cassiodorus are especially illustrative of the perpetual comings and goings of the bureaucracy. Civil servants abounded in all the traditional departments in dismaying numbers. But in some cases the old Roman structures stood in the way of Theodoric's policy of joint governmental powers at the top.

The numerous members of the military *scholares* attached to the western emperors no longer had a function under the Ostrogoths and scarcely any in the East. Theodoric allowed those in Rome to remain as a symbol of his desired continuity with the empire, but he apparently pensioned them off at a very low rate of pay as they grew old.[24] As a further gesture, he continued the pensions to their heirs in order to avoid any ill will, since these positions were hereditary, like so many other posts in the cumbersome bureaucracy. There was absolutely no need for the *protectores domestici*, since whatever remained of their role as imperial bodyguards was taken over by Ostrogoths around Theodoric. They were likewise pensioned off, with provisions for their descendants. They even haggled over their small sums. Their head, the office of *comes domesticorum*, was, however, retained as a convenient titular post for awarding the lowest rank of *vir inlustris*.[25] The *silentiarii*, ushers in the consistory, were probably replaced by members of Theodoric's own Germanic household staff, collectively the *maiores domus regiae*. Naturally the retired *silentiarii* and their ancestors received appropriate grants.[26]

A *comitatus* somewhat modified by these deductions and replacements was the heart of the government of Italy. Under Theodoric, as under the emperors, the *comitatus* represented all aspects of government and was attached to the ruler. The elimination of the *scholae*, *domestici*, and *silentiarii* provided an opportunity to replace these lesser military and custodial functionaries with Gothic retainers. Nor of course was there a *magister militum praesentalis*, for Theodoric was himself the *magister*, as had been Odovacar. The *comitiaci* attached to the *magister* were retained and their roles expanded. The head of the *comitiaci* at court was the *princeps cardinalis*, and there was a vicarate at Rome with its own staff.[27] In its civilian aspects, the *comitatus* remained intact. The formal household, *sacrum cubiculum* with its *praepositus* and eunuch chamberlains (*cubicularii*), stood watch over the palace. They had to be trusted, for often, at least under the emperors, they controlled most access to the ruler. Not surprisingly, two *cubicularii* are known by name, and both are Goths: Wiliarit and Seda. The latter died in 541 at age forty after serving Theodoric as a young man.[28] Triwilla was a *saio* before becoming *praepositus cubiculi* at Ravenna (520–23), thus reemphasizing its importance to Theodoric.[29] The two great heads of the bureaucracy were present as ever: the praetorian prefect and the *magister officiorum*. Their duties were outlined in the *formulae* for bestowing their offices (*Var.* 6. 3, *praet.*; 6. 6, *mag.off.*), but in each case the *formulae* are anachronistic and do not reflect the powers of the *comitiaci* now attached to the monarch himself, nor do they take into account the other modest reorganizations made under Theodoric. So too the *formulae* reveal a considerable overlap in the duties of the urban prefect and the *vicarius* (6. 4 and 15). Formulae are preserved for a host of traditional offices, including *comes rei privatae*, *referendarii*, and the provincial *consularis* and *rectores* charged with various fiscal and judicial responsibilities. In sum, the *formulae* help to complete a picture of the survival of the Roman bureaucratic structure with but few changes.[30]

The *comes sacrarum largitionum* was responsible for mines and mints (gold and probably silver) and certain taxes and payments, including donatives. He had to be highly capable and extremely trustworthy. Cyprianus, the son of Opilio (*comes sar. larg.* under Odovacar) and one of very few Romans to know Gothic, was a holder of the office.[31] The *comes rei privatae* was a member of the *comitatus* and managed the estates of the imperial fisc, then in Theodoric's hands. The consistory was another important imperial legacy present in the *comitatus*. By this time, membership in the consistory was restricted to counts of the first order of the three ranks of counts. The *comes primi ordinis*, and, in fact, under Theodoric only those actually serving in the provinces, and the counselors of the praetorian prefect were automatically members.[32] Cassiodorus preserved the formula for awarding the title:

> The rank of Comes is one which is reached by Governors (*Rectores*) of Provinces after a year's tenure in office, and by the Counsellors of the Praefect, whose functions are so important that we look upon them as almost Quaestors. Their rank gives the holder of it, though only a Spectabilis, admission to our Consistory, where he sits side by side with all the Illustres.
>
> We bestow it upon you, and name you a Comes Primi Ordinis, thereby indicating that you are to take your place at the head of all the other Spectabiles and next after the Illustres. See that you are not surpassed in excellence of character by any of those below you.[33]

The *quaestor* was obviously also present as secretary to the monarch under the Ostrogoths. Its most famous holder was none other than Cassiodorus himself during his early career.[34]

At least one important Ostrogoth was a count of the first order, a certain Gudila.[35] Gudila is probably typical rather than unique, as our isolated inscriptional evidence would suggest. The literary sources make repeated reference to Gothic counts, unfortunately without the specificity of inscriptions in regard to complete titles. The various Roman offices represented in the *comitatus* were themselves complex bureaus with numerous subalterns and clerks. The consistory had an independent staff of secretaries. Ostrogoths whose counsel helped determine policy also attended the *comitatus*. When a difficult matter arose, even one such as that involving Theodahad, royal nephew and future king, the parties were summoned to present their case before the *comitatus*.[36] Thus in the central institution of his government, Theodoric enhanced the effectiveness of late Roman forms and adapted them with only slight modification to the new conditions in Italy. If he so wished, the Goths too were subject to its rule.

Theodoric maintained a personal treasury, the *patrimonium*, under the *comes patrimonii*. The *patrimonium* apparently took over the lands of the imperial *domus divina* but had new and important sources of income as well. Its additional revenues included the taxes from outside Italy, specifically from Sicily (*Variae* 8. 23; 9. 3; 12. 4), Spain (*Variae* 5. 39), Dalmatia (*Variae* 9. 9), Savia (*Variae* 5. 14), and Pannonia (*Variae* 4. 13). Inheritances, gifts, and confiscations also flowed into this treasury. Its known *comites* are Bergantinus, Julianus, Senarius, and Wilia.[37] Wilia and Julianus, if the same as the *comes* of *Variae* 5. 23, were certainly Goths, and Senarius, too, perhaps. The *comes patrimonii* had a variety of duties not obvious in his title.[38] For example, Theodoric ordered Senarius to establish supplies for the army moving to Pannonia under *comes* Colosseus and to compensate some shippers for their losses while transporting grain from Sicily to the army in Gaul.[39] Thus it was with pride that Senarius was remembered as an adviser sought out in war and peace. A very important man indeed, he was *comes rexi patrimonia clarus et mea patricio*.[40] Cassiodorus also addressed Senarius as *comes rei privatae* on three occasions in his *Variae* (4. 3, 7, 14), indicating that Senarius may have held that post as well. Surely, however, his epitaph would have included such a noteworthy honor, but it did not.

Not all the office holders were capable or caring. So at least recorded Cassiodorus, who claimed that he spent much of his time while *quaestor* assisting others. Nonetheless, the picture emerging from Cassiodorus, indeed from all our sources, is one of consistently good government, often unusually attentive and effective. The traditional Roman courts rendered justice within their respective jurisdictions. The provincial courts and governors toiled in Gaul, Pannonia,

Dalmatia, indeed wherever Ostrogothic rule had peacefully supplanted the Roman emperors. So too the courts of the vicars and praetorian prefect hammered out justice according to the law of the *Codex Theodosiani* and its *Novellae*. The letters of Ennodius to his friend Faustus, then praetorian prefect, attest to the endless stream of correspondence and petitions submitted to these officials. Their tasks were difficult at best. In emergencies they might have to act on their own authority in matters beyond their customary jurisdiction. Thus, Cassiodorus found himself deeply involved in a military crisis during his term as praetorian prefect.[41] Characteristically, Theodoric sought to secure and regularize the distribution of public grain and paid close attention to the traffic on the Po and to keeping the mouth of the Tiber clear of fishing nets and stakes, thus slowing the silting up.[42] No one failed to realize why all of these activities went on so smoothly. The answer was Theodoric. Whether it was the transport of public grain, the provisioning of garrisons and frontier troops, the law courts, the circus in Rome, famine relief, or whatever else Romans expected of government, Theodoric shouldered the burden. He probably cared even more about the Goths, but his approach was different, more personal and sensitive to their peculiar problems and traditions.

Goths were not usually summoned to the *comitatus*; nor were Romans, for it was essentially a court of final jurisdiction in cases involving the nobilities. Instead, provincial *iudices* heard Gothic cases and decided them on the basis of custom and the *edicta* of Theodoric and his successors.[43] Now that recent research has cast doubt on the traditional attribution of the famous *Edictum* to Theodoric the Great and has sought to bestow it on Theodoric II at Toulouse, Ostrogothic legal proceedings are even less securely defined. Theodoric was popularly praised and remembered for his *edicta* establishing justice for the Goths. The legend of his Solomonesque justice and impatience for legal obstruction and delay was equally endearing to the Romans.

One story even spread to the eastern Mediterranean. A Roman matron, Juvenalia, had grown old awaiting a decision on a lawsuit against one Firmus, a patrician. Utterly exasperated after thirty years, she appealed to Theodoric to hasten the litigation. He issued an ultimatum giving the lawyers only two days more. They were now suitably inspired, and a settlement issued forthwith. A short while later, Juvenalia came to thank the king, who promptly summoned the lawyers. "Why could you do in two days what was impossible in thirty years?" he demanded. They were executed.[44]

Although most details of his legislation are lost, he directly confronted the problem of merging the *iudices* and other legal officers into the customary legal framework of his people. The new system involved appealing decisions from the local level, decisions of the *iudices* to the *comites Gothorum* or, in special instances, to the *comitatus* itself. His *edicta* must also have detailed procedures and jurisdictions in cases involving Romans and Goths, since these were specifically left to the *comites Gothorum*. The reason these cases were so troublesome was the fact that for many matters there were two bodies of law.[45] The Romans followed the Theodosian Code and the Novellae. The Goths adhered to their customs and whatever instructions were contained in the lost royal enactments. Cassiodorus recorded the formula for the appointment of a *comes Gothorum* and carefully outlined the legal procedures to be followed.

> As we know that, by God's help, Goths are dwelling intermingled among you, in order to prevent the trouble (*indisciplinatio*) which is wont to arise among partners (*consortes*) we have thought it right to send to you as Count, A B, a sublime person, a man already proved to be of high character, in order that he may terminate (*amputare*) any contests arising between two Goths according to our edicts; but that, if any matter should arise between a Goth and a born Roman, he may, after associating with himself a Roman jurisconsult, decide the strife by fair reason. As between two Romans let the decision rest with the Roman examiners (*cognitores*), whom we appoint in the various Provinces; that thus each may keep his own laws, and with various Judges one Justice may embrace the whole realm. Thus, sharing one common peace, may both nations, if God favour us, enjoy the sweets of tranquility. Let both nations hear what we have at heart. You oh Goths! have the Romans as neighbours to your lands; even so let them be joined to you in affection. You too, oh Romans! ought dearly to love the Goths, who in peace swell the numbers of your people and in war defend the whole Republic. It is fitting therefore that you obey the Judge whom we have appointed to you, that you may ordain for the preservation of the laws; and thus you will be found to have promoted your own interests while obeying our command.[46]

Failing decisive action at the comital level, the Gothic plaintiff could appeal directly to the monarch. The typical appeal involved the actions of the local nobility, who were so powerful in their areas that greater authority was often required. A case involving an old Gothic soldier, gone blind, is illustrative. The elderly man charged two other Goths, Gudila and Oppas, with attempted enslavement. The *comes Gothorum* in the area, a certain Pythius, was unable to free the veteran and, it seems, urged him to petition Theodoric (ca. 523–26). Indeed, if the old man was imprisoned, as the letter implies, the *comes* may actually have taken the matter in hand himself.[47] Other Goths were similarly seeking redress from Theodoric for what they regarded as enslavement by the Gothic nobility with their loyal bands of warriors.[48] However, despite the widening gulf between the lower class and the Gothic nobility that was apparent in dress, rank, and way of life, the ample records preserved for us in Cassiodorus's *Variae* reveal that as long as Theodoric lived, the checks on the nobility's aggressive behavior effectively protected the Goths beneath them.

The pattern of settlement and defense left the Goths in more isolated settings than those of the migration, where king, nobles, and the ordinary Goths often shared the camps. The legal apparatus was adapted accordingly. The cases of appeal from the general settlement areas in which there were large numbers of Gothic communities required the regionalized *comes Gothorum*, i.e., one of provincial scope, *comites provinciarum*.[49] Along the frontiers and outlying provinces, they also commanded the Gothic troops. The government at Ravenna extended this structure to include the frontier areas as well. Everywhere the provincial *comites* were the supreme governmental officials whenever present. In the frontier areas, the *comes* had legal jurisdiction and probably held overall command unless, as was sometimes the case, a *dux* was present specifically as commander. In Dalmatia, the *comes* was superior to the *principes* and the Roman governor (*praeses*), who was increasingly a fiscal officer having some responsibility for tax collection. The *principes* of Dalmatia maintained the Roman legal structure alongside the Gothic command embodied in the *comes*.[50] A *princeps* may have been assigned to each major city, since the office of *princeps* was held by several men at one time. They were under the *comes*. The provincial governor (*praeses*) retained some civil authority and shared some responsibility for tax collection. The principal city in Dalmatia was Salona, where the *comes* and Gothic garrison resided.[51]

Savia, the area of the middle Sava and Drava basin, was administered by its own *comes* but remained largely "Pannonian," with few Goths. Further down the Sava there was perhaps some settlement around Sirmium in Pannonia Secunda in the wake of the Sirmium War (504–05).[52] Prior to this time, the area around Sirmium seems to have been semiautonomous, acting as a forward outpost under an alliance of senior Roman nobles. These lords allowed the Gepids to move into Sirmium itself and ultimately to provoke retaliation from Theodoric's appointed commander, Pitzia. Upon driving out the Gepids and their Byzantine allies, Pitzia set about reestablishing government. He allowed the Romans to return to their own legal customs, while he himself apparently took up residence in the area and returned some wasteland to cultivation.[53] A certain Fridibad became *comes* of Savia (ca. 507–11), thereby perhaps even extending regular Ostrogothic administration as far as Sirmium.[54] Shortly after his elevation, Athalaric consolidated Savia and Dalmatia under *comes* Osiun.[55] Perhaps he, in effect, acknowledged in this way that the revival of Gepidic power around Sirmium made the old province of Savia no longer tenable as a separate administrative unit. Before the Sirmium War, Savia definitely had a separate provincial government, and Sirmium in Pannonia Secunda was an outpost in loose allegiance to Theodoric. Theodoric alone minted coins at Sirmium; the last was a half-siliqua piece with Theodoric and Justinus I (518–27). By early 535 the Byzantines were again nominally in control of Sirmium through their allies the Gepids, Erulians, and Sclaveni.[56]

Because Savia required repeated attention, detailed instructions for its administration survive. In general, the governmental system operated as in Italy, with similar problems and abuses. The indigenous populations lived under their own laws as elaborated by the *curiales*, who continued to exist in Savia. The rich coerced the poor into paying a greater share of taxes. The *iudices* toured the province, rendering justice and abusing their rights to three days' free maintenance in each town. Barbarians married wealthy Roman women to add to their own holdings but refused to pay taxes on their new lands. They probably claimed that the lands were legally part of their *sortes* of the settlements and as such were nontaxable. Some Goths were even less subtle and simply forced the Romans to sell, probably at a bargain.[57] All of this illegality introduced a flood of litigation before the *comes* and his staff. Behind them stood the distant monarch, who could summon the troublemakers before him, but in reality, Theodoric delegated government to the *comes* and the very nobles whose actions were decried. Everywhere the royal authority was too intrinsically weak to prevent personal disputes over land and private abuses of power. Sending an expeditionary force under a man like Pitzia was always theoretically possible but expensive. Even then the result might well have been the replacement of one group of nobles by another. Theodoric rarely resorted to such drastic measures as martial intervention in an entire area. He seems to have preferred to bring the offenders before his *comitatus* and thereby remove them from their power bases in the provinces.

In Provence the provincial *comes* Marabad worked closely with the Roman *vicarius* Gemellus in difficult legal actions as they jointly struggled against famine and Frankish invasion.[58] Perhaps Istria, Noricum Mediterranean, and Switzerland also had a provincial *comes* as a regular feature of their government.[59] Gaul was a special case, for it remained under the *praefectus praetorio Galliarum*. From 510 to 534, the noteworthy Liberius held the post and as such represented the royal authority at the highest levels in such important matters as the settlement of Ostrogoths, Orthodox religious conclaves, and major military campaigns.[60] As *vicarius*, Gemellus was under his jurisdiction and handled the routine tasks of civil government as well as the details of coordination between the civil and military structures.

The Goths established garrisons in important cities throughout their rule. Such special cities as Naples, Pavia, and Syracuse had their own *comes*, as did Massilia, Arelate, the Insulae Curicta, and Celsina. These *comites Gothorum* were legal officers, as were the provincial *comites*, and they also commanded whatever garrisons were stationed there. At distant Syracuse, *comes* Gildias was at pains to control his men. Garrisons were probably comprised largely of warrior groups personally tied to their commanders. That was perhaps especially true of small units assigned to guard key roads and estates. Gildias was instructed to look after his garrison's regular provisioning so that they would be less likely to plunder the neighboring farms.[61] The problem of Goths appealing against their own noble leaders was less likely to arise in areas far distant from the frontiers than in the settlements in Liguria, Picenum, and Ravenna, and even there it was rare. The enslavement of the old warrior by Gudila and Oppas warranted such action. Perhaps the rank of *comes secundi ordinis* was accorded to the urban *comites*, whereas the provincial became *comes primi*. The various *comites Gothorum* and other high Gothic officials may have employed their traditional associations of warriors as *buccellarii*, as was common in the East. Indeed, Procopius and other sources abound with examples of such attendants, variously called, accompanying Byzantine leaders, especially Belisarius. Unfortunately, the sources are inadequate to prove their widespread existence among the Ostrogoths, although the actions of the nobility and the official holders are more understandable if we accept that the coercive power of the followers was close at hand. Oppas, who was executed following his personal rebellion against Theodoric, was perhaps a *buccellarius* of the monarch.[62] The use of *buccellarii* would have been an acceptable redirection of the energies of the warbands into more defined government under the primary direction of the monarchy.

At least in some areas, lesser officials called *priores* assisted the provincial *comites*. In a highly rhetorical letter dated ca. 526, Athanaric addressed all the inhabitants of Reate (now Rieti) and Nursia, announcing proudly that, as they wished, he was appointing Quidila, the son of Sibia, *prior* over both cities.[63] Alas, Cassiodorus could not resist this opportunity to present a general exhortation on governmental virtues. He alluded to their many victories and the donatives made possible by the Roman tribute (the general tax). All were under the law and the *iudices*. All that we may safely conclude is that the *prior* was a minor provincial official with limited legal and fiscal duties. Perhaps he also had some military function in regard to payment of donatives, although this role was more narrowly in the hands of the *millenarii*.[64]

The office of *defensor civitatis* was another feature of late Roman government adapted by the Ostrogoths. The office was originally created by Valentinian in 364 to defend the citizens of the communities from the unlawful incursions of imperial officials. But over the next century, the office slipped into disuse until reestablished by Majorian in 458. The *defensor civitatis* continued to exist in most early Germanic kingdoms, as well as in the Eastern Empire, but each area witnessed a different evolution. In Gaul, where the institution lasted the longest in the West, the *defensor* merely enrolled acts in the municipal registers with the aid of the local curia.[65] In Italy the Ostrogoths continued the office as a local "protector." *Defensores* were supposed to protect the community from oppression, just as Valentinian had planned, but their protection included the seasonal fixing of prices and often the forced requisition of military supplies.[66] In small towns, the *defensor* and the curia were the government: the *defensor* represented the central government; the curia, of course, was drawn from the locality.[67] Roman senators also were accorded the honor of having a *defensor*. In the only case in which a *defensor* is known by name, *saio* Tezutzat replaced Amara as *defensor* for Senator Petrus. Amara had "protected" his ward by occasionally beating him![68] Since only Amara and Tezutzat are known (the *saio* was clearly an Ostrogoth), it is perhaps unwarranted to assume that all *defensores* were Goths. However, Theodoric and his successors could not allow men of questionable loyalty to hold the office, for the *defensor* alone represented the central government in many towns. In times of famine, the town probably sought tax reductions through its *defensor*. However, the decision whether to grant a reduction for a given indiction rested exclusively with the central government and its representatives the counts, provincial judges, and the Roman governors.[69]

So far it would seem that the Goths governed themselves in a remarkably Roman manner, with clearly defined chains of command within the institution of law and civil government. That was indeed a goal; however, the majority of the Goths were unaccustomed to such delineation. The nobility, in particular, must have regarded much of this government from Ravenna as a gross intrusion into their preserve. Making the system work meant reenforcing the sinews between the localities and the central government with personal agents of the crown. *Comites Gothorum*, perhaps usually urban *comites*, were dispatched on errands throughout the kingdom. These missions are so numerous as to suggest that a third type of *comes* should be added to the urban and provincial—the *comites* undertaking special assignments.[70] However, the actual royal "firefighters" were the *saiones*, whose responsibilities were left undefined and who neither held nor apparently desired lofty ranks and titles. They were the king's men. Wherever they went, they took charge for the king himself. Unless the king retained their loyalty and obedience and the respect they inspired, he could not rule. They represented the personal leadership invested in the royal power without which the Goths would withdraw into the enclaves of traditional local and regional government under the nobility.

Many *saiones* are known by name, but by almost nothing else. Perhaps three held other posts: *saio* Triwilla became *praepositus cubiculi* (ca. 520–23);[71] *saio* Tezutzat definitely became a *defensor civitatis* (*Var.* 4. 27–28); and finally, Athalaric may have appointed *saio* Quidila as *prior* over Reate and Nursia (*Var.* 5. 10–11). The institution, if the *saiones* can be so classified, existed as early as 508, when Theodoric instructed *saio* Nandus to assemble troops for the invasion of Gaul.[72] *Saiones* or similar royal servants existed among many Germanic peoples throughout the early Middle Ages and seem to have emerged out of the royal band in response to basic needs for personal and trusted contact with the royalty. None of the Ostrogothic *saiones* ever achieved comital or ducal status, which suggests that they were of lowly origins. In each of the three cases above, they undertook office specifically during crises (Tezutzat and Quidila) or held a post in the heart of the palace structure (Triwilla). As a group, the *saiones* were remarkably versatile.

In ca. 507–11 Theodoric sent a *saio* to assist in tax collection—a function the *saiones* were still undertaking as late as 533–37.[73] Fruirarith was asked by Theodoric to judge a case involving a Roman court official.[74] Unigilis directed the provisioning for Theodoric's roving court on one of his visits to Liguria.[75] *Saio* Grenoda along with a special military aide investigated charges against ex-praetorian prefect Faustus.[76] Leodifrid supervised the building of the new fortifications at Verruca, although theoretically the palace architect was in charge of the construction of fortifications.[77] Gesila was sent to Picenum and

Tuscany to force certain Goths to pay taxes.[78] Duda, a *saio* of exceptional talents, unsuccessfully brought a case against Theodahad, then *dux* in Liguria. Duda also channeled a troublesome legal case to the proper court and supervised grave robbing to ensure that the treasure went to the crown![79] Veranus supervised the movement of the Gepids across Venetia and Liguria when Theodoric (ca. 523–26) sought to strengthen his Frankish frontier.[80] Dumerit was sent to Faventia to punish the plunderers of small farmers "whether the culprits were Goth or Roman."[81] The last datable reference to *saiones* is under Athalaric, when he sent one to correct *comes* Gildila at Syracuse (ca. 533).[82] Although this reference is among the last to *saiones*, Cassiodorus, our only source, left very few letters for the later kings and none after Witigis. Occasionally the *saiones* were paired on their missions with *comitiaci*.[83] The number of examples could be expanded, but there is no need to belabor the point that the *saiones* were a very versatile group with authority unlimited by institutional or ethnic boundaries.

Generally the *comites* on special assignment undertook more delicate and complex operations, often but not always involving the upper levels of the Roman bureaucracy and the senatorial class. The *comites* too were quite adept. For example, when Venantius, son of Liberius, who had supervised the settlement of the Goths, faced charges of gross misconduct, *comes* Arigern headed the investigation. Venantius became a senator.[84] Anabilis coordinated shipping along the entire western coast when Theodoric sought to relieve a famine in Gaul.[85] *Comes Gothorum* Julian, who was perhaps the same as Julian *comes patrimonii*, conducted special military exercises, for which *saio* Tato alerted praetorian prefect Abundantius to ready supplies.[86] Luvirit and Ampelius investigated and fined merchants for failing to deliver grain taken on in Spain.[87] These are enough examples, perhaps, to demonstrate the extraordinary flexibility brought to Gothic government by the personal emissaries of the monarch. The *saiones* and *comites Gothorum* with some assistance from the *comitiaci* enabled Theodoric to make the system work.

Their service gave him the tools necessary to ease the stress points of crisis. During the three decades of Theodoric's rule in Italy, the Goths began the long process of accommodating their lives to institutional mechanisms. The old blind warrior used the system, as did the nobility. Indeed, that the "Goths remembered him for his *edicta*" is itself an eloquent epitaph of Theodoric's success. Perhaps we can see an echo of this learning process in the case of *inlustris femina* Gundihild and her sons Lendarit and Landerit recorded in the *Acta* of Rieti, dated 6 December 557.[88] She did not hesitate to use Roman legal process to counter the threat of the local nobles Aderid, *vir inluster*, and Gunderit, *vir magnificus*, and their followers. Thus within five years of Totila's defeat, people of obvious Germanic, if not Gothic, descent were effectively engaged in the Roman courts and against each other.

Although the long-term adaptations to some basic features of regular government continued after Theodoric's death in 526, the crown quickly lost its ability to control the structure and command the loyalty and obedience of its representatives. Symptomatic of the diminished royal authority, ten-year-old Athalaric had to create a *patricius praesentalis* to command the army.[89] The *saiones* were quick to take advantage of their weak young king. In one of his earliest edicts (ca. 527), Athalaric ordered the *comes patrimonii* to protect the *curiales* from the oppression of *saiones* and other officials extorting taxes.[90] The main tax fell on the land and was collected through the communities, where the *curiales*, town councilors, were still responsible for their payment. The members of one curial family won their plea to be removed from the curial list only to be reminded that they would now face the *compulsores*, before sent at their behest.[91] Two tax collectors, *censitores*, in Sicily, Victor and Witigisdus (certainly a Goth), *viri spectabiles*, refused a summons to the *comitatus* to face charges of extortion and oppression of the provincials.[92] Gildias, *comes* for Syracuse, used an alleged need for wall repairs to raise taxes and then did not rebuild the walls. He also was accused of confiscating the property of the deceased, even those with legally valid testaments, when it suited him.[93] He was chastened with a reminder that "the true praise of the Goths is lawabidingness."[94]

The Edict of Athalaric (ca. 526) was an outline of disintegration from beginning to end. The prologue set the tone:

> For long an ominous whisper has reached our ears that certain persons, despising *civilitas*, affect a life of beastly barbarism, returning to the wild beginnings of society, and looking with a fierce hatred on all human laws. . . . The internal enemy is even more dangerous than the external.[95]

Athalaric went on to decry the forced appropriations of land, abuse of the royal prerogative to affix titles to property, unauthorized editing of royal decrees, forced donations, and abuse of those under royal protection (*tuitio*). He continued by spelling out abuses in the appeals system and a variety of moral failings. Sorcery was on the rise and had to be suppressed. In another pronouncement he revealed that despite his appointment of numerous *iudices* to the provinces, he was perpetually inundated with law suits.[96] Obviously the *iudices* lacked the power to implement justice that they had possessed under Theodoric. The nobility had little difficulty taking charge of the young king, insisting that he be educated among some young Gothic nobles rather than being trained in Roman letters as his mother, Amalasuintha, had been. They acted in part at least in repudiation of her father's policies, but also and more simply because as a woman she did not command the respect of warriors. Athalaric died on 2 October 534, his death probably hastened by alcohol.[97]

Amalasuintha foresaw her son's death and cast about for protection. She turned to Justinian and secretly offered him the kingdom in return for his protection, but before these negotiations bore fruit, she set about eliminating the three principal nobles in opposition and then turned to securing her kingdom internally. After Athalaric's death, she entered into an alliance with her cousin Theodahad and declared him king.[98] He hardly cut an appropriate figure for a Gothic king. He had two loves, Roman culture and the expansion of his estates in Liguria, for which Theodoric had once summoned him to the *comitatus*. Even the aggressive expansion of his estates was perhaps illusionary, disguising his inability to control his own followers. He had no better luck as king. Even the members of his private household did as they pleased.[99] He tried to build on Theodoric's image, even to the point of using Theodoric's monogram on his coins, but failed.[100] The senate distrusted him as much as the Goths.[101] The *saiones* grew more brazen and feckless. By now their duties were apparently concentrated in tax collecting and in enforcing the rulings of the *iudices*, who were themselves heavily involved in the tax system. At least, that was the official limit of their powers. In fact, they did as they pleased, "swaggering through the streets exulting that people dare not look them in the eye."[102] Royal offers of better pay for better performance doubtless met with laughter. Under Theodoric the issue of pay never arose. At Justinian's urging, Theodahad even agreed to return the property of a Gothic woman, Veranilda, confiscated under Theodoric when she had converted from Arianism to Orthodoxy.[103]

The war against the Byzantines demanded a more vigorous and commanding leader. The nobility rose, murdered Theodahad, and declared one of their own king. In a gesture perhaps harking back to the warbands and the origins of the Ostrogothic confederacy, they raised Witigis aloft on a shield and raised their swords around him in salute.[104] Witigis as king saw that victory and ultimately peace and prosperity were attainable only in a symbiosis of Romans and Goths in Italy. Cassiodorus was ordered to announce him to the troops in the manner of an emperor. So, too, Cassiodorus celebrated his royal wedding to Matasuentha, sister of Athalaric, in courtly style with images of the imperial palace uniting the scene.[105] The coinage continued to reflect the vision of Theodoric. Indeed, it did so until the very end of the kingdom, steadfastly acknowledging that despite the horrors of war, Gothic and Roman traditions could and should coexist.[106] But the kings had forever lost the internal struggle with the aristocracy and with it the power to further the policies of Theodoric.

War took its toll on all aspects of government. The tax system strained to meet the demands for more revenue from less territory and increasingly devastated populations as the war, famine, and pestilence—even the bubonic plague—destroyed the economy.[107] Finally, the system of tax-farming gave way to direct payment and outright confiscations. At the beginning of the war, the government was able to stockpile supplies in advance of its troops and to avert famine.[108] Roads and bridges were checked and repaired along the lines of the march.[109] In the end there was no logistical support, and even the royal treasury was gone.[110]

Each crack in the edifice forced the Ostrogoths, including their kings, back upon the support of the nobility. The nobility had controlled the settlement areas for years, and now that the tax system was in disarray, supplies and men came almost entirely from these very areas. Belisarius understood the situation well. The nobility's voice in council, advisory to Theodoric in the *comitatus*, no longer merely offered opinions. Witigis asked their consent to surrender Gaul to the Franks in an attempt to achieve peace on that front and consolidate his troops.[111] Totila appointed the most notable Goths commanders of the army he sent to Picenum, including dukes Scipuar, Gibal, and Gundulf, who had been a bodyguard to Belisarius.[112] He was strongly opposed by the council when he sought to imprison one of his own bodyguards. He suffered further rebuke for not totally leveling Rome. After Totila's death in battle, the nobles had no trouble continuing and negotiating a surrender the following day.[113] The transition from duke or member of the council to king was easy for Witigis, Hildibadus, and Eraric. The dukes owed their thrones to the necessity for coordinated command and the tradition of Ostrogothic monarchy. Prior to the War of Justinian, the Amali could claim the kingship by inheritance without special ceremonies. Only now did Ostrogothic dukes grasp the royal cloak. But regardless of their title or the ceremony of kingship each underwent, later Ostrogothic kings never matched the power and authority of Theodoric, especially over their noble counterparts. With the death of Teias in 554, the kingship expired. Aligernus, the brother of Teias, went over to the Byzantines against the Franks. He knew that with the wealth of the Amali long spent, there was no hope for kingship or victory.[114] Other Goths served the Franks under *dux* Ragnaris, who was himself of Hunnic descent. These 7,000 pitiful remnants held out at Campsas and were ultimately sent to Constantinople as hostages. But by then most Goths had already returned to their homes in peace, their governmental aspirations forgotten.[115]

In the final analysis, war or the threat of war created and destroyed the Ostrogothic monarchy and its governmental system. Not surprisingly, we will discover many parallels to the ebb and flow of government while analyzing Gothic military evolution. In many respects, the creation of a diplomatic and military network to defend Italy from invasion was Theodoric's crowning achievement. Along the frontiers of Italy and beyond, he was able to blend his personal leadership with structural patterns modeled on Roman achievements. Storm clouds were visible on the horizon even before he died, but in the aftershock of his death the structure collapsed.

As to government, it is important to stress in conclusion that no other barbarian peoples, not even the Visigoths, retained so much of the Roman government as an active part of society. Nowhere else in the West did the praetorian prefect and *magister officiorum* attend the *comitatus* and manage a bureaucracy basically unchanged. The intimate presence of a functioning system of such complexity, regardless of its obvious arterial sclerosis, was a major ingredient in Theodoric's vision and in the evolution of the Ostrogothic people.

8

Warriors and the Military System

WARFARE WAS A characteristic feature of Ostrogothic life, but only rarely did it flare into a societal struggle of tribal proportions. Even the chroniclelike *Getica* of Jordanes makes it clear that major struggles were infrequent and brief. Cattle rustling, petty raids, and militant competition among warbands, on the other hand, were commonplace. Theodoric himself was a fierce and respected warrior of great renown, but no one ever made that claim for any of his numerous grandsons or his nephew Theodahad. Indeed, even Witigis, held aloft on a shield by the soldiers and hailed king, failed as a commander. Only Totila deserved his acclaim as an able field commander. History usually celebrates Ostrogothic defeats rather than praising their victories: Ermanaric's heroic stand and suicide before the Huns; Theodoric the Amal swallowing his pride before his rival Theodoric Triarius near Sondis; the staggering losses of the Hunnic allies at the Catalaunian Fields; and the victories of Belisarius and Narses. To be sure, there were great moments. The dash of Greuthingi cavalry at the exposed Roman flank decided the battle of Adrianople. Nevertheless, if anything distinguished the Ostrogoths from the other Germanic peoples, it was their tenacity and ultimately their ability to manipulate surviving Roman systems of government and defense to their own uses.

That is not to say that they preserved the Roman army or concepts of frontier defense intact. They did not. Nor, for that matter, did any other barbarian group.[1] Yet the bits and pieces remaining were made to operate in conjunction with the military and diplomatic initiatives of the monarchy. The defense of the Alpine areas, the Rhone Valley, and ultimately Italy itself was responsive to these initiatives, which, until the crisis of the War of Justinian, provided reasonable security for the Ostrogothic Kingdom. These defenses were directed against the threat of invasion from other barbarians, against whom the Ostrogoths were indeed almost universally victorious. Theodoric, his father, and his uncles in the Balkans defeated Sadagi, Suevi, Sarmatians, and various other fragments of the old federate system.[2] Finally at the Ulca River in 489, they humbled the defiant Gepids. They even more than held their own against the Franks in the distant Rhone valley. However, against Roman arms they were much less successful, especially when the empire mounted a concerted attack over a prolonged period. Thus, until his death in 481, Sabinianus, *magister militum per Thracias*, penned the Ostrogoths near Epirus Nova. Belisarius and Narses were in the field for two decades, during which they destroyed most of the Roman government supporting the Ostrogothic Kingdom and redirected at least some of the loyalty of the Italo-Romans away from their Gothic hosts. In effect, Justinian's successful prosecution of the war inevitably destroyed the underlying symbiotic relationship that had nourished Italy since the coming of the Ostrogoths. The extraordinary duration of the struggle is, in part, a testament to the partial fruition of Theodoric's vision of competitive cooperation.

Ultimately, every able-bodied male Ostrogoth was a soldier. Although the almost complete lack of weapons in Gothic burials prohibits precise reconstruction of the battle dress, many aspects of the military life are nonetheless discernible. Prowess was still a determinant of social eminence.[3] Arms and armor varied from individual to individual, but their worth and beauty set the nobility apart on the fields of honor. Totila died fighting in the ranks of the common soldiers, having exchanged his princely golden armor for that of an ordinary soldier. Indeed, competition in dress reached its height in military garb throughout Ostrogothic history: the armbands of the fourth and early fifth century, the prestigious medallions from Szilágysomlyó, the "mask" fibulae, and the exquisite spangenhelmets produced in Italy attest to the continuing need to display rank in conspicuous dress.[4] If for any reason other than injury a soldier was discharged from the army, he lost his annual donative and suffered severe rebuke.[5]

The strengths and weaknesses of barbarian armies were well

known already to Tacitus and had become common fare in Byzantine military manuals by A.D. 600. In essence, the barbarians were seen to lack cohesive command, technological elements such as effective siege craft, and the patience required for utilizing a tactical reserve. During the encounters of the third century, these failings produced some pitiful, almost comical, incidents. The German "plan of attack" usually consisted of a human-wave assault with much yelling and throwing of stones, spears, and arrows. Obviously this approach had little success against walled towns, so they resorted to various means in numerous ill-fated efforts. At Marcianopolis in 248, the Goths piled stones against the wall, but their attempt to build a ramp and so take the city failed.[6] At Philippopolis in 250, a ramp of dirt and wood eventually carried them over the walls, but not, however, before the defenders had crushed their crude, unprotected scaling towers with boulders.[7] At Side in Lycia, the Goths pushed armored towers up to the walls yet still failed.[8] In 269 they again used armored towers, this time against Thessalonika. The struggle raged as the defenders hurled fireballs of wicker soaked with olive oil against the towers. The Goths dug reservoirs behind them for water to contain the flames—doubtless a hindrance to their safe removal at night as well. Thessalonika held.[9] The Herulians took Athens in 270. The somewhat comical story of their almost burning the Athenians' books enthralled numerous Byzantine chroniclers for over a millennium.[10]

The great Gothic victory over Decius in 251 was more of an accident than the result of a coherent plan. The Goths had had a good winter in and around recently captured Philippopolis and were eager to return home once the passes were free of snow. In April or May the conditions were right for their victorious withdrawal, but the emperor Decius had not yet given up. Although defeated at Philippopolis and near Beroea, the Romans could still mount a formidable force by stripping the remaining garrisons and passes of their defenders. It seems that Decius was determined to make the Gothic exodus as difficult as possible. He could not afford a direct confrontation and chose instead to shadow the baggage train and harass straying elements and thereby limit plundering and increase hunger. The Goths apparently set an ambush in the swamp near Abrittus and struck the Romans strung out along the only pathway from several areas of solid ground known only to the Goths. The rout was complete with Decius dying among his troops.[11] Moesia and Thrace were again ravaged. The victorious Goths from Abrittus recrossed the Danube in the vicinity of Durostorum, just east of where they had crossed two or three years before.[12] There were at least three other principal groups of Goths involved in the invasions. The others proceeded independently, crossing and recrossing the Danube months and years apart. Ultimately the raids turned into family migrations. These were doomed when Roman power concentrated its resources for prolonged warfare under Claudius, Aurelian, and Probus. Many starved to death or were sold into slavery throughout the empire. Others were granted official reception and dispersed along the frontiers as peasant-soldiers.

The underlying weakness of Gothic society during these troubled decades was its lack of ethnic unity and unwillingness to cooperate even for its own salvation. Without unity, the Goths fell easy victims to Roman tactics of containment and dispersal and eventually to the reassertion of traditional Roman diplomacy that began recreating a client network almost at once. Their technological shortcomings could be temporarily offset by stratagems or ruses and probably partially overcome through the employment of Roman technicians, shipwrights, sailors, and even soldiers and brigands.[13] But disunited, they could not sustain the invasions and were typically unable to develop tactics beyond the "hurrah and charge" of their ancestors. After all, since manliness was synonymous with military prowess as proven on the battlefield, who wanted to wait in reserve and perhaps miss priceless opportunities? Obviously, no one. Nor did any leader have the power so to order another free man, even in his warband. Thus it is hardly surprising that Germanic tactics varied so little regardless of the particular tribe or location. Besieging Roman cities was especially trying. Gothic siege craft were inadequate and poorly employed, but to invest a city with a blockade meant months or even years of living together in close quarters with ever increasing logistical problems of supply in a hostile country. Occasionally the besiegers starved before the surrounded urbanites, with dire consequences for the commanders. That happened even to Maximinus's troops before Aquileia in 238 and almost struck Attila there in the fifth century.[14] None of these military failings could be remedied before and until significant changes occurred in the political and social domains. All of these things took time—indeed, centuries were hardly enough.

Ermanaric took advantage of the fluid ethnic circumstances to bind together the Ostrogothic confederacy around the old Greuthingi. However, the details of his ill-fated resistance to the Huns are largely lost. Ammianus reported a wall built by the Greuthingi at this time, and that farther west Athanaric ordered another wall constructed to check the Hunnic advance.[15] There are numerous walls in the area of the Dniester, all subject to heated scholarly debate. A reasonable hypothesis is that the earthen wall running between modern Brăhăsesti on the Seret river and Stoicani on the Prut, a distance of 85 km, was erected under Athanaric. The Ostrogoths may have thrown up the rampart and ditch between Leova on the Prut and Chircăesti on the Dniester. Recent excavation of the former, the so-called wall of Moldavia Inferior, has revealed that the ditch was on the south side, thus adding some credence to Ammianus's account that Athanaric sought to protect his southern flank with a wall, beyond which lived the Taifali, while his people prepared to defend their heartland in the forests of what is now central Moldavia.[16] Nevertheless, without some better data for dating, the testimony of Ammianus must stand without secure buttressing from archaeology.

Clearly both Gothic confederacies rallied significant support in their bids to thwart Hunnic aggression. Thousands of hands were needed to complete so many kilometers of walls in the short time available before the expected attacks. The leaders, perhaps including the same *megistanes* who persecuted Saba, could have forced the villages within their domains into action. The servile and the indigenous peoples, about whom so little is known, doubtless contributed their labor. Ammianus's frightening picture of the invaders—short, bowlegged, and scarred, terrible creatures who lived astride their horses and ate raw meat—probably derived from some terrified Goth he interviewed years later. Such horror stories help account for the wholesale collapse of the Germanic peoples and must have given added incentive to the wall builders. Yet the Gothic confederacies still broke apart. Athanaric remained in the ancestral forests, leaving his rivals Alavivus and Fritigern to lead most of his confederacy into Roman *receptio*.[17] Ermanaric's heirs quarreled, and only the young Videric with his tutors Alatheus and Saphrax continued to resist, and they too joined the exodus crossing the Danube.

Their small group played a decisive role in Fritigern's victory at Adrianople in 378. Even then the overall problems of Gothic command left the military initiatives clearly in Roman hands throughout the two difficult years between the crossing and the great battle. Indeed, even after the mechanisms of *receptio* choked and collapsed completely, the Romans were able to shift tactics to a plan of containment and starvation by holding the key passes and striking at small foraging parties with their cavalry. The hit-and-run operations were a brilliant demonstration of Roman defensive strategy in action.[18] The very concept of reserve units and the *comitatensis* rested on the assumption of initially large-scale barbarian breakthroughs and the loss of many minor fortifications and supply depots. But the very number of such units, many having had their strength greatly enhanced under Valentinian and Valens, virtually guaranteed the prolonged survival of some. These could assist the advanced units of the Roman field armies. Between 376 and the summer of 378, the Roman commanders Richomeres and then Sebastianus presumably made use of any surviving Roman enclaves in their efforts. Sebastianus even tried to dissuade Valens from marching out against Fritigern before Gratian arrived. Alas for Valens, jealousy clouded his vision.[19] The Goths could do little more than consolidate their scattered forces and hope for an early and decisive confrontation. When the dusty and thirsty Roman troops spotted the Goths some miles outside Adrianople, perhaps near the modern village of Demeranliga, the Goths were surprised in their laager.[20]

The famous Gothic cavalry under Alatheus and Saphrax does not seem to have been a large force. In fact, the cavalry probably consisted of the nobility following the young Videric, a few Visigothic nobles who had found remounts, and the allied Huns and Alans also in the Alatheus-Saphrax group. If the archaeological data currently attributed to them are suggestive of anything, it is that this group was itself further subdivided during its settlement in northern Pannonia and for the most part rapidly assimilated into the existing elements of the Roman army stationed in the vicinity. They may have fought as a unit under Theodosius in his campaign against Eugenius, but the evidence for such independence is lacking or ambiguous.[21] The problems of unity and sustained military and political coordination had not yet found solutions.

The Ostrogoths within the Hunnic Empire may have occasionally encountered more sophisticated military techniques, such as Attila's siege at Naissus. At least under Attila, the Huns too actively employed Romans in their campaigns. Moreover, small advances in military technology were combined with a tightfisted political command structure built around the Germanic élites. The hierarchic social and political system imposed by the Huns fostered a greater sense of rank and its outward display in exclusive dress styles. Presumably the concomitant development in warfare was a greater adherence to the principles of a chain of command. Unfortunately, the extant records for the Ostrogoths are insufficient really to test such a hypothesis. The wars resulting from the settlement in Pannonia were primarily small-scale raids—certainly nothing to tax the command strengths of the Amali line. The battles against the Huns lingering in the area were more demanding and may have entered into Germanic sagas.[22] Nevertheless, details of actual battles are too sketchy to have much substantive value for factual evaluation. Theodoric's campaigns against the Sarmatians and his long feud with Theodoric Triarius were similarly recorded. Even his final raids from his base at Novae in 486–87 appear as mere shadows on the landscape, surely little more than large-scale raids. Only with the confrontations with the Gepids at Cybalae during the march to Italy in 488–89 and the Sirmium War of 504–05 against these same foes does Theodoric's ability to translate political power into military capacity begin to emerge from the sources.

The wicker shields of the Goths failed to stop the spears thrown across the muddy stream bottom of the Ulca River near Cybalae. Even after repeated assaults, the Gepids held throughout the daylong struggle until finally Theodoric discovered a ford of solid ground. He then rallied his men and with great personal courage led them through the enemy's ranks to their baggage. The Gepidic wagons were piled high with recently harvested grain, a welcome booty indeed for the hungry Goths.[23] In itself this sketch, all that survives of the battle, reveals a resolve rare among the Goths of earlier times. Those not loyal to Theodoric were not present on the Ulca. Nobles like Bessas had refused to follow him to Italy. These were desperate hours for the Ostrogoths, for there was no alternative to victory except gradual starvation in the barren Balkans. The Gepids were equally resolute. Victory was a result not of weapons or brilliant tactics but of tenacity and personal sacrifice.

The Goths and Gepids remained far from peaceful coexistence in the Sirmium area. By 504–05 a new war had begun here on the outskirts of Theodoric's kingdom. Unfortunately, Ennodius, bishop of Pavia, is again virtually our only source.[24] Although his account of the Sirmium War itself is even more disappointing than his reflections on the battle near Cybalae, other data are available for reconstructing the general situation. Moreover, Illyria in the era of the Sirmium War reflected in considerable detail the complex defensive system that was peculiarly Ostrogothic. In outline, the same pattern governed the defense of the northern frontiers with the Alamanni and Franks. Originally the Rhone Valley also fitted into this profile, but shortly after Clovis began to press the Burgundians, the Ostrogoths were forced to escalate their involvement and ultimately to settle in the area of Arles. In no case, however, are all the details known.[25]

The need for defending Italy from attacks across northern Pannonia, specifically along the Drava (Drau) and Sava (Save) rivers and the road systems along their paths, was hardly a new problem. By the reign of Diocletian, the Romans had fortified a series of strong points and built sections of walls as barriers across the main passes through the Julian Alps.[26] The struggle between Magnentius and Constantius II during the middle of the fourth century took its toll on the defenses as again and again the units stationed there were removed to fight in the civil wars.[27] Raiding parties of Quadi and Sarmatians ravaged the area in 374–75. Still, the passes were so clearly important that the units were restored once peace returned. That was not the case, however, when Theodosius stripped the fortifications in his preparations against the usurper Eugenius. Prior to their fateful meeting in September 394, near the Frigidus River, Eugenius and his German backer the *magister* Arbogast took control of the Alpine passes, where they hoped to block Theodosius's advance. When they mistook some of his troop deployments as a flanking movement against their southern defenses and shifted troops accordingly, Theodosius hit the center with a crushing blow.[28] He died 17 January 395, before he could refurbish the Alpine defenses with new troop dispositions, and although some forts were manned eventually, the system as a whole collapsed. The struggles under Stilicho took troops from throughout the West; the passes were now secondary. When Alaric marched to Italy in 401, the defenses were weak.[29]

Aetius apparently sent garrisons to some cities in an effort to contain the Huns of Attila, but even that proved too little too late. In reality, the fifth century, at least up to the time of the frontier wars in Noricum and Illyricum under Odovacar and his brother Onoulph, witnessed the virtual abandonment of direct Roman control in Pannonia north of the Sava and east of the old Alpine defenses on the Nauportus-Tarsatica line. Beginning with the settlement of the Visigoths and the Ostrogoths of Alatheus and Saphrax, the only effective powers in this salient were barbarians. Many of these groups were theoretically "federates" of the empire. They included various peoples, some of whom disappear from the records in the course of the century, perhaps victims of the almost constant strife among them or because they lost their identity through merging with others.

The original purpose of "inviting" the barbarians to the area seems to have been the strenthening of the *limes* from Aquincum southward in the only manner still feasible, i.e., establishing a series of federate allies from among the barbarians assaulting the area. Hunnic power in Pannonia peaked from the 430s until the death of Attila and made a sham of Roman hopes. But once the rebellious Hunnic allies had defeated their quarreling masters at Nedao in 454 (probably just northwest of Sopianae), the Romans had another chance. The emperor Marcian "received" the Ostrogoths into the area, perhaps settling them in three groups as Jordanes recorded, in the vicinity of the old federate areas.[30] As we have seen, the wars and raids with the Sadagi, Sciri, remnants of the Huns, and finally with the Sarmatians intensified before the Ostrogoths moved off their assigned lands for new settlements around Pella in Macedonia. They reentered Roman strategic concerns in the general Illyrian area briefly during their sojourn in Epirus Nova. Presumably the Rugians fleeing Odovacar passed through Pannonia on their way to join Theodoric at Novae in Moesia in 488. At about that time, the Gepids moved into the area of Sirmium and established themselves to the northwest around Cybalae, where the Roman highway branched, with one road leading up the Drava and the other passing through modern Levcono and following the Sava valley westward.

Theodoric set about to stabilize the area in much the same manner as had the eastern emperors and perhaps Odovacar. The defenses in the Julian Alps stretched from Tarsatica at the head of the Adriatic northward through Nauportus and then up to Zarakovec to northwest of Cividale (Forum Julium), but not all elements in the system were manned. To date, the archaeology of these fortifications and barriers is incomplete and the resulting picture imprecise. At a few locations there seems to have been an Ostrogothic presence as early as the reign of Arcadius (491–518); others remained uninhabited after the withdrawal of troops under Theodosius until late medieval times.[31] In the present state of excavation, it seems safe to conclude only that the Ostrogoths did not systematically garrison the passes, nor, for that matter, did the Lombards who succeeded them. Theodoric did, however, maintain Forum Julium as the strategic center for the northern sector of the defenses. Aquileia, the principal regional city, held an Ostrogothic garrison.[32]

The Ostrogoths also maintained outposts at key stations along the Sava. At Kranj and Dravlje, belt buckles and bow fibulae attest to an Ostrogothic presence in the early sixth century.[33] Archaeology at Rifnik also reveals a continuity of settlement under the Ostrogoths.[34] Near the eastern border of Ostrogothic control lay Sirmium. South of the Sava basin, only scattered finds date to the Ostrogothic period. A few burials in Bosnia and Hercegovina may be Ostrogothic, as might several walls as far south as Dubrovnik. Still farther south, several Ostrogothic coins reveal a trade relationship and perhaps an occasional visitor, but they certainly do not constitute proof of settlement.[35] For that matter, Ostrogothic bronze pieces have come to light at Corinth and in the Athenian agora.[36]

The old province of Valeria, where the federates had been established during the late fourth century, remained beyond the Ostrogothic sphere. The inhabitants there were probably confronting endemic internecine warfare. The town of Sopianae survived the establishment of federates in the 380s but deteriorated rapidly until it faded into oblivion sometime during the first half of the fifth century. An epidemic still traceable in the last burials may have hastened its demise.[37] Nothing indicates an Ostrogothic presence at Sopianae, nor have any characteristic artifacts come to light at Intercisa to the northeast of Sopianae and along the Danube itself. The few barbarian pieces that appear to be East Germanic may best be assigned to the late fourth and early fifth centuries, perhaps to the federates settled in Valeria after 380. The site itself was inhabited at least through the sixth century, when the Lombards exerted some influence. The Roman population survived despite the obvious barbarian presence and dominance in the area. No precise terminus can yet be assigned to the city.[38] To the east of Valeria, in Pannonia Prima, lay Savaria. A principal Roman city during the fourth century, Savaria commanded the central hub of the road system running southward from Vindobona and Carnuntum to Poetovio and Emona. By the mid-fifth century, the city was abandoned and in ruins.[39] Thus, in general, the areas of northern and eastern Pannonia were in chaos. Several of the great Roman centers had ceased to exist before the Ostrogoths even entered Pannonia, and others may have lived out their final days in the intense struggles of the midcentury in part spawned by the Ostrogothic arrival. Theodoric saw little need to worry about these areas in the sixth century. Nevertheless, some Ostrogoths may have lived to the north of the Drava, manning outposts along the roads leading to Emona and the Alpine passes. Fenékpuszta, lying at the southwestern end of Lake Balaton (Pelso Lacus in antiquity), may have been such a place, but as our previous discussion of Fenékpuszta revealed, it and other sites in the area were ethnically diffuse, with only minor Ostrogothic presence.

Thus in central Illyricum the Ostrogoths loosely controlled a wedge of land largely confined to the Drava and Sava basins and extending along this corridor to the immediate area of Sirmium, which according to Ennodius was at the extreme edge of the Ostrogothic dominion.[40] To the south lay Dalmatia, another area of scattered Ostrogothic settlements and influence. The administration of Dalmatia and Pannonia Savia evinced a typical symbiosis of traditional Roman government and the Gothic military command necessary in these exposed areas. Salona was the principal city of Dalmatia, and it definitely held a Gothic garrison, as well as other Goths not in the garrison. In a letter to Osuin, *vir illustris* and *comes* at Salona, Theodoric instructed him to arm the inhabitants of the city and instruct them in the use of weapons.[41] The order to train and equip the inhabitants may have applied only to the Goths, but surely the garrison was already armed. Therefore, the instruction of the inhabitants must have referred to the nongarrison personnel. The exposed situation of Dalmatia probably demanded a militia reserve of all able-bodied males, including those of the native population.

Salona was the scene of the first battles in the Justinianic War, when the Goths under Asinarius, Gripas, and others engaged the Roman forces under Mundo while negotiations were being conducted between Theodahad and Justinian. At that time the walls of Salona fell into disrepair and had to be rebuilt by the Byzantine general Constantianus after he had driven out Gripas for the last time.[42] The actions of Gripas and the other Gothic leaders were in accord with the independent command of marcher-lords of a later date. The border areas were supposedly commanded by those closest to the throne, a policy that recognized the value of their loyalty as well as the need for proven commanders along the frontier. The Roman legal structure seems to have continued to exist alongside the Gothic military command in Dalmatia.

Sirmium geographically and strategically was at the extreme end of a frail line stretching outward from Theodoric's court. If the Gepids or the Byzantines mounted a resurgence in the upper Balkans, the area around Sirmium would be the first to be affected. The city was guarded by an alliance of senior lords under a *retenator* charged with the defense of the city. These Roman lords probably commanded what, if anything, remained of Roman forces and the local militia. The inhabited portion of Sirmium must have been only a small fraction of this once-prosperous administrative center. Ennodius, a pitiful and terribly sketchy authority but nonetheless unique, reported that the rulers had so completely neglected the defenses that the Gepids moved in unopposed. Once established in the city, they used it as a base for random attacks into the countryside. Theodoric grew incensed when the Roman rulers proved impotent against his lifelong foes, who now threatened his hold over the provinces and roads leading to Italy. Perhaps he even knew the Gepidic *ductor* Gundeuth personally from the battles on the Ulca. From his *comitatus*, Theodoric appointed Pitzia to take command of a Gothic army dispatched from Italy and in his name drive the Gepids back and reestablish Gothic control permanently.[43]

At the opening of the Sirmium War, a new element disrupted the equilibrium in the area. Mundo, a Hun by ancestry, broke his pact with the Gepids and struck out on his own, with recruits drawn from barbarians and brigands from beyond the Danube, probably an area considered within the Gepidic sphere. Mundo threatened to destroy the Byzantine-Gepid control of the area lying beyond Sirmium in the vicinity of Singidunum and Dacia Ripensis. The Byzantines countered his moves with the dispatch of Sabinianus, *magister militum per Thraciam*, and their newest allies, the Bulgars. They defeated Mundo, but at an abandoned watchtower on the Danube called Herta he joined forces with Pitzia. According to Jordanes, Pitzia's troops numbered 2,000 foot and 500 horse. Although the Ostrogothic contingent did defeat the opposing Bulgars, the battle was inconclusive.[44] Since both sides were unable or unwilling to sacrifice more lives, the *status quo ante* returned. Sabinianus accepted the restoration of Ostrogothic control at Sirmium, and the Ostrogoths gave up any designs on expanding their power in the area beyond Sirmium. The Sirmians, that is to say, the Roman indigenous population, received anew their rights and traditions, *praecepta*, held from the Ostrogoths.[45] These probably included the appointment of a new *retenator* from among them. In general, however, the indigenous peoples suffered more from the abuses of war.[46] Pitzia may have stayed in the area, perhaps heading a modest settlement of Ostrogoths in the countryside, for his name never reentered the historical record. Some of his men did return to Italy; a few rose to prominence.[47] By the spring of 535, Sirmium was again nominally Byzantine, but in reality it and Dacia Ripensis were under the Gepids.[48]

The Sirmium War illustrates the Ostrogothic military and political structures at work under Theodoric perhaps better than any other incident. The eastern frontier was an area of vital concern for the Ostrogothic Kingdom, but there was no thought of a massive settlement or of rigorous military garrisoning. The Ostrogoths were too few and their center of power in northern Italy too far removed to monitor events directly and exert lasting military pressure. Moreover, they maintained the outlines of Roman administration and even apparently entrusted the defense of key cities like Sirmium to Romans. Their own "soldiers" in the area were widely dispersed, but when occasion demanded, the central government dispatched effective personnel to resurrect Ostrogothic fortunes. Despite their intrinsic weakness throughout the northern half of Illyricum, the Ostrogoths were the most important single power. Modest indications of their influence do extend beyond their areas of physical occupation. Culturally, at least, the Ostrogoths extended the traditional links between Italy and her neighbors to the northeast. Italy was safe from attack from the east.[49]

Theodoric was eventually able to recruit some Gepids to serve in southern Gaul. The *saio* Veranus supervised their march through Venetia and Liguria and ordered the local Goths and Romans to make supplies available for their purchase. Three gold solidi were set aside for their expenses, rather than the customary rations in kind.[50] Purchasing supplies instead of carrying a large baggage train would have hastened their passage. Theodoric was hopeful that under such circumstances the transfer to Gaul would be peaceful. These events are usually placed near the end of his reign (ca. 523–26) and reemphasize that the true nature of the Gotho-Gepidic wars was essentially that of a series of feuds and rivalries among the nobilities and their warbands. The majority of the Goths and Gepids shared a common lifestyle and could readily communicate and, at least in this instance, cooperate.

The northern Alpine areas, roughly modern Austria and Switzerland, also aroused Ostrogothic concern. The meager results of place-name studies support the overall conclusion that in the north, as in northern Illyricum, the Ostrogoths were thinly scattered and relied heavily upon small units and the active participation of the indigenous inhabitants in their own defense.[51] The safety of the Alpine areas and ultimately northern Italy itself rested upon Theodoric's attempt to create a network of buffer kingdoms along the northern periphery to check the Franks and others. Secondly, garrisons were established in key passes and road junctions.[52] The Raetians were the cornerstone of the defensive system within the boundaries of immediate Ostrogothic control. They were to entangle "the wild and cruel nations beyond" until the Ostrogoths could march to their aid. A *ducatus Raetiarum* was appointed on each indiction with the rank of *vir spectabilis.*[53] The *ducatus* Servatus, either a Roman or Romanized Raetian, appears in the *Variae,* where he is ordered to investigate a charge of slave stealing brought against the Breones (a people living near the Brenner Pass) by one Maniarius.[54] Although the *ducatus Raetiarum* was a distinct office needing a special formula for its bestowal, the general outline for Raetia is similar to that of other frontier provinces, including Pannonia Savia and Noricum Mediterraneum, with a *praeses* (provincial governor) involved in tax collection and a Gothic *comes* commanding the garrisons.[55]

Fixing the location of residences has attracted considerable attention. A reasonable hypothesis would place the *praeses* at Chur and the *dux* nearer the frontier, perhaps at Bregenz. Chur has long been popularly identified as the Theodoricopolis of the Anonymous Geographer of Ravenna.[56] In truth, the riddle of Theodoricopolis is still not completely resolved. Moreover, excavations at Chur prove that despite at least two decades of Ostrogothic rule, there was never a Gothic settlement there.[57] At Teurnia, the last capital of Noricum Mediterraneum, an inscription dating to the early sixth century was set up honoring a certain Ursus *vir spectabilis*, thereby suggesting that a basically similar administrative structure prevailed to the south. The exact boundaries of Ostrogothic Raetia are also still in dispute.[58] Nonetheless, it seems safe to conclude that most of eastern Switzerland fell under his jurisdiction and that Theodoric may have sought to strengthen its defenses by settling some Alamanni there after their disastrous struggles against Clovis, whom he admonished to keep his hands off. Perhaps he established them in the Rheintal just south of the Bodensee.[59] Theodoric, an old federate commander himself, would not have had to ponder long on how to utilize such homeless bands.

Thus Theodoric extended his sway to Raetia I and opened diplomatic ties with the peoples beyond the Rhine, including the Thuringians, Burgundians, and the Alamanni.[60] Garrisons in the Alpine passes monitored the flow of people and trade. Verruca, a fort (*castellum*) on the Adige River guarding a major descent route above Trent, was "a key that unlocks a kingdom."[61] At Aosta, sixty men and their families stood watch over the traffic going through the Bernard passes.[62] The strategic area between the upper Drava and the Danube was also garrisoned with small settlements along the Glan, Gorschita, and Gurk rivers in Carinthia.[63] In these outposts the Goths set up house, just as had the *limitanei* under the Romans.[64] They could not repel a concerted invasion but might hold out behind the enemy's advancing forces to harass his supplies. More typically, however, they kept brigands at bay and traffic flowing. The stabilization of the Alpine areas and the Rhone valley stimulated a resurgence of transalpine trade. Ostrogothic materials arrived in the north soon after Theodoric's assumption of power in Italy. Raetia in particular entered into a prolonged trade relationship still demonstrable in the numerous fibulae, Ostrogothic coins, and various other items of dress.[65] Indeed, as we have seen, materials from Ostrogothic workshops were widely disseminated, especially bow fibulae, coins, and the rare but important spangenhelmets.

The movement of Gepids across northern Italy toward the northwest as well as the settlement of Alamannic refugees in parts of Switzerland attest that Provence and the western Alpine areas were very troublesome frontier provinces needing constant attention. At the very outset of the kingdom, the Burgundians had posed such a threat to northwestern Italy that Theodoric bought peace and helped ransom captives from their raids.[66] Beyond the Burgundians, the Franks seemed to be chafing for a fight. By 509 the Burgundians and Ostrogoths had struck an alliance of mutual convenience against the Franks. In that year the Ostrogothic *dux* Mammo invaded Provence and began a long period of direct Ostrogothic activity, usually in concert with the Burgundians. In 534, after the Ostrogoths had been withdrawn to fight in Italy, the Burgundian Kingdom fell to the Franks.[67] Until their withdrawal, the Ostrogoths had maintained the Roman governmental apparatus.

Gaul continued to have a praetorian prefect under the Ostrogoths; indeed, none other than Liberius—the mastermind of settlements—held the post from ca. 510 until 534. As prefect, Liberius played an important role in planning and implementing military campaigns.[68] Beneath the praetorian prefect, the *vicarius praefectorum* was charged with the routine tasks of government, including logistical support for the Gothic troops. A certain Gemellus, who had already served Theodoric in lesser capacities, was *vicarius* in 508–511 and held the rank of *vir spectabilis*. Half a dozen requests for action are addressed to him in the *Variae* by Theodoric. He continued in office briefly after Liberius became prefect—ransoming captives, overseeing tax relief, and holding legal hearings.[69] As *vicarius*, Gemellus was charged with organizing the supply of the garrisons along the Durance River. He was instructed to dispatch ships from Marseilles forthwith.[70] A Gothic *comes* also served in Provence; *comes* Marabad is known by name. Toward the end of Theodoric's reign, conditions so deteriorated that a permanent *dux* was stationed there and seems to have taken over even the legal functions of the *comes*.[71] The system of marginal Ostrogothic presence superimposed on existing populations still responsible for government and local defense soon proved insufficient in Provence. The letters of Ennodius to Liberius attest that the Ostrogoths physically settled around Arles, Ennodius's ancestral home and the residence of his family. In 510–11 the Franks wrought unusual destruction throughout the province, forcing Theodoric to grant a provincial tax reduction instead of allowing only individuals to seek case-by-case relief.[72] When Clovis destroyed the crops, grain was shipped from the Italian ports to Arles to relieve famine. Under such trying circumstances, the Ostrogothic commander of the garrison at Avignon was admonished to tighten the discipline of his troops who were plundering the Romans. Life in Provence was the very contrast to garrison duty elsewhere.[73] At places like Aosta, regular pay (usually in kind) and proper supplies were the principal concerns of the commanders; the monotonous routines of pass defense and watching merchants trudge along the highways were seldom broken.[74] But the Franks kept the Goths in Provence at the ready until sometime shortly after Witigis mounted the throne and the garrisons were ordered back to face Belisarius.

Since military prowess was the essential quality of leadership, service on the frontiers provided an important path to advancement. Tulum's rise to the rank of *dux* began when as a youth he fought with Pitzia in the Sirmium War. Next he commanded one of several campaigns against Clovis, in which he ably defended a key bridge on the Rhone near Arles. Later he returned to Gaul as Theodoric's commander to overhaul the provincial defenses. Once it became clear that a permanent solution demanded a resident ducal commander rather than the usual *comes* paired with the Roman governor, Theodoric appointed *dux* Wilitancus, and rewarded Tulum with large tracts of land, probably in southern Gaul, where his experience and followers were so desperately needed.[75] The Roman Cyprianus also served at Sirmium and rose to high office.[76] The future king Witigis likewise proved his mettle around Sirmium.

The *duces* were the highest military leaders in Ostrogothic society, and their very presence in a frontier zone attested to the gravity of the situation. Their functions were primarily but not exclusively military. Wilitancus was ordered to see justice done in a case of adultery. While a Gothic soldier was fighting in Gaul, his spouse had found another.[77] The *duces*' power over their men was virtually unchallengeable and the subject of abuse. Theodoric doubtless regretted his appointment of Gudui as *dux* when charges of enslavement of his fellow Goths reached the king's ear.[78] Other *duces* are also known. Tremonus commanded the Goths at Aterna in Samnium during the Justinianic War. *Duces* Uraias, nephew of Witigis, and Hildibadus, commander of the strategic garrison at Verona, vied for the kingship until the latter's kinship to Theudis, regent and later king in Spain, gave him an edge during the crises following the capture of Witigis and Ravenna. *Dux* Hunila commanded the force dispatched to Perusia by Witigis. Finally there is the case of *dux* Eraric, whose followers declared him king in 541 after the murder of Hildibadus.[79]

Eraric was a subtribal *dux* of the Rogi, who had only joined the

Ostrogothic confederacy under Theodoric. The Rogi had steadfastly refused to intermarry with other Goths and preserved their own customs. At his elevation, Eraric was obviously the leader of a traditional subunit of the confederacy, which had presumably settled together and still constituted an identifiable military and social group.[80] The other *duces* probably also belonged to the leading families of the Ostrogoths, and some at least could probably recall lineages going far back in Gothic history—perhaps to some of the great families mentioned in the *Getica*. By elevating such men to the rank of *dux*, as Theodoric clearly did Gudui, the monarchy placed tribal leadership upon the secure foundations of traditional regional and local allegiance. Under lesser men than Theodoric, such concentrations of power proved dangerous and, at least in the struggle between Uraias and Hildibadus, destructive of whatever unity still prevailed among the Goths.

In conclusion prior to the War of Justinian, the Ostrogoths had made considerable strides in developing military strategy and defense. The type of success witnessed at Sirmium and in the Alpine areas, indeed even in the troublesome Rhone valley, was an accomplishment of no mean proportion. To be sure, the basic technological aspects of warfare had not changed. The Goths still fought with the same weapons and in the same manner as their ancestors had at Adrianople. The Ostrogoths apparently used swords produced either in Roman shops or with very similar techniques. Although the absence of weapons in burials prohibits specific comparisons, the great ado made over the damascene sword from the Thuringians speaks eloquently enough. The pattern-welding method that increased the carbon content and hence the strength of the steel blade was mysterious and unknown among the Goths.[81]

The Ostrogothic military achieved a reputation of strength against other barbarians primarily through building upon their own traditions, but they also accepted certain Roman organizational and support systems. The Gothic offices of *comes* and *dux* were tied more closely to the central authority, which at least under Theodoric appointed them, and evolved in conjunction with the surviving aspects of Roman government. Thus, the frontier provinces, like Italy itself, prospered from the symbiosis of Goth and Roman. Indeed, if the Ostrogoths were more capable militarily than other barbarians, it was an outgrowth of their ability to work with Romans in an atmosphere of cooperation—the very essence of Theodoric's vision. The War of Justinian destroyed the Ostrogothic Kingdom, but try as they might, the Byzantines were unable to dissolve the bonds of Italian society that now included many Goths. For the Italians, at least, the line between aggressor and savior remained blurred until the very end of Ostrogothic rule.

9

The End of the Ostrogothic Kingdom

THEODORIC BUILT HIS kingdom upon the personal capacities of the monarch to control both Goths and Romans. He manipulated both to add their particular strengths to the state through the central government, but except for the instance of his daughter, he rejected the complete merging of the two traditions as unworkable. Indeed, the success of his government and that of the Ostrogothic Kingdom as a whole depended upon the fair-minded juxtaposition of personnel and functions into an overlapping system. The monarch assumed a position similar to that of a man walking on stilts, one support Gothic, the other Roman. He alone controlled the direction of policy and could see over the shoulders of his ministers toward a distant objective of peace secured through competitive cooperation between Goths and Romans. His vision allowed the Roman senatorial class to achieve greater influence in matters of state and government than their peers in the East. In this respect they continued in the steps of their fifth-century forebears, who had reentered active government as the emperors in Ravenna riveted their attention on the disintegration of the West and the endless intrigues of court. The Goths enjoyed the fruits of the settlement, lived in several enclaves, and still prided themselves on their prowess. Many members of the nobility grew from warlords of the migrations into powerful regional leaders. Some went on to participate in government and Roman culture.

By the time of his death, Theodoric had established his vision as a governmental norm, and as such it survived his feeble successors. Nevertheless, without a respected and resolute king on the throne, latent forces, only temporarily subdued under Theodoric, quickly emerged. Amalasuintha and Athalaric proved themselves unable to wear Theodoric's mantle. Athalaric increasingly fell into the hands of the nobility, who educated him in "manly ways" as opposed to the culture of Roman sterility taught by his mother. When the struggle for his mind proved too much for the youthful king, Athalaric turned to drink and debauchery. His early demise left his mother alone at the apex of a masculine society still governed, in part, by the sword. She turned to her cousin Theodahad as the oldest male heir to Theodoric. Perhaps she deceived herself into believing that she could dominate this would-be "Roman man of letters," a devotee of Plato and the greatest landowner in Liguria. Her mistake in judgment led to her death and gave legal pretext for Justinian's invasion. There is little reason to recount in any detail the long and bitter struggle of the war against Justinian, except to illustrate once more the underlying features of Ostrogothic society and the promise they held out to Italy. Procopius has provided an account of several hundred pages for the analyst and the curious, but his narrative is not free from prejudice.

Procopius was well aware that the Goths had built a strong base of support among various elements of the Roman population, which of course he regarded as shortsighted and foolish. He recounts a story told of Theodahad. The king placed great store in sorcery and prophecy and one day summoned a noted Hebrew prophet, who said:

> "Confine three groups of ten swine each in three huts. After giving them respectively the names of Goths, Romans, and the soldiers of the emperor, wait for a specific number of days before disturbing them in any way." Theodahad waited as instructed. Then on the appointed day they went into the huts and examined the swine. They found those named for Goths dead except for two and of those named for the emperor's soldiers only a few had died. When they looked at those called by Roman names they discovered that despite a general loss of hair most had lived.[1]

The story goes on to report that in this way Theodahad foresaw the outcome of the war and so lost what little resolve he had for battle: the Romans would lose half their people and possessions, and only a few Goths would survive. Such accuracy suggests considerable hindsight, yet the narrative is instructive. The Goths and Romans were collectively the losers, while the soldiers of the emperor, most of whom were barbarian mercenaries, were the victors. The hoped-for fundamental alliance of the two peoples of Italy was reasserted under Totila, but with increasing difficulty brought on by the miseries and outrages of war.

Totila had just retaken Naples and was about to march northward toward Rome when he dispatched a letter to the Roman senate. He pointedly asked the senate to remember the benefactions of Theodoric and Amalasuintha in contrast to the tax levies of Justinian's paymaster Alexander (538–41). He spoke of one and the same cause for Goths and Italians—the restoration of olden times and the expulsion of the Greeks.[2] For him and the senators, he hoped, the dreams of imperial unity were dead, victims of war, replaced by the proven potentials of peaceful coexistence in Italy. Later, after his second capture of the city, Totila refused to destroy Rome, and instead repaired the damages and established Goths and Romans there, including members of the senate he had held as hostages in Campania. According to Procopius, he did so in order to increase his own prestige in the eyes of the Franks, but certainly a more immediate concern was the persuasion of the Roman population itself. Finally in 549, as had Theodoric during his ceremonial visit to Rome, Totila held games in the circus—the last ever held.[3] His coins also continued to protray the theme of concord for all to see. The war provided numerous examples of Gothic-Roman cooperation, not all of it forced and artificial.

When Justinian launched his armies against the Ostrogoths, he may have envisioned a quick victory of Belisarius, like that he had achieved over the Vandals. If so, the emperor was gravely mistaken but not foolishly naive. After all, Theodahad was well known. Even before he was made king, he had entered into negotiations with Justinian to hand over all his lands in Tuscany in return for a sizable sum, so that he himself could retire to Constantinople and there presumably read Plato in the company of scholars.[4] Soon after Theodahad's mistreatment and slaying of Amalasuintha gave Justinian a *casus belli*, he offered to place 3,000 troops at the emperor's disposal, to pay an annual tribute in gold, to accord the emperor the honor of designating candidates for the patriciate and membership in the senate, to have the people acclaim the emperor before the king in all public ceremonies, and, finally, to grant immunity from royal taxation to senators and churchmen, thus securing their loyalty and support for the emperor. As if this were not enough, Theodahad suggested to the imperial envoy Peter that still further concessions might be made if

Justinian rejected his offer, essentially a return to federate status. Theodahad would then relinquish all Italy in return for lands in the East where he could forget the stress of kingship and enjoy the bucolic life of a gentleman farmer. Justinian was happy to reject the return of sovereignty in return for absolute possession and so instructed his officials to find royal lands for Theodahad. Belisarius was to depart Sicily and seize the reins of government at Ravenna from the would-be philosopher.[5] Obviously there was, indeed, none of the resolve and militancy of Theodoric in his nephew. No wonder Theodoric shunned a complete fusion of races and traditions with this painful reminder present. Justinian held an easy victory in his hands. However, even before he could contemplate his success, the real power holders in Ostrogothic Italy—the Ostrogothic nobility—took action.

Far away at Salona in Dalmatia, the Gothic marcher-lords, Asinarius and Gripas, went into battle without consulting Ravenna, in fact, while Theodahad was still involved in negotiations. They engaged Mundo, a Hun and former ally in the Sirmium War, who now led the Roman forces along with his son. A general melée shed much blood but produced little of consequence, although Mundo and his son fell in the battle, as did many Gothic leaders. Gripas counterattacked and cleared much of Dalmatia of Roman troops. Salona returned to Gothic hands, but her defenses were in desperate disrepair. When the Byzantines launched another offensive, Gripas quickly retired to Ravenna. The Greek commander, Constantine, reoccupied Salona and repaired the fortifications. Round one had gone to the imperial forces, but they were unable to sustain the offensive. The garrisons in the Julian Alps and the valleys beyond barred the gates, so that Italy remained beyond reach from the northeast. Salona itself soon witnessed renewed Gothic attacks.[6]

Italy's relative invulnerability from the north until Witigis ordered the garrisons to depart derived from the successful frontier program begun under Theodoric. However, the Byzantines also had other and more direct approaches. Rome was the hub of the transportation system for all but the Po Valley and remained the demographic and cultural center of Italy. Despite centuries of gradual erosion of her monuments and a declining population, Rome still held more people than her environs could hope to support. Since the granaries in North Africa had long ago opened their doors to others, first Vandals and more recently Belisarius, Ostrogothic Rome depended upon Sicily for food and shippers to transport it to Portus. Gradual silting had closed Ostia to traffic. All of these things were public knowledge. Alaric had unsuccessfully tried to capture Sicily after his sack of Rome, and now Belisarius and later Totila pursued the same relentless strategic logic.

Tactically, however, the Byzantine army led by Belisarius always had to overcome the enemy without jeopardizing many lives. In short, manpower was never adequate to sustain a major campaign. Belisarius's personal guard of some 7,000 formed the heart of the army. In addition to these men, paid at his own expense, the general had 4,000 cavalry and perhaps 3,000 infantry. Minor additions of Huns, Slavs, Antes, and even a few Goths like Bessas rounded out a force totaling approximately 15,000 men. Opposing them were potentially at least twice their number of Goths. Neither side held a clear dominance. On the battlefield the difference was, according to Belisarius, that "practically all the Romans and their allies, the Huns, are good mounted bowmen, but not a man among the Goths has had practice in this brand, for their horsemen are accustomed to use only spears and swords, while their bowmen enter battle on foot and under cover of the heavy-armed men."[7] Yet despite this failing, the Goths usually held their own.

The shortage of manpower prolonged the war in Italy for decades. Rome dominated their thinking, but neither side possessed the necessary forces to man the long stretches of walls. Witigis's siege of Rome took the form of a guessing game. Where and when would the attack come? Or how might the defenders be deceived into leaving a section of wall undefended long enough for the attackers to marshal an overwhelming assault? Once the enemy withdrew from Rome, a new task confronted the occupiers. In order to secure Rome and win true victory, merely taking Rome itself was not enough; the would-be conquerors had also to control the interlocking network of roads. The only way to achieve this control was to drive opposing garrisons from the cities along the key routes and garrison them oneself. Alas, garrisons further decreased the troop strength available for sustained offensive action and weakened the hold on Rome itself. The Goths proved themselves equally as adept and troubled with the game as the imperial forces.[8] For years the war seemingly walked very slowly counterclockwise up the Via Flaminia, then northwest on the Via Aemilia, and finally back to Rome. The Byzantines periodically tried to root out Gothic resilience by attacking their settlement areas along the Po and especially in Picenum and Samnium where often women and children remained virtually undefended, but the Greeks met with only marginal success.[9] The Goths rallied behind their nobility. *Dux* Tremenus held Aterna in Samnium, for example. At Uriventus the Goths with Albilias fought on even after their supplies ran short.[10]

Sometimes the Gothic garrisons held out for many months, as did the men at Uriventus, but at other places they vanished into the mountains, only to reappear once the imperial forces had departed. Logistical problems soon came to the fore, overriding all other considerations. After the early campaigns, the supply system strained and snapped, leaving both sides to scrounge the countryside for food. The Byzantines were only marginally better off. In fact, the Ostrogoths had sold supplies to Belisarius during a crucial stage in his war against the Vandals. Horses were then in such limited numbers that the Ostrogoths had set up open markets.[11] Sieges and countersieges often hinged on the supply trains' getting through. That was especially true around Rome, where living off the swampy land was virtually impossible. The Moors in Belisarius's army were particularly aggressive against Gothic supply areas, killing the guards at night and driving off the flocks.[12] The real losers, true perhaps to the Hebrew prophecy, were the Roman indigenous populations, who for two decades faced a political dilemma in allegiance—how to accommodate the current victor without completely severing ties with the opposition and all the while hoping to avoid starvation and disease. Few were exempt from suffering, not even the senatorial families. Witigis had many senatorial hostages massacred at Ravenna, and this act temporarily brought many Romans over to the Greek cause.[13]

Although the army was always predominantly Gothic, non-Gothic personnel had figured into defensive planning from the beginning, especially in the frontier areas. The war compelled the Goths and Byzantines to force urban militias to help man the walls of their cities. Farmers and civilians also dug ditches and pits.[14] During the early phases of the war, Witigis recalled the frontier troops from both Gaul and Venetia to fight in Italy.[15] But by the late 540s, manpower was again critical, so desperate in fact that Totila, like his adversaries, accepted deserters from the other side. Totila treated these "with full and complete equality with the Goths."[16] When not even such drastic measures as recruiting deserters could fill the gaps, both sides opened their ranks to slaves and tenants. Totila knew that their labor was sorely needed on the crops, but he reluctantly agreed to enroll them.[17] However, they remained servile in status, for Totila had no illusions of leading a peasant revolt or establishing an egalitarian state.[18] Not surprisingly, the Roman tax system broke down completely, replaced by direct expropriation by treasury or military officials.[19] The hoarded wealth of the monarchy was gone forever. Totila had to try to reconstitute a war chest from his collections in southern Italy, but they were sufficient only for the present. The Gothic army ran short of horses and weapons, yet the Romans were often even worse off.[20] Roman supply problems escalated once Totila established a naval blockade of some four hundred ships from Naples to divide Rome from her Sicilian grain. Even a special relief force mounted by Pope Vigilius was denied entry. Indeed, entire crews were slain, and the hands of the bishop in charge were severed as a brutal warning not to succor Rome.[21]

Already at Naples in 536, the complexity of the situation was obvious. Before marching on Naples, Belisarius had encountered but slight opposition. His conquest of Sicily had gone smoothly. Only at Palermo did the Gothic garrison offer any resistance, but they were bested when Belisarius used his ships to outflank their position by fixing them with platforms high on the masts for his archers. With Sicilian grain now at his disposal and denied to the Ostrogoths, Naples, with a magnificent harbor and port facilities, became the major goal. Unless Naples were taken, the Gothic garrison there could harass imperial supplies at will, but if the city lay in imperial hands, the march on Rome could proceed forthwith. Time and supplies went hand in hand. So when Stephen, a prominent citizen of Naples, implored Belisarius to pass his city by, the general could not agree. He proffered as excuse that the imperial sovereignty was at issue. Stephen accepted his words and returned to Naples and his fellow citizens.

The discussions among the citizenry were dominated by Pastor and Asclepiodotus, speaking astutely to the Romans of the probable imperial government of Naples after the war and of the possible benefits of loyalty to the Goths. The Goths, for their part, wavered. At first they seemed content to accept Belisarius's offer of amnesty and freedom to go home. After all, they were outnumbered, and the king's own son-in-law Ebrimuth had recently surrendered Rhegium without a fight. They were just part of the crowd listening to Pastor and Asclepiodotus, citizens too, and in a special dilemma at that, for Theodahad held members of their families as hostages to guarantee their loyalty. How much lower could Gothic kingship sink? But when the Jewish representatives volunteered supplies and assistance in manning the walls, the Gothic troops pledged to fight. The whole city rallied, and for twenty days the walls held. Chance worked against the defenders when a curious Isaurian in Belisarius's force happened upon an unguarded entry through a severed aqueduct.[22] Nevertheless, until the final moments of the struggle, when the mob murdered Pastor and Asclepiodotus, Naples stood firm and basically united. At Naples the Ostrogothic-Roman symbiosis proved strong and resilient, even under a pathetic monarch.

Good relations with the Roman population of the towns paid dividends at Naples, but elsewhere garrisons occasionally collected a different bounty. At Rhegium, Ebrimuth, son-in-law of Theodahad, governed with his followers (literally those sworn to him) and generated open hostility.[23] Similarly, the command of the garrison at Avignon in the Rhone Valley had once been reminded by Theodoric to show the people that the Goths were their protectors, not plunderers.[24] From time to time there was terrible slaughter of civilians on both sides. In 539, Uraias allowed his soldiers to slay the male inhabitants of Milan; Totila's men left Tibur piled with corpses.[25] Belisarius's atrocities after he finally took Naples in 536 might have gone unrecorded except for the brief entry in the *Liber Pontificalis* that "he slew both the Goths and all the inhabitants of Naples and sacked it and spared not even the churches." His men killed priests and captives and apparently took delight in dispatching "husbands in the presence of their wives."[26] The majority of the Roman population displayed no real enthusiasm for either side but wanted peace, and that they could not have. As late as Totila's first siege of Rome (545–46), there were still Arian priests in the city, unharmed until the Byzantine general John then expelled them. Perhaps he feared that they might become a rallying point for the Gothic sympathies still current. Totila was, indeed, trying to enlist the Romans against the Greeks at this very time. His first attempt to revive their memories of Theodoric failed when John captured the messengers, but his expedient worked of having his offer of amnesty painted in large script on walls around the city.[27] Surely the presence of Arian priests in Rome testifies to the success of Ostrogothic policies of peaceful cooperation. If there had been much anti-Gothic sentiment, the priests would have vanished years before. Where there were no Goths, the inhabitants had no tangible feelings either for or against the Goths. Official Gothic tolerance and generally enlightened regard for Roman traditions went unnoticed. Apulia and Campania were such areas; they did not hesitate to welcome Byzantine forces and remained faithful to them despite mistreatment. Obviously fair government from Ravenna was not a sufficient cause for loyalty.[28] Indeed, a reading of Procopius raises the question whether anyone other than the respective nobilities envisioned loyalty to the state at all. The Ostrogoths did not win over many Romans from their own mundane concerns, nor did Belisarius or Narses, but the leaders of both sides tried. The fact is that the longer the war raged, the more society simply unraveled into personal dilemmas. The atrocities at Milan, Naples, Rome, and elsewhere probably do not reflect anything more than the violence and frustrations of often ill-supplied and vengeful soldiers. This war was, in that regard, too much like so many others.[29]

Totila's siege of Rome brought terrible suffering upon the Roman population. Gradual starvation and relentless requisitions of supplies and men by Bessas, the notorious Ostrogoth in command of the Roman garrison, reduced the people to dire circumstances. Even members of the senate were reportedly begging for bread; among them was Rusticiana, the daughter of Symmachus and widow of Boethius. She had given freely of her wealth to the poor as long as she had had anything to give. The first sweep of the bubonic plague struck an already frail city. The corpses dramatized the rapid disintegration of a great urban center. Bessas could not hold the loyalty of his troops as well as Belisarius, and when the last attempts to relieve the beleaguered fortress failed, the Isaurians opened the gates to the Goths. After the death of Theodoric perhaps only Totila had the power to demand compliance to his orders. In accordance with his commands, Roman women were safe. Despite their cravings, the Ostrogothic soldiers abstained from rapine, which was so frequently the victor's tax upon the conquered. Not even Rusticiana fell into their hands, although the demands for her death were loud. The Goths knew well her destruction of Theodoric's statues, inviolate until she bribed the Roman guards to allow her to destroy them in vengeance for her father and husband. Totila spared her as well. In his victory speech he echoed his belief that the war was against the Greeks, not the Romans. He reminded the Romans of the benefits of Gothic rule, their prosperity, and the offices and honors they had held. Finally, Totila dispatched two Romans to Justinian with a letter. He asked the emperor to recall the peace and prosperity of the joint rule of Anastasius and Theodoric and offered him a chance to return to those days and an alliance against any other imperial foe.[30]

While the embassy traveled to Constantinople, events elsewhere decided Totila upon Rome's destruction. The Greek general John and a few Antae seized a key pass in Lucania and beat off a small force of Goths and many rustics from the indigenous population trying to dislodge them.[31] Totila knew that his forces were incapable of defending Rome and simultaneously attacking southward. The only solution at hand was to make Rome indefensible and worthless. The same logic became increasingly applicable as the war dragged on. Witigis had already proven at Pesaro, Fano, and Milan that towns without walls were not likely to be reoccupied by the Romans after the Goths left.[32] Totila leveled the walls of Spoleto, Beneventum, and Tibur (Tivoli) and parts of those at Naples and Rome. That is not to say that he gave up the garrisoning of towns. In fact, he later rebuilt the walls at Tibur to hold a garrison. His strategy was to limit the number of towns to a strategic group, which he had forces to hold, and thereby deny the Romans the opportunities for counterblockades from nearby fortresses.[33] The walls of Rome were more than his forces could destroy. Finally he listened to Belisarius's urgings from Portus to refrain from destroying such a noble city, whose image gave its ruler fame and whose mistreatment would brand him forever. With the senate in tow, Totila moved south. Along the way, the senatorial families were placed under guard in Campania while Totila attacked the Byzantines in Apulia in an effort to eject John and cut off supplies coming from southern Italy and Sicily. Rome stood empty; not a single soul remained.[34] Belisarius hesitated to reoccupy the city for over a month. Perhaps fear of disease gave him pause.

If the war produced any victors among the Goths, they were select members of the nobility. As we have seen, the traditional leaders of Gothic society found Athalaric and his mother unacceptable, so much so that some of them took the youth into their own custody. These same noblemen ultimately rejected Theodahad and elevated Witigis, who had himself won his spurs in battle at Sirmium against the Gepids. Procopius again went to the heart of the Ostrogothic Kingdom when he called Witigis king of both Goths and Italians,[35] but in fact his power was based on the tenuous allegiance of his nobility and their followers. Circumstance and his own strategic failing worked against Witigis from the start and undermined his limited power over the nobility. His withdrawal of frontier forces left the entire arch of the Alpine areas ripe for new conquerors and was accomplished only with the consent of the nobles.[36] The Burgundians lost their independence to the Franks with at least tacit Ostrogothic compliance. The Alamanni too were restless and eager to exploit Ostrogothic weakness in the central Alpine areas.[37] Sirmium again fell nominally within the Byzantine sphere no later than 535, but in reality the Gepids, Erulians, and Sclaveni had by then challenged the Ostrogoths for control.[38] Alas, Witigis wasted his preciously garnered forces against the walls of Rome and Belisarius's guile. Gothic siege tactics against Rome were pathetic. Their rude towers drawn by oxen had little chance. The poor creatures fell to arrows as soon as they approached the walls.

When Witigis proved unable to take Rome and hold the Ostrogothic armies together, the Gothic nobility reasserted its power and cast him into Belisarius's hands. The Byzantines took Ravenna without opposition, leaving only the nobles Hildibadus and Uraias holding out as independent Gothic commanders at war. If the Byzantines had marshaled their strength and attacked the Gothic strongholds around Verona, surely the Ostrogothic Kingdom would have ended then and there. Witigis and his wife Matasuentha seemed quite content in Constantinople. Witigis led Byzantine forces in Asia Minor until his death. Matasuentha was remarried to Germanus, nephew of Justinian and a probable heir to the throne. However, as far as the Goths were concerned, Witigis's reign began and ended at the hands of the Gothic nobility.

The Byzantines lost precious time dividing their booty and quarreling among themselves until Ostrogothic resistance hardened with renewed Roman support. Justinian expected the Italians to pay for their liberation, and his tax collector Alexander was ruthless even by sixth-century standards. Once again the Ostrogoths rallied around their nobility and posed a threat. More than a few Romans were also distressed over Byzantine rule. With the selection of Totila (ca. 545), the Goths chose a gifted warrior and governor, second in their history only to Theodoric himself. However, Totila, like Witigis, Hildibadus, and Eraric, was a member of the nobility, not an Amali. Totila appointed his principal commanders from their ranks, including dukes Scipuar, Gibal, and Gundulf, who had been a bodyguard to Belisarius only a short time before.[39] Even in matters of discipline, the nobles acting through the council were able to oppose his wishes.[40] When he left Rome's walls still basically intact, he again heard their discontent.[41] Theodoric had often asked their advice, but no noble ever raised a strident voice to his and lived to speak again.[42] The war, with its extreme deprivations of the general populace, offered a few nobles a chance to consolidate their holdings and show off their armor. Some of them can still be seen at the head of their warriors even after the last Ostrogothic insurgents surrendered at Campsas in 553.[43]

Despite the handicaps placed upon his leadership by the nobility, Totila was a first-rate general. His long-range siege of Rome and the employment of a sizable fleet manned apparently by Goths ultimately succeeded in bringing Rome to its knees. Unlike Witigis, whose tactics were an outgrowth of the old needs for displaying personal valor in frontal assault and direct combat, Totila waited. He had little choice. He relied on ambush to chop away at the Byzantine cavalry. After leaving Rome, he attacked Lucania at night while the Romans slept. His fame grew, and his forces remained loyal until he could challenge the Romans in open combat—perhaps he had not so appreciated Roman mounted archers as had Belisarius.[44] Certainly there was no point in laying siege to Roman towns, for the sieges of Rome under Witigis had shown beyond question that the Goths still should have followed Fritigern's admonition to "keep peace with walls" delivered before Adrianople in 376.[45] His forces held firm until the Romans were forced to abandon the towns and fight in the open. Throughout these campaigns, the Goths usually held a numerical superiority and were fine warriors individually. Their equipment varied according to rank and service. The infantry still played a key role in Gothic warfare. Soldiers with their long shields formed a wall for the spearmen behind. The cavalry was the elite force and home of the principal nobility, but quite often the cavalry had to retreat within the shield defenses against the Byzantine mounted archers. Some members of the nobility wore armor of gold and silver, with a few spangenhelmets probably atop certain princely heads. Under Totila's command, the Gothic army retrieved some of its reputation. Justinian needed Belisarius elsewhere and searched for a new leader; perhaps he even toyed with the idea of accommodating the Ostrogoths and Italians.

The emperor turned first to aged Liberius. The elderly senator had after all orchestrated the settlements of Odovacar and then Theodoric and had been praetorian prefect of Italy (493–500) and later of Ostrogothic Gaul (510–534) before turning to the East, where he was *praefectus augustalis* (538/39) under Justinian. In 549 Justinian twice designated him to command against the Goths but always delayed assigning him the new troops the task required. In 550 Justinian gave him a fleet to check the Gothic invasion of Sicily but recalled him as too old. Nevertheless, the old gentleman managed to enter Syracuse harbor and attempted to relieve the Gothic siege before withdrawing. When news of his dismissal reached him, he returned to Constantinople, only to be reassigned in the spring of 552 to Spain. His efforts to assist Athanagild in the Visigothic civil war were inconclusive. He witnessed Justinian announce his pragmatic sanction for the governing of reconquered Italy in August 554 and played a major role in its instrumentation before his death at age eighty-nine. He and his wife were buried at Rimini.[46]

Next Justinian looked to his nephew Germanus, second husband of Matasuentha. Germanus began preparations in earnest. Now for the first time the Byzantines had a numerical advantage as well as the tactical benefits of mounted archers. Progress was made against the Goths south of Ravenna, and in the Adriatic the Byzantine navy reestablished control. Then Germanus died, leaving only an unborn son as a hope. Jordanes, in particular, recorded the expectation that perhaps even this baby could somehow rally the forces of reason.

Possibly the two races—Goths and Romans—could indeed live together, just as their noble blood now flowed in unison.[47] His dream was merely that, a flickering vision. Narses, a eunuch and palace chamberlain, took over Germanus's army and added substantial other forces. In 551 he arrived in Italy.

Totila's only hope was to attack immediately, before the full strength of Byzantine arms could assemble. Narses wasted no time in courtly dalliance in Ravenna. By early spring he had stripped numerous garrisons in the north and was busy around Rome. He too feared a war of attrition, for Italy was barren. Justinian might need his troops in Persia at any moment. The battle at Busta Gallorum saw the Romans fighting primarily in mixed array, with a part of the cavalry fighting as infantry in the shield wall. Outnumbered, Totila stalled until an additional 2,000 Goths could assemble from nearby camps. According to Procopius, Totila mounted his great horse and in full dress armor rode out between the armies and began to perform a dance:

> He wheeled his horse around in a circle and then turned him again to the other side and so made him run round and round. And as he rode he hurled his javelin into the air and caught it again as it quivered above him, then passed it rapidly from hand to hand, shifting it with consummate skill, and he gloried in his practice in such matters, falling back on his shoulders, spreading his legs and leaning from side to side.[48]

Where Totila had learned this dance Procopius did not say, but surely he conveyed something purely Gothic to his men as he spun his horse on the plain. Despite his belief in coexistence with Romans and Roman culture, Totila, like Theodoric, remained a Goth. Theodoric would not have had it any other way. The Gothic cavalry, using spears, carried the initial struggle to the enemy but was forced back into the temporary safety of the Gothic infantry. Narses advanced against the Gothic line, now outnumbered and virtually engulfed. The Gothic infantry fought bravely but gave way. Totila himself shed his golden armor and died fighting in the ranks along with some 6,000 others, including almost all the Roman deserters. One account further states that he fell victim to a Byzantine arrow.[49]

Teias became king at the hands of the nobility and ruled briefly from Pavia. His coins were circulated widely, even making their way along the Alpine trade routes into Gaul. His silver coins proclaimed his kingship on the obverse and presented Anastasius I on the reverse. Perhaps that was a final longing to remind people of the good times of Theodoric and Anastasius, just as had Totila on his issues.[50] Teias fell in battle at Mons Lactarius later in 552.[51] The Goths with him were allowed to return to their homes in peace. Some 7,000 held out at Campsas under *dux* Ragnaris, himself a Bittuguric Hun, until 553. Others followed *dux* Aligernus in alliance with Narses in a struggle to protect their homes in northern Italy from their erstwhile allies the Franks. By 554 the Ostrogothic Kingdom was gone. A few Gothic garrisons held out in the north for almost seven years. Finally in 561, the garrisons at Verona and Brixia capitulated. For the most part the Ostrogoths quietly merged into the population of Italy as the synthesis begun under Theodoric continued without direction and without official notice. A few people still claimed to live under "Gothic law" as late as 769, but they were only one small and peculiar group.[52] The Italians—Goths and Romans—now were forced to pay for the war. The victor had other wars to fight.

EPILOGUE

THE OSTROGOTHS TRAVELED a peculiar route in their migrations and in their evolution. To be sure, their history has many parallels to that of other barbarian peoples, particularly their cousins the Visigoths. Yet the Hunnic overlordship, the long experience on the steppes of Russia, and the settlement in Italy gave a distinctive cast to the Ostrogoths. On the one hand, they readily accepted others into the heart of their society, and on the other, the Ostrogoths developed a strong central monarchy under Amalian leadership. Theodoric was unquestionably the greatest Germanic leader of his day. Totila, whose struggles were waged during some of the bleakest hours in western history, also ranks among the best of his contemporaries in Europe. Moreover, the Ostrogoths as a people, not merely their greatest leaders, helped produce some lasting features of the Middle Ages.

Theodoric's enlightened policies toward Roman letters contributed immeasurably to the last flowering of Roman secular culture in the West. His support of the schools and professors in Rome was continued under the Byzantine emperors. Cassiodorus rose to literary renown as a royal servant. Boethius wrote and died a martyr to the senatorial aristocracy and an exemplar of Roman culture along with his father-in-law Symmachus. Theodoric encouraged them and their cultural peers at every turn. Important religious exiles flocked to Italy from the persecutions in the East. Among the foremost refugees was Dionysius Exiguus, whose collection of canons began a chain of law as yet unbroken.[1] Religious toleration was a cornerstone in the restoration of Roman society and the acceptance of Ostrogothic rule. The fruit of this farsightedness showed clearly at Naples when the Jews of the city volunteered to fight alongside the Goths. So too the Ostrogothic acceptance of the Constantinian Compromise in church-state relations built strong foundations of support among many members of the Roman clergy.

A peaceful Italy gave popes like Gelasius and Symmachus time to hammer out a uniquely western position of papal independence. They and their colleagues could even thwart the desire of the secular lords to recover the lands their ancestors had once given to the church.

But many of the great men of this era—Cassiodorus, Boethius, Gelasius, even Pope Symmachus—pointed in a new direction, toward the medieval Christian synthesis. Cassiodorus, without whose *Variae* this study would not exist, turned late in life to his Vivarium and there experimented with the first "Christian university." Indeed, his *Institutes* became a central work for the entire Middle Ages, although his program itself failed to endure. He and his school were probably too scholastic to appeal during the times of trouble to come. Boethius also turned his talents to religion and theological debates in his *Tractates*.

Paul the Deacon, writing in the late eighth century, still regarded Arator, a pupil of Ennodius, as one of the world's greatest poets. Arator was captured in the last siege of Rome and was taken as a hostage with the senatorial assemblage to Campania. Totila either spared his life or he escaped. At any rate, he kept a vow made in captivity to write a metrical version of the *Acts of the Apostles*. He presented the finished copy to Pope Vigilius in 544 and was immediately beset with requests for recitals.[2] His mentor Ennodius left a corpus second in volume only to that of Cassiodorus.

The curious figure of Jordanes haunts us still. The only Germanic historian, he was so deeply imbued with Cassiodorus that their respective contributions to the *Getica* and *Romana* are the subject of endless dispute. Jordanes seems to have entered the priesthood after his conversion to Orthodoxy. Together Jordanes and Cassiodorus shared a vision of peaceful coexistence between the Goths and the Romans, and ultimately perhaps they shared in the despair of seeing bloodshed wash away their dreams. Religious withdrawal held the only true hope for peace. Perhaps that is the true importance of the alleged meeting between King Totila and Saint Benedict of Nursia.

According to Gregory the Great, in 542 Totila sought out Saint Benedict to test his powers and hear his words. As proof of Benedict's divine guidance, Totila sent his swordbearer in his place disguised as king and accompanied by three *comites Gothorum* as escorts. The impostor approached the holy man along with the noble entourage of the *comites* Vulteric, Ruderic, and Blidin. But once in Benedict's presence, the swordbearer fell to his knees in supplication. So too, according to tradition, Totila himself ultimately lay prostrate before the man of God and listened to a sermon on his sins and received his blessing and a prophecy. Totila would rule for nine more years and die in his tenth year. Next Benedict reassured the frightened bishop of Canusinae (Canossa) that Totila would not destroy Rome but that nature would gradually reclaim her.[3] Gregory wrote of these happenings decades later, when the church stood almost alone. Seen in this light, the Ostrogothic Kingdom was indeed a period of transition.

The Ostrogoths preserved many Roman administrative techniques virtually intact. The essential knowledge of urban government and bureaucratic systems never left Italy, not even under the Lombards. In papal lands, Gregory was able to reorganize the system along Roman lines. Justinian accepted the exchange ratios of gold, silver, and bronze coinage as established under Theodoric. In fact, they continued throughout the remainder of Byzantine rule in Italy. Ostrogothic tastes in art and personal dress influenced peoples well beyond the Italian peninsula. Their craftsmen were on the threshold of the "animal style" popularized under the Lombards. Ostrogothic shops produced helmets and fibulae of extraordinary quality. Their spangenhelmets formed an important stage in the evolution of noble battle dress that culminated in the early Middle Ages and to which the great helmet at Sutton Hoo stands as final testament. Ostrogothic control of the Alpine passes quickened economic activity far into Gaul and Germania.

However, the impact of Roman civilization upon the Ostrogoths was uneven. A divergence in the rapidity of Romanization was apparent very early in the Gothic history. That does not mean that only the nobility changed, but they were closer to the principal conveyors of *Romanitas* in late antiquity—the army, the priesthood, and the government—and changed more dramatically, yet they too never completely abandoned their "Gothic" heritage. The gap between the nobles and the common Goths widened in Italy in a great many respects, socially as well as culturally. Yet whenever records reveal ordinary Ostrogoths, they too are reacting to stimuli from Roman civilization. Whether in the everyday functioning of the economy or through their Arian form of Christianity, they could not avoid interacting with the Roman world. Some sought to reject the most flagrant forms of Romanization, such as classical education and what they may have regarded as an effeminate military tradition. Nevertheless, all the inhabitants of Italy lived within the peace and prosperity of the Ostrogothic Kingdom and suffered during its dissolution.

In the final analysis, the history of the Ostrogoths manifests the potentials and pitfalls of the symbiosis of Germans and Romans in a uniquely late Roman setting. In virtually every aspect of society, Goths were learning Roman techniques. That was true even in the craft specialties, as artisans reflected the changing tastes of their clients. The frontiers were safe; Italy prospered. Although Theodoric failed to establish a completely satisfactory framework for competitive cooperation, the process took place regardless. Nevertheless, and despite his brutal execution of his trusted advisor Boethius and the impossibility of many aspects of his vision, the image of Theodoric deserved to be enshrined in myth. Like his great mausoleum in Ravenna, he is still mysterious and awe-inspiring. Alas, the Middle Ages lost sight of his humane and sagacious tolerance. After the Ostrogoths had ceased to exist as a people, a few obviously lingered on in Italy under their own peculiar customs. Certain noble families apparently intermarried with the Lombards and thereby joined the next generation of Germanic élites. As a group the Gothic nobility perhaps emerged after the war as powerful locally as they were before. Although they now were subject to different constraints, nobody in Byzantine Ravenna seriously objected to their imperious treatment of fellow Goths. Thus the resultant merging of populations in Italy gave final form to the early divisions of Gothic society. The vanished governmental apparatus devised under Theodoric, but always basically ad hoc, had done much to maintain a balance within Gothic society as well as between the Goths and the Romans. Now the fundamental irregularities of agriculture that had long polarized agrarian life worked without hindrance. The Ostrogoths became Italians.

The traditional account of Ostrogothic history maintains that the reign of Theodoric was essentially the entire story, that his policy of separating Goths and Romans produced a dualistic society with little interaction between the two peoples, and that Theodoric's basic goal was the preservation of an unaltered Roman civilization by Gothic arms. The truth was far more complex. Theodoric's program was the culmination of over two centuries of evolution. There were insoluble problems with his plan of separation, which, in effect, sought to control the Romanization of his people. His reign was hardly content with the preservation of ancient forms, for, although he built his regime upon Roman foundations, he made the bureaucracy function more efficiently and replaced outmoded concepts and institutions with Gothic innovations and personnel.

Perhaps the saddest aspect of the traditional history of the Ostrogoths is that it relegates them to a minor role in the transformation of the ancient world. In fact, they exerted their cultural, political, and military strength far beyond the boundaries of their settlements, whether in the Balkans or in Italy. Jordanes and Cassiodorus saw clearly what we have too often overlooked. The Ostrogoths were one of the few peoples capable of creating a synthesis of Germans and Romans within the framework of late antiquity. For men like Cassiodorus and Jordanes, the failure of the Ostrogothic Kingdom destroyed what little confidence remained in the progress of mankind in this world. The history of the Ostrogoths was indeed a rich and intricate blending of diverse traditions, many of which never found a home in the medieval synthesis.

NOTES

1. ROME AND THE NORTHERN BARBARIANS

1. Ernst Badian, *Roman Imperialism in the Late Republic.*

2. Julius Caesar *Bellum Gallicum* 4. 2–3; and for Britain, 4. 20.

3. Ibid., I, 23; see further Carole L. Crumley, *Celtic Social Structure.*

4. Caesar *B.G.* 1. 3.

5. Livy, II, 22. 1; for this preconception as a continuing problem, see W. C. Sturtevant, "Anthropology, History, and Ethnohistory," *Ethnohistory* 13 (1966): 1–51.

6. Santo Mazzarino, *The End of the Ancient World,* on Cicero, esp. pp. 22–34. Caesar begins his accounts with a clear statement of the bipolarity of Gaul, *B.G.*, I, 1.

7. The author's views are set forth in detail in Thomas S. Burns, "Pursuing the Early Gothic Migrations" and "Theories and Facts: The Early Gothic Migrations."

8. Suetonius *v. Julii Caesaris* 22, 54, 80.

9. Rolf Hachmann, *The Germanic Peoples*; and C. M. Wells, *The German Policy of Augustus*, pp. 14–31.

10. A general survey of the Roman frontier has yet to be written. A convenient guide to recent excavations in Germany is Philipp Filtzinger, *Limesmuseum Aalen.* For greater detail and bibliography, see Harald von Petrokovits, "Germania (Romana)"; R. Günther, ed., *Die Römer an Rhein und Donau*; and H. Schönberger, "The Roman Frontier in Germany."

11. Anthony Birley, *Marcus Aurelius*, p. 285.

12. The literature on the Celtic world grows daily; for a reliable introduction, see T. G. E. Powell, *The Celts.*

13. Dimitru Tudor, "Preuves archéologiques attestant la continuité de la domination romaine au nord du Danube après l'abandon de la Dacie sous Aurélian (IIIe–Ve siècles)."

14. For a detailed critique, see Thomas S. Burns, "The Germans and Roman Frontier Policy (ca. A.D. 350–378)." For similar transfrontier activities under Diocletian and Constantine, see Peter Brennan, "Combined Legionary Detachments as Artillery Units in Late Roman Danubian Bridgehead Dispositions."

15. For a convenient survey of the evolution of Roman towns in Germany, see F. Bömer and L. Voit, eds., *Germania Romana*, vol. 1. Augusta Vindelicum is discussed by W. Schleiermacher, pp. 78–93.

16. Cassius Dio *Historia Romana* 69.6. 3; in general, see Fergus Millar, *The Emperor in the Roman World, 31 B.C.–A.D. 337*, who begins his study with this anecdote.

17. *Historia Augusta, v. Hadriani* 6. 8; 12. 7; 14. 1–5. On the *Historia Augusta, v. Hadriani* in general, see Herbert W. Benario, *A Commentary on the Vita Hadriani in the Historia Augusta*. For the *H.A.* on the barbarians, see Thomas S. Burns, "The Barbarians and the *Scriptores Historiae Augustae.*"

18. For a detailed analysis of Roman activities in this area of the German frontier, see Philipp Filtzinger, ed., *Die Römer in Baden-Württemberg.*

19. Tacitus *Annales* 12. 45; Cassius Dio 56. 22. 2; Ammianus Marcellinus 17. 6. 1; 29. 6. 12; see also E. A. Thompson, *The Early Germans*, and Peter Goessler, "Zur Belagerungskunst der Germanen."

20. Ammianus 31. 6. 4–5. Typical late-fourth-century fortifications are examined in Karl Stehlin, *Die spätrömischen Wachttürmen am Rhein von Basel bis zum Bodensee*, and Sándor Soproni, *Der spätrömische Limes zwischen Esztergom und Szentendre.*

21. Ramsay MacMullen, *Soldier and Civilian in the Later Roman Empire*; J. C. Mann, "The Role of the Frontier Zones in Army Recruitment."

22. See the detailed citations to the sources for the late fourth century in Burns, "Roman Frontier Policy," and Ramsay MacMullen, "Barbarian Enclaves in the Northern Roman Empire."

23. Jerome *Ep.* 123, 15 dtd 410; Rutilius *De reditu suo* 1. 413–414; and Libanius *Or.* 18. 35. On the major clashes between Magnentius and Constantius II, see Jaroslav Šašel, "The Struggle between Magnentius and Constantius II for Italy and Illyricum."

24. See Burns, "Roman Frontier Policy."

25. Ammianus 16. 11. 9; 16. 11. 8–10; 17. 1. 7; 18. 2. 3–7, 2. 17, 2. 19; 20. 10. 1–3; and further, 17. 1. 4–8; 12. 1–8; 13. 12–14.

26. In support of this view, see further the arguments advanced by F. Vercauteren, "La Ruine des villes de la Gaule."

27. Ausonius *Mosella* 455.

28. Ammianus 14. 10. 8. This incident is one of only four such betrayals recorded in Ammianus for all the Germanic soldiers: the others are 16. 12. 2; 29. 4. 7; 31. 10. 3.

29. On the developing cultures in central Europe, see Kazimierz Godłowski, *The Chronology of the Late Roman and Early Migration Periods in Central Europe.* The extent of Roman trade and its distribution and impact are examined by Hans Jürgen Eggers, *Der römische Import im freien Germanien*, and Ryszard Wołagiewicz, "Der Zufluss römischer Importe in das Gebiet nördlich der mittleren Donau in der älteren Kaiserzeit."

30. Max Martin, "Die spätrömisch-frühmittelalterliche Besiedlung am Hochrhein und im schweizerishen Jura and Mittelland," pp. 432–34; and Rudolf Moosbrugger-Leu, "Die Alamannen und Franken," pp. 40–43.

31. Ammianus 15. 4. 1; 18. 2. 15. Caesar, writing four centuries before, noted the absence of measured land units, *B.G.* 4. 1.

32. This subject will occupy us later in detail; in general, see A. R. Korsunskii, "Visigothic Social Structure in the Fourth Century."

33. Considerable work now exists on the chip-carved style. Much of the literature is cited in Hermann Bullinger, *Spätantike Gurtelbeschlage.* See also the regional typologies in Herbert Kühn, *Die germanischen Bügelfibeln der Völkerwanderungszeit in Süddeutschland.*

34. Michel Bréal, "Premières influences de Rome sur la monde germanique." Boris Gerov, "L'Aspect éthnique et linguistique dans la région entre le Danube et les Balkans à l'époque romaine (I[e]–III[e]s.)."

35. Joachim Werner, "Zur Entstehung der Reihengräberzivilisation," pp. 285–321, with an extensive update to 1972 and a comprehensive bibliography, pp. 321–25.

36. For the gradual retreat southward of the senatorial nobility in the fifth century, see Karl F. Stroheker, *Der senatorische Adel im spätantiken Gallien*. See also C. E. Stevens, *Sidonius Apollinaris and His Age*.

37. Pierre Riché, *Education and Culture in the Barbarian West*, especially pp. 184–209.

38. For Hydatius, see E. A. Thompson, "The End of Roman Spain." For Severinus, a good place to start is Friedrich Lotter, *Severinus von Noricum*. See also Karl Pömer, ed., *Severin zwischen Römerzeit und Völkerwanderung*.

39. The most detailed survey remains F. Lot, "Du Régime de l'hospitalité." On the Burgundians, see "Burgunden," in *Reallexikon der Germanischen Altertumskunde*, ed. H. Beck, vol. 4, pp. 224–71.

40. So at least for Paulus Orosius 7. 43. 3–7, discussed at length in Emilienne Demougeot, *La Formation de l'Europe et les invasions barbares*, vol. 2, pp. 464–67.

41. Peter Lasko, *The Kingdom of the Franks*, pp. 13–41, and Kurt Böhner et al., *Gallien in der Spätantike: von Kaiser Constantin zu Frankenkönig Childerich*. On Childeric, see also Kurt Böhner, "Childerich von Tournai."

42. Lucien Musset, *The Germanic Invasions*, pp. 22–24.

43. For the importance to the Merovingians of the Roman garrisons in the south, see Bernard S. Bachrach, *Merovingian Military Organization, 481–751*. On the survival of certain Roman governmental forms and institutions, see also Émile Chénon, "Étude historique sur le *defensor civitatis*."

44. Eugen Ewig, "Résidence et capitale dans le haut Moyen Âge," surveys the lure towns had for medieval kings in search of the symbols of power. See also Kurt Böhner, "Urban and Rural Settlement in the Frankish Kingdom."

45. See especially the fundamental work by Heinz Löwe, "Von Theoderich dem Grossen zu Karl dem Grossen."

2. The Presettlement Phase

1. See, for example, Rolf Hachmann, *The Germanic Peoples*, and his *Die Goten und Skandinavien*.

2. In general, see Kazimierz Godłowski, *The Chronology of the Late Roman and Early Migration Periods in Central Europe*. For Pollwitten, see Hans Jürgens Eggers, "Das kaiserzeitliche Gräberfeld von Pollwitten, Kreis Mohrungen, Ostpreussen." A very detailed study and inventory of the Przeworsk Culture is now available: Roman Kenk, "Studien zum Beginn der jüngeren römischen Kaiserzeit in der Przeworsk-Kultur."

3. M. Stenberger, *Vallhagar*, and Berta Stjernquist, *Simris*.

4. Thomas S. Burns, "Pursuing the Early Gothic Migrations"; and R. Wenskus, *Stammesbildung und Verfassung*, pp. 462–69.

5. A very useful introduction is Marshall D. Sahlins, *Tribesmen*. For the Germanic groups in general, see Wenskus, *Stammesbildung*, and the still-valuable Bertha S. Phillpotts, *Kindred and Clan in the Middle Ages and After*.

6. The example of "Moka" among the inhabitants of parts of New Guinea is an interesting comparative system of gift exchange, peculiar in that it emphasizes the increasing value of gifts. See further R. N. H. Bulmer, "Political Aspects of the Moka Ceremonial Exchange System among the Kyaka People of the Western Highlands of New Guinea."

7. Tacitus documented various stages in this process in his *Germania*. In gen-

eral, the closer a group was to Roman influence, the more durable and complex were its structures. See especially E. A. Thompson, *The Early Germans.*

8. Such interaction between newcomers and the indigenous populations may account for the peculiar distribution of graves (styles and sites) at Weisory; see Jerzy Kmieciński, "Niektóre spoleczne aspekty epizodu gokiego w okresie srodkoworzymskim na comorzu" [Some social aspects of the Gothic Episode in Pomerania in the Middle Roman Period], *Zeszyty Naukove Universytetu Lodzkiego, Nauki Humanist-Spol.*, ser. 1, 12 (1959): 3–22.

9. Godłowski, *Chronology*, p. 32.

10. For the types of chronologies of Roman items, see Ryszard Wołagiewicz, "Der Zufluss römischen Importe in das Gebiet nördlich der mittleren Donau in der älteren Kaiserzeit," and Jerzy Kolendo, "Les Influences de Rome sur les peuples de l'Europe centrale habitant loin des frontières de l'Empire."

11. Bucur Mitrea, "La Migration des Goths reflétée par les trésors de monnaies romaines enfouis en Moldavie."

12. Ibid., p. 233, and V. V. Kropotkin, "Topografiia rimskikh i rannevizantiiskikh monet na territorii SSSR." Tribal dislocations were noted by Roman authors, eg., Dio Cassius 72. 3. 3, and *H.A., vita Commodi* 13. 5–7.

13. Viktor Francevich Gajdukevich, *Das bosporanische Reich*, pp. 333–458, and T. Lewicki, "Zagandnienie Gotów na Krymie."

14. E. Belin du Ballu, *Olbia, cité antique du littoral nord de la Mer Noire*, pp. 181–82, and P. D. Karyshkorskii, "Sur l'histoire tardive d'Olbia."

15. In general, see I. B. Brashkinskii, "Recherches soviétiques sur les monuments antiques des régions de la Mer Noire."

16. For the initial survey, see V. V. Khvoika, "Polia pogrebenii v srednem Pridneprov'e." P. Reinecke quickly offered his conflicting dates: "Aus der russischen archäologischen Litteratur."

17. M. B. Schukin, "Das Problem der Černjachov-Kultur in der sowjetischen archäologischen Literatur"; K. Ambroz, "Problems of the Early Medieval Chronology of Eastern Europe," pp. 350–57; Gheorghe Diaconu, "On the Socio-economic Relations between Natives and Goths in Dacia"; Bucur Mitrea and Constantin Preda, "Quelques problèmes ayant trait aux nécropoles de type Sîntana-Tcherniakhov découvertes en Valachie"; and E. A. Symonovich, "Toward the Question of the Scythian Affiliation of the Cherniakhov Culture."

18. Mitrea and Preda, *Sîntana-Tcherniakhov*, p. 222.

19. This subject will find proper treatment in chapter 5, but see also Ion Ioniţă, "The Social-Economic Structure of Society during the Goths' Migration in the Carpatho-Danubian Area," pp. 79–81.

20. Ioniţă, *Goths' Migration*, pp. 77–78, and work cited. For the Carpi, see Gheorghe Bichir, "La Civilisation des Carpes (IIe–IIIe siècle de n.è.) à la lumière des fouilles archéologiques de Poiana-Dulceşti de Butnăreşti et de Pădureni," and more recently his *Archaeology and History of the Carpi from the Second to the Fourth Century A.D.*, pp. 165–71.

21. See especially Evangelos K. Chrysos, "Gothia Romana. Zur Rechtslage des Föderatenlandes der Westgoten im 4. Jh.," and his more expansive *To Byzantion kai hoi Gotthoi.*

22. Mitrea and Preda, *Sîntana-Tcherniakhov*, p. 18.

23. Ioniţă, *Goths' Migration*, p. 83.

24. Jordanes *Getica* 89–100. The Gepids of course saw themselves as "openhanded, rich and ready to give," István Bóna, *The Dawn of The Dark Ages*; p. 14.

25. Harold Mattingly, C. H. V. Sutherland, and R. A. G. Carson, *The Roman Imperial Coinage*, vols. 4–7. Splendid examples with more recent finds can be found in Jenö Fitz, *Der Geldumlauf der römischen Provinzen im Donaugebiet Mitte des 3. Jahrhunderts*. On the escalating violence under Gallienus, see Constantin Preda and G. Simion, "Le Trésor de monnaies romaines impériales découvert à Isaccea (distr. de Tulcea) et l'attaque des Goths sous le règne de Gallien." So too a verse in hexameter written under Claudius II praising his victory and recovery of insignia from the Goths was set up in Rome (*C.I.L.*, VI, 31421).

26. Sextus Aurelius Victor *Liber de Caesaribus* 27. 2 (Teubner edition).

27. The scanty details concerning these developments are emerging gradually from the numismatic record; see especially the works of Boris Gerov, "Die gotische Invasion in Mösien und Thrakien unter Decius im Lichte der Hortfunde," and more recently his very helpful survey of the published data with a site gazetteer, "Die Einfälle der Nordvölker in den Ostbalkanraum im Lichte der Münzschatzfunde I. Das II. und III. Jahrhundert (101–284)." These events are discussed in some detail in Thomas S. Burns, *The Ostrogoths*; pp. 12–19.

28. Boris Gerov, "L'Aspect éthnique et linguistique dans la région entre le Danube et les Balkans à l'epoque romaine (I[e]–III[e]s.)."

29. The best, at least most reasonable, account of Decius's demise is the *Tactica* of the pseudo-Maurice (ca. 600), Mauricius, IV, 3. 1 (ed. George T. Dennis and Ernst Gamillscheg, pp. 109–110). Other accounts are: Zosimus 1. 23; Sextus Aurelius Victor 29. 1–5; and Jordanes *Getica* 101–103.

30. Gerov, "Gotische Invasion," pp. 138–39.

31. B. Rappaport, *Die Einfälle der Goten in das römische Reich bis auf Constantin*, remains very useful for untangling the scraps of literary evidence and for a tentative chronology. More recent surveys include A. M. Remennikov, *Borba plemen Severnogo Prichenomoria s Rimom v III veke n.e.*, and Andrew Alföldi, "The Invasion of Peoples from the Rhine to the Black Sea."

32. Gregorius Thaumaturgus *Epistola Canonica* (ed. J. P. Migne, cols. 1019–48).

33. Maciej Salamon, "The Chronology of Gothic Incursions into Asia Minor."

34. Zonaras 12. 26; Cedrenus 454; Leo Grammaticus, p. 78 (ed. Bonn); and Georgius Monachus 160.

35. So conclude Brashkinskii, "Monuments antiques," and others with ready access to the sites.

36. Al. Suceveanu, "Observations sur la stratigraphie des cités de la Dobrogea aux IIe–IVe siècle à la lumière des fouilles d'Histria"; and Halina Gajewska, *Topographie des fortifications romaines en Dobroudja*.

37. See especially the very interesting article by László Barkóczi, "Transplantations of Sarmatians and Roxolans in the Danube Basin"; on the Carpi, see Aurelius Victor 39, 40.

38. So concludes Andrei Bodor, "Emperor Aurelian and the Abandonment of Dacia."

39. Although the account of Claudius's career in the *H.A., v. Claudiani* 9. 3, is embellished, the same outline of events is catalogued in Zosimus, I, 46. On the problems and potential of the *Historia Augusta*, see Thomas S. Burns, "The Barbarians and the *Scriptores Historiae Augustae*."

40. *H.A., v. Claudii*, VI, 2; *III Panegyricus Maximiano Dictus* 17. 1 (in *Panégyriques Latins*).

41. The meanings of the names Tervingi and Greuthingi are controversial, but the simple renderings by Radu Vulpe are convincing; see Radu Vulpe, *Le Vallum*

de la Moldavie inférieure et le "mur" d'Athanaric, p. 25, with references.

42. *H.A., v. Aureliani* 22. 2; 33, 3–5. In general, see Burns, "Barbarians and *Scriptores*."

43. Bodor, "Emperor Aurelian," p. 37. Bodor's dates for the artifacts have not won universal acceptance. Several scholars prefer to date the materials to the last quarter of the third century and place the Goths in former Dacia no later than 291.

44. Diaconu, "Natives and Goths," pp. 67–68.

45. *H.A., v. Taciti* 13; Zosimus 1. 63–64; Zonaras 12. 28.

46. *H.A., v. Probi* 18, 2.

47. Many aspects of this development figure prominently in later chapters. For the present, see Ioniţă, *Goths' Migration*, pp. 85–89.

48. So at least among the Visigoths at the time of Saint Saba's martyrdom, ca. 370. Thomas S. Burns, *The Ostrogoths*, pp. 36–43; E. A. Thompson, *The Visigoths in the Time of Ulfila*; both drawing upon the life of the saint in H. Delehaye, "Saints de Thrace et de Mésie." See also Petre S. Năsturel, "Les Actes de St. Sabas le Goth," and Zeev Rubin, "The Conversion of the Visigoths to Christianity."

49. The literature on Constantine grows rapidly; for a general, useful, and readable account, see Ramsay MacMullen, *Constantine*. The first clashes between Constantine and Licinius seem now to have followed the incursions of 315. So too the program of reducing legionary size seems to have begun ca. 320, at least at Novae in Moesia. See further Tadeusz Sarnowski, "Le destruction des *principia* à Novae vers 316/317 de notre ère. Révolte militaire ou invasion gothe?"

50. Constantine's building program restored much of the lost prosperity to Roman towns; see Gajewska, *Topographie*, and a brief survey in Paul MacKendrick, *The Dacian Stones Speak*, pp. 163–86.

51. MacKendrick, *Dacian Stones*, and Dimitru Tudor, "Preuves archéologiques attestant la continuité de la domination romaine au nord du Danube après l'abandon de la Dacie sous Aurélian (IIIe–Ve siècles)."

52. For the events of ca. 291, see Mamertinus *Pan. Max.* 3. 17. 1, and for the Constantinian struggles, Jordanes *Getica* 79; Anonymous Valesianus 31.

53. These incidents are briefly surveyed by E. A. Thompson, "Constantine, Constantius II, and the Lower Danube Frontier"; for more discussion, see Chrysos, *To Byzantion*, pp. 41–76.

54. Peter Brennan, "Combined Legionary Detachments as Artillery Units in Late-Roman Danubian Bridgehead Dispositions."

55. Timothy D. Barnes, "The Victories of Constantine."

56. *Chron. Min.*, I, 234; Anon. Vales 31; see further references and discussion in Thompson, "Constantine, Constantius II," p. 373. This action is a rare example of Roman intervention beyond the frontier to assist their allies.

57. Eusebius v. *Const.* 4, 5. I agree with the arguments advanced by Thompson, "Constantine, Constantius II," p. 375, based on Eusebius, Julian, and Jordanes.

58. Libanius *Orat.* 90.

59. Tudor, "Preuves archéologiques," pp. 155–61.

60. Treated at length in Thomas S. Burns, "The Germans and Roman Frontier Policy (ca. A.D. 350–378)."

61. Ammianus 27. 5. 1. Peace existed despite Julian's apparently disdainful attitude. If there is any truth to Libanius *Or.* 12. 78, Julian once told a Gothic embassy that if the Goths were upset by the current treaty, they could go to war.

62. Ammianus 26. 10. 3.

63. Ibid., 27. 5. 2–5. See now the interesting discussion by Narciso Santos Yanguas, *Los pueblos germanicos en la segunda mitad del siglo IV D.C.*

64. *Ammianus* 27. 5. 6, and on "Gothia" among the Romans, see Chrysos, "Gothia Romana." On the *iudex* among the Visigoths, see also Burns, *Ostrogoths*, pp. 37–39. Themistius, especially *Or.* 10 (ed. Dindorf, p. 160), stands in a long series of Roman authors using foreigners as literary foils to criticize Roman society. See further Gilbert Dagron, "L'Empire romain d'orient au IVe siècle et les traditions politiques de l'Hellenisme," and Lawrence J. Daly, "The Mandarin and the Barbarian."

65. Ammianus 27. 5. 7.

66. Ibid., 27. 5. 9–10.

67. Ammianus 31. 5. 7; Sozomenus is more helpful, *Hist. Eccles.* 37. 5 (ed. J. Bidez).

68. C. Brady, *The Legends of Ermanaric*, and Georges Zink, *Les Légendes héroïques de Dietrich et d'Ermrich dans les littératures germaniques.*

69. Jordanes *Getica* 79.

70. On the Peucini, see Claudianus *VI cons. Hon.*, 105 f., and E. Polaschek, "Peucini." For the various groups referred to in Jordanes *Getica* 116, see Irma Korkkanen, *The Peoples of Hermanaric.*

71. In addition to the works of Diaconu, Ioniţă, Preda, and Schukin, see also the detailed report by Bucur Mitrea, "Mogil'nik v sele independenťsa i pogredenie v sele kokon k voprosy o kul'ture cyntana-de-muresh-Chernîakhovo."

72. Ammianus 31. 3. 1.

73. Emilienne Demougeot, *La Formation de l'Europe et les invasions barbares*, vol. 2, p. 349. On the restructuring following Ermanaric, see also Wenskus, *Stammesbildung*, pp. 478–81.

74. Ammianus 31. 3. 3.

75. Demougeot, *Formation de l'Europe*, pp. 355–59; László Várady, *Das Letzte Jahrhundert Pannoniens (376–476)*, pp. 19–23, 31–33; and Otto J. Maenchen-Helfen, "Germanic and Hunnic Names of Iranian Origin."

3. Bondage and Struggle

1. Ammianus Marcellinus 31. 4. 12 and 5. 3.

2. Ibid., 31. 4. 4.

3. Ibid., 31. 4. 2. *vagari cum caritatibus suis disseminantes.*

4. Ibid., 31. 4. 11.

5. Ibid., 29. 6. 5.

6. Zosimus *Historia Nova* 4. 11 (trans. J. Buchanan and H. T. Davis, pp. 145–46), and for the text, see the Teubner edition by L. Mendelssohn.

7. Ammianus 31. 5. 3.

8. Ammianus, 31. 12. 17.

9. For the details of the battle, see Thomas S. Burns, "The Battle of Adrianople."

10. There is no doubt that some Goths, Alans, and Huns found refuge within the empire under Theodosius and were settled in Pannonia, where they served as allies of Rome; Pacatus, *Pan. Theodosio Dictus* (in *Panégyriques latins*) 12. 32. However, this identification as including those Ostrogoths with Alatheus and Saphrax, the date of the settlement, and their role and significance in Pannonia are subjects of great debate. They are very important for László Várady, *Das letzte Jahrhundert Pannoniens 376–476*, pp. 375–02. Others are more critical, however; see particularly J. Harmatta, "The Last Century of Pannonia" and "Goten und Hunnen in Pannonien," with a survey of the archaeological data including grave

styles; T. Nagy, "The Last Century of Pannonia in the Judgment of a New Monograph" and "Reoccupation of Pannonia from the Huns in 427." On the problems with Pacatus as a source, see also Adolf Lippold, "Herrscherideal und Traditionsverbundenheit im Panegyricus des Pacatus."

11. Here I have followed Várady, who cites the extant literary sources; however, it must be noted that the sources usually do not refer to the specific groups led by Alatheus and Saphrax but vaguely to Goths, Huns, etc. The linking by Várady has convinced most, but I cannot accept the independent role he asserts for the "Pannonian federates" in dealing with the Roman command or with the Huns and later Radagaius. The archaeological record would be far different if they were so unified and numerically significant.

12. Most Ostrogothic materials that have come to light are more convincingly assigned to the post–Nedao settlements (455–71) and the later period of Ostrogothic hegemony in Pannonia, which disintegrated shortly after the death of Theodoric in 526. See further László Barkóczi, "History of Pannonia," pp. 117–20, and Agnes Salamon and Agnes A. Sós, "Pannonia—Fifth to Ninth Centuries," pp. 400–404. So too the second treasure from Szilágysomlyó; for this find, see Nándor Fettich, *A szilágysomlyói második kincs—Der zweite Schatz von Szilágysomlyó*. But for dating, see Volker Bierbrauer, *Die ostgotischen Grab und Schatzfunde in Italien*, pp. 114–22.

13. J. Hampel, *Die Alterthümer des frühen Mittelalters in Ungarn* (Braunschweig, 1905), vol. 2, pp. 15–26. On late Roman medallions in general, see Jocelyn M. C. Toynbee, *Roman Medallions*, pp. 118–21, 184–90.

14. Olympiodorus, frag. 3 (ed. L. Dindorf, *Historici Graeci Minores*, Teubner edition, p. 451); Ammianus 17. 12. 21 (Quadi), 16. 12. 26 (Alamanni).

15. W. Kubitschek, *Ausgewählte römische Medaillons der kaiserlichen Münzensammlung in Wien*; and John C. Kent, Bernhard Overbeck, and Armin V. Stylow, *Die römische Münze*, no. 712, discussed by Overbeck, p. 172.

16. Gyula Mészáros, "A Regölyi korai népvándorlaskori fejedelmi sír"; and see Bierbrauer, *Schatzfunde*, p. 191. On Csákár, see Á. Salamon and L. Barkóczi, "Bestattungen von Csákvár aus dem Ende des 4. und dem Anfang des 5. Jahrhunderts," and Á. Salamon and I. Lengyel, "Kinship Interrelations in a Fifth-Century 'Pannonian' Cemetery."

17. *Historia Augusta, v. Claudii* 6. 2. The author has discussed the *Historia Augusta* in "The Barbarians and the *Scriptores Historiae Augustae*." This dual listing might well be the work of later emendation.

18. Claudianus *in Eutrop*., II, 153.

19. Zosimus 4. 35; Claudianus *iv Hon*. 623–36. Chroniclers also recorded the victory; see *Consularia Const*. and Hydatius *Chronicon*, an. 386 (ed. Th. Mommsen, *M.G.H., A.A.*, vols. 9 and 11 [Chronica Minora, vols. 1 and 2]). Scenes of the Roman victory in 386 were prominent on the obelisk set up by Theodosius on the spina of the hippodrome in Constantinople in 390. Additional fragments depicting dead soldiers, soldiers on a boat, etc. were discovered in excavation. See Gerda Bruns, *Der Obelisk und seine Basis auf dem Hippodrom zu Konstantinopel*, fig. 43, and J. Kollwitz, *Oströmische Plastik der theodosianischen Zeit*, vol. 1, pp. 3–16. For more recent developments and explanations, see V. Velkov, "Ein Beitrag zum Aufenthalt des Kaisers Theodosius I in der Provinz Skythien im Jahr 386 im Lichte neuer Erkenntnisse," reprinted in his *Roman Cities in Bulgaria*, pp. 215–28; Velkov suggested that the essential theme was the commemoration of the Gothic campaigns, culminating with the rout on the Danube in 386.

20. Zosimus 4. 38–39.

21. So concludes V. Velkov, *Cities in Thrace and Dacia in Late Antiquity* (Amsterdam, 1977), p. 37; Claudianus *in Eutrop.* 2. 153.

22. Eunapius, frag. 60 (ed. L. Dindorf, *Historici Graeci Minores*, Teubner edition, vol. 1, pp. 252–53).

23. For Athanaric, see Jordanes *Getica* 142–45. Butherichus, killed at Thessalonika, is another example of a German in favor under Theodosius; Sozomenus *Historia Ecclesiastica* 7. 25. 3 (ed. J. Bidez).

24. Jordanes *Getica* 145; Paulus Orosius *Historiarum adversum paganos libri vii* 7. 35. 13. The most extensive survey of these developments is Massimiliano Pavan, *La Politica Gotica di Teodosio nella Pubblicisticà del suo Tempo*.

25. The sources on these events are notoriously vague; Orosius 7. 34; Claudianus *in Ruf.* 316–22; *iv Cons. Hon.* 105, *de Bello Gothico* 524–26. The data were surveyed by Stewart I. Oost, *Galla Placidia Augusta*.

26. Priscus, frag. 39 (trans. C. D. Gordon, *The Age of Attila*, p. 136). For the text, see L. Dindorf, ed., *Historici Graeci Minores* (Teubner edition), vol. 1, p. 348.

27. Jordanes *Getica* 199–200.

28. See sources cited in A. H. M. Jones, J. R. Martindale, and J. Morris, *The Prosopography of the Later Roman Empire*, vol. 1, pp. 379–80.

29. Zosimus 5. 21–22.

30. There are numerous works on the Huns, but to cite only a few, see: E. A. Thompson, *A History of Attila and the Huns*; Joachim Werner, *Beiträge zur Archäologie des Attila-Reiches*; J. Harmatta, "The Dissolution of the Hun Empire"; Otto J. Maenchen-Helfen, *The World of the Huns*.

31. On Priscus's journey and the location of Attila's roving camp, at the time probably in former Visigothic territory in Eastern Wallachia, see R. Browning, "Where Was Attila's Camp?" On Ardaric, Valamir, and others, see Jordanes *Getica* 199–201, and for Ardaric at Nedao, 262.

32. See references and discussion by Harmatta and Nagy in their articles cited above, n. 10.

33. Jordanes *Getica* 249.

34. Kurt Horedt and Dumitru Protase, "Ein völkerwanderungszeitlicher Schatzfund aus Cluj-Someşeni" and "Das zweite Furstengrab von Apahida (Siebenbürgen)."

35. Ion Ioniţă, "The Social-Economic Structure of Society during the Goths' Migration in the Carpatho-Danubian Area," pp. 79–80; Radu Harhoiu, *The Treasure from Pietroasa Romania*, p. 23, and "Aspects of the Socio-political Situation in Transylvania during the Fifth Century."

36. For a discussion of the sites in Hungary with many finds probably belonging to an Ostrogothic ruling class of the mid-fifth century, see I. Kovrig, "Nouvelles trouvailles du Ve siècle découvertes en Hongrie." Kovrig based his identifications, in part, upon stylistic and manufacturing similarities to early finds from Apahida published in the 1930s. On the role of allies within the Hunnic federation, see Suzana Dolinescu-Ferche, "On Socio-economic Relations between Natives and Huns at the Lower Danube."

37. E. M. Zaharia and N. Zaharia, "La Nécropoles des IVe–Ve siècles de Botoşani-Dealul (Cărămidărieé)." The presence of several skeletons with obvious signs of cranial deformation characteristic of the Huns is unsettling. That the Ostrogoths, at this early stage, would adopt such a practice in imitation is possible, as the authors suggest, but is still problematic. Until more and similarly dated finds are discovered, much will remain unclear, especially precise ethnic identification of these finds and others of the period.

38. See Jordanes *Getica* 247–49.

39. For example, see Volker Bierbrauer, "Zur chronologischen, soziologischen und regionalen Gliederung des ostgermanischen Fundstoffs des 5. Jahrhunderts in Südosteuropa," for the existence of a dispersed upper crust of East Germans in the March Feld and serving the Huns. The similarities of jewelry between this site and other Ostrogothic finds is at present convincing.

40. On the Ostrogoths, see Kurt Horedt, "Neue Goldschätze des 5. Jahrhunderts aus Rumänien (ein Beitrag zur Geschichte der Ostgoten und Gepiden)," extended chronologically and geographically in his "Wandervölker und Romanen im 5. bis 6. Jahrhundert in Siebenbürgen."

41. Along this line, see particularly the carefully reserved study by Bierbrauer, "Gliederung des ostgermanischen."

42. There is now a considerable literature on population survival: I. Nestor, "Les Données archéologiques et le problème de la formation du peuple roumain"; Dan Gheorghe Teodor, *The East Carpathian Area of Romania in the V–XI Centuries* A.D.; and Radu Harhoiu, "Das norddonauländische Gebiet im 5. Jahrhundert und seine Beziehungen zum spätrömischen Kaiserreich." And on the Hunnic settlements, see also Zaharia and Zaharia, "Botoşani-Dealul (Cărămidărieé)."

43. Joachim Werner, "Neue Analyse des Childerichgrabes von Tournai"; F. Dumas, *Le tombeau de Childéric. La Normandie Soutterraine* (Musée Departemental des Antiquités, Rouen, 1975). The Hunnic invasions stimulated the development of Germanic aristocracies and warbands all along the Danube. So also concludes J. Harmatta, "Les Huns et le changement et conflict à la frontière Danubienne au IVe siècle après J.C." On Childeric, see Kurt Böhner, "Childerich von Tournai."

44. Harhoiu, *Treasure*, but also for an earlier date, see David Brown, "The Brooches in the Pietroasa Treasure," and the highly technical study by B. Arrhenius, *Granatschmuck und Gemmen aus nordischen Funden des frühen Mittelalters*. The primary work on Pietroasa by Alexandru Odobesco, *Le Trésor de Pétrossa*, has been republished with updated comments in his *Opera*, vol. 4.

45. Harhoiu, *Treasure*, p. 9.

46. For a general discussion of brooches and fashions, see J. Heurgon, *Le Trésor de Tĕnès*.

47. Ambrosius Sanctus (ed. P. Labbe, P. Cossart, and G. D. Mansi, p. 617 c–d).

48. Zosimus 4. 40.

49. Harhoiu, *Treasure*, pp. 19–22.

50. Jordanes *Getica* 259.

51. Perhaps that explains some of the finds in Hungary reported by Joachim Werner, "Studien zu Grabfunden des V. Jahrhunderts aus der Slowakei und der Karpatenukraine." It may also help to clarify some of the unresolved problems of ethnic affiliation surrounding Apahida II and other finds from the last half of the fifth century.

52. Sidonius Apollinaris *Panegyricus* 471–79 (in *Sidoine Apollinaire*).

53. Jordanes *Getica* 272. On the archaeological dimensions of the settlement, see Attila Kiss, "Ein Versuch die Funde und das Siedlungsgebiet der Ostgoten in Pannonien zwischen 456–471 zu bestimmen." For a very helpful attempt to unravel the historical events of this era in northern Pannonia, see Jaroslav Šašel, "Antiqui Barbari. Zur Besiedlungsgeschichte Ostnoricums und Pannoniens im 5. und 6. Jahrhundert nach den Schriftquellen."

54. Jordanes *Getica* 268.

55. Maenchen-Helfen, *World of the Huns*, p. 158.

56. Ibid., pp. 152–61, 164.

57. Jordanes *Getica* 271; Priscus, frag. 28 (ed. L. Dindorf, *Historici Graeci Minores*, Teubner edition, vol. 1, p. 338); Ennodius *Pan. Theod.*, 7 (ed. F. Vogel). Their rebellion may have begun in 459 when Dyrrhachium was sacked.

58. Jordanes *Getica* 272.

59. Agathias *Historiarum Libri Quinque* (ed. R. Keydell) 2. 13. 1–14. 5.

60. Jordanes *Getica* 273–76; Priscus, frag. 35.

61. Jordanes *Getica* 277–78.

62. Priscus, frag. 35.

63. J. B. Bury, *The Later Roman Empire*, pp. 227–33.

64. Marcellinus Comes *Chronicon* 471 (ed. Th. Mommsen, *Chronica Minora*, vol. 2 [*M.G.H., A.A.*, vol. 11]).

65. Jordanes *Getica* 282.

66. Horedt and Protase (*Germania*, 1970); see particularly the front of the cloak ornament, pl. 21, fig. a; also pl. 23, figs. 19a–24b; and pl. 24, figs. 1–3. On the strong revival of Byzantine influence, see particularly Ligia Bârzu, *Continuity of the Romanian People's Material and Spiritual Production in the Territory of Former Dacia*.

67. For examples of Gepidic workmanship, see Dezsö Csallány, *Archäologische Denkmäler der Gepiden im Mitteldonaubecken (454–568 u.z.)*.

68. Werner, "Studien zu Grabfunden," p. 435, pl. 3, fig. 2.

69. For example, compare Werner's fibula from Gyulavári on pl. 3 to N. Riépnikoff, fig. 43, in "Quelques cimetières du pays des Goths de Crimée."

70. Werner, "Studien zu Grabfunden."

71. A. A. Vasiliev, *The Goths in the Crimea*, pp. 33–70.

72. *Getica* 282.

73. Eugippius *Vita Severini* 31. 1–6, 24. 1, 25. 3, 27. 1, 42. 1 (ed. R. Noll).

74. Jordanes *Getica* 284–87.

75. Jordanes *Getica* 287–88. Nicholas G. L. Hammond, *A History of Macedonia*, pp. 108–09, does not believe that the Ostrogoths reached Thessaly.

76. Malchus Philadelphis, frag. 11 (ed. C. Müller, *Fragmenta Historicorum Graecorum*, vol. 4, pp. 119–20).

77. On Triarius in general, see Ludwig Schmidt, *Geschichte der deutschen Stämme bis zum Ausgang der Völkerwanderung*, pp. 278ff.

78. Malchus, frag. 14.

79. Malchus, frag. 16.

80. Malchus, frag. 15.

81. Malchus, frag. 16.

82. Malchus, frags. 7, 8.

83. Malchus, frag. 15.

84. Malchus, frag. 17.

85. Malchus, frag. 18.

86. E. Kitzinger, "A Survey of the Early Christian Town of Stobi," confirms much of the violence reported in Malchus, frag. 18, as it pertained to Stobi. Although Stobi was ravaged, it flowered anew under Justinian.

87. Malchus, frag. 18; Müller, p. 125.

88. Malchus, frag. 18; Müller, p. 126.

89. R. F. Hoddinott, *Bulgaria in Antiquity*, pp. 178–83.

90. Malchus, frag. 18; for the route and description of the Via Egnatia, see Hammond, *Macedonia*, with maps.

91. Malchus, frag. 17; Müller, pp. 125–30.

92. Malchus, frag. 18; on Dardania, see Hammond, *Macedonia*, pp. 62 ff.

93. Malchus, frag. 18; Müller, p. 129.

94. Malchus, frag. 18; Müller, p. 130. Nepos would not have needed Theodoric unless he wanted real control instead of titular recognition. See further John C. Kent, "Julius Nepos and the Fall of the Western Empire."

95. These events in *Vita Severini* are among the saddest chapters of the fifth century. The archaeological record demonstrates the contrasts of waning Roman influence and sharp cessation from one community to another. See, for example, Johanna Haberl, *Wien-Favianis und Vindobona*; Friedrich Lotter, *Severinus von Noricum*; and the contributions in Karl Pömer, ed., *Severin zwischen Römerzeit und Völkerwanderung*.

96. Much is available on the career of Zeno, but still useful is E. W. Brooks, "The Emperor Zeno and the Isaurians," and Bury, *Later Roman Empire*, pp. 263–94.

97. Joannes Antiochenus, frag. 213 (ed. C. Müller, *Fragmenta Historicorum Graecorum*, vol. 4, (p. 620) and Malchus, frag. 19–21.

98. Joannes Ant., frag. 213; Marcellinus Comes 482 (ed. Th. Mommsen, *Chronica Minora*, vol. 2 [*M.G.H., A.A.*, vol. 11]). See also V. Beseveliev, "Les cités antiques en Mésie et en Thrace et leur sort à l'époque du haut moyen âge," for an archaeological survey.

99. Joannes Ant., frag. 214 (3).

100. Joannes Ant., frag. 214 (6). I disagree with E. Brooks ("Emperor Zeno," pp. 209–238), who disavowed the recall of Theodoric. His preference here for the later account in Theophanes is unjustified.

101. Bury, *Later Roman Empire*, pp. 255–258.

102. Marcellinus Comes 483.

103. Joannes Ant., frag. 214 (7); Marcellinus Comes 487.

104. So concludes Beseveliev, "Cités Antiques."

105. Velkov, *Thrace and Dacia*, p. 101, with references to literature. Most recently, see Stefan Parnicki-Pudełko, "Les Recherches archéologiques polonaises à *Novae* (Bulgarie) en 1978." Parts of the early Christian basilica seem to date from the early sixth century, with a coin of Arcadius giving the *terminus post quem*.

106. Eugippius *Vita Severini* 42. 4.

107. Joannes Ant., frag. 214 (8), recalls her role in the negotiations over Dardania.

108. On the Roman imperial fleet up to the end of the fourth century, see Dietmar Kienast, *Untersuchungen zu den Kriegsflotten der römischen Kaiserzeit*.

109. Velkov, *Thrace and Dacia*, pp. 142–45; *Cod. Theod* 7. 17. 1; Vegetius *de re militari* 4. 46.

110. *Nov. Theod.* 24. 5.

111. Theophylactus Simocatta 7. 10. 3; 8. 6. 8 (Teubner edition).

112. Eugippius *Vita Severini* 22. 2, 28. 2.

113. Joannes Ant., frag. 213.

114. The initiator of the march to Italy remains disputed. For Theodoric: Malchus, frag. 18, Müller, p. 129; and Jordanes *Getica* 290–91. For Zeno: Anonymus Valesianus 49; Procopius *Bellum Gothicum*, V, 1. 10. Finally, Evagrius *Historica Ecclesiastica* 3. 27, gives both but favors Theodoric. All references to Procopius are to the ubiquitous Loeb edition. The Teubner text used in the Loeb underwent revision in 1962–64 by G. Wirth. The citations have been checked in both, but for convenience I have chosen to cite the more readily available Loeb text.

115. For example, Bessas refused to leave and later allied with Belisarius, Procopius *B.G.*, V, 16. 2.

116. See Thomas S. Burns, "Calculating Ostrogothic Population."

117. Ennodius *Pan.* 29 (chap. 7. 1) 206 (ed. F. Vogel). On the location of the Ulca and the battle there, see Heinz Löwe, "Theoderichs Gepidensieg in Winter 488/89." So too *Tabula Imperii Romani.*

118. Ennodius *Pan.* 7. 206–07.

119. Anonymus Valesianus 50.

4. Theodoric's Kingdom Surveyed

1. Anonymus Valesianus 50 (Loeb edition). The last wagons did not reach the staging area until late summer. Despite the revision of the Jacques Moreau text of the *Excerpta Valesiana* by V. Velkov (Teubner edition), there remains no completely satisfactory text. However, the important work by J. N. Adams, *The Text and Language of a Vulgar Latin Chronicle (Anonymus Valesianus II)*, demonstrates a likelihood that a single author drew from numerous chronicles available in Ravenna, ca. 540. The stories about Theodoric contained in Anonymus are often too colorful to accept wholeheartedly, yet to reject them out of hand because of their brutality is equally uncritical. They are cited here as examples of one aspect of the popular traditions surrounding Theodoric.

2. Zacharias of Mytilene *Hist. Eccles.* 16. 10 (trans. F. Hamilton and E. Brooks, pp. 317–18).

3. Ennodius *Panegyricus dictus Theodorico* (ed. F. Vogel, pp. 203–14); Q. Aurelius Symmachus *Laudatio in Valentinianum Seniorem Augustum, I et II* (ed. O. Seeck, pp. 318–30).

4. *Gesta de Xysti Purgatione*, pp. 117–20. See further Giuseppe Zecchini, "I 'gesti de Xysti purgatione' e le fazione aristocratiche a Roma alla metà del V secolo," pp. 60–74. Zecchini traces the evolution of factions within the aristocracy from the reign of Honorius and the breakdown in order following his death.

5. Anonymus Valesianus 60, *Excerpta Valesiana* (Teubner edition).

6. John Matthews, *Western Aristocracies and Imperial Court* A.D. 364–425, discusses in detail the careers of the nobility in the age of Valentinian I.

7. Thanks to A. H. M. Jones, J. R. Martindale, and J. Morris, *The Prosopography of the Later Roman Empire*, vol. 2 (Cambridge, 1980), we can follow the careers of important individuals with considerable ease up to 527. For the remainder of the sixth century, see Johannes Sundwall, *Abhandlungen zur Geschichte des ausgehenden Römertums.*

8. Despite the difficulty in dating the Ennodian corpus, this ebb and flow in correspondence is clear; especially instructive are the letters addressed to Faustus. On dating, see F. Vogel, "Chronologische Untersuchungen zu Ennodius," pp. 53–74, and Sundwall, *Abhandlungen*, pp. 1–83.

9. On the *saiones* and *defensores civitatis*, see Thomas S. Burns, *The Ostrogoths*, pp. 114–26. See also R. Morosi, "I *saiones*, speciali agenti di polizia presso i Goti." Morosi sees a strong repressive involvement in Italy of both *agentes in rebus* and *saiones*. The worst features of both, however, were subdued under Theodoric.

10. Cassiodorus *Variae* 1. 1. 3 (ed. Th. Mommsen). So too concludes the Anonymus 66.

11. Procopius *B.G.*, V, 2. 6–15 (Loeb edition). Cassiodorus *Variae* 10. 4; 11. 1

(ed. Th. Mommsen). The payments were taken over by the Byzantine government. *Codex Iustinianus* (ed. P. Krüger, *Novellae* A 7. 22).

12. Wolfgang Hahn, *Moneta Imperii Byzantini*, vol. 1: *Von Anastasius I bis Justinianus I (491–565)* (Vienna 1975), pp. 77–88.

13. Malchus Philadelphensis, frag. 16 (ed. C. Müller, *Fragmenta Historicorum Graecorum*, vol. 4).

14. Not all came, as the case of Bessas attests (Procopius *B.G.*, VII, 20. 12). Most did, however, and are visible only in the artifacts; Giovanni Annibaldi and Joachim Werner, "Ostgotische Grabfunde aus Acquasanta, Prov. Ascoli Piceno (Marche)."

15. Dietrich Claude, "Die Ostrogotischen Königserhebungen," stresses the evolution of investiture of kings beginning with Theodoric under the constant influence of the Eastern Empire as seen in the dress used in coronations and in the act itself, here specifically pp. 181–86.

16. Anonymus 50; Joannes Antiochenus, frag. 214a (ed. C. Müller, *Fragmenta Historicorum Graecorum*, vol. 4).

17. Canadidus, frag. 1, Photius, codex 79 (ed. C. Müller, *Fragmenta Historicorum Graecorum*, vol. 4); Joannes Antiochenus, frag. 209; Ennodius *Pan.* 8 (ed. F. Vogel); Anonymus 36–48. There are two complete modern editions of Ennodius's works; besides Vogel, see W. Hartel, *Corpus Scriptorum Ecclesiasticorum Latinorum*, vol. 6 (Vindobonae, 1882). All references are to Vogel's edition.

18. Cassiodorus *Variae* 3. 35 confirms a grant to him and his mother by Liberius; see also Anonymus 38, 45, and Marcellinus Comes, *Chronicon* 476 (ed. Th. Mommsen, *Chronica Minora*, vol. 2 [*M.G.H., A.A.*, vol. 11]).

19. John C. Kent, "Julius Nepos and the Fall of the Western Empire."

20. A. Chastagnol, *Le Senát romain sous le règne d'Odoacre. Recherches sur l'épigraphie du Colisée au Ve siècle*. Many individual careers can be traced in Jones, Martindale, and Morris, *Prosopography*, vol. 2, and for the sixth century, see Sundwall, *Abhandlungen*.

21. Kent, "Julius Nepos," stresses the importance of Rome.

22. Franz F. Kraus, *Die Münzen Odovacars und des Ostgotenreiches in Italien*, pp. 52–58; W. Wroth, *Catalogue of the Coins of the Vandals, Ostrogoths, and Lombards and of the Emperors of Thessalonica, Nicaea and Trebizond in the British Museum*.

23. Kraus, *Münzen Odovacars*, p. 18, with a chart of monograms beginning on p. 228. See Odovacar's coins no. 25, 25a, 26, 27, and 35 on pl. 1.

24. Ennodius *Vita S. Epifani* 104–108; Pierre LeGentilhomme, "Le Monnayage et la circulation monetaire dans les royames barbares en Occident (Ve–VIIIe siècle)," pp. 86–92.

25. Ernst Stein, *Histoire du Bas-Empire*, vol. 2, pp. 117–22. See also Manfred Clauss, *Der Magister Officiorum in der Spätantike (4–6 JH.)*.

26. Ennodius *Vita S. Epifani* 106–108; William G. Sinnigen, "Administrative Shifts of Competence under Theodoric."

27. So conclude numerous studies of the economy, for example, Kund Hannestad, *L'Évolution des ressources agricoles de l'Italie du IVe au VIe siècle de notre ère*, and L. Cracco Ruggini, *Economia e società nell "Italia annonaria."*

28. *The Theodosian Code and Novels and the Sirmondian Constitutions.*

29. *Notitia Dignitatum*, occ., 9. 28 (ed. O. Seeck). On their impact upon artistic motifs, particularly the early introduction of zoomorphic patterns, see N. Degrassi, "Rinvenimento di un tesoretto. Le oreficerie tardo-Romane di Pavia."

30. Procopius *B.G.*, V, 1. 28.

31. *PLRE*, II, 806.

32. Malchus, frag. 18.
33. Eugippius *Vita Severini* 42. 4, 44. 4–5 (ed. R. Noll).
34. Eugippius *Vita Severini* 24. 1, 25. 3, 27. 1, 42. 1.
35. Ibid., 44.
36. Ibid., 42.
37. Ibid., 46.
38. The best account of the Acacian Schism is the recent contribution by Jeffrey Richards, *The Popes and the Papacy in the Early Middle Ages, 476–752*, pp. 55–136. Others have also recognized its importance; see, for example, Peter A. B. Llewellyn, *Rome in the Dark Ages*, pp. 21–51.
39. Kurt Horedt and Dumitru Protase, "Ein völkerwanderungszeitlicher Schatzfund aus Cluj-Someşeni." On the possible reestablishment of a federate tie to Byzantium among the peoples in the area, some at least Eastern Germanic, see Ligia Bârzu, *Continuity of the Romanian People's Material and Spiritual Production in the Territory of Former Dacia*. The profound resurgence of Byzantine influence in former Dacia after the departure of the Ostrogoths from Moesia is dramatically attested in the influx of Byzantine coins into the area from the reign of Anastasius onward. See Constantine Preda, "The Byzantine Coins—an Expression of the Relations between the Empire and the Populations North of the Danube in the Sixth–Thirteenth Centuries."
40. Ennodius *Epist*. 6. 5 to Aurelianus urged him to accept Theodoric's decision graciously regardless of its verdict. If Theodoric then so wished, Aurelianus might receive land elsewhere.
41. Ennodius *Vita S. Epifani* 111, *Videres urbem familiarum coetibus scatentem*; see also D. A. Bullough, "Urban Change in Early Medieval Italy: The Example of Pavia."
42. *PLRE*, II, 1131, follows M. Schönfeld, *Wörterbuch der altgermanischen Personen—und Völkernamen*, p. 242, in suggesting that Tufa is a Latin name. The problem of ethnic attribution is extremely perplexing, since Goths often took Latin-Christian names, used with their Gothic name, but named all their children, born Orthodox Christians with only Latin names. For example, *C.I.L.*, III, 12396, probably late fourth century, set up in honor of a veteran, records one Valerius Vitalis, who had been named Tzita, and his three sons Florentius, Vitalis, and Laurentius.
43. Ennodius *Vita S. Epifani* 122–34.
44. Ibid., 135.
45. G. M. Cook, *The Life of Saint Epiphanius by Ennodius*, p. 214.
46. Malchus, frag. 15.
47. Cassiodorus *Variae* 2. 16. 5; so too Ennodius *Epist*. 9. 23.
48. Procopius *B.G.*, V, 1. 28.
49. Anonymus 57. That was the third and final time Theodoric underwent a special ceremony of kingship. The first occurred when he was designated heir by his father through a transference of followers: Jordanes *Getica* 282 (ed. Th. Mommsen). The second occurred at his dying father's side (Jordanes *Getica* 288). At each stage he expanded his rule until with the followers of Odovacar, Rugians, etc. he ruled all the Germanic peoples of Italy as one.
50. For comparative data, see the *Liber Constitutionum sive Lex Gundobada*, LIV–LV (ed. L. R. de Salis, *Leges Burgundionum, M. G. H. Legum*, Sec. I, II, i). The controversial *Edictum Theodorici Regis* 150, 151 (ed. F. Bluhme) reveals the need to shift labor from one area to another to pool the scant supply of able workers. This condition might relate directly to the early stages of the settlement

in Italy ca. 500, unless the document is Visigothic and dates to the reign of Theodoric II at Toulouse. Theodoric was concerned to redeem laborers captured by the Burgundians, Ennodius *Vita S. Epifani* 147–73.

51. Sale was a customary and expected aspect of most testamentary issues in Roman law and underlies the complex procedures outlined in the Roman law on property. See Ernst Levy, *West Roman Vulgar Law*.

52. The 40,000 is an estimate based on extrapolations of treaties with the Byzantines; see further Thomas S. Burns, "Calculating Ostrogothic Population."

53. The settlements in these areas emerge clearly from the literary and archaeological data. This pattern was seen first by Ludwig Schmidt, *Die Ostgermanen*, and was confirmed more recently with increased archaeological data: Volker Bierbrauer, "Die Ansiedlung der Ostgothen in Italien." Such a settlement guaranteed control of the road network of central and northern Italy and also preserved the ethnic cohesion of the Goths.

54. See chap. 8 on the military.

55. Volker Bierbrauer, *Die ostgotischen Grab- und Schatzfunde in Italien*, p. 283: at San Andrea di Grottainare, some of the graves may be of Ostrogothic military personnel stationed to monitor the nearby *via Adriatica*; p. 313, similarly at Rosara, near the *via Salaria*; so also at Acquasanta, see Annibaldi and Werner, "Ostgotische Grabfunde."

56. Ennodius is especially helpful on the impact of the settlement around Arles. See Thomas S. Burns, "Ennodius and the Ostrogothic Settlement."

57. Cassiodorus *Variae* 5. 10 and 11. The unit is mysterious. Alexander Souter, A *Glossary of Later Latin to 600 A.D.*, p. 69, suggests that it was a Gothic measure of land. But it may have been an otherwise unknown survival of Roman agrarian practice; see A. R. Korsunskii, "Small Landed Property in the Western Provinces of the Late Roman Empire." For a revisionist view stressing that revenues were the overwhelming concern, see Walter Goffart, *Barbarians and Romans, A.D. 418–584*. In this context Goffart suggests that the *condomae* may have derived from late Roman administrative patterns and thereby corresponded to "tents" or "mess" used to distribute rations in the Roman army (*Barbarians and Romans*, pp. 221–22).

58. Jan-Olof Tjäder, ed., *Die nichtliterarischen lateinischen Papyri Italiens aus der Zeit 445–700*, vol. 1, papyri no. 13. The twelfth was an arbitrary division used for testament. According to *Institutiones* (2. 14. 5), the custom derived from the unit *As*, which had twelve divisions. Since no one could be partially intestate in Roman law, if the units of an estate added up to less than twelve *unciae*, then the stipulated heirs divided the remainder according to their share of the assigned portion. If the units totaled more than twelve *unciae*, the *As* was doubled or tripled and the estate divided according to the percentage of the *As* units, now twenty-four or thirty-six *unciae* per *As*.

59. *Edictum Theodorici Regis* 10–12; and *Leges Visigothorum, Codicis Euriciani Fragmenta* 277 (ed. K. Zeumer). On the attribution of the *Edictum*, see Giulio Vismara, "El 'Edictum Theodorici,'" and his *Edictum Theodorici*. Vismara presents a strong case for Theodoric II, the Visigothic king at Toulouse, ca. 458–59. This view has won many converts but certainly not all; for example, see Bernard S. Bachrach, *Early Medieval Jewish Policy in Western Europe*, pp. 29–30, 153 n. 6, and Hermann Nehlsen, *Sklavenrecht zwischen Antike und Mittelalter*, vol. 1. All discussion based on the *Edictum* must remain inconclusive without additional support.

60. Ennodius *Epist*. 2. 23.

61. Ibid.; *Epist.* 3. 20 is a similar letter written for another friend troubled over the settlement.

62. Ibid., 9. 23.

63. Ibid., 2. 23. The letter (8. 13) congratulating his friend Aurelianus for his restored prosperity marks a successful conclusion of still another appeal. We are, unfortunately, left in the dark as to whether Aurelianus had received his wish for a greater share or had received new lands far removed from his host and tormentor.

64. For example, Cassiodorus *Variae* 1. 18; 4. 39; 9. 18; and Procopius *B.G.*, V, 32. 4. 12. The most forceful reprimand came late in his reign (*Variae* 5. 12), in which he ordered his nephew Theodahad to restore the lands seized by his men at the estate of Palentia. Palentia itself was a recompense for the taking of the estate of Arbitana.

65. The problem of Goth preying upon Goth may have extended even beyond the fall of the kingdom. See papyrus no. 7 in the Tjäder collection, dated 557 from Rieti. Gundihild, widow of Gudahals, asked the curia of Rieti to take action against four Germans (Ostrogoths?) threatening the estates of her two sons Lendarit and Landerit. Rieti was a known Gothic enclave.

66. Gelasius *Epist.* 14. 1 (ed. A. Thiel, p. 362). The mechanics of papal government are illuminated in this correspondence; see particularly J. J. Taylor, "The Early Papacy at Work: Gelasius I."

67. Ennodius *Vita Epif.* 147–73, the embassy to Gundobad, king of the Burgundians.

68. Letters relating to his health problems are 6. 4, 7; 8. 16, 21, 22, 24, 25, 27; 9. 14.

69. *Epist.* 8. 12, 31, 37, 40; 9. 22.

70. Chastangnol 80; *PLRE*, II, 454–56; Sundwall, *Abhandlungen*, pp. 117–20.

71. *PLRE*, II, 454–56.

72. Richards, *Popes and Papacy*.

73. András Mócsy, "Der Name Flavius als Rangbezeichnung in der Spätantike."

74. Cassiodorus *Variae* 3. 20.

75. *PLRE*, II, 482 (Florus 4).

76. Anonymus 53; *PLRE*, II, 467–69.

77. Anonymus 92; *PLRE*, II, 1044–46 (Symmachus 9).

78. Cassiodorus *Variae* 10. 31. Cassiodorus drafted only five letters for him. The symbolism of 10. 31 is itself significant, in that it reaffirms the dualism of Gothic/Roman rule even during the great war and seeks to grasp the mantle of Theodoric as the exemplar for all. Thus there was an official proclamation to the Goths despite the fact that they had recently hailed him king on a raised shield within a circle of swords. On Cassiodorus in general, see James J. O'Donnell, *Cassiodorus*.

79. Anonymus 53.

80. Anonymus 57; Richards, *Popes and Papacy*, pp. 23–24, 93–96. Gelasius was pope from 492–96.

81. Anonymus 54.

82. Richards, *Popes and Papacy*, p. 92.

83. Anonymus 64.

84. Richards, *Popes and Papacy*, 93–96.

85. R. M. Harrison, "The Emperor Zeno's Real Name."

86. Richards, *Popes and Papacy*, pp. 104–108.

87. *Die Canonessammlung des Dionysius Exiguus in der ersten Redaktion*, ed. A. Strewe (Berlin, 1931). His table of ninety-five years marks the introduction in

the West of reckoning the years from the Incarnation. See Reginald L. Poole, *Chronicles and Annals*, pp. 22–23.

88. Wroth, *Catalogue of Coins*, pp. xxxi–xxxiii; LeGentilhomme, "Monnayage," pp. 86–92. New plates with cross listings to Kraus, Wroth, and others are now available in Ermanno A. Arslan, *Le Monete di ostrogoti, longobardi e vandali*. Note that Theodoric only occasionally used his monogram on gold issues.

89. See further Zecchini, "Xysti purgatione."

90. Ennodius *Vita Epif.* 110.

91. Richards, *Popes and Papacy*, pp. 83–91.

92. Ibid., pp. 69–82.

93. The dilemma of the late Roman aristocracy during the collapse in the West is ably analyzed by M. A. Wes, *Das Ende des Kaisertums im Westen des römischen Reiches*. On the Symmachian Schism in this light, see Peter A. B. Llewellyn, "The Roman Church during the Laurentian Schism: Priests and Senators."

94. Anonymus 65–67 (Loeb edition).

95. Cassiodorus *Variae* 1. 3 perhaps best illustrates his love of the city and his desires for her to reunite mankind. In regard to the flourishing intellectual life and the schools in Rome, see Pierre Riché, *Education and Culture in the Barbarian West, Sixth through Eighth Centuries*, especially pp. 26–30 but in general pp. 17–78. The special role of patronage is stressed by M. Stanislas Léglise, "Saint Ennodius et la haute éducation littéraire dans la monde romain au commencement du VIe siècle." On the medallion, see further Jocelyn M. C. Toynbee, *Roman Medallions*, p. 189, but this medallion certainly did not end the "empire."

96. Theophylactus Simocatta *Historiarum libri octo* 6. 3 (Teubner edition).

97. All of that made Ennodius particularly joyous as one of the principal supporters of Symmachus and a close correspondent of Faustus and the royal court. The data concerning the councils are analyzed by Adolf Lumpe, "Die konziliengeschichtliche Bedeutung des Ennodius."

98. Richards, *Popes and Papacy*, p. 79.

99. Anonymus 60, *ut etiam a Romanis Traianus vel Valentinianus, quorum tempora sectatus est*. The *Gesta de Xysti purgatione*, part of the so-called "Symmachian apocrypha," casts Theodoric as Valentinian in the schism: Richards, *Popes and Papacy*, p. 81. In many ways, the imagery was very appropriate, for both had great martial vigor and restrained judgment until broken late in life by the frustrations of rule. See also Zecchini, "Xysti purgatione." Zecchini traces the evolution of factions within the aristocracy from the reign of Honorius and the breakdown in order following his death.

100. Richards, *Popes and Papacy*, pp. 69–79.

101. Ibid., pp. 86–88.

102. C. Pietri, "Le Sénat, le peuple chrétien et les partis du cirque à Rome sous le pape Symmaque (498–514)," sees these outbursts as clearly connected to political factions, with the Blues synonymous with the Laurentians. Alan Cameron, *Circus Factions*, p. 97, cautions against assuming that this outburst was necessarily related to class strife. The *variae* 1. 30, 31, 32 are inconclusive. The Roman circus remained calm when compared to the Constantinopolitan, where thousands died in the riots of 501 alone.

103. The correspondence of Pope Hormisdas reflects his careful steps toward reconciliation in full knowledge of Theodoric, *Epistolae Romanorum pontificum, a S. Hilario usque ad S. Hormisdam*, ed. A. Thiel (Brunsbergae, 1868).

104. Anonymus 80.

105. Jordanes *Getica* 174.

106. O'Donnell, *Cassiodorus*, pp. 44–46, presents a strong case that the writing of the *Getica* too reached a culmination in 519 and was completed much later by Jordanes. On the *Panegyric*, see the comments to his edition by Th. Mommsen (*M.G.H., A.A.*, vol. 12, p. 463), and also E. Chatelain, "Notes sur quelques palimpsestes de Turin, IV. Fragments des panégyriques de Cassiodore."

107. See further Hahn, *Moneta Imperii*, #74a and b.

108. Ibid., #75.

109. Ibid., #76.

110. Anonymus 80.

111. The legends of Ermanaric and Theodoric (Dietrich) invoked deeds of prowess and dreams of honor generation after generation across all Europe. See Georges Zink, *Les Légendes héroïques de Dietrich et d'Ermrich dans les littératures germaniques*, and C. Brady, *The Legends of Ermanaric*. Volker Bierbrauer explores Ostrogothic relations with other states, especially under Theodoric, in his "Zur ostgotischen Geschichte in Italien."

112. Procopius *B.G.*, V, 4. 12–15; *PLRE*, II, 1068.

113. On Audefleda, see Anonymus 63; Gregorius Turonensis *Historiae Francorum* 3. 31; Jordanes *Getica* 295–96 (not, however, Clovis's daughter, but his sister). On Amalafrida, see Anonymus 68; *PLRE*, II, 63. The relationship with the Franks is discussed by Alexander Schenk Graf von Stauffenberg, *Das Imperium und die Völkerwanderung* (Munich, 1947), pp. 143–56.

114. Greg. Tur. *H.F.* 3. 4; *PLRE*, II, 63.

115. Procopius *B.G.*, V, 13. 2. There seems to have been a considerable amount of economic and cultural contact between the Thuringians and Ostrogoths, with artistic influences going in both directions. See Joachim Werner in his preface to Mario Degani, *Il tesoro romano-barbarico di Reggio Emilia*, pp. 8–12.

116. Procopius *B.G.*, VIII, 25. 11–12.

117. Greg. Tur. *H.F.* 3. 4, 7–8; Procopius *B.G.*, V, 13. 1. 3.

118. Cassiodorus *Variae* 9. 1. See further Franz Xaver Zimmerman, "Der Grabstein der ostgotischen Königstocher Amalafrida Theodenanda in Genazzano bei Rom," for a discussion of the possible dates of the great Amalafrida's death.

119. Marius Aventicensis *Chronica* 509 (ed. Th. Mommsen, *M.G.H., A.A.*, vol. 11 [*Chronica Minora*, 2]). Cassiodorus *Variae* 1. 24 probably relates to this campaign.

120. *Greg. Tur.* 3. 5; *Marius Avent.* 522.

121. *PLRE*, II, 64–65.

122. On the Ostrogothic period of Visigothic history, see E. A. Thompson, *The Goths in Spain*, and José Orlandis, *Historia de España*, pp. 66–81.

123. Procopius *B.G.*, V, 12. 50; Jordanes *Getica* 302; *PLRE*, II, 1112.

124. Procopius *B.G.*, V, 12. 36–48.

125. Anonymus 27; *B.G.*, V, 12. 51–4; Procopius *B.G.*, V, 12. 49.

126. Procopius *B.G.*, V, 12. 50–52.

127. Cassiodorus *Variae* 5. 35.

128. Greg. Tur. *H.F.* 3. 1–10.

129. Ibid.

130. Procopius *B.G.*, V, 13. 6–7; Jordanes *Getica* 302.

131. Orlandis, *Historia*, p. 74. Similar "restraints" on bribery existed in Italy.

132. Thompson, *Goths in Spain*, p. 15; Procopius *B.V.*, III, 24. 7–17.

133. Procopius *B.G.*, VI, 30. 15.

134. Isidorus of Seville *Historia Gothorum Wandalorum Sueborum* 44 (ed. C. Rodríguez Alonso). See further Thompson, *Goths in Spain*, p. 16, n. 4.

135. Cassiodorus *Variae* 1. 45.
136. *PLRE*, II, 233–36.
137. Boethius *Philosophiae Consolatio* 2. 3. 25–35.
138. Boethius *P.C.*, I, 4. 40–75.
139. Ibid. There is no longer any doubt that Boethius wrote various religious tracts, including *De trinitate* and *De fide Catholica*.
140. On Theopaschism and Boethius, see Richards, *Popes and Papacy*, pp. 107–27, and W. Bark, "Theodoric v. Boethius: Vindication and Apology."
141. Richards, *Popes and Papacy*, p. 108.
142. *PLRE*, II, 456 (Faustus 9).
143. Bark, "Theodoric v. Boethius," p. 416.
144. Ibid., pp. 416–22.
145. Anonymus 85.
146. Richards, p. 118; the reconstruction of events and chronology in *PLRE*, II, 233–36 is not convincing.
147. Anonymus 87; Procopius *B.G.*, V, 4. 45. Amalasuintha restored the property to his family, *B.G.*, V, 2. 5.
148. Anonymus 90.
149. Anonymus 93: *quod videntes populi et senatores, coeperunt reliquias de veste eius tollere*.
150. Ibid., 95.
151. Ibid., 87.
152. Boethius, *P.C.*, II, 50–65 (Loeb edition, p. 147).
153. Cassiodorus *Variae* 8. 21; *PLRE*, II, 332 (Cyprianus 2).
154. *PLRE*, II, 808 (Opilio 4).
155. *PLRE*, II, 495 (Gaudentius 11).
156. Cassiodorus *Variae* 8. 28.
157. *PLRE*, II, 1126 (Triwilla). John Moorhead, "Boethius and Romans in Ostrogothic Service," points out that Boethius was out of touch with those who found favor through men like Triwilla.
158. Boethius *P.C.*, I, 34–40.
159. Except, of course, for the Anonymus 85–87.
160. Boethius *P.C.* 1. 34–40; Anonymus 85–87.
161. Cassiodorus *Variae* 5. 16.
162. Ibid. On the Vandal fleet, see especially J. Rougé, "Quelques aspects de la navigation en Méditerranée au Ve siècle et dans la première moitié du VIe siècle." I cannot accept John Moorhead, "The Last Years of Theodoric," that the fleet was directed primarily against the Vandals because of their seizure of Amalafrida. The relevant *Variae* (5. 17) to Abundantius does mention obliquely the Greeks and Vandals: *Non habet quod nobis Graecus imputet aut Afer insultet*. Procopius *B.G.* 3. 8. 12, however, explicitly denies that Theodoric attempted to build a fleet against the Vandals to take revenge. I am convinced, nevertheless, by Moorhead's detective work that Senarius, one of Theodoric's longstanding aides and possibly of Germanic stock, was in the plot. That perhaps strengthens the thesis that Germanic participation in factional disputes greatly angered Theodoric.
163. Cassiodorus *Variae* 10. 31. Although Witigis in this letter to the Goths called the ceremony "our ancestral custom," the raising aloft on a shield was by then a well-established "Roman tradition" as well. Already in the fourth century Julian and Valentinian I were similarly saluted as emperors by their troops, many of whom were Germans. The precise origin of the ceremony among the Germans and Romans is still a subject of debate. See further the discussion of the

ceremony, particularly as revived in Byzantium in the fourteenth century, by Christopher Walter, "Raising on a Shield in Byzantine Iconography," most importantly pp. 157–59.

164. Th. Mommsen, *M.G.H., A.A.*, vol. 12, p. 463.

165. Theophylactus Simocatta 8. 8–15.

166. Anonymus Val. 61 (Loeb edition, p. 547).

167. Procopius *B.G.*, V, 1. 32–35.

5. The Metamorphosis of Ostrogothic Society

1. See further Gheorghe Diaconu, "Über die scheibengedrehte Keramik in der Sîntana de Mures-Tschernjachowkultur."

2. This fact is reflected in Libanius *Orationes* 18. 78. For a survey of the recent archaeological data, see Ligia Bârzu, *Continuity of the Romanian People's Material and Spiritual Production in the Territory of Former Dacia*. See also Gheorghe Diaconu, "On the Socio-economic Relations between Natives and Goths in Dacia." The outlines of the process have been long debated; see the philological analysis in R. Löwe, *Die Reste der Germanen am Schwarzen Meere*.

3. Viktor Francevich Gajdukevich, *Das bosporanische Reich*, pp. 371–459. E. Belin du Ballu, *Olbia, cité antique du littoral nord de la Mer Noire*, and P. D. Karyshkorskii, "Sur l'histoire tardive d'Olbia." In general, I. B. Brashkinskii, "Recherches soviétiques sur les monuments antiques des régions de la Mer Noire."

4. Jordanes *Getica* 267.

5. Diaconu, "Socio-economic Relations," pp. 70–73, but without reference to specific excavations. See also Ion Ioniţă, "The Social-Economic Structure of Society during the Goths' Migration in the Carpatho-Danubian Area."

6. Gheorghe Bichir, "La Civilisation des Carpes (IIe–IIIe siècle de n. è.) à la lumière des fouilles archéologiques de Poiana-Dulceşti, de Bulnareşti et de Pădureni." The various "hut-type" coinage of the mid-fourth century affords a Roman vision of contemporary barbarian dwellings. For example, see fig. 11.

7. Bârzu, *Continuity*, pp. 49–53. However, the thesis that "Roman rule" extended to all former Dacia between 275–602 is difficult to accept, especially after the collapse of the Constantinian dynasty.

8. See further A. Wasowicz, *Olbia pontique et son territoire*, and most recently Christopher Prestige Jones, *The Roman World of Dio Chrysostom*, pp. 62–64, with a very useful bibliography.

9. Jordanes *Getica* 116. On this important passage, see Irma Korkkanen, *The Peoples of Hermanaric: Jordanes, Getica 116.* On the possible ethnic affiliations of various leaders, see further Emilienne Demougeot, *La Formation de l'Europe et les invasions barbares*, vol. 2, pp. 355–65.

10. E. M. Zaharia and N. Zaharia, "Les Nécropoles des IVe–Ve siècles de Botoşani-Dealul Cărămidărieé)." Volker Bierbrauer, "Zur chronologischen, soziologischen und regionalen Gliederung des ostgermanischen Fundstoffs des 5. Jahrhunderts in Südosteuropa." Kurt Horedt, "Wandervölker und Romanen im 5. bis 6. Jahrhundert in Siebenbürgen." Note from the discussion in chap. 3 the extraordinary difficulty in assigning any specific ethnic attribution to these finds. Others are more willing to advance tribal identifications: see Herwig Wolfram, *Geschichte der Goten*, pp. 315–19.

11. In addition to the works cited above on the problem of Hunnic redistribution of Roman tribute, see further Joan M. Fagerlie, *Late Roman and Byzantine*

Solidi Found in Sweden and Denmark, and Joachim Werner, "Zu den auf Öland und Gotland gefundenen byzantinischen Goldmünzen."

12. Joachim Werner, "Der goldene Armring des Frankenkönigs Childerich und die germanischen Handgelenkringe der jüngeren Kaiserzeit."

13. Ambrosius Sanctus (P. Labbe, G. Cossart, and G. D. Mansi, eds., p. 617 c–d).

14. Eunapius, frag. 60 (ed. L. Dindorf), and Zosimus 4. 56. 1–3 (Teubner edition); see further the essay by Massimiliano Pavan, *La Politica Gotica di Teodosio nella Pubblicisticà del suo Tempo*, and Adolf Lippold, *Theodosius der Grosse und seine Zeit*, pp. 138–54.

15. For specific references to Ammianus Marcellinus, see Thomas S. Burns, "The Battle of Adrianople."

16. Claudian *B.G.* 537–39 (Loeb edition).

17. In addition to the works cited above concerning the Goths in former Dacia, see also Ramsay MacMullen, "Barbarian Enclaves in the Northern Roman Empire"; and for a somewhat later period, I. Kovrig, "Nouvelles trouvailles du Ve siècle découvertes en Hongrie." See also David Brown, "The Brooches in the Pietroasa Treasure," and the survey of brooch development in late antiquity by J. Heurgon, *Le Trésor de Ténès*.

18. Gerda Bruns, *Der Obelisk und seine Basis auf dem Hippodrom zu Konstantinopel*, and the cogent reconstruction by H. Kähler, "Der Sockel des Theodosiusobelisken in Konstantinopel als Denkmal der Spätantike."

19. For convenient modern surveys of some of these developments, see especially Radu Harhoiu, *The Fifth-Century* A.D. *Treasure from Pietroasa, Romania*, and Harhoiu and Diaconu's updating in Alexandru Odobesco, *Opera*, vol. 4, pp. 1011–72. The Italian phases are ably discussed in Volker Bierbrauer, *Die ostgotischen Grab- und Schatzfunde in Italien*.

20. Robert Göbl, *Antike Numismatik*, pls. 15–17, discussed in vol. 2, pp. 134–35; and J. Hampel, *Die Alterthümer des frühen Mittelalters in Ungarn*, vol. 2, pp. 15–26.

21. On the comparison of Gepidic and Ostrogothic materials, see the useful introduction by István Bóna, *The Dawn of the Dark Ages*, pp. 55–60. For manufacturing techniques, see especially B. Arrhenius, *Granatschmuck und Gemmen aus nordischen Funden des frühen Mittelalters*. For the Goths, János Dombay, "Der gotische Grabfund von Domolospuszta."

22. Bona, *Dawn*, p. 58.

23. Volker Bierbrauer, "Reperti Alemanni del primo periodo ostrogoto provenienti dell'Italia Settentrionale," pl. 109, fig. 7, from tomb 126 Basel-Kleinhüningen.

24. So apparently at Straubing-Alburg in Bavaria; see the brief announcement by R. Christlein in *Das archäologische Jahr in Bayern 1980*. For Gothic fibulae in the north, see further Joachim Werner, "Fernhandel und Naturalwirtschaft in östlichen Merowingerreich nach archäologischen und numismatischen Zeugnissen," and the relevant portions of the encyclopedic study of Herbert Kühn, *Die germanischen Bügelfibeln der Völkerwanderungszeit*. Especially useful is the succinct discussion of styles with illustrations by Volker Bierbrauer, "Zu den Vorkommen ostgotischer Bügelfibeln in Raetia II," *Bayerische Vorgeschichteblätter* 36 (1971):134–65.

25. Diaconu, "Socio-economic Relations," p. 71, n. 30, and for cloth manufacturing along the Dniester, see A. R. Korsunskii, "Visigothic Social Structure in the Fourth Century," p. 57.

26. There is a continuing effort to quarry the Gothic language for clues to their

society; most recently, see Korsunskii, "Social Structure"; and Herwig Wolfram, "Gotische Studien," pt. 2, and further, "Gotische Studien," pt. 3.

27. Valens had to cross on a pontoon bridge in 367: Ammianus 27. 5. 2.

28. Dimitru Tudor, *Sucidava, une cité daco-romaine et byzantine en Dacie*, pp. 85–101, and further his "Preuves archéologiques attestant la continuité de la domination Romaine au nord du Danube après l'abandon de la Dacie sous Aurelien (IIIe–Ve siècles)." See also Andrei Bodor, "Emperor Aurelian and the Abandonment of Dacia," and Dumitru Protase, "Considérations sur la continuité des Daco-Romains en Dacie post–aurelienne, à la lumière des recherches archéologiques et numismatiques."

29. Ammianus 17. 1. 8.

30. Ammianus 18. 2. 17.

31. See further Bârzu, *Continuity*, pp. 46–58, and for a general survey, Jerzy Kolendo, "Les influences de Rome sur les peuples de l'Europe centrale habitant loin des frontières de l'Empire." A comparative perspective can be seen along the upper Rhine: Rudolf Moosbrugger-Leu, "Die Alamannen und Franken"; Max Martin, "Die spätrömisch-frühmittelalterliche Besiedlung am Hochrhein und im schweizerischen Jura und Mittelland"; and Max Martin, "Die alten Kastellstädte und die germanische Besiedlung," in *Archäologie der Schweiz*, vol. 6, pp. 97–132.

32. In general, see Ramsay MacMullen, *Soldier and Civilian in the Later Roman Empire.*

33. To Martin Bang, *Die Germanen im römischen Dienst bis zum Regierungsantritt Constantins I*, add *C.I.L.*, III, 1296, the case of Tzita from the late fourth century and an inscription from Tomi (Fiebiger and Schmidt, 1939, no. 49) set up to honor the death of one Atala, son of Tzeiuk, at age twenty-five. Atala was also the name of an eponymous ancestor of Theodoric (Jordanes *Getica* 79 and Cassiodorus *Variae* 11. 1. 19).

34. Ammianus 27. 5. 7. and *C.I.L.*, III, (6159) 7494, which commemorated his victories.

35. For example, *C.I.L.*, III, 12483, dated 337–40 from Troesmia in Lower Moesia, preceded a punitive expedition of Constantius.

36. See further MacMullen, "Enclaves." I have explored some aspects of these developments in "The Germans and Roman Frontier Policy (ca. A.D. 350–378)."

37. Marriage to barbarians was prohibited, doubtless to no avail, in 368 (*Cod. Theod.* 3. 14. 1), perhaps in the wake of sorties against the Goths.

38. Bârzu, *Continuity*, p. 61.

39. See also the discussion by E. A. Thompson, "Constantine, Constantius II, and the Lower Danube Frontier."

40. Ammianus 27. 5. 1.

41. One Roman response was to retreat into small fortified centers during these crises. For an example, see D. Paunier, "Un refuge du Bas-Empire au Mont-Musiège (Haute-Savoie)."

42. Ammianus 21. 4. 2.

43. For an example, see Ammianus 30. 5. 14.

44. Ammianus 27. 5. 4–5. So too Athanaric and his followers retreated into the forests when facing Hunnic invasion.

45. Michel Bréal, "Premières influences de Rome sur le monde germanique."

46. Fagerlie, *Solidi*, p. 166. It is possible that some of these coins were carried by soldiers returning to distant kinsmen during the second half of the fifth century. They may have also influenced military construction, particularly at Isman-

torp on Öland. For this hypothesis, see Werner, "Öland und Gotland."

47. Otto J. Maenchen-Helfen, *The World of the Huns*, pp. 182–87. See also Göbl, *Antike Numismatik*, vol. 1, pp. 145–46, and vol. 2, pl. 39, nos. 472–79, discussed on p. 148; and O. Iliescu, "Nouvelles information relatives aux lingots romaine d'or, trouvés en Transylvanie."

48. See further András Mócsy, *Pannonia and Upper Moesia*, pp. 339–58, and B. Thomas, *Römische Villen in Pannonien*, pp. 389–92.

49. Jordanes *Getica* 271–76. On the various settlement areas of the numerous barbarian peoples, see the reconstruction of Jaroslav Šašel, "Antiqui Barbari." On overall Roman policy in the area, see in particular Friedrich Lotter, "Zur Rolle der Donausueben in der Völkerwanderungzeit."

50. Kühn, *Bügelfibeln*, vol. 1, pp. 95–106; and more recently and specifically Attila Kiss, "Ein Versuch die Funde und das Siedlungsgebiet der Ostgoten in Pannonien zwischen 456–471 zu bestimmen."

51. Eugippius *Vita Severini* 4. 1 is but one example (ed. R. Noll).

52. Malchus, frag. 18 (ed. Müller, p. 129).

53. Malchus, frag. 17 (ed. Müller, p. 124).

54. Malchus, frag. 15 (trans. C. D. Gordon, *The Age of Attila*, pp. 165–66).

55. M. A. Wes, *Das Ende des Kaisertums im Westen des römischen Reichs.*

56. So conclude Anne Kahane, Leslie M. Threipland, and John Ward-Perkins, "The Ager Veientanus, North and East of Rome."

57. Ennodius *Epist* 2. 22, 2. 33, 3. 20, 6. 5, 8. 13 (ed. F. Vogel).

58. Paulinus Pellaeus *Eucharisticus* 575–80 (Loeb edition, in vol. 2 of Ausonius *Opuscula*, ed. H. G. White).

59. For a late example involving obviously Germanic (Gothic?) owners, see papyrus no. 13 in the Tjäder collection dated 4 April 553 or papyrus no. 7 dated 557. There is no question but that similar forms of routine Roman government continued throughout the Ostrogothic Kingdom, papyri nos. 4–5, BV, 7–11 dated 520–26 and no. 12 dated January 491, J. O. Tjäder, ed., *Die nichtiterarischen lateinischen Papyri Italiens aus der Zeit 445–700.*

60. On *condamae*, see Cassiodorus *Variae* 5. 10; 5. 11.

61. Although I obviously hesitate to reject Giulio Vismara, *Edictum Theoderici*, whose work reassigned the *Edictum* to Theodoric II, Hermann Nehlsen, *Sklavenrecht zwischen Antike und Mittelalter*, vol. 1, has indeed raised new doubts. If the *Edictum* is Ostrogothic, dated ca. 503, then "comparative value" is an error, and rather the arguments here advanced are directly applicable.

62. *Edictum Theodorici Regis* 94 (ed. F. Bluhme) remains the standard edition.

63. Ibid., 75; see further G. Cardascia, "L'Apparition dans le droit des classes d' '*honestiores*' et d' '*humiliores*,'" and Peter Garnsey, *Social Status and Legal Privilege in the Roman Empire.*

64. *Edictum* 142.

65. Ibid., 70, 148. On slavery, see especially Nehlsen, *Sklavenrecht*, pp. 120–52.

66. *Edictum* 150.

67. Ibid., 151.

68. Ibid., 136–41.

69. Ibid., 32.

70. Ibid., 34.

71. Ibid., 56–58.

72. Ibid., 104.

73. Ibid., 75.

74. Ennodius *Vita S. Epifani* 147–73.

75. Ennodius *Epist.* 2. 23.

76. See further, Jaroslav Šašel, "Alpes Juliani." Ravennas Anonymus 4. 22–41 (ed. Otto Cuntz and Joseph Schnetz, *Itineraria Romana*, vol. 2).

77. So concludes Fabien Thibault, "L'Impôt direct dans les royaumes des Ostrogoths, des Wisigoths et des Burgundes." Cassiodorus *Variae* 4. 14 and 1. 19.

78. *Variae* 5. 14.

79. *Variae* 5. 26 and 5. 27. See also Procopius *B.G.*, V, 12. 46–48.

80. Wolfgang Hahn, *Moneta Imperii Byzantini*, vol. 1, pp. 77–79.

81. See further H. Geiss, *Geld-und-naturwissenschaftliche Erscheinungsformen im staatlichen Aufbau Italiens während der Gotenzeit*, and Pierre LeGentilhomme, "Le Monnayage et la circulation monétaire dans les royames barbares en Occident (V[e]–VIIIe siècle)."

82. Georg Pfeilschifter, *Der Ostgotenkönig Theoderich der Grosse und die katholische Kirche*, p. 50, and Jacques Zeiller, "Étude sur l'arianisme en Italie à l'époque ostrogotique et à l'époque lombarde," p. 134.

83. Other pieces also betray Ostrogoths or indigenous Romans operating under the Ostrogoths; see for further examples Joachim Werner, "Eine ostgotische Prunkschnalle von Köln-Severinstor." Further discussion of the problems of the spangenhelmets can be found in the following chapter on religion. The relevant bibliography is cited there.

84. Fagerlie, *Solidi.*

85. J. Werner, "Fernhandel" and "Ostgotische Bügelfibeln aus bajuwarischen Reihengräbern."

86. See further the discussion in Otto von Hessen, Wilhelm Kurze, and Carlo Alberto Mastrelli, *Il Tesoro di Golognano*, pp. 33–58, on the evolution from secular to religious usage, and pp. 94–101 on the personal names; for the discussion of spoons from Desana and elsewhere, see Bierbrauer, *Schatzfunde*, pp. 180–88, 263–72. The religious invocations on the Golognano items mark a late stage in the evolution to a purely religious usage.

87. Cassiodorus *Variae* 4. 10, probably a case of not Gothic coercion but Roman.

88. *Variae* 5. 29, 30.

89. *Variae* 9. 2.

90. *Variae* 9. 20.

91. *Variae* 9. 18.

92. Procopius *B.G.*, VII, 1. 37–47.

93. Other examples of concern for appropriate dress include Procopius *B.G.*, VI, 23. 37; VI, 30. 7; VI, 30. 17; VIII, 32. 2; and Agathias I, 20. 10.

94. Tjäder, *Papyri Italiens*, papyrus no. 8.

95. Ibid., papyrus no. 9.

96. *Historiae Patriae Monumenta*, XII, "Codex diplomaticus Langobardiae," 37, Stavile [. . .] legem vivens Gothorum [. . .] civis Brixianus, dated 769. The scattered pieces of Ostrogothic jewelry in late burials may also reflect continued Gothic family ties under the early Lombards.

97. Giovanni Annibaldi and Joachim Werner, "Ostgotische Grabfunde aus Acquasanta, Prov. Ascoli Piceno (Marche)." Especially interesting in this context is the chip-carved buckle with attenuated animals, virtually Salin Style I except for the chip-carving.

98. Bierbrauer, *Schatzfunde*, pp. 264–66. This developmental phase is "Zelldekor," which reached its high point in sixth-century Italy. According to Bierbrauer, "Die ostgotischen Funde von Domagnano, Republik San Marino," the Zelldekor itself also ultimately derived from late antique craft traditions.

99. B. Schmidt, "Theoderich der Grosse und die damaszierten Schwerter der Thüringer."

100. Fagerlie, *Solidi*.

101. See further B. Thomas, *Römische Villen in Pannonien*, pp. 389–92.

102. László Barkóczi, "A Sixth Century Cemetery from Keszthely-Fenekpuszta."

103. Ibid., pp. 281, 286.

104. I. Lengyel, "Chemico-analytical Aspects of Human Bone Finds from the Sixth Century 'Pannonian' Cemeteries," p. 158, table iv, and p. 160, fig. 2.

105. L. Barkóczi and A. Salamon, "Remarks on the Sixth Century History of 'Pannonia.'"

106. Zdenko Vinski, "Die völkerwanderungszeitliche Nekropole in Kranj und der Reihengräberfelder Horizont des 6. Jahrhunderts im westlichen Jugoslawien"; and Lojze Bolta, "Spätantikes Gräberfeld auf Rifnik bei Sentzur," pp. 138–40. On Dravlje, see Marijan Slabe, "La Nécropole de la période de la migration des peuples à Dravlje," p. 150.

107. Bona, *Dawn*, p. 57. On the eagle-headed buckles, see also M. Rusu, "Pontische Gürtelschnallen mit Adlerkopf (VI–VIII Jh. n.C.)."

108. Cassiodorus *Variae* 5. 10 and 11; Bona, *Dawn*, pp. 57–59, 84. One might add the possible burial of a noble Gepidic female near the Villa Clelia in Imola. See also Karl Hauck, "Mainz und Odense," p. 82.

109. Hampel, *Alterthumer*, vol. 2, pp. 15–17; vol. 3, pl. 14.

6. Religion

1. There exists to date little to recommend on the general subject. Among the best modern studies are Knut Schäferdick, "Der germanische Arianismus," and E. A. Thompson, "Christianity and the Northern Barbarians." See also J. de Vries, *Altgermanische Religionsgeschichte*.

2. Tacitus *Germania* 7 (ed. M. Winterbottom).

3. Malcolm Todd, *Everyday Life of the Barbarians* (Putnam, N.Y., 1972), pp. 129–36. On the "cult league of the Goths," see further Rolf Hachmann, *The Germanic Peoples* and *Die Goten und Skandinavien*.

4. For a full elaboration of the importance of these subtribal "kernels" in the evolution of the Gothic people, see particularly Herwig Wolfram, *Geschichte der Goten*. Others have seen this in a still broader context. See further Reinhard Wenskus, *Stammesbildung und Verfassung*, and his "Amaler," pp. 247–48. There is no doubt that these great families and their leaders followed Theodoric to Italy. They may even have left their mark on the archaeological record; see Giovanni Annibaldi and Joachim Werner, "Ostgotische Grabfunde aus Acquasanta, Prov. Ascoli Piceno (Marche)."

5. Similar cult communities are emerging in the archaeological patterns. See especially Karl Hauck, *Goldbrakteaten aus Sievern*, who sees the tribe as essentially a religious cult group.

6. Francis P. Magoun, Jr., "On the Old Germanic Altar—or Oath-Ring (Stallahringr)." Most importantly, Radu Harhoiu, *The Fifth-Century A.D. Treasure from Pietroasa Romania*, pp. 13–14.

7. Pointed out by Emilian Popescu, "Das Problem der Kontinuität in Rumänien im Lichte der epigraphischen Entdeckungen."

8. Eunapius, frag. 55 (ed. L. Dindorf). Also S. Paulinus of Nola commented on the conversion of certain Visigoths to Bishop Nicetas (*Carmina* 17) and Vic-

toricius (*Epist.* 18) in the fourth century as a necessary step toward peace and concord. The *Epistulae* and *Carmina* were edited by G. von Hartel, *CSEL*, vols. 29–30 (Leipzig, 1894).

9. Sozomenus *Historia Ecclesiastica* 6. 21 (ed. J. Bidez).

10. Jordanes *Getica* 267.

11. At least according to Sozomenus 37. 7.

12. Ibid., 37. 12–14.

13. Eunapius, frag. 55.

14. *Passio*, ed. H. Delehaye, in "Saints de Thrace et de Mésie," pp. 217–20.

15. One of the first to explore the *Passio* was E. A. Thompson, *The Visigoths in the Time of Ulfila*; more recently see Zeev Rubin, "The Conversion of the Visigoths to Christianity."

16. The various martyrologies and the Gothic Calendar are discussed by several authorities, among them: H. Achelis, "Der älteste deutsche Kalender" and *Die Martyrologien*. For these specific references, see Richard Löwe, "Gotische Namen in hagiographischen Texten." The recent arguments advanced by Rubin, "Conversion," pp. 39–44, add appreciably to Löwe's work.

17. R. Löwe, "Der gotische Kalender," pp. 245, 259–61; Rubin, "Conversion," pp. 52–53. The Calendar is edited along with the Bible in W. Streitberg, *Die gotische Bibel*, p. 472.

18. Ammianus 28. 5. 14.

19. So the third-century writer Gregorius Thaumaturgus *Epist. Canon*, cols. 1019–49 (ed. J. P. Migne).

20. Elsewhere we can see even among the pagan priests, uniquely able to write in runes, the profound influence of Christianity. See further S. Opitz, *Südgermanische Runeninschriften im älteren Futhark aus der Merowingerzeit*, for interesting comparative data.

21. Sozomenus 7. 24.

22. Jordanes *Getica* 282, 288; Anonymus Valesianus 57.

23. Cassiodorus *Variae* 10. 31; *Paneg.* to Witigis and Matasuentha, 475–76 (ed. Th. Mommsen, *M.G.H., A.A.*, vol. 12). See further Sabine MacCormick, *Art and Ceremony in the Late Roman Empire*, pp. 229–40, and Dietrich Claude, "Die Ostrogotischen Königserhebungen," pp. 181–86.

24. Ennodius *Paneg.* 87–93 (ed. F. Vogel, pp. 213–14).

25. *Liber Pontificalis* 86, *partes ulteriores* (ed. L. Duchesne, 2 vols. [1886, 1892, Bibl. des Écoles fr. d'Athènes et de Rome, 2e série]).

26. The pillar at Theodoric's tomb is now lost, but its discoverers were careful to record the scene in line drawings. See Robert Heidenreich and Heinz Johannes, *Das Grabmal Theoderichs zu Ravenna*, pp. 18–21. The pillar was one of several placed at prescribed intervals around the tomb. For an example from Gaul, see I, 183 in *Recueil des inscriptions chrétiennes de la Gaule anterieurs à la renaissance carolingienne*, p. 458.

27. See further S. V. Grancsay, "A Barbarian's Chieftain's Helmet"; Joachim Werner, "Zur Herkunft der frühmittelalterlichen Spangenhelme," with citations to earlier literature and present locations. Werner proposes an evolutionary route from Persia to the late Roman and Byzantine empires to Ostrogothic Italy. The helmets manufactured in Ostrogothic Italy were decorated for Germanic tastes and often traded to outlying areas, where the style continued to evolve. An example found at Planig bei Kreuznach offers many parallels to that from Montepagano, including an eight-pointed star or sun, crosses, and trees, all bound by a similar headband. The Planig piece is in the Mittelrheinisches Landesmuseum,

Mainz, and is best photographed in Friedrich Behn, *Römertum und Völkerwanderung*, pl. 67. An example from Stössen, Kr. Hohenmölsen also has a headband identical to that of Montepagano and Planig but with the added similarity to Montepagano of an A-ω cross stimpled on the front. For a fine illustration of the Stössen piece, see Friedrich Schlette, *Germanen zwischen Thorsberg und Ravenna*, pl. 5. Paul Post, "Der kupferne Spangenhelm," goes so far as to suggest specific battles during which these rare helmets may have been lost. We might add the magnificent gold-cloisonné fish found in Switzerland to the inventory of fish symbolism. They are, however, not securely Ostrogothic. See Max Martin, *Die Schweiz im Frühmittelalter*, figs. 47, 67.

28. For an example of the Ostrogothic use of the lion symbol, see the bronze coin issued under Totila, ca. 552, no. 91 in Wolfgang Hahn, *Moneta Imperii Byzantini*, vol. 1.

29. Joachim Werner, "Fernhandel und Naturalwirtschaft im östlichen Merowingerreich nach archäologischen und numismatischen Zeugnissen."

30. Zdenko Vinskí, "Zikadenschmuck aus Jugoslawien." Volker Bierbrauer, *Die ostgotischen Grab- und Schatzfunde in Italien*, Vecchiazzano pp. 332–34, Udine pp. 329–31.

31. For a discussion of "masked fibulae," see further Annibaldi and Werner, *Grabfunde*, and Otto J. Maenchen-Helfen, *The World of the Huns*, pp. 280–86.

32. On the changing interpretations of these animal portrayals, see further Wera von Blankenburg, *Heilige und dämonische Tiere.*

33. Note, however, that the basic Burgundian styles remained essentially abstract and pagan for centuries. On the complex archaeological data for the Burgundians, including a discussion of these traditions, see Max Martin, "Burgunden," pp. 248–71.

34. Theodoros Lector *Historia Ecclesiastica* 165–226 (ed. G. Hansen).

35. *PLRE*, II, Barbara 209–210, for references to Ennodian correspondence; Procopius *B.G.*, VI, 6. 18–19.

36. See further, with references to Orthodox literature, Jacques Zeiller, "Étude sur l'arianisme en Italie à l'époque ostrogothique et à l'époque lombarde," pp. 134–35.

37. It should be noted that here once again Theodoric viewed the Jews as separate but protected and with their own customs guaranteed; Cassiodorus *Variae* 2. 27, 4. 33, 5. 37.

38. Sidonius Apollinaris *Epist.* 7. 6. (ed. C. Luetjohann).

39. Despite the miracles, the essentially political aspects of the ultimate Visigothic conversion are clear. See further E. A. Thompson, "The Conversion of the Visigoths to Catholicism," and J. N. Hillgarth, "La Conversion de los visigodos." For the actions at Toledo, see the acta of the council, *Concilios visigóticos e hispano-romanos*, ed. J. Vives, pp. 107–145. Reccared's personal conversion, on the other hand, was a private matter: Fredegarius *Chronicon* 4. 8 (ed. J. M. Wallace-Hadrill).

40. Victor Vitensis *Historia persecutiones Wandalicae*, I (ed. C. Halm, pp. 1–58). On Victor, see further Christian Courtois, *Victor de Vita et son oeuvre.*

41. Victor, II, 8–9, discussed in Mechtild Overbeck, *Untersuchungen zum afrikanischen Senatsadel in der Spätantike*, pp. 65–66.

42. Cassiodorus *Variae* 9. 1. On the Vandals in general, see Christian Courtois, *Les Vandales et l'Afrique.*

43. Procopius, VI, 6. 18–19; *C.I.L.*, 5. 6470.

44. Jan-Olof Tjäder, ed., *Die nichtliterarischen lateinischen Papyri Italiens aus der*

Zeit 445–700, papyri no. 3 and 7; *C.I.L.* 11. 5976; 5. 7793; 5. 6176; 5. 1583; 9. 2817.

45. *Documentum Neapolitanum* 82–85 (as reprinted in P. Scardigli, *Die Goten. Sprache und Kultur* [München, 1973], p. 277).

46. *Documentum Aretinum*, as in Scardigli, pp. 279–80. On nomenclature and the possible taking over of Gothic forms, ibid., pp. 280–301.

47. The commentaries are Visigothic and are edited with the Bible in Wilhelm August Streitberg, *Die gotische Bibel*. On Arian bishops, see also Georg Pfeilschifter, *Der Ostgotenkönig Theoderich der Grosse und die katholische Kirche*, p. 50.

7. Leadership and Government

1. Eunapius, frag. 55 (ed. L. Dindorf).

2. Ibid., frag. 60 (Dindorf, p. 252).

3. For references, see G. H. Balg, *A Comparative Glossary of the Gothic Language*.

4. See the discussions of these terms in Richard Löwe, "Der gotische Kalender," pp. 245, 259–261. In addition to those sources discussed by Löwe, add the rather careful use of *duces* to describe Germanic leaders, especially Goths and Franks, beneath the *rex* in the Continuator of Prosper, *M.G.H., A.A.*, 9. 199, 302.

5. *Passio s. Sabae* 218. 5; 8 (ed. H. Delehaye, in "Saints de Thrace et de Mésie"); Balg, *Glossary*; Zeev Rubin, "The Conversion of the Visigoths to Christianity," p. 38, n. 26.

6. We can catch a glimpse of similar, if not identical, internal social units among the Lombards where there are more ample data. See further the discussion by G. P. Bognetti, "L'Influsso delle istituzioni militari romane sulle istituzioni longobarde del secolo VIe la natura della 'fara.'" The Lombardic *farae*, like the Gothic *φυλαί*, were subtribal groups combining familial units and warbands.

7. Olympiodorus is preserved in Photius *Bibliothèque*, Codex 80 (57a), vol. 1, p. 168, 1. 1–16 (ed. R. Henry).

8. Ibid., 57a, 1. 36–39, 168: *ὅτι τῶν μετὰ* Ροδογάϊσον Γότθων *ὁι κεφαλαιῶται ὀπτίματοι ἐκαλοῦντο, εἰς δώδεκα συντείνοντες χιλιάδας, ὅυς καταπολεμήθας* Στελίχων Ροδογάϊσον *προσηταιρίσατο.*

9. Wilhelm August Streitberg, *Die gotische Bibel*, p. 472.

10. Ammianus Marcellinus 31. 6. 3; 31. 7. 1–16.

11. Eunapius, frag. 60 (ed. Dindorf, pp. 252–53). These actions took place under Theodosius and thus long after the crossing of the Danube, p. 251.

12. Joachim Werner, *Die Langobarden in Pannonien*, pp. 119–20. Although I do not agree with the basic reassessment of the settlement process as articulated by W. Goffart, *Barbarians and Romans, A.D. 418–584*, his discussion of the Lombards 176–205 adds appreciably to our view of the *farae*.

13. Paulus Diaconus *Historia Langobardorum 2.9* (ed. L. Bethmann and G. Waitz).

14. Georg Waitz, *Deutsche Verfassungsgeschichte*, p. 118, n. 37 on the fara with references to texts.

15. *C.I.L.* 5. 7417.

16. Ferdinand Wrede, *Über die Sprache der Ostgoten in Italien*, p. 134.

17. *C.I.L.* 11. 3567.

18. Mario Degani, *Il tesoro romano-barbarico di Reggio Emilia*, pp. 75, 79, and Volker Bierbrauer, *Die ostgotischen Grab- und Schatzfunde in Italien*, p. 308.

19. Jordanes *Getica* 21–24; now see also the discussion of "tradition centers"

as a formulative aspect of Germanic society in Herwig Wolfram, *Geschichte der Goten*, especially pp. 1–30.

20. For a fuller discussion of the author's views, see Thomas S. Burns, "Pursuing the Early Gothic Migrations," pp. 197–99.

21. C. Brady, *The Legends of Ermanaric*.

22. Procopius *B.G.*, VII, 20. 19–20 (Loeb edition), sent to Armenia, VIII, 9. 4. He went on to redeem himself in the East, VII, 12. 30–34.

23. Anonymus Valesianus 68–69 (Teubner edition).

24. Procopius *Anecdota* 26. 27; Cassiodorus *Variae* 6. 6.

25. A. H. M. Jones, *The Later Roman Empire*, p. 256, n. 45.

26. Procopius *Anecdota* 26. 28; Symmachus *Epist*. 5. 7 (ed. O. Seeck).

27. See further William G. Sinnigen, "Administrative Shifts of Competence under Theodoric."

28. *C.I.L.* 6. 9379 (*PLRE*, II, 1167); *C.I.L.* 11. 310 (*PLRE*, II, 987).

29. *PLRE*, II, 1126.

30. For all the surviving offices, see first the fundamental work by A. H. M. Jones, *The Later Roman Empire*.

31. Cassiodorus *Variae* 8. 22.

32. See William G. Sinnigen, "Comites Consistoriani in Ostrogothic Italy"; and Theodor Mommsen, "Ostgothische Studien," p. 419, n. 6.

33. Cassiodorus *Variae* 6. 12 (in Thomas Hodgkin, *The Letters of Cassiodorus*, p. 308).

34. Cassiodorus *Variae* 6. 5.

35. *C.I.L.* 11. 268. vir sub(limis) Gudila com(es) [ord(inis) pr(imi) et cura]tor r(ei) p(u)b(licae) hanc sta[tuam terrae m]oto . . . . See also the commentary by O. Fiebiger and L. Schmidt, "Inschriftensammlung zur Geschichte der Ostgermanen," p. 94 (no. 182).

36. Cassiodorus *Variae* 4. 39.

37. On Bergantinus, *PLRE*, II, 225; Julianus, *PLRE*, II, (Iulianus, 24), 640.

38. In general, see Jones, *Empire*, vol. 1, p. 255. The office was functioning during the reign of Athalaric (Cassiodorus *Variae* 9. 13) and continued under Justinian.

39. Cassiodorus *Variae* 4. 7 and 13.

40. So he is remembered on an inscription, *Fiebiger* (1944), no. 8.

41. Cassiodorus *Variae* 9. 24–25.

42. *Variae* 4. 15; and see also J. E. Eubanks, "Navigation on the Tiber."

43. Anonymus Valesianus 60.

44. Joannes Malalas *Chronographia* 384 (ed. C. de Boor, *CSHB*, vol. 28 [Berlin, 1905]).

45. If the *Edictum* is indeed Ostrogothic, then, of course, it represents an early attempt to bring the same aspects of the various legal processes under central control through royal legislation.

46. Cassiodorus *Variae* 7. 3 (Hodgkin, *Letters*, pp. 321–22).

47. *Variae* 5. 29.

48. *Variae* 5. 30.

49. *Variae* 7. 26–28.

50. *Variae* 7. 24–25; 8. 4; 9. 9.

51. *Variae* 1. 40; 5. 24; *C.I.L.* 3. 9563; see also John J. Wilkes, *Dalmatia*, p. 427.

52. Procopius *B.G.*, V, 15. 27–28.

53. Ennodius *Paneg*. 21 (65).

54. *Variae* 4. 49. PLRE, II, 485 suggests that he was a *comes provinciae*.

55. Cassiodorus *Variae* 9. 8.
56. Franz F. Kraus, *Die Münzen Odovacars und des Ostrogotenreiches in Italien*, pp. 6, 94–95. On the Byzantine reestablishment, *Novellae* 11 (14 April 535), *Codex Iustinianus* (ed. P. Krüger), creating a new metropolitan see including Sirmium. The real powers were the Gepids, Erulians, and Sclaveni; see Procopius *B.G.*, VII, 33. 7. 13; *Aedif*, III, 2. 1.
57. *Variae* 4. 49; 5. 14 and 15.
58. *Variae* 4. 12 and 46.
59. Ludwig Schmidt, "Die Comites Gothorum," p. 127.
60. Liberius 3, *PLRE*, II, 678–79; Gemellus 2, 499–500.
61. For possible remains of garrisons guarding estates, see, for example, Stezzano in Bierbrauer, *Schatzfunde*, p. 315; military road stations, the example of San Andrea di Grottamare, p. 283, and probably Acquasanta as well, see Giovanni Annibaldi and Joachim Werner, "Ostgotische Grabfunde aus Acquasanta, Prov. Ascoli Piceno (Marche)." *Variae* 9. 10.
62. See further on the development of the *buccellarii*, including the case of Oppas and the Ostrogoths, H.-J. Diesner, "Das Buccellariertum von Stilicho und Sarus bis auf Aëtius."
63. *Variae* 8. 26.
64. *Variae* 5. 26 and 27; Procopius *B.G.*, V, 12. 46–48. The *millenarii* are discussed in greater detail in the following chapter.
65. Émile Chénon, "Étude historique sur le defensor civitatis."
66. *Variae* 4. 43; 7. 11.
67. *Variae* 7. 12.
68. *Variae* 4. 27–28.
69. *Variae* 1. 16; 4. 19; 9. 10; 12. 2.
70. For example, *Variae* 3. 36 (allegation of high-level misconduct); 4. 5 (famine relief); 5. 23 (military supplies); 5. 35 (legal misconduct concerning Spain).
71. *PLRE*, II, 1126.
72. *Variae* 1. 24.
73. *Variae* 2. 4; 12. 3.
74. *Variae* 2. 13.
75. *Variae* 2. 20.
76. *Variae* 3. 20.
77. *Variae* 3. 48; 7. 15.
78. *Variae* 4. 14.
79. *Variae* 4. 32, 34, 39.
80. *Variae* 5. 10.
81. *Variae* 5. 27.
82. *Variae* 9. 10.
83. *Variae* 3. 20; 7. 39; 8. 27.
84. *Variae* 3. 36.
85. *Variae* 4. 5.
86. *Variae* 5. 23.
87. *Variae* 5. 35.
88. Jan-Olof Tjäder, ed., *Die nichtliterarischen lateinischen Papyri Italiens aus der Zeit 445–700*, papyrus no. 7.
89. *Variae* 8. 9–10; 11. 1.
90. *Variae* 9. 2.
91. *Variae* 9. 3.
92. *Variae* 9. 12.

93. *Variae* 9. 14.
94. *Variae* 9. 14(5).
95. *Variae* 9. 18.
96. *Variae* 9. 20.
97. Procopius *B.G.*, V, 2. 1–10, 19; V, 3. 10, 4. 5, 4. 4, 19.
98. Ibid., V, 2. 20–22; 3. 12. *Variae* 10. 3.
99. *Variae* 4. 39; 5. 12, 10. 5.
100. W. Wroth, *Catalogue of the Coins of the Vandals, Ostrogoths, and Lombards and of the Emperors of Thessalonica, Nicea, and Trebizond in the British Museum*, pp. 36–39, and the discussion of Theodahad in Wolfgang Hahn, *Moneta Imperii Byzantini*, pp. 87–89. His copper coinage introduced the "royal bust" first seen on Theodoric's great triple solidus.
101. *Variae* 10. 18.
102. *Variae* 12. 2–3.
103. *Variae* 10. 26.
104. *Variae* 10. 31.
105. Only fragments of Cassiodorus's panegyric are preserved; ed. Th. Mommsen, p. 463.
106. Witigis minted a quarter siliqua with the monogram of Theodoric; Hahn, *Moneta*, p. 87.
107. *Variae* 12. 10, trying to collect arrears in the *tributum*. See also *Variae* 12. 8 and Procopius *B.G.*, VII, 6. 5.
108. *Variae* 10. 18, 27; 12. 7.
109. *Variae* 12. 18–19.
110. Procopius *B.G.*, VII, 8. 15–25; Agathias *Hist. Libri Quinque*, I, 20. 10 (ed. R. Keydell).
111. Procopius *B.G.*, V, 13. 17–25.
112. Ibid., VIII, 23. 1.
113. Ibid., VII, 8. 12–25; 24. 27; 35. 31–33.
114. Agathias *Libri Quinque*, I, 20. 1.
115. Ibid., II, 13–14; I, 1.

8. Warriors and the Military System

1. There were, of course, other peoples trying to control the fragmented remains of Roman units. For example, Coroticus and his followers in Britain were in demand at the time of Saint Patrick (see his letter to Coroticus, ed. R. Hanson, *Sources Chrétiennes*, p. 249, Paris, 1978). The Franks manipulated the surviving military forces under the Patrician in southern Gaul (see further Bernard S. Bachrach, *Merovingian Military Organization, 481–751.*
2. See Jaroslav Šašel, "Antiqui Barbari." Šašel (pp. 135 ff.) believes that the "antiqui barbari" were the remains of Germanic-Hunnic fragments of Attila's confederacy not yet completely assimilated.
3. Cassiodorus *Variae* 1. 24; 1. 38 (ed. Th. Mommsen).
4. For examples of concern for dress and rank, see Procopius *B.G.* (Loeb edition), VI, 23. 37; 30. 7; 30. 17; VIII, 32. 2; and Agathias *Historiarum Libri Quinque*, I, 20. 10 (ed. R. Keydell).
5. *Variae* 5. 36.
6. Dexippus, frag. 25 (ed. F. Jacoby, *Fragmente der griechischen Historiker*, vol. 2A), and Jordanes *Getica* 92 (ed. Th. Mommsen).
7. Dexippus, frag. 27 (ed. Jacoby, pp. 470–72); *Getica* 102–03.

8. Dexippus, frag. 29 (ed. Jacoby, p. 474).

9. Zosimus *Historia Nova* 1. 43 (Teubner edition). Details are preserved in a certain Eusebius 101 F. 2 (ed. Jacoby, p. 481).

10. Zonaras *Epitomae historiarum* 12. 26 (ed. T. Büttner-Wobst); Cedrenus *Compendium Historiarum* 454 (ed. J. P. Migne); see also Leo Grammaticus *Chronographia* 78 (ed. Bekker) and Georgius Monachus 160. Recounted in detail in chap. 2.

11. Mauricius *Strategicum* 4. 3. 1 (ed. George T. Dennis and Ernst Gamillscheg) is the best account of the disaster. Others include the *Getica* 101–103 and Zosimus 1. 23, and Sextus Aurelius Victor 29. 1–5 (Teubner edition). See further Friedrich Lammert, "Zum Kampf der Goten bei Abrittus im J. 251." On the Germans' use of ambush in general, see Hans Georg Gundel, "Die Bedeutung des Geländes in der Kriegskunst der Germanen."

12. We have discussed these events in chap. 2. See again the numismatic data assembled by Boris Gerov, "Die gotische Invasion in Mösien und Thrakien unter Decius im Lichte der Hortfunde."

13. For examples, see Zosimus 1. 33–34, 70; *Getica* 90.

14. Herodianus 8. 5. 3 (Loeb edition), *Getica* 221. Alaric had similar problems in Liguria; see Claudianus *vi cons. Hon.* 238 (Loeb edition).

15. Ammianus Marcellinus 31. 3. 5 (ed. W. Seyfarth).

16. See further Radu Vulpe, *Le Vallum de la Moldavie inférieure et le "mur" d'Athanaric*, and his "Les *Valla* de la Valachie, de la Basse-Moldavie et du Boudjak."

17. Ammianus 31. 4. 2 reported that similar retreats into the forests characterized the reactions of warbands along the Rhine to Roman attacks.

18. Ammianus 31. 8. 1–2; Zosimus 4. 23; see also Thomas S. Burns, "The Battle of Adrianople: A Reconsideration," with complete citations to the sources and discussion.

19. The bickering between the imperial colleagues is reflected in their coinage and probably explains Valens's rashness at Adrianople. See Harold Mattingly, C. H. V. Sutherland, and R. A. G. Carson, *The Roman Imperial Coinage*, vol. 9, pp. xv–xxii.

20. On the location of the battle, see F. Runkel, *Die Schlacht bei Adrianopel.*

21. As we have seen in chap. 3, the important work by László Várady, *Das letzte Jahrhundert Pannoniens, 376–476*, overextends the evidence for these peoples.

22. Ch. Tolkin, "The Battle of the Goths and the Huns."

23. Ennodius *Pan.* 7 (ed. F. Vogel).

24. Ibid., *Pan.* 62 (chap. 29) 210.

25. There are numerous scholarly clarifications on the various "boundaries" of the Ostrogothic Kingdom; see, for example, H. Zeiss, "Die Nordgrenze des Ostgotenreiches"; E. Schaffran, "Zur Nordgrenze des ostgotischen Reiches in Kärnten"; and Volker Bierbrauer, "Zur ostgotischen Geschichte in Italien."

26. Jaroslav Šašel, *Claustra Alpium Iuliarum*, with all the pertinent literary sources.

27. Zosimus 2. 45; see further Jaroslav Šašel, "The Struggle between Magnentius and Constantius II for Italy and Illyricum"; and Thomas S. Burns, "The Germans and Roman Frontier Policy (ca. A.D. 350–378)."

28. Paulus Orosius *Historiarum adversum paganos libri vii* 7. 35. 13 (ed. C. Zangemeister); Ambrosius Sanctus *De obitu Theodosii* (ed. J. P. Migne, vol. 16, col. 1386 ff.); texts also collected in Šašel, *Claustra*, pp. 28–40.

29. Texts of Turranius Rufinus, Zosimus, and others are in Šašel, *Claustra*, pp. 33–39.

30. Jordanes *Getica* 268–71. Šašel's (see "Antiqui Barbari") placement of the three does not accord with the *Getica*, which had the Sadagi living between two settlements of Ostrogoths.

31. Thilo Ulbert, "Zur Siedlungskontinuität im südöstlichen Alpenraum (vom 2. bis 6. Jahrhundert n. Chr.). Dargestellt am Beispiel von Vranje (ehem. Untersteiermark)," pp. 150–57, especially Ajdovski Gradec bei Vranje, along the main route to Italy. On Ad Pirum, see Thilo Ulbert, ed., *Ad Pirum (Hrušica)*, pp. 47–50.

32. Šašel, *Claustra*, pp. 85–86; for Trieste, see *Tabula Imperii Romani* L. 33 (Rome, 1961). The finds, for the most part, are published in Volker Bierbrauer, *Die ostgotischen Grab- und Schatzfunde in Italien*.

33. Zdenko Vinski, "Die völkerwanderungszeitliche Nekropole in Kranj und der Reihengräberfelder Horizont des 6. Jahrhunderts in westlichen Jugoslawien," pp. 259–65; Marijan Slabe, "La Nécropole de la période de la migration des peuples à Dravlje."

34. Lojze Bolta, "Spätantikes Gräberfeld auf Rifnik bei Sentzur."

35. Jovan Kovačevič, *Varvarska Kolonizacija Južnoslovenskih Oblasti od IV do početka VII veká*, pp. 64–65.

36. Katherine M. Edwards, *Corinth*, vol. 6: *Coins*, p. 120, item no. 766, a five-nummi piece of Theodoric; Margaret Thompson, *The Athenian Agora*, vol. 2: *Coins*, pp. 66–67, nine Ostrogothic bronze coins of various issues, including Theodoric and Totila.

37. Ferenc Fülep, *Roman Cemeteries on the Territory of Pécs (Sopianae)*, pp. 9–10; Ferenc Fülep, *Sopianae*, p. 38.

38. Surely we cannot assign the polyhedron earrings, perhaps dating to the early sixth century, to any particular group. Esyter B. Vágó and István Bóna, *Die Gräberfelder von Intercisa*, vol. 1, pp. 131–34, 168–75, 196–209.

39. Lajos Balla, T. P. Buocz, Z. Kádár, A. Mócsy, and T. Szentléleky, *Die römischen Steindenkmäler von Savaria*, pp. 32–34.

40. Ennodius *Pan*. 12 (60–62) 210.

41. Cassiodorus *Variae* 1. 40 to Osuin; see also *C.I.L*. 3. 9593 = 12867 for Ostrogoths in the area.

42. Procopius *B.G*., V, 6. 2; 7. 22–36. See further E. Dyggve, "L'Influence des Goths à Salone."

43. Ennodius *Pan*. 12 (60–62); *Getica* 300.

44. Jordanes *Getica* 300–301.

45. Ennodius *Pan*. 21. (65) 211, lines 5–13.

46. Procopius *B.G*., V, 3. 15–17.

47. For example, Witigis and Tulum; Cassiodorus *Chronica*, s.a. 504 (ed. Th. Mommsen, *M.G.H., A.A*., vol. 11) and *Variae* 8. 10; see also Procopius *B.G*., V, 11. 5.

48. *Novellae*, XI (14 April 535), *Codex Iustinianus* (ed. P. Krüger), creating a new metropolitan see, including Sirmium. The Gepids, Erulians, and Sclaveni, however, dominated the area militarily; Procopius *B.G*., VII, 33. 7–13; *Aedif*., III, 2. 1.

49. See also Endre Tóth, "Zur Geschichte des nordpannonischen Raumes im 5. und 6. Jahrhundert," who concluded that at least under Theodoric the cultural orb of the Gothic Kingdom linked Ravenna with the northern half of Pannonia.

50. *Variae* 5. 10 and 11. Exactly how the payment of three solidi was disbursed is unknown. I agree with G. Sartorius, *Versuch über die Regierung der Ostgothen während ihrer Herrschaft in Italien*, p. 289, that the most likely interpretation is that

the three solidi represented the amount of state funds assigned to Veranus, the addressee, to take care of Gepids. Surely three solidi were not paid to each Gepid.

51. For an attempt to gauge settlement density through place-name analysis, see Josef Rungg, *Ortsnamen der Goten, Römer, Franken in Rätien, Noricum, besonders Tirol.* The Gothic place names are dubious and of little independent value. G. Schneider-Schnekenburger, *Churrätien im Frühmittelalter auf Grund der archäologischen Funde*, pp. 12–13, does not even mention them in her discussion of place names.

52. Sixty men were thus stationed at Aosta to monitor the southern approaches of the Bernard passes; *Variae* 2. 5.

53. *Variae* 7. 4; see further Richard Heuberger, "Das ostgotische Rätien," pp. 81, 109, and his *Rätien im Altertum und Frühmittelalter*, pp. 120–30.

54. *Variae* 1. 11.

55. There is no absolute proof that these officials existed in Raetia under the Ostrogoths, but they are attested to before and after. See further Otto P. Clavadetscher, "Churrätien in Übergang von der Spätantike zum Mittelalter nach den Schriftquellen," p. 162.

56. Ravennas Anonymus, IV, 26. 45 (ed. O. Cuntz and J. Schnetz, p. 61 emendation).

57. Clavadetscher, "Übergang," p. 164; Schneider-Schnekenburger, *Frühmittelalter*, p. 8, as a purely military presence.

58. Heuberger suggested Maxima Sequanorum, and this explanation is generally accepted; see Clavadetscher, "Übergang," pp. 160–66.

59. *Variae* 2. 41; see further Clavadetscher, "Ubergang," p. 161, for a full discussion.

60. For the Thuringians, see *Variae* 3. 3, and for the marriage alliance, *Variae* 4. 1. For the Alamanni, see *Variae* 3. 3, 50. On the problems of the Alamanni with a catalogue of finds and references to the literary sources, see Volker Bierbrauer, "Alamannische Funde der frühen Ostgotenzeit aus Oberitalien." The Burgundians are discussed further below.

61. *Variae* 3. 48.

62. *Variae* 2. 5.

63. Schaffran, "Nordgrenze."

64. Procopius *B.G.*, VI, 27. 28–29.

65. Volker Bierbrauer, "Zu den Vorkommen ostgotischer Bügelfibeln in Raetia II."

66. Ennodius *Vita S. Epifani* 155–57 (ed. F. Vogel, *M.G.H., A.A.*, vol. 7).

67. Marius Aventicensis *Chronicon* 509 (ed. Th. Mommsen, *M.G.H., A.A.*, vol. 11); *Variae* 1. 24 probably refers to this campaign.

68. *PLRE*, II, 679–81.

69. *PLRE*, II, Gemellus 2, 499–500.

70. *Variae* 3. 41.

71. *PLRE*, II, 706. See further Ludwig Schmidt, "Die Comites Gothorum"; J. Declareuil, "Des Comtes de cités à la fin du Ve siècle," especially pp. 814–28; and Rolf Sprandel, "Dux und Comes in der Merovingerzeit," especially pp. 56–65.

72. *Variae* 3. 40 and 42.

73. *Variae* 3. 44; 4. 5 and 7. Also relating to Provence are *Variae* 3. 17 and 18, 4. 19, 5. 10, 8. 7, 9. 1. On the use of rations, see further Walter Goffart, *Barbarians and Romans,* A.D. *418–584*, pp. 46–50.

74. *Variae* 2. 5.

75. *PLRE*, II, Tulum, 1131–33.
76. *PLRE*, II, Cyprianus 2, 332.
77. *Variae* 5. 33.
78. *Variae* 5. 30.
79. For Tremonus, see Marcellinus Comes 538 (ed. Th. Mommsen, *M.G.H., A.A.*, vol. 11, p. 105); on Uraias, see Procopius *B.G.*, VI, 18. 19 ff.; on Hildibadus, Procopius *B.G.*, VI, 29. 41 ff.; on Hunila, see Jordanes *Getica* 312; and on Eraric, see Procopius *B.G.*, VII, 2. 1 ff.
80. Procopius, VII, 2. 1–4; VI, 14. 24.
81. *Variae* 3.3; see further B. Schmidt, "Theodorich der Grosse und die damaszierten Schwerter der Thüringer." On the probable techniques used in the early Middle Ages in the north, see J. W. Anstee and L. Biek, "A Study in Pattern-welding."

9. The End of the Ostrogothic Kingdom

1. Procopius *Bellum Gothicum*, V, 9. 2–7 (Loeb edition).
2. Ibid., VII, 9. 10–15.
3. Ibid., VII, 36. 28–37. 4.
4. Ibid., V, 3. 2–4.
5. Ibid., V, 6. 22–26.
6. Ibid., V, 6. 2; V, 7. 22–36. Witigis later attempted to retake the city with a combined land and sea blockade; V, 16. 11.
7. Ibid., V, 27. 27–29.
8. Ibid., V, 11. 1–3.
9. Ibid., VI, 7. 28–34; 10. 1; 13. 4 and 16–18.
10. Ibid., VI, 18. 12–13.
11. Procopius, *B.V.*, III, 14. 5–6; *B.G.*, V, 3. 22.
12. Ibid., V, 25. 8.
13. Ibid., V, 26. 1; 28. 1; VI, 3. 14.
14. Cassiodorus *Variae* 12. 17 (ed. Th. Mommsen).
15. Procopius *B.G.*, V, 11. 14–15.
16. Ibid., VII, 36. 24–27; 23. 3–6.
17. Ibid., VII, 22. 4–6, 20; 16. 15; 13. 1.
18. But see Zinaida V. Udalcova, "La Campagne de Narses et l'écrasement de Totila."
19. Procopius *B.G.*, VII, 6. 5.
20. Ibid., VII, 8. 8–20; 12. 1–10.
21. Ibid., VII, 14. 5–7; 37. 5. The Roman navy could defeat the Goths and did so on those infrequent occasions when they could intercept them; see VIII, 23. 31–34.
22. Ibid., V, 8. 7–10. 48. The Jews doubtless compared their lot under the Ostrogoths favorably to that of their kinsmen in the East.
23. Ibid., V, 8. 2–3.
24. *Variae* 3. 38.
25. Procopius *B.G.*, VI, 21. 39; VII, 10. 19.
26. *Liber Pontificalis* 60 (Silverius 536–37) (ed. Th. Mommsen).
27. Procopius *B.G.*, VI, 9. 10–22.
28. Ibid., VI, 7. 35; VII, 6. 5; 18. 21.
29. But see E. A. Thompson, *Romans and Barbarians*, p. 89.
30. Procopius *B.G.*, VII, 20. 26–21. 23.

31. Ibid., VII, 22. 1–3.
32. Ibid., VII, 11. 32; 25. 7; and Marcellinus Comes 539 (ed. Th. Mommsen, *M.G.H., A.A.*, vol. 11 [Chronica Minora, vol. 2]).
33. Procopius *B.G.*, VII, 24. 32.
34. Ibid., VII, 22. 3–20.
35. Ibid., V, 11. 5.
36. Ibid., V, 13. 17–25.
37. Ibid., V, 12. 29–30.
38. Ibid., VII, 33. 7–13; *de Aedif* III, 2. 1.
39. Ibid., VIII, 23. 1.
40. Ibid., VII, 8. 12–25.
41. Ibid., VII 24. 27.
42. Odoin's rebellion ended in his beheading under Theodoric; Anonymus Valesianus 68–69 (Teubner edition). Only Theudis, safe in distant Spain, is recorded in tacit opposition.
43. In addition to those forces mentioned in Byzantine service by Agathias *Historiarum Libri Quinque* (ed. R. Keydell), we might add those in some of the midcentury papyri from Ravenna as discussed previously. The nobles serving in Totila's fleet also saw special service.
44. Procopius *B.G.*, VII, 4. 31; 5. 13; 13. 3; 15. 7; 26. 15; 28. 13.
45. Ammianus Marcellinus 31. 6. 4–5 (ed. W. Seyfarth). On this pitiful episode, see further E. A. Thompson, *Romans and Barbarians*, p. 83.
46. Procopius *B.G.*, VIII, 36. 6–37. 26–27; see also for full details *PLRE*, 2, 679–81. See further on his extraordinary career James J. O'Donnell, "Liberius the Patrician."
47. Jordanes *Getica* 314 (ed. Th. Mommsen).
48. Procopius *B.G.*, VII, 31. 18–21.
49. Ibid., VIII, 31. 18; 32. 34.
50. For examples, see #63–64 Totila, #68–69 Teias in Wolfgang Hahn, *Moneta Imperii Byzantini*, vol. 1. On Teias's coinage in transalpine areas, see further Joachim Werner, "Fernhandel und Naturalwirtschaft im östlichen Merowingerreich nach archäologischen und numismatischen Zeugnissen."
51. Procopius *B.G.*, VIII, 35. 24.
52. *Historiae Patriae Monumenta*, vol. 12, "Codex diplomaticus Langobardiae" (Torino, 1873), 37. As we have seen, certain archaeological remains also suggest survivals under the early Lombards. For the lingering resistance after the death of Teias, see Agathias, I, 8–20.

Epilogue

1. See further Wilhelm M. Pietz, *Dionysius Exiguus-Studien*.
2. Paulus Diaconus *Historia Langobardorum* 1. 25 (ed. L. Bethmann and G. Waitz). Arator's works were edited by J. Arnzt, *P.L.* 68, cols. 63–251.
3. Gregorius *Dialogus II, P.L.*, vol. 66, cols. 160–62.

Table 4: The Roman Emperors

Maximinus	235–238	Carus	282–283
Gordian I and II	238	Numerianus	283–284
Balbinus and Pupienus	238	Carinus	283–285
Gordian III	238–244	Diocletian	284–305
Philip	244–249	Maximian	286–305
Decius	249–251	Constantius	305–306
Gallus	251–253	Galerius	305–311
Aemilianus	253	Severus	306–307
Valerian	253–260	Licinius	308–324
Gallienus	253–268	Maximinus Daia	310–313
Claudius II Gothicus	268–270	Constantine	306–337
Quintillus	270	Constantine II	337–340
Aurelian	270–275	Constans	337–350
Tacitus	275–276	Constantius II	337–361
Florianus	276	Magnentius	350–353
Probus	276–282	Julian	361–363
		Jovian	363–364
East		*West*	
Valens	364–378	Valentinian I	364–375
Theodosius I	379–395	Gratian	367–383
		Valentinian II	383–392
		Eugenius	392–394
		Theodosius I	394–395
Arcadius	395–408	Honorius	395–423
Theodosius II	408–450	Valentinian III	425–455
Marcian	450–457	Maximus	455–457
Leo I	457–474	Majorian	457–461
		Severus	461–467
		Anthemius	467–472
		Olybrius	472–473
Leo II	474	Glycerius	473–474
Zeno	474–491	Julius Nepos	474–475
(Basiliscus	475–476)	Romulus Augustulus	475–476
Anastasius I	491–518		
Justin I	518–527		
Justinian I	527–565		

BIBLIOGRAPHY

Primary Sources (Texts and Collections)

Agathias. *Historiarum Libri Quinque*. Edited by R. Keydell. CFHB, vol. 2. Berlin, 1967.

Ambrosius Sanctus (Bishop of Milan). In *Sacrorum Conciliorum Nova et Amplissima Collectio*, ed. P. Labbe, P. Cossart, and G. D. Mansi, vol. 3. Firenze, 1759.

Ambrosius Sanctus (Bishop of Milan). *Opera omnia*. Edited by J. P. Migne. In *P.L.*, vols. 14–17. Paris, 1845–66.

Ammianus Marcellinus. Loeb edition. Translated by John C. Rolfe. Cambridge, Mass., 1935–40.

Ammianus Marcellinus. Edited by Wolfgang Seyfarth. In *Römische Geschichte*. Darmstadt, 1970–78.

Anonymi Valesiani pars posterior. Edited by Th. Mommsen. In *M.G.H., A.A.*, vol. 9 (Chronica Minora, vol. 1). Berlin 1892. Reprint 1961.

Anonymi Valesiani pars posterior. Loeb edition. Translated by John C. Rolfe. Cambridge, Mass., 1964 revision.

Anonymus Valesianus. *Excerpta Valesiana*. Teubner edition. Edited by Jacques Moreau, revised by V. Velkov. Leipzig, 1968.

Arator. *De Actibus Apostolorum*. Edited by J. P. Migne. In *P.L.*, vol. 68, pp. 45–252. Paris, 1847.

Ausonius. *Opuscula*. Loeb edition. Translated by H. G. Evelyn-White. New York, 1921.

Auxentius (Bishop of Silistria). *Aus der Schule des Wulfila. Auxenti Dorostorensis Epistola de fide vita et obitu Wulfilae . . . .* Edited by F. Kauffmann. Strassburg, 1899.

Boethius. *Philosophiae Consolatio*. Loeb edition. Translated by H. F. Stuart. Cambridge, Mass., 1953.

Boethius. *Philosophiae Consolatio*. Edited by L. Bieler. In *Anicii Manlii Severini Boethii Philosophiae consolatio. Corpus Christianorum, Series Latina*, vol. 94. Turnhout, 1957.

Caesar, C. Julius. *Bellum Gallicum*. Teubner edition. Edited by Otto Seel. Leipzig, 1961.

Cassiodorus. *Cassiodori Senatoris variae*. Edited by Th. Mommsen. In *M.G.H., A.A.*, vol. 12. Berlin, 1894.

Cassius Dio. *Historia Romana*. Loeb edition. Translated by E. Cary. New York, 1914–25.

Cedrenus, Georgius. *Compendium Historiarum*. Edited by J. P. Migne. In *P.G.*, cols. 121–22. Paris, 1889.

Chronica Minora. Edited by Th. Mommsen. In *M.G.H., A.A.*, vol. 9 (Chronica Minora, vol. 1). Berlin, 1892.

Claudianus, Claudius. *Carmina*. Loeb edition. Translated by M. Platnauer. Cambridge, Mass., 1922.

Codex Iustinianus. Edited by Paul Krüger. In *Corpus Iuris Civilis*, vol. 2. Berlin, 1915. 12th ed., 1959.

Codex Theodosianus. Edited by Paul Krüger. Berlin, 1923–26.

Concilios visigóticos e hispano-romanos. Edited by J. Vives. España cristiana, Textos 1. Madrid, 1963.

Constantius VII, Porphyrogenitus. *Excerpta de legationibus*. In *Excerpta historica*, vol. 1, ed. C. de Boor and T. Büttner-Wobst. Berlin, 1903–10.

Constantius VII, Porphyrogenitus. *De Administrando Imperio*. Edited by R. Jenkins and G. Moravcsik. 2d ed. Washington, D.C., 1967.

Corpus inscriptionum latinarum consilio et auctoritate Academiae litterarum regiae Borussicae editum . . . . Berlin 1862–.

Delehaye, H. "Saints de Thrace et de Mésie." *Analecta Bollandiana* 31 (1912): 161–300.

Dindorf, L. *Historici Graeci Minores*. Teubner edition. Leipzig, 1870.

Diocleatis, Presbyteri. *Regnum Slavorum*. Edited by J. G. Schwandther. In *Scriptores rerum hungaricarum veteres* . . . , vol. 3. Vindobonae, 1748.

Dionysius Exiguus. *Die Canonessammlung des Dionysius Exiguus in der ersten Redaktion*. Edited by Adolf Streuwe. Berlin, 1931.

Edictum Theodorici Regis. Edited by F. Bluhme. In *M.G.H., Legum*, vol. 5. Hanover, 1875–89.

Ennodius. *Opera*. Edited by W. Hartel. In *Corpus Scriptorum Ecclesiasticorum Latinorum*, vol. 6. Vindobonae, 1882.

Ennodius. *Opera*. Edited by F. Vogel. In *M.G.H., A.A.*, vol. 7. Berlin, 1885.

Eugippius. *Vita Severini*. Edited by Th. Mommsen. In *M.G.H., Scriptores rerum Germanicarum in usum scholarum*. Berlin, 1898.

Eugippius. *Vita Severini*. Edited by R. Noll. In *Eugippius. Das Leben des heiligen Severin. Schriften und Quellen der alten Welt*, vol. 11. Berlin, 1963.

Eunapius. Edited by L. Dindorf. In *Historici Graeci Minores*, Teubner edition. Leipzig, 1870.

Eusebius Pamphili (Bishop of Caesarea). *Vita Constantini*. Edited by F. Winkelmann. *Die Textbezeugung der Vita Constantini des Eusebius von Caesarea: Texte und Untersuchungen*, vol. 84. Berlin, 1962.

Evagrius Scholasticus. *Historia Ecclesiastica*. Edited by J. Bidez and L. Parmentier. London, 1898.

Fiebiger, O., and Schmidt, L. "Inschriftensammlung zur Geschichte der Ostgermanen." *Denkschriften der kaiserlichen Akademie der Wissenschaften in Wien, philosophisch-historische Klasse*, vol. 60, Abh. 3 (1917). Continued by Fiebiger alone in vol. 70, Abh. 3 (1939) and vol. 72 (1944).

Fredegarius. *Chronicon, The Fourth Book of the Chronicle of Fredegar with Its Continuations*. Edited and translated by J. M. Wallace-Hadrill. London, 1960.

Frontinus, Sextus Julius. *Strategemata*. Edited by G. Gundermann. Teubner edition. Leipzig, 1888.

Gelasius (Pope). *Epistulae*. Edited by A. Thiel. In *Epistulae Romanorum pontificum, a S. Hilario usque ad S. Hormisdam*. Brunsbergae, 1868.

Georgius Monachus. *Chronicon*. Teubner edition. Edited by Carolus de Boor. Leipzig, 1904.

Gesta de Xysti Purgatione. Edited by P. Coustant. In *Pontificum Romanum Epistulae Genuinae*. Göttingen, 1791.

Gregorius Thaumaturgus, Saint (Bishop of Neocaesarea). *Opera quae reperiri potuerunt omnia*. Edited by J. P. Migne. In *P.G.*, vol. 10. Paris, 1857.

Gregorius Turonensis. *Historiae Francorum*. Edited and translated by R. Buchner. In *Gregor von Tours: Zehn Bücher Geschichten*, 2d ed. Berlin, 1967.

Gregorius I, Pope. *Dialogi*, vol. 2. Edited by J. P. Migne. In *P.L.*, vol. 76. Paris, 1896.

Herodianus. Loeb edition. Edited by C. R. Whittaker. Cambridge, Mass., 1970.

Hieronymus. *Epistulae*. Edited by J. P. Migne. In *P.L.*, vol. 22. Paris, 1864.

Historiae Patriae Monumenta, vols. 12–13, "Codex diplomaticus Langobardiae." Torino, 1873.

Isidorus. *Historia Gothorum Wandalorum Sueborum*. Edited by Th. Mommsen. In *M.G.H., A.A.*, vol. 11 (Chronica Minora, vol. 2). Berlin, 1894.

Isidorus. *Historia Gothorum Wandalorum Sueborum*. Edited by C. Rodríguez Alonso. In *Las historias de los Godos, Vandalos y Suevas de Isidoro de Sevilla*. León, 1975.

Jacoby, F. *Die Fragmente der griechischen Historiker*. Berlin, 1923–1958.

Joannes Malalas. *Chronographia*. Edited by C. de Boor. In *CSHB*, vol. 28. Berlin, 1905.

Jordanes. *Jordanis Romana et Getica*. Edited by Th. Mommsen. In *M.G.H., A.A.*, vol. 5. Berlin, 1882.

Leges Burgundionum. Edited by L. R. de Salis. In *M.G.H., Legum*, Sectio 1. 2, pars 1. Hanover, 1892.

Leges Visigothorum. Edited by K. Zeumer. In *M.G.H., Legum*, Sectio 1.1 *Legum Nationum Germanicarum*. Hanover, Leipzig, 1902.

Leo Grammaticus. *Chronographia*. Edited by I. Bekker. In *Corpus Scriptorum Historiae Byzantinae*, vol. 46. Bonn, 1842.

Libanius. *Opera*. Teubner edition. Edited by R. Foerster. Leipzig, 1903–27.

Liber Pontificalis. Edited by Th. Mommsen. In *M.G.H., gesta pontif.*, vol. 1. Berlin, 1898.

Livius, Titus. *Ab urbe condita*. Loeb edition, vol. 1. Translated by B. O. Foster. New York, 1919.

Mansi, Johannes. *Sacrorum Conciliorum Nova et Amplissima Collectio*. Edited by P. Labbe, P. Cossart, and G. D. Mansi. Firenze, 1758–1798. Reprint. Graz, 1901.

Marini, Gaetano Luigi. *I Papiri diplomatici*. Rome, 1805.

Mauricius, Flavius Tiberius (Emperor). *Arriani Tactica et Mauricii Ars militaris*. Edited by J. Scheffer. 1664. Reprint. Osnabrück, 1967.

Mauricius, Flavius Tiberius (Emperor). *Das Strategikon des Maurikios*. Edited and translated by George T. Dennis and Ernst Gamillscheg. In *Corpus Fontium Historicae Byzantinae*, Series Vindobonesis, vol. 17. Vienna, 1981.

Müller, Carl. *Fragmenta Historicorum Graecorum*. Paris, 1853–1883.

Notitia Dignitatum. Edited by O. Seeck. Frankfurt am Main, 1876. Reprint 1962.

Panegyrici Latini. Teubner edition. Edited by W. A. Baehrens. Leipzig, 1911.

Panégyriques Latins. Edited by E. Galletier. Collection G. Budé. Paris, 1949–55.

Patrick, Saint. *Confession et lettre à Coroticus*. 2d ed. Translated and with criticism and commentary by Richard Hanson. Sources Chrétiennes, vol. 249. Paris, 1978.

Paulinus (Bishop of Nola). *Epistulae et Carmina*. Edited by G. Hartel. In *Corpus Scriptorum Ecclesiasticorum Latinorum*, vols. 29–30. Leipzig, 1894.

Paulinus Pellaeus. Loeb edition. Translated by H. G. Evelyn-White. Cambridge, Mass., 1921.

Paulus Diaconus. *Pauli Historia Langobardorum*. Edited by L. Bethmann and G. Waitz. In *MGH, Scriptores rerum Langobardicarum et Italicarum, saec. vi–ix*. Hanover, 1878.

Paulus Orosius. *Historiarum adversum paganos libri vii*. Edited by C. Zangemeister. In *Corpus Scriptorum Ecclesiasticorum Latinorum*, vol. 5. Vienna, 1882.

Petrus Patricius. *Historiae*. Edited by C. de Boor and T. Büttner-Wobst. In *Excerpta historica*. Berlin, 1903–10.

Philostorgius. *Historia Ecclesiastica*. In J. Bidez, *Die griechischen christlichen*

Schriftsteller der ersten Jahrhunderte. Leipzig, 1913. Rev. ed. by F. Winkelmann, Berlin, 1972.

Photius. *Bibliothèque*. Text established and translated by R. Henry. Collection G. Budé. Paris, 1959–1977.

Pithou, P. *Epigrammata vetera*. Paris, 1590.

Procopius. *History of the Wars*. Loeb edition. Translated by H. B. Dewing. Cambridge, Mass., 1914–40. Reprint 1953–54.

Procopius. *Opera omnia*. Teubner edition. Revised and edited by G. Wirth. Leipzig, 1962–64.

Ravennas Anonymus. *Cosmographia*. Edited by Otto Cuntz and Joseph Schnetz. In *Itineraria Romana*, vol. 2. Leipzig, 1929–40.

Recueil des inscriptions chrétiennes de la Gaule anterieurs à la renaissance carolingienne. Vol. 1, *Première belgique*. Edited by N. Gauthier. Paris, 1975.

Rutilius Namatianus. In *Minor Latin Poets*, Loeb edition, trans. J. W. Duff and A. M. Duff. Cambridge, Mass., 1935.

Rutilius Namatianus. *De reditu suo sive Iter Gallicum*. Edited by E. Doblhofer. Heidelberg, 1972–77.

Scriptores Historiae Augustae. Loeb edition. Translated by D. Magie. Cambridge, Mass., 1921–1932.

Sextus Aurelius Victor. *Liber de Caesaribus*. Teubner edition. Edited by R. Gruendel. Leipzig, 1961.

Sidonius Apollinaris. *Opera*. Edited by C. Luetjohann. In *M.G.H., A.A.*, vol. 8. Berlin, 1887.

Sidonius Apollinaris. *Opera*. Text established and translated by André Loyen. In *Sidoine Apollinaire*. Paris, 1960.

Sozomenus. *Historia Ecclesiastica*. Edited by J. Bidez. In *Kirchengeschichte, Die griechischen christlichen Schriftsteller der ersten Jahrhunderte*, vol. 50. Berlin, 1960.

Suetonius, Tranquillus. *De vita Caesarum*. Teubner edition. Edited by Maximilian Ihm. Leipzig, 1908.

Symmachus, Q. Aurelius. *Opera*. Edited by O. Seeck. Vol. 6. Berlin, 1883.

Synesius of Cyrene (Bishop of Ptolemais). *Opera*. Edited by J. P. Migne. In *P.G.*, vol. 66. Paris, 1857.

Tabula Imperii Romani. Foglio L32, Mediolanum (Aventicum-Brigantium). Rome, 1966.

Tabula Imperii Romani. Foglio L34 (Aquincum-Sarmizegetusa-Sirmium). Amsterdam, 1968.

Tacitus, Cornelius. *Annales*. Teubner edition. Edited by Erich Koestermann. Leipzig, 1960.

Tacitus, Cornelius. *Germania*. Edited by M. Winterbottom. Oxford, 1975.

Themistius. *Orationes*. Edited by W. Dindorf. Leipzig, 1832. Reprint. Hildesheim, 1961.

Theodoros Lector. *Historia Ecclesiastica*. Edited by G. Hansen. In *Kirchengeschichte, Die griechischen christlichen Schriftstellar der ersten Jahrhunderte*, vol. 54. Berlin, 1971.

Theophylactus Simocatta. *Historiarum libri octo*. Teubner edition. Edited by C. de Boor, revised by P. Wirth. Leipzig, 1972.

Tjäder, Jan-Olof, ed. *Die nichtliterarischen lateinischen Papyri Italiens aus der Zeit 445–700*. Vol. 1, papyri 1–28, *Srikfter utgivna av Svenska Institutet i Rom, Acta Instituti Romani Regni Sueciae*, 4, 19, 1. Lund, 1955.

Translatio sancti Epiphani. Edited by J. Pertz. In *M.G.H., Scriptores*, vol. 4. Hanover, 1841.

Vegetius, Flavius Renatus. *Epitoma Rei Militaris*. Teubner edition. Edited by C. Lang. Leipzig, 1967.

Victor (Bishop of Vita). *Historia persecutionis Wandalicae*. Edited by C. Halm. In *M.G.H., A.A.*, vol. 3, pt. 1. Berlin, 1879.

Vita S. Caesarii. Edited by J. P. Migne. In *P.L.*, vol. 67. Paris, 1865.

Zacharias (Bishop of Mytilene). *Historia Ecclesiastica, The Syriac Chronicle*. Translated by F. J. Hamilton and E. W. Brooks. London, 1899.

Zonaras. *Epitome historiarum*. Edited by T. Büttner-Wobst. In *Corpus Scriptorum Historiae Byzantinae*, vol. 50. Bonn, 1897.

Zosimus. *Historia Nova*. Text established and translated by F. Paschoud. Collection G. Budé. Paris, 1971–.

Zosimus. *Historia Nova*. Teubner edition. Edited by L. Mendelssohn. Leipzig, 1887.

Zosimus. *Historia Nova*. Translated by J. J. Buchanan and Harold T. Davis. San Antonio, Texas, 1967.

Secondary Works

Åberg, N. *Die Goten und Langobarden in Italien*. Arbeten utg. med understöd af Vilhelm Ekmans universitetsfond, vol. 29. Uppsala, 1923.

Achelis, H. "Der älteste deutsche Kalender." *Zeitschrift für die neutestamentliche Wissenschaft und die Kunde des Urchristentums* 1 (1900):308–335.

———. *Die Martyrologien: Ihre Geschichte und ihr Wert*. Gesellschaft der Wissenschaften zu Göttingen, philologisch-historische Klasse, Abhandlungen N.F.3,3. 1899–1901.

Adams, J. N. *The Text and Language of a Vulgar Latin Chronicle (Anonymus Valesianus II)*. University of London Institute of Classical Studies Bulletin, Supp. 36. London, 1976.

Alföldi, Andrew. "The Invasion of Peoples from the Rhine to the Black Sea." In *Cambridge Ancient History*, vol. 12, pp. 138–64. Cambridge, 1939.

Alföldi, Andrew, and Straub, J., eds. *Transformation et conflicts au IVe siècle ap. J. C.* Antiquitas, ser. 1, vol. 29. Bonn, 1978.

Alföldy, Geza. *Noricum*. Translated by Anthony Birley. London, Boston, 1974.

Almren, O. *Studien über nordeuropäische Fibelformen*. Mannus-Bibliothek, no. 32. Leipzig 1923. Reprint. Bonn, 1973.

Ambrosino, G., and Weil, A. R. "Nature et portée d'analyses nondestructives de méteux précieux." *Bulletin du laboratoire du musée du Louvre* 1 (1956):53–62.

Ambroz, K., "Problems of the Early Medieval Chronology of Eastern Europe," pt. 1. *Soviet Anthropology and Archaeology* 10 (1972):336–90.

Andersson, Theodore M. "Cassiodorus and the Gothic Legend of Ermanaric." *Euphorion* 57 (1963):28–43.

Annibaldi, Giovanni, and Werner, Joachim. "Ostgotische Grabfunde aus Acquasanta, Prov. Ascoli Piceno (Marche)." *Germania* 41 (1963):356–73.

Anstee, J. W., and Biek, L., "A Study in Pattern-welding." *Medieval Archaeology* 5 (1961):72–94.

Antoniervicz, J. "Tribal Territories of the Baltic Peoples in the Hallstatt-La Tène and Roman Periods in the Light of Archaeology and Toponomy." *Acta Baltico-Slavica* 4 (1966):7–27.

Arrhenius, B. *Granatschmuck und Gemmen aus nordischen Funden des frühen Mittelalters*. Stockholm, 1971.

Arslan, Ermanno A. *Le Monete di ostrogoti, longobardi e vandali*. Milano, 1978.

Austin, N. J. E. "In support of Ammianus' Veracity." *Historia* 22 (1973):331–35.

Bach, E. "Théodoric, romain ou barbare?" *Byzantion* 25–27 (1935–37):413–20.

Bachrach, Bernard S. *Early Medieval Jewish Policy in Western Europe*. Minneapolis, Minnesota, 1977.

———. *Merovingian Military Organization, 481–751*. Minneapolis, Minnesota, 1972.

Badian, Ernst. *Roman Imperialism in the Late Republic*. 2d ed. Oxford, 1968.

Balg, G. H. *A Comparative Glossary of the Gothic Language*. Mayville, Wisconsin, 1887–1889.

Balla, Lajos, Buocz, T. P., Kádár, Z., Mócsy, A., and Szentléleky, T. *Die römischen Steindenkmäler von Savaria*. Amsterdam, 1971.

Balzert, Monika. *Die Komposition des claudianischen Gotenkriegsgedichtes*. Hildesheim, 1974.

Bang, Martin. *Die Germanen im römischen Dienst bis zum Regierungsantritt Constantins I*. Berlin, 1906.

Bark, W. "Theodoric v. Boethius: Vindication and Apology." *American Historical Review* 49 (1944):410–26.

Barkóczi, László. "History of Pannonia." In *The Archaeology of Roman Pannonia*, ed. A. Lengyel and G. T. Radan, pp. 85–124. Lexington, Ky., 1980.

———. "A Sixth Century Cemetery from Keszthely-Fenekpuszta." *Acta Archaeologica* 20 (1968):275–86.

———. "Transplantations of Sarmatians and Roxolans in the Danube Basin." *Acta Antiqua* 7 (1959):443–53.

Barkóczi, László, and Salamon, A. "Remarks on the Sixth Century History of 'Pannonia.'" *Acta Archaeologica* 23 (1971):139–53.

Barnes, Timothy D. "The Lost Kaisergeschichte and the Latin Historical Tradition." *Bonner Historia-Augusta-Colloquium*, 1968/69, pp. 13–43. Antiquitas, pt. 4, no. 7. Bonn, 1970.

———. "The Victories of Constantine." *Zeitschrift für Papyrologie und Epigraphik* 20 (1976):149–55.

Bârzu, Ligia. *Continuity of the Romanian People's Material and Spiritual Production in the Territory of Former Dacia*. Bucharest, 1980.

Behn, Friedrich. *Römertum und Völkerwanderung: Mitteleuropa zwischen Augustus und Karl dem Grossen*. Stuttgart, 1963.

Behrens, G. "Spätrömische Kerbschnittschnallen." *Schumacher-Festschrift*, edited by the director of the Roman-German Central Museum in Mainz, pp. 285–94. Mainz, 1930.

Belin du Ballu, E. *Olbia, cité antique du littoral nord de la Mer Noire*. Leyde, 1972.

Benario, Herbert W. *A Commentary on the Vita Hadriani in the Historia Augusta*. American Classical Studies, no. 7. Missoula, Mont., 1980.

Berger, Adolf. *Encyclopedic Dictionary of Roman Law*. Transactions of the American Philosophical Society, n.s. 43.2. Philadelphia, 1953.

Bersu, G. "A Sixth-Century German Settlement of Foederati: Golemanoso Kale." *Antiquity* 17 (1938):31–43.

Besevliev, V. "Les cités antiques en Mésie et en Thrace et leur sort à l'époque du haut moyen âge." *Études Balkaniques* 5 (1966):207–220.

Beyerele, Franz. "Süddeutschland in der politischen Konzeption Theodorichs des Grossen." *Vorträge und Forschungen* 1 (1955):65–81.

Bichir, Gheorghe. *Archaeology and History of the Carpi from the Second to the Fourth Century A.D.* British Archaeological Reports, supplementary series, no. 16. Oxford, 1976.

———. "La Civilisation des Carpes (IIe–IIIe siècle de n.é.) à la lumière des fouilles archéologiques de Poinana-Dulceşti, de Butnăreşti et de Pădureni." *Dacia,* n.s. 11 (1967):177–224.

Bieler, Ludwig. *Eugippius' The Life of St. Severinus.* Translated by L. Bieler with collaboration of L. Krestan. Fathers of the Church, vol. 55. Washington, D.C., 1965.

Bierbrauer, Volker. "Alamannische Funde der frühen Ostgotenzeit aus Oberitalien." In *Studien zur vor-und frühgeschichtlichen Archäologie, Festschrift für Joachim Werner zum 65. Geburtstag,* vol. 2, pp. 559–77. Munich, 1974.

———. "Die Ansiedlung der Ostgothen in Italien." In *Les Relations entre l'empire romain tardif, l'empire franc et ses voisins,* pp. 42–70. Nice, 1976.

———. "Die ostgotischen Funde von Domagnano, Republik San Marino." *Germania* 51 (1973):499–523.

———. *Die ostgotischen Grab- und Schatzfunde in Italien.* Biblioteca degli Studi Medievali, no. 7. Spoleto, 1975.

———. "Ostrogotische und ostgotenzeitliche Grabfunde von Tortona, Prov. Alessandria." *Boll. della Soc. Pavese di Storia Patria* 22/23 (1973):3–30.

———. "Reperti Alemanni del primo periodo ostrogoto provenienti dell'Italia settentrionale." In *I Longobardi e la Lombardia,* pp. 241–60. Milan, 1978.

———. "Zu den Vorkommen ostgotischer Bügelfibeln in Raetia II," *Bayerische Vorgeschichtblätter* 36 (1971):134–65.

———. "Zur chronologischen, soziologischen und regionalen Gliederung des ostgermanischen Fundstoffs des 5. Jahrhunderts in Südosteuropa." In *Die Völker an der mittleren und unteren Donau im 5. und 6. Jahrhundert,* ed. H. Wolfram and F. Daim, pp. 131–42. Vienna, 1980.

———. "Zur ostgotischen Geschichte in Italien." *Studi Medievali,* ser. 3, vol. 14 (1973):1–37.

Biondi, Biondo. *Il diritto romano.* Bologna, 1957.

———. *Successione testamentaria, donazioni.* 2d. ed. Milan, 1955.

Biraben, J. N., and Le Goff, Jacques. "La Peste du haut moyen âge." *Annales, Économies, Sociétés, Civilisations* 24 (1969):1484–510.

Birley, Anthony. *Marcus Aurelius.* Boston, 1966.

Blankenburg, Wera von. *Heilige und dämonische Tiere: Die Symbolsprache der deutschen Ornamentik im frühen Mittelalter.* 2d. ed. Cologne, 1975.

Bloch, Marc. "Économie de nature ou économie d'argent. . . ." *Annales d'histoire sociale* 1 (1939):7–16.

Blockley, R. C. "Dexippus of Athens and Eunapius of Sardis." *Latomus* 30 (1971):710–15.

———. *The Fragmentary Classicising Historians of the Later Roman Empire: Eunapius, Olympiodorus, Priscus, and Malchus.* Classical and Medieval Texts, Papers, and Monographs, no. 6. Trowbridge, England, 1981.

Blume, Erich. *Die germanischen Stämme und die Kulturen zwischen Oder und Passarge zur römischen Kaiserzeit.* Mannus-Bücherei, nos. 8 and 14. Würzburg, 1912 and 1915.

Bodor, Andrei. "Emperor Aurelian and the Abandonment of Dacia." *Dacoromania* 1 (1973):29–40.

Bognetti, G. P. "L'Influsso delle istituzioni militari romane sulle istituzioni longobarde del secolo VI la natura della 'fara,'" *Atti del Congresso internazionale di diritto romano e di storia del diritto* 4 (Milano, 1953):167–210.

Böhner, Kurt. "Childerich von Tournai." In *Reallexikon der Germanischen Altertumskunde,* pp. 441–60. Berlin, 1980.

Böhner, Kurt. "Urban and Rural Settlement in the Frankish Kingdom." In *European Towns: The Archaeology and Early History*, ed. M. Barley, pp. 185–202. New York, 1977.

Böhner, Kurt, and Weidemann, Konrad, eds. *Gallien in der Spätantike: von Kaiser Constantin zu Frankenkönig Childerich.* Mainz am Rhein, 1980.

Bolta, Lojze. "Spätantikes Gräberfeld auf Rifnik bei Sentzur" [in Slovene with German summary]. *Arheološki Vestnik* 21–22 (1970–71):127–40.

Bömer, F., and Voit, L., eds. *Germania Romana*, vol. 1, *Romerstädte in Deutschland.* Gymnasium, Zeitschrift für Kultur der Antike und Humanistische Bildung, Beiheft, no. 1. Heidelberg, 1960.

Bona, István. *The Dawn of the Dark Ages: The Gepids and the Lombards in the Carpathian Basin.* Budapest, 1976.

Bonanni, Susanna. "Ammiano Marcellino e i Barbari." *Rivista di cultura classica e medioevale* 23 (1981):125–42.

Bradley, D. R. "The Composition of the Getica." *Eranos* 64 (1966):67–79.

Brady, C. *The Legends of Ermanaric.* Los Angeles, 1943.

Brand, C. E. *Roman Military Law.* Austin, Texas, 1968.

Brashkinskii, I. B. "Recherches soviétiques sur les monuments antiques des régions de la Mer Noire." *Eirene: Studia Graeca et Latina* 7 (1968):81–118.

Bréal, Michel. "Premières influences de Rome sur le monde germanique." *Mémoires de la société de linguistique de Paris* 7 (1892):135–48.

Brennan, Peter. "Combined Legionary Detachments as Artillery Units in Late Roman Danubian Bridgehead Dispositions." *Chiron* 10 (1980):553–67.

Brogan, O. "Trade between the Roman Empire and the Free Germans." *Journal of Roman Studies* 26 (1936):195–223.

Brøgger, A. W., and Shetelig, H. *The Viking Ships, Their Ancestry and Evolution.* Oslo, 1953.

Brooks, E. W. "The Emperor Zeno and the Isaurians." *English Historical Review* 7 (1893):209–38.

Broom, Leonard, et al. "Acculturation: An Exploratory Formulation." *American Anthropologist* 56 (1954):973–1000.

Brown, David. "The Brooches in the Pietroasa Treasure." *Antiquity* 46 (1972): 111–16.

Brown, Peter. "The Rise and Function of the Holy Man in Late Antiquity." *Journal of Roman Studies* 61 (1971):80–101.

Browning, R. "Where Was Attila's Camp?" *Journal of Hellenic Studies* 73 (1953):143–45.

Bruns, Gerda. *Der Obelisk und seine Basis auf dem Hippodrom zu Konstantinopel.* Istanbul, 1935.

Bullinger, Hermann. *Spätantike Gürtelbeschläge: Typen, Herstellung, Tragweise und Datierung.* Diss. Archaeol. Gandenses, no. 12. Brugge, 1969.

Bullough, D. A. "Early Medieval Social Groupings: The Terminology of Kinship." *Past and Present* 45 (1969):3–18.

———. "Urban Change in Early Medieval Italy: The Example of Pavia." *Papers of the British School at Rome* 34 (1966):82–130.

Bulmer, R. N. H. "Political Aspects of the Moka Ceremonial Exchange System among the Kyaka People of the Western Highlands of New Guinea." *Oceania* 31 (1960–61):1–13.

Burger, A. Sz. "The Late Roman Cemetery at Ságvár." *Acta Archaeologica* 18 (1966):99–234.

Burgundian Code. Translated by Katherine F. Drew. Philadelphia, 1972.

Burns, Thomas S. "The Alpine Frontiers and Early Medieval Italy to the Middle of the Seventh Century." In *The Frontier: Comparative Studies*, vol. 2, pp. 51–68. Norman, Oklahoma, 1979.

———. "The Barbarians and the *Scriptores Historiae Augustae*." In *Studies in Latin Literature and Roman History*, vol. 1, ed. C. Deroux, pp. 521–40. Collection Latomus, vol. 164. Brussels, 1979.

———. "The Battle of Adrianople: A Reconsideration." *Historia* 22 (1973): 336–45.

———. "Calculating Ostrogothic Population." *Acta Antiqua* 26 (1978):457–63.

———. "Ennodius and the Ostrogothic Settlement." *Classical Folia* 32 (1978): 153–68.

———. "The Germans and Roman Frontier Policy (ca. A.D. 350–378)." *Arheološki Vestnik* 32 (1981):390–404.

———. *The Ostrogoths: Kingship and Society*. Historia Einzelschriften, no. 36. Wiesbaden, 1980.

———. "Pursuing the Early Gothic Migrations." *Acta Archaeologica* 31 (1979): 189–99.

———. "Theories and Facts: The Early Gothic Migrations." *History in Africa* 9 (1982):1–20.

Bury, J. B. *The Later Roman Empire*. London, 1889. Reprint. New York, 1958.

Calandra, C. *Di una necropoli barbarica scoperta a Testona*. Atti della Società di archaeologia e belle arti per la provincia di Torino, vol. 4. Torino, 1880.

Calasso, Francesco. *Il medio evo del diritto*. Vol. 1, *Le fonti*. Milan, 1954.

Cameron, Alan. *Circus Factions: Blues and Greens at Rome and Byzantium*. Oxford, 1976.

———. *Claudian: Poetry and Propaganda at the Court of Honorius*. Oxford, 1970.

———. "A New Fragment of Eunapius [Suidas m.203]." *Classical Review* 17 (1967):10–11.

Cameron, Averil. *Agathias*. Oxford, 1970.

———. "Agathias on the Early Merovingians." *Annali della Scuola Normale di Pisa* 2, no. 37 (1968):95–140.

Cardascia, G. "L'Apparition dans le droit des classes d'*honestiores* et d'*humiliores*." *Revue historique de droit français et étranger* 28 (1950):305–337, 461–85.

Charles-Edwards, T. M. "Kinship, Status, and the Origins of the Hide." *Past and Present* 56 (1972):3–33.

Chastagnol, A. *Le Sénat romain sous le règne d'Odoacre: Recherches sur l'épigraphie du Colisée au Ve siècle*. Antiquitas, pt. 3, no. 3. Bonn, 1966.

———. *Recherches sur l'histoire Auguste* avec un rapport de la Histoire Auguste-Forschung depuis 1963. Antiquitas, pt. 4, no. 6. Bonn, 1970.

Chatelain, E. "Notes sur quelques palimpsestes de Turin. IV. Fragments des panégyriques de Cassiodore." *Revue de philologique, d'histoire et de littérature anciennes* 27 (1903):45–48.

Chénon, Émile. "Étude historique sur le *defensor civitatis*." *Revue historique de droit* 13 (1889):515–37.

Christlein, R. "Straubing-Alburg." *Das archäologische Jahr in Bayern 1980* 1 (1981): 154.

Chrysos, Evangelos K. "Gothia Romana: Zur Rechtslage des Föderatenlandes der Westgoten im 4. Jh." *Dacoromania* 1 (1973):52–64.

———. *To Byzantion kai hoi Gotthoi: symbole eis ten exoteriken politiken tou Byzantiou kata ton 4. aiona*. Thessalonika, 1972.

Claude, Dietrich. "Zur Königserhebung Theoderichs des Grossen im Geschichtsschreibung und Geistigen Leben im Mittelalalter." In *Festschrift für Heinz Löwe zum 65. Geburtstag*, ed. Karl Hauck and Hubert Mordek, pp. 1–13. Cologne, 1978.

———. "Universale und partikulare Züge in der Politik Theoderichs." *Francia* 6 (1978):19–59.

———. "Die ostrogotischen Königserhebungen." In *Die Völker an der mittleren und unteren Donau im 5. und 6. Jahrhundert*, ed. H. Wolfram and F. Daim, pp. 149–86. Vienna, 1980.

Clauss, Manfred. *Der Magister Officiorum in der Spätantike (4–6 Jh.): Das Amt und sein Einfluss auf die kaiserliche Politik*. Vestigia, no. 32. Munich, 1980.

Clavadetscher, Otto P. "Churrätien im Übergang von der Spätantike zum Mittelalter nach den Schriftquellen." In *Von der Spätantike zum frühen Mittelalter*, ed. J. Werner and E. Ewig, pp. 159–78. Sigmaringen, 1979.

Clover, Frank M. "Geiseric the Statesmen: A Study of Vandal Foreign Policy." Unpublished Ph.D. thesis. University of Chicago, 1966.

Comsa, M. "Zur Romanisierung der Gebiete nördlich der Donau (Multenien, Südmoldau) im 4. Jahrhundert." *Dacia* 9 (1965):283–98.

Constantinescu, M., ed. *Relations between the Autochthonous Population and the Migratory Populations on the Territory of Romania*. Bibliotheca Historica Romaniae, Monographs, no. 16. Bucharest, 1975.

Cook, G. M. *The Life of Saint Epiphanius by Ennodius*. Washington, D.C., 1942.

Courtois, Christian. "Auteurs et scribes: Remarques sur la chronique d'Hydace." *Byzantion* 21 (1951):23–54.

———. *Les Vandales et l'Afrique*. Paris, 1955.

———. *Victor de Vita et son oeuvre: Étude critique*. Alger, 1954.

Croke, Brian. "Mundo the Gepid: From Freebooter to Roman General." *Chiron* 12 (1982):123–35.

Cross, Samuel H. "Gothic Loan-words in the Slavic Vocabulary." *Harvard Studies and Notes in Philology and Literature* 16 (1934):37–49.

Crumley, Carole L. *Celtic Social Structure: The Generation of Archaeologically Testable Hypotheses from Literary Evidence*. Ann Arbor, Mich., 1974.

Crump, G. A. "Ammianus and the Late Roman Army." *Historia* 22 (1973):91–103.

Csallány, Dezsö. *Archäologische Denkmäler der Gepiden im Mitteldonaubecken (454–568 u. Z.)*. Archaeologica Hungarica, no. 38. Budapest, 1961.

Czarnecki, Jan. *The Goths in Ancient Poland*. Miami, Florida, 1975.

Dagron, Gilbert. "Discours utopique et récit des origines." Part 1, "Une lecture de Cassiodore-Jordanès. Les Goths de Scandza à Ravenne." *Annales, Économies, Sociétés, Civilisations* 6 (1971):290–305.

———. "L'Empire romain d'orient au IVe siècle et les traditions politiques de l'Hellenisme: le témoignage de Themistius." *Travaux et Mémoires* 3 (1967): 1–242.

Dahn, Felix. *Die Könige der Germanen bis auf die Feudalzeit*, vol. 4. Würzburg, 1866.

Daly, Lawrence J. "The Mandarin and the Barbarian: The Response of Themistius to the Gothic Challenge." *Historia* 21 (1972):351–79.

Davies, Oliver. *Roman Mines in Europe*. Oxford, 1935.

Declareuil, J. "Des comtes de cités à la fin du Ve siècle." *Revue historique de droit* 34 (1910):794–836.

Degani, Mario. *Il tesoro romano-barbarico di Reggio Emilia*. Firenze, 1965.

Degrassi, N. "Rinvenimento di un tesoretto: Le oreficerie tardo-Romane di Pavia." *Notizie degli scavi di antichità*, ser. 7, vol. 2 (1941):303–310.

Deloche, M. *La Trustis et l'antrustion royale sous les deux premières races.* Paris, 1873.

Demandt, Alexander. "Magister militum." *R-E*, suppl. 12 (1970):553–790.

Demougeot, Emilienne. *La Formation de l'Europe et les invasions barbares.* Vol. 2, *De l'Avénement de Dioclétien (284) à l'occupation germanique de l'Empire roman d'Occident (dèbut du VIe siècle).* Paris, 1979.

———. *De l'unité à la division de l'empire romain 395–410: Essai sur le gouvernement impérial.* Paris, 1951.

Dessau, H. "Über die Scriptores Historiae Augustae." *Hermes* 27 (1892):561–605.

———. "Über Zeit und Persönlichkeit der Scriptores Historiae Augustae." *Hermes* 24 (1889):337–92.

Diaconu, Gheorghe. "Einheimische und Wandervölker im 4. Jahrhundert auf dem Gebiete Rumäniens." *Dacia* 8 (1964):195–210.

———. "On the Socio-economic Relations between Natives and Goths in Dacia." In *Relations between the Autochthonous Population and the Migratory Populations on the Territory of Romania . . .*, ed. M. Constantinescu, pp. 67–75. Bucharest, 1975.

———. *Tîrgşor necropola din secolele III–IV.* Bucharest, 1965.

———. "Über die scheibengedrehte Keramik in der Sîntana de Mures-Tschernjachowkultur." *Dacia* 14 (1970):243–50.

Diculescu, C. *Die Wandalen und Die Goten in Ungarn und Rumänien.* Mannus Bibl., no. 34. Leipzig, 1923.

Diesner, H. J. "Das Buccellariertum von Stilicho und Sarus bis auf Aëtius." *Klio* 54 (1972):321–50.

Digges, Thomas G., and Rosenberg, Samuel J. *Heat Treatment and Properties of Iron and Steel.* National Bureau of Standards Monograph, no. 18. Washington D.C., 1960.

Dölger, F. "Byzantine Literature." *Cambridge Medieval History*, vol. 4, pt. 2, ed. J. M. Hussey, pp. 206–263. Cambridge, 1967.

Dolinescu-Ferche, Suzana. "On Socio-economic Relations between Natives and Huns at the Lower Danube." In *Relations between the Autochthonous Population and the Migratory Populations on the Territory of Romania*, ed. M. Constantinescu, pp. 91–98. Bucharest, 1975.

Dombay, János. "Der gotische Grabfund von Domolospuszta: Der Fundort und die Umstände des Fundes." *Janus Pannonius Muzeum Evkonyve* 1 (1956):104–30.

d'Ors, Alvaro. *Estudios visigóticos.* No. 2, *El Código de Eurico.* Cuadernos del Instituto Juridico Español, no. 12. Rome, Madrid, 1960.

Dubois, Augustin. *La Latinité d'Ennodius.* Clermont, 1903.

Dumoulin, Maurice. "Le Gouvernement de Théodoric et la domination des Ostrogoths en Italie d'après les oeuvres d'Ennodius." *Revue historique* 78 (1902): 1–7, 241–65, and 79 (1903):1–22.

Dyggve, Ejnar. *History of Salonitan Christianity.* Cambridge, 1951.

———. "L'Influence des Goths à Salone." *Byzantion* 19 (1949):73–77.

Eadie, John W. "Roman Agricultural Implements from Sirmium." *Sirmium II.* Belgrade, 1971.

Ebel, J. "Die Fremdwörter bei Ulfilas in phonetischer Hinsicht." *Zeitschrift für vergleichende Sprachforschung* 4 (1855):282–88.

Ebert, M. "Ausgrabungen bei dem 'Gorodok Nikolajewka' am Dnjepr." *Prähistorische Zeitschrift* 5 (1913):80–113.

Edwards, Katherine M. *Corinth.* Vol. 6, *Coins.* Cambridge, Mass., 1933.

Eggers, Hans Jürgen. "Das kaiserzeitliche Gräberfeld von Pollwitten, Kreis

Mohrungen, Ostpreussen." *Jahrbuch des Römisch-Germanischen Zentralmuseums Mainz* 11 (1966):154–75.

———. *Der römische Import im freien Germanien*. Atlas der Urgeschichte, vol. 1. Hamburg, 1951.

———. "Zur absoluten Chronologie der römischen Kaiserzeit im freien Germanien." *Jahrbuch des Römisch-Germanischen Zentralmuseums Mainz* 2 (1955):196–244. Reprinted with an updating of sites by H. Jankuhn in *Aufstieg und Niedergang der römischen Welt*, pt. 2, vol. 5, pp. 3–64. Berlin, New York, 1976.

Ekholm, Gunnar. *Handelsförbindelsen mellan Skandinavien och Romerska riket*. Verdandis scriftserie, no. 15. Stockholm, 1961.

Enmann, A. "Eine verlorene Geschichte d. röm. Kaiser." *Philologus*, suppl. 4 (1883):335–501.

Ensslin, W. "Die Ostgoten in Pannonia." *Byzantinisch-neugriechische Jahrbücher* 6 (1927–8):146–59.

———. *Theoderich der Grosse*. 2d ed. Munich, 1959.

———. "Zum Heermeisteramt des spätrömischen Reiches," pts. 2 and 3. *Klio* 24 (1931):102–47, 467–502.

Eubanks, J. E. "Navigation on the Tiber." *Classical Journal* 25 (1930):684–90.

Evans, James A. S. *Procopius*. New York, 1972.

Ewig, Eugen. "Résidence et capitale dans le haut moyen âge." *Revue historique* 230:(1963) 25–72.

Fagerlie, Joan M. *Late Roman and Byzantine Solidi Found in Sweden and Denmark*. Numismatic Notes and Monographs, no. 157. New York, 1967.

Fertig, Michael. *Magnus Felix Ennodius' Lobrede auf Theoderich den Grossen, König der Ostgoten*. Landshut, 1858.

Fettich, Nándor. *A szilágysomlyoí második kincs—Der zweite Schatz von Szílágysomlyó*. Archaeologia Hungarica, no. 8. Budapest, 1932.

Filtzinger, Philipp. *Limesmuseum Aalen*. 2d ed. Stuttgart, 1975.

———. *Die Römer in Baden-Württemberg*. Stuttgart, 1976.

Fitz, Jenö. *Der Geldumlauf der römischen Provinzen im Donaugebiet Mitte des 3. Jahrhunderts*. Budapest, 1978.

Folz, R. *De l'Antiquité au monde médieval*. Paris, 1972.

Fowkes, R. A. "Crimean Gothic Cadarion 'Miles, Soldier,'" *Journal of English and German Philology* 45 (1946):448–49.

France-Lanord, A. "Le Polissage électrolytique et les répliques transparentes." *Conservation (Études de)*, vol. 7, pt. 4 (1962):121–33.

Freeman, J. D. "On the Concept of the Kindred." *Journal of the Royal Anthropological Institute of Great Britain and Ireland* 91 (1961):192–220.

Fridh, Åke. *Contributions à la critique et à l'interprétation des Variae de Cassiodore*. Acta Regiae Societatis Scientiarum et Litterarum Gothoburgensis. Humaniora, no. 4. Göteborg, 1968.

———. *Études critiques et syntaxiques sur les Variae de Cassiodore*. Göteborgs kungl. vetenskapsoch vitterhetssamhälle. Handlinger, 6 följden, ser. A, vol. 4, no. 2. Göteborg 1950.

———. *Terminologie et formules dans les Variae de Cassiodore; études sur la développment du style administratif aux derniers siècles de l'antiquité*. Studia graeca et latina Gothoburgensia, no. 2. Stockholm, 1956.

Fried, Morton. *The Notion of Tribe*. Cummings, 1975.

———. "Warfare, Military Organization, and the Evolution of Society." *Anthropologica* 3 (1961):134–47.

Fuchs, S. *Kunst der Ostgotenzeit*. Berlin, 1944.

Fülep, Ferenc. *Roman Cemeteries on the Territory of Pécs (Sopianae)*. Budapest, 1972.

———. *Sopianae: Die Stadt Pécs zur Römerzeit*. Budapest, 1975.

Gajdukevich, Viktor Francevich. *Das bosporanische Reich*. Berlin, Amsterdam, 1971.

Gajewska, Halina. *Topographie des fortifications romaines en Dobroudja*. Wrocław, 1974.

Gamillscheg, Ernest. *Romania germanica: Sprach- und Siedlungsgeschichte der Germanen auf dem Boden des alten Römerreichs*. Berlin, 1934.

Garnsey, Peter. *Social Status and Legal Privilege in the Roman Empire*. Oxford, 1970.

Gaudenzi, A. "Die Entstehungszeit des Edictum Theoderici." *Zeitschrift der Savigny-Stiftung für Rechtsgeschichte, Germ. Abt.* 7 (1887):29–52.

Gaupp, Ernst Theodor. *Die germanischen Ansiedlungen und Landtheilungen in den Provinzen des römischen Westreiches in ihrer völkerrechtlichen Eigenthümlichkeit und mit Rücksicht auf verwandte Erscheinungen der alten Welt und des späteren Mittelalters dargestellt*. Breslau, 1844.

Geiss, H. *Geld-und-naturwissenschaftliche Erscheinungsformen im staatlichen Aufbau Italiens während der Gotenzeit*. Vierteljahrsschrift für Sozial-und Wirtschaftsgeschichte, Beiheft 27. Stuttgart 1931.

Gerov, Boris. "L'Aspect éthnique et linguistique dans la région entre le Danube et les Balkans à l'époque romaine (I[e]–IIIe s.)." *Studi urbinati di storia, filosofia e letteratura*, n.s. B., 33 (1959):173–91.

———. "Die Einfälle der Nordvölker in den Ostbalkanraum im Lichte der Münzschatzfunde. I. Das II. und III. Jahrhundert (101–284)." In *Aufstieg und Niedergang der römischen Welt*, pt. 2, vol. 6, pp. 110–81. Berlin, 1977.

———. "Die gotische Invasion in Mösien und Thrakien unter Decius im Lichte der Hortfunde." *Acta Antiqua Philippopolitana, Studia histor. et. philol. Serdicae* 4 (1963):127–46.

Göbl, Robert. *Antike Numismatik*. Munich, 1978.

Godłowski, Kazimierz. *The Chronology of the Late Roman and Early Migration Periods in Central Europe*. Translated by Maria Wałega. Cracow, 1970.

Goessler, Peter. "Zur Belagerungskunst der Germanen." *Klio* 35 (1942):103–114.

Goffart, Walter. *Barbarians and Romans, A.D. 418–584: The Techniques of Accommodation*. Princeton, 1980.

Gordon, C. D., *The Age of Attila: Fifth-Century Byzantium and the Barbarians*. Ann Arbor, Mich., 1966.

Götze, Alfred. *Gotische Schnallen*. Berlin, 1913.

Grancsay, S. V. "A Barbarian Chieftain's Helmet." *Metropolitan Museum of Art, Bulletin* 7 (1949):272–81.

Grosse, Robert. *Römische Militärgeschichte von Gallienus bis zum Beginn der byzantinischen Themenverfassung*. Berlin, 1920.

Grumel, V. "L'Illyricum de la mort de Valentinian Ier (375) à la mort de Stilicon (408)." *Revue des études byzantines* 11 (1951):164–76.

Gschwantler, O. "Zum Namen der Rosomonen und an. Jonakr." *Die Sprache: Zeitschrift für Sprachwissenschaft* 17 (1971):164–76.

Guillou, André. *Régionalisme et indépendance dans l'empire byzantine au VIIe siècle: L'exemple de l'Exarchat et de la Pentapole d'Italie*. Rome, 1969.

Gundel, Hans Georg. "Die Bedeutung des Geländes in der Kriegskunst der Germanen." *Neue Jahrbücher für Antike und deutsche Bildung* 3 (1940):188–96.

———. *Untersuchungen zur Taktik und Strategie der Germanen nach den antiken Quellen*. Marburg, 1937.

Günther, R., ed. *Die Römer an Rhein und Donau: Zur politischen, wirtschaftlichen und sozialen Entwicklung in den römischen Provinzen am Rhein, Mosel und oberer Donau in 3. u. 4.J.* Berlin, 1975.

Haberl, Johanna. *Wien-Favianis und Vindobona: Eine archäologische Illustration zur Vita Severini des Eugippius.* Leiden, 1976.

Hachmann, Rolf. *The Germanic Peoples.* Translated by J. Hogarth. Geneva, 1971.

———. *Die Goten und Skandinavien.* Quellen und Forschungen zur Sprach-und Kulturgeschichte der germanischen Völker, no. 158. Berlin, 1970.

Hagberg, Ulf Erik, ed. *Studia Gotica: Die eisenzeitlichen Verbindungen zwischen Schweden und Südosteuropa.* Antikvariska serien, no. 25. Stockholm, 1972.

Hahn, Wolfgang. *Moneta Imperii Byzantini*, vols. 1–3. Österreichische Akad. d. Wis., phil-hist. Klasse, Denkschriften, vols. 109, 119, 148. Vienna, 1973, 1975, 1981.

Hammond, Nicholas G. L. *A History of Macedonia.* Vol. 1, *Historical Geography and Prehistory.* Oxford, 1972.

Hampel, Joseph. *Die Alterthümer des frühen Mittelalters in Ungarn.* Braunschweig, 1905. Reprint 1971.

Hannestad, Knud. *L'Évolution des ressources agricoles de l'Italie du IVe au VIe siècle de notre ère.* Historisk-filosofiske Meddelelser udgivet af Det Kongelige Danske Vindenskabernes Selskab, vol. 40, no. 1. Copenhagen, 1962.

———. "Les Forces militaires d'après la guerre gothique de Procope." *Classica et Medievalia* 29 (1960):136–83.

Harhoiu, Radu. "Aspects of the Socio-political Situation in Transylvania during the Fifth Century." In *Relations between the Autochthonous Populations and the Migratory Populations on the Territory of Romania*, ed. M. Constantinescu, pp. 99–109. Bucharest, 1975.

———. *The Fifth-Century A.D. Treasure from Pietroasa Romania.* British Archaeological Reports, supplementary series, no. 24. Oxford, 1977.

———. "Das norddonauländische Gebiet im 5. Jahrhundert und seine Beziehungen zum spätrömischen Kaiserreich." In *Die Völker an der mittleren und unteren Donau im 5. und 6. Jahrhundert*, ed. H. Wolfram and F. Daim, pp. 101–115. Vienna, 1980.

Harmatta, J. "The Dissolution of the Hun Empire," pt. 1: "Hun Society in the Age of Attila." *Acta Archaeologica* 2 (1952):277–305.

———. "Goten und Hunnen in Pannonien." *Acta Antiqua* 19 (1971):293–97.

———. "The Last Century of Pannonia." *Acta Antiqua* 18 (1970):361–69.

———. "Les Huns et le changement et conflict à la frontière Danubienne au IVe siècle après J.C." In *Transformation et conflicts au IVe siècle après J.C.*, ed. A. Alföldi and J. Straub, pp. 95–101. Bonn, 1978.

———. *Studies on the History of the Sarmatians.* Budapest, 1950.

Harrison, R. M. "The Emperor Zeno's Real Name." *Byzantinische Zeitschrift* 74 (1981):27–28.

Hartmann, L. M. "Anonymus Valesianus." *R-E* 1, pt. 2 (1894):2333–34.

———. *Geschichte Italiens im Mittelalter.* Gotha, 1903.

Hauck, Karl. *Goldbrakteaten aus Sievern.* Münstersche Mittelalterschriften, no. 1. Münster, 1970.

———. "Mainz und Odense. Brakteaten als Devotionalien aus christlichen und heidnischen Zentren." In *Münzen in Brauch und Aberglauben*, ed. H. Maúe and L. Veit, pp. 81–93. Mainz am Rhein, 1982.

Hauptmann, Ludmil. "Kroaten, Goten und Sarmaten." *Germanoslavica* 3 (1935): 95–127, 315–53.

Hawkes, Sonia Chadwick. "Soldier and Settlers in Britain, Fourth to Fifth Century: With a Catalogue of Animal-Ornamented Buckles and Related Belt-Fittings." *Medieval Archaeology* 5 (1961):1–71.

Heidenreich, Robert, and Johannes, Heinz. *Das Grabmal Theoderichs zu Ravenna.* Veröff. d. deutschen Archäolog. Instituts, no. 8, 1895. Wiesbaden, 1971.

Helbling, Hanno. *Goten und Wandalen.* Zürich, 1954.

Herlihy, David. "The Carolingian Mansus." *Economic History Review* 13 (1961): 79–89.

Hessen, Otto von; Kurze, Wilhelm; and Mastrelli, Carlo Alberto. *Il Tesoro di Golognano.* Firenze, 1977.

Heuberger, Richard. "Das ostgotische Rätien." *Klio* 30 (1937):77–109.

———. *Rätien im Altertum und Frühmittelalter.* Innsbruck, 1932. Reprint. Aalen, 1971.

Heurgon, J. *Le Trésor de Ténès.* Paris, 1958.

Heym, W. "Der ältere Abschnitt der Völkerwanderungszeit auf dem rechten Ufer der unteren Weichsel." *Mannus* 31 (1939):3–28.

Hillgarth, J. N. "La Conversión de los visigodos: Notas criticas." *Analecta Sacra Tarracenensia* 34 (1961):21–46.

Hitzinger, P. "Der Kampf des Kaisers Theodosius gegen den Tyrannen Eugenius am Flusse Frigidus." *Mittheilungen des historischen Vereines für Krain* 10 (1855): 81–85.

Hoddinott, R. F. *Bulgaria in Antiquity: An Archaeological Introduction.* New York, 1975.

Hodgkin, Thomas. *Italy and Her Invaders, 376–814.* Vol. 3, *The Ostrogothic Invasion 476–535.* New York, 1885.

———. *The Letters of Cassiodorus.* London, 1886.

Hoepffner, André. "Les 'Magistri militum praesentales' au IVe siècle." *Byzantion* 11 (1936):483–98.

Höfler, O. "Der Sakralcharakter des germanischen Königtums." In *Das Königtum, seine geistigen und rechtlichen Grundlagen,* Vorträge und Forschungen, vol. 3, ed. Th. Mayer, pp. 75–104. Lindau, Konstanz, 1956.

den Hollander, A. N. J. "The Great Hungarian Plain: A European Frontier Area." *Comparative Studies in Society and History* 3 (1960):74–88, 135–69.

Horedt, Kurt. "Neue Goldschätze des 5. Jahrhunderts aus Rumänien (ein Beitrag zur Geschichte der Ostgoten und Gepiden." In *Studia Gotica: Die eisenzeitlichen Verbindungen zwischen Schweden und Südosteuropa,* ed. Ulf E. Hagberg, pp. 105–116. Stockholm, 1972.

———. "Wandervölker und Romanen im 5. bis 6. Jahrhundert in Siebenburgen." In *Die Völker an der mittleren und unteren Donau im 5. und 6. Jahrhundert,* ed. H. Wolfram and F. Daim, pp. 117–21. Vienna, 1980.

Horedt, Kurt, and Protase, Dumitru. "Ein völkerwanderungszeitlicher Schatzfund aus Cluj-Someşeni." *Germania* 48 (1970):85–98.

———. "Das zweite Fürstengrab von Apahida (Siebenbürgen)." *Germania* 50 (1972):174–220.

Huebner, R. *A History of Germanic Private Law.* The Continental Legal History Series, vol. 4. Boston, 1918.

Iliescu, O. "Nouvelles informations relatives aux lingots romains d'or, trouvés en Transylvanie." *Revue des études sud-est européenes* 3 (1965):269–81.

Ioniţă, Ion. "The Social-Economic Structure of Society during the Goths' Migration in the Carpatho-Danubian Area." In *Relations between the Autochthonous Population and the Migratory Populations on the Territory of Romania,* ed., M. Constantinescu, pp. 77–89. Bucharest, 1975.

Jaskanis, Jan. "Human Burials with Horses in Prussia and Sudovia in the First

Millennium of our Era." *Acta Baltico-Slavica* 4 (1966):29–65.
Jellinek, Max Hermann. *Geschichte der gotischen Sprache*. Berlin, 1926.
Jones, A. H. M. "The Constitutional Position of Odoacer and Theodoric." *Journal of Roman Studies* 52 (1962):126–30.
———. *The Later Roman Empire: A Social, Economic, and Administrative Survey*. Norman, Oklahoma, 1964.
Jones, A. H. M.; Martindale, J. R.; and Morris, J. *The Prosopography of the Later Roman Empire*. 2 vols. Cambridge, 1971, 1980.
Jones, Christopher Prestige. *The Roman World of Dio Chrysostom*. Cambridge, Mass., 1978.
Jordanes. *Gothic History in English Version*. Translated by Charles C. Mierow, 2d. ed. Princeton, N.J., 1915. Reprint. New York, 1960.
Kaegi, Walter Emil. *Byzantium and the Decline of Rome*. Princeton, 1968.
Kahane, Anne; Threipland, Leslie M.; and Ward-Perkins, John. "The Ager Veientanus, North and East of Rome." *Papers of the British School at Rome* 36 (1968): 1–218.
Kähler, H. "Der Sockel des Theodosiusobelisken in Konstantinopel als Denkmal der Spätantike." *Acta ad archaeologiam et artium historiam pertinentia* 6 (1975): 45–55.
Karlsson, Gustav. "Goten, die in Osten blieben." In *Studia Gotica: Die eisenzeitlichen Verbindungen zwischen Schweden und Südosteuropa*, ed. Ulf E. Hagberg, pp. 165–74. Stockholm, 1972.
Karyshkorskii, P. D. "Sur l'histoire tardive d'Olbia." *Vestnik drevnei istorii* 103 (1968):167–79.
Kelemina, J. "Goti na Balkanu." *Casopis za zgodovino in Narodopisje* 27 (1932): 121–36.
Kempisty, A. "Some Problems of Research on the Roman Period in Masouria and Podlachia." *Acta Baltico-Slavica* 4 (1966):67–78.
Kenk, Roman. "Studien zum Beginn der jüngeren römischen Kaiserzeit in der Przeworsk-Kultur." *Bericht der römischen-germanischen Kommission* 58 (1977): 161–446.
Kent, John C. "The Coinage of Theodoric in the Names of Anastasius and Justin I." In *Mints, Dies, and Currency: Essays Dedicated to the Memory of Albert Baldwin*, ed. R. A. G. Carson, pp. 67–74. London, 1971.
———. "Julius Nepos and the Fall of the Western Empire." In *Corolla Memoriae Erich Swoboda dedicata*, pp. 146–50. Graz, 1966.
Kent, John C.; Overbeck, Bernhard; and v. Stylow, Armin. *Die römische Münze*. Munich, 1973.
Khvoika, V. V. "Polia pogrebenii v srednem Pridneprove." *Zapiski Russkogo arckheologicheskogo obshchestva* 12 (1906):42–50.
Kienast, Dietmar. *Untersuchungen zu den Kriegsflotten der römischen Kaiserzeit*. Antiquitas, ser. 1, vol. 13. Bonn, 1966.
Kiss, Attila. "Ein Versuch die Funde und das Siedlungsgebiet der Ostgoten in Pannonien zwischen 456–471 zu bestimmen." *Acta Archaeologica* 31 (1979): 329–39.
Kitzinger, E. "A Survey of the Early Christian Town of Stobi." *Dumbarton Oaks Papers* 3 (1946):81–182.
Kmieciński, Jerzy. "Niektoŕe spoleczne aspekty epizodu goekiego w orkesie środknworzymskim na Pomorzu." *Zeszyty Naukowe Uniwersytetu Lódzkiego, Nauki Humanist-Spol.*, ser. 1, vol. 12 (1959):3–22.
———. ed. *Odry Cmentarzysko kurhanowe z okresu rzymskiego*. Łódź, 1968.

———. "Problem of the So-called Gotho-Gepidian Culture in the Light of Recent Research." *Archaeologia Polona* 4 (1962):270–85.
———. *Zagadnienie tzw. Kultury gocko-gepid-zkiej na Pomorzu Wschodnim w okresie wczesnorzymsk'n.* Societas Scientiarum Lodziensis, sec. 2, vol. 46, Acta Archaeologica Lodziendzia, no. 11. Łódź, 1962.
Kolendo, Jerzy. "Les Influences de Rome sur les peuples de l'Europe centrale habitant loin des frontières de l'Empire." *Klio* 63 (1981):453–72.
Kollwitz, J. *Oströmische Plastik der theodosianischen Zeit.* Vol. 1, *Die Theodosiussäule.* Berlin, 1941.
Korkkanen, Irma. *The Peoples of Hermanaric: Jordanes, Getica 116.* Suomalainen tiedeakatemian toimituksia, Annales Academiae Scientiarum Fennicae, Ser. B., no. 187. Helsinki, 1975.
Korsunskii, A. R. "The Visigoths and the Roman Empire in the Late Fourth to Early Fifth Century" [in Russian]. *Vestnik Moskovskogo Universiteta* (istor. sektsiia) 3 (1963):87–95.
———. "Visigothic Social Structure in the Fourth Century" [in Russian]. *Vestnik drevnei istorii* 93 (1965):54–74.
———. "Small Landed Property in the Western Provinces of the Late Roman Empire" [in Russian]. *Vestnik drevnei istorii* 112 (1970):167–74.
Kossina, Gustaf. "Die ethnologische Stellung der Ostgermanen." *Indogermanische Forschungen* 7 (1897):276–312.
———. *Das Weichselland, ein uralter Heimatboden der Germanen.* Danzig, 1919.
Kostrzewski, Józef. "Le Problème du séjour des Germains sur les terres de Pologne." *Archaeologia Polona* 4 (1962):7–44.
Kovačevič, Jovan. *Varvarska Kolonizacija Južnoslovenskih Oblasti od IV do početka VII veka.* Musée de Voivodina Monographie, no. 2. Novi Sad, 1960.
Kovács, István. "A. M. Marosszentannai népvándozlaskori temetö." *Dolgozatok (Cluj)* 3 (1912):250–367.
Kovrig, I. "Nouvelles trouvailles du Ve siècle découvertes en Hongrie." *Acta Archaeologica* 10 (1959):209–225.
Kraus, Franz F. *Die Münzen Odovacars und des Ostgotenreiches in Italien.* Halle, 1928.
Krautschick, Stefan. *Cassiodor und die Politik seiner Zeit.* Habelts Dissertationsdrucke, Reihe alte Geschichte, no. 17. Bonn, 1983.
Kropotkin, V. V. "Topografiia rimskikh i rannevizantiiskikh monet na territorii SSSR." *Vestnik drevnei istorii* 3, no. 49 (1954):152–80.
Kubitschek, W. *Ausgewählte römische Medaillons der kaiserlichen Münzensammlung in Wien.* Vienna, 1909.
Kuharenko, Iurij V. "Le Problème de la civilisation gotho-gépide en Polésie et en Volhynie." *Acta Baltico-Slavica* 56 (1967):19–40.
Kühn, Herbert. *Die germanischen Bügelfibeln der Völkerwanderungszeit in der Rheinprovinz.* Die germanischen Bügelfibeln der Völkerwanderungszeit, vol. 1. Bonn, 1940. Revised reprint. Graz, 1962.
———. *Die germanischen Bügelfibeln der Völkerwanderungszeit in Süddeutschland.* Die germanischen Bügelfibeln der Völkerwanderungszeit, vol. 2. Graz, 1974.
de Laet, S. J.; Dhondt, J.; and Nenquin, J. "Les Laeti du Namurois et l'origine de la civilisation mérovingienne." *Études d'histoire de d'archéologie dediées à Ferdinand Courtoy* (Namur, 1952):149–72.
Lammert, Friedrich. "Zum Kampf der Goten bei Abrittus im J. 251." *Klio* 34 (1942):125–26.

Langenfelt, Gösta. "On the Origin of Tribal Names." *Anthropos* 14/15 (1919–20):295–313.

Laqueur, Richard. "Suidas (Lexikograph)." *R-E*, vol. 4, A 1 (1931):675–717.

Lasko, Peter. *The Kingdom of the Franks: North-West Europe before Charlemagne.* London, 1971.

Lattimore, Owen. *Studies in Frontier History*. Paris, 1962.

Lavagnini, B. *Belisario in Italia*. Pt. 1, *Storia di un anno (535–36)*. Atti Accad. di Scienze, Lett. & Arti di Palermo Ser. 4, vol. 8, no. 2, 1947–48. Palermo, 1948.

Leach, E. R. *Political Systems of Highland Burma: A Study of Kachin Social Structure.* Cambridge, Mass., 1954.

Lecce, M. "La vita economica dell'Italia durante la dominazione dei Goti nelle 'Variae' di Cassiodoro." *Economia e Storia, Rivista Italiana di Storia Economica e Sociale* 3, no. 4 (1956):354–408.

LeGentilhomme, Pierre. "Le Monnayage et la circulation monétaire dans les royames barbares en Occident (V[e]–VIIIe siècle)." *Revue numismatique* 7 (1943): 45–112.

Léglise, M. Stanislas. *Oeuvres complètes de Saint Ennodius évêque de Pavie*. Vol. 1: *Lettres*. Paris, 1906.

———. "Saint Ennodius et la haute éducation littéraire dans la monde romain au commencement du VIe siècle." *Revue des facultés catholiques (l'université catholique)* 5 (1892):209–228, 375–97, 568–90.

———. "Saint Ennodius et la suprématie pontificale au VIe siècle (499–503)." *Revue des facultés catholiques (l'université catholique)* 2 (1889):220–42, 400–415, 569–93; 3 (1890):513–23; 4 (1891):55–66.

Le Goff, Jacques. "Travail, techniques et artisans dan les systèmes de valeur du haut moyen âge (V[e]–Xe siècles)." *Settimane di Studio* 18 (1971):239–66.

Leighton, Albert C. *Transport and Communication in Early Medieval Europe, A.D. 500–1100*. New York, 1972.

Lengyel, Alfonz, and Radan, George, eds. *The Archaeology of Roman Pannonia.* Lexington, Kentucky and Budapest, 1980.

Lengyel, I. "Chemico-analytical Aspects of Human Bone Finds from the Sixth Century 'Pannonian' Cemeteries." *Acta Archaeologica* 23 (1971):155–66.

Levy, Ernst. Review of Alvaro d'Ors, *El Código de Eurico*. In *Zeitschrift der Savigny-Stiftung für Rechtsgeschichte, Röm. Abt.* 79 (1962):479–88.

———. *West Roman Vulgar Law: The Law of Property*. Philadelphia, 1951.

Lewicki, T. "Zagandnienie Gotów na Krymie." *Przegląd Zachodni* 7 (1951):78–99.

Liber Pontificalis. Translated and with introduction by Louise R. Loomis. New York, 1916. Reprint 1965.

Lippold, Adolf. "Herrscherideal und Traditionsverbundenheit im Panegyricus des Pacatus." *Historia* 17 (1968):228–50.

———. *Theodosius der Grosse und seine Zeit*. 2d ed. Munich, 1980.

Llewellyn, Peter A. B. "The Roman Church during the Laurentian Schism: Priests and Senators." *Church History* 45 (1976):417–27.

———. *Rome in the Dark Ages*. London, 1970.

Lot, F. "Du Régime de l'hospitalité." *Revue belge de philologie et d'histoire* 7 (1928):975–1011.

Lotter, Friedrich. "Zur Rolle der Donausueben in der Völkerwanderungszeit." *Mitteilungen des Instituts für österreichische Geschichtsforschung* 76 (1968):275–98.

———. *Severinus von Noricum, Legende und historische Wirklichkeit*. Untersuchungen zur Phase des Übergangs von spätantiken zu mittelalterlichen Denk- und Lebensformen, Monographien zur Geschichte des Mittelalters, no. 12. Stuttgart, 1976.

Löwe, Heinz. "Theoderichs Gepidensieg in Winter 488/89: Eine historisch-geographische Studie." In *Historische Forschungen und Probleme: Peter Rassow z. 70 Geburtstage dargebracht von Kollegen, Freunden und Schülern*, pp. 1–16. Cologne, 1961.

———. "Von Theoderich dem Grossen zu Karl dem Grossen: Das Werden des Abendlandes im Geschichtsbild des frühen Mittelalters." *Deutsches Archiv für Erforschung des Mittelalters* 9 (1952):353–401.

Löwe, Richard. "Der gotische Kalender." *Zeitschrift für deutsches Altertum und deutsche Litteratur* 59 (1922):245–90.

———. "Gotische Namen in hagiographischen Texten." *Beiträge zur Geschichte d. deutsche Sprache u. Litteratur* 47 (1923):407–433.

———. *Die Reste der Germanen am Schwarzen Meere*. Halle, 1896.

Lumpe, Adolf. "Die konziliengeschichtliche Bedeutung des Ennodius." *Annuarium Historiae Conciliorum* 1 (1969):15–36.

MacCormick, Sabine. *Art and Ceremony in the Late Roman Empire*. Berkeley, 1981.

MacKendrick, Paul. *The Dacian Stones Speak*. Chapel Hill, North Carolina, 1975.

MacMullen, Ramsay. "Barbarian Enclaves in the Northern Roman Empire." *Antiquité classique* 32 (1963):552–61.

———. *Constantine*. New York, 1969.

———. *Soldier and Civilian in the Later Roman Empire*. Cambridge, Mass., 1963.

Maenchen-Helfen, Otto J. "Germanic and Hunnic Names of Iranian Origin." *Oriens* 10 (1957):280–83.

———. *The World of the Huns: Studies in Their History and Culture*. Berkeley, 1973.

Magoun, Francis P., Jr. "On the Old-Germanic Altar—or Oath-Ring (Stallahringr)." *Acta Philologica Scandinavica* 20 (1949):277–93.

Mann, J. C. "The Role of the Frontier Zones in Army Recruitment." *Quintus Congressus Internationalis Limitis Romani Studiosorum*, 1961 pp. 145–50. Zagreb, 1963.

Manso-Zisi, Dorde. "O Granicama Periodizacije anticke Kulture." *Materjali IV. VII Kongres archaeologa Jugoslavije. Actes IV. VIIe Congrès des archéologiques yugoslaves*. Herceg-Novi, 1966, pp. 225–28. Belgrade, 1967.

Martin, Max, et al. "Burgunden." In *Reallexikon der germanischen Altertumskunde*, vol. 4, ed. H. Beck, pp. 224–71. Berlin, 1980.

Martin, Max. *Die Schweiz im Frühmittelalter*. Bern, 1975.

———. "Die spätrömisch-frühmittelalterliche Besiedlung am Hochrhein und im schweizerischen Jura und Mittelland." In *Von der Spätantike zum frühen Mittelalter*, ed. J. Werner and E. Ewig, Vortrage und Forschungen, vol. 25, pp. 411–46. Sigmaringen, 1979.

Matthews, J. F. "Olympiodorus of Thebes and the History of the West (407–425)." *Journal of Roman Studies* 60 (1970):79–97.

Matthews, John. *Western Aristocracies and Imperial Court, A.D. 364–425*. Oxford, 1975.

Mattingly, Harold; Sutherland, C. H. V.; and Carson, R. A. G. *The Roman Imperial Coinage*. London, 1936–66. Reprint 1972.

Mazzarino, Santo. *The End of the Ancient World*. Translated by G. Holmes. New York, 1966. Reprint. Westport, Conn., 1976.

Menner, R. J. "Crimean Gothic cadarion (cadariou), Latin centurio, Greek *κεντύριον*." *Journal of English and Germanic Philology* 36 (1937):168–75.

Mészáros, Gyula. "A Regölyi korai népvándorláskori fejedelmi sír [mit deuts. Auszug, 'Das Fürstengrab von Regöly aus der Frühvölkerwanderungszeit']." *Archaeologiai Értesítö* 97 (1970):66–93.

Metlen, M. "Letter of St. Jerome to the Gothic Clergymen Sunnia and Frithila Concerning Places in their Copy of the Psalter . . . ." *Journal of English and Germanic Philology* 36 (1937):515–42.

Millar, Fergus. *The Emperor in the Roman World, 31 B.C.–A.D. 337*. Ithaca, NY, 1977.

———. "P. Herennius Dexippus: The Greek World and the Third-Century Invasions." *Journal of Roman Studies* 59 (1969):12–29.

Miller, K. *Die Peutingersche Tafel*. Stuttgart, 1962.

Mirković, Miroslava. "Die Ostgoten in Pannonien nach dem Jahre 455." *Recueil des travaux de la faculté de philosophie* 10, no. 1 (Belgrade, 1968):119–28.

———. "Sirmium: Its History from the First Century A.D. to 582 A.D." *Sirmium I* (Belgrade, 1961):5–90.

Mitrea, Bucur. "La Migration des Goths reflétée par les trésors de monnaies romaines enfouis en Moldavie." *Dacia*, n.s. 1 (1957):229–36.

———. "Mogil'nik v sele independentsa i pogredenie v sele kokon k voprosy o kul'ture cyntana-de-muresh-Cherniakhovo" [Grave in the village of Independence and the burial in the village of Kokon, concerning the Sîntana de Mures-Cherniakhovo Culture]. *Dacia* 3 (1959):473–83.

Mitrea, Bucur, and Preda, Constantin. "Quelques problèmes ayant trait aux nécropoles de type Sîntana-Tcherniakhov découvertes en Valachie." *Dacia* 8 (1964):211–37.

Mócsy, András. "Der Name Flavius als Rangbezeichnung in der Spätantike." *Akten des IV. internationalen Kongresses für grieschische und lateinische Epigraphik*, pp. 257–63. Vienna, 1962.

———. *Pannonia and Upper Moesia*. London, 1974.

———. *Die spätrömische Festung und das Gräberfeld von Tokod*. Budapest, 1981.

Mohler, S. L. "The Iuvenes and Roman Education." *Transactions of the American Philological Association* 68 (1937):442–79.

Momigliano, A. D. "An Unsolved Problem of Historical Forgery: The Scriptores Historiae Augustae." *Journal of the Warburg and Courtauld Institutes* 17 (1954):22–46.

———. "Cassiodorus and Italian Culture of His Time." *Proceedings of the British Academy* 41 (1955):207–45. Reprinted in his *Studies in Historiography* (New York, 1966), pp. 181–210.

Mommsen, Theodor. "Der Begriff des Limes." *Westdeutsche Zeitschrift für Geschichte und Kunst* 13 (1894):134–43. Reprinted in *Gesammelte Schriften*, vol. 5 (*Historische Schriften*, vol. 2) (Berlin, 1908), pp. 456–64.

———. "Ostgotische Studien." *Neues Archiv der Gesellschaft für ältere deutsche Geschichtskunde* 14 (1888):225–43, 453–544. Nachträge 15 (1890):181–86. Reprinted in *Gesammelte Schriften*, vol. 6 (*Historische Schriften*, vol. 3) (Berlin, 1908), pp. 372–482.

Mongait, A. L. *Archaeology in the USSR*. Translated by M. W. Thompson. Harmondsworth. 1961.

Moorhead, John. "Boethius and Romans in Ostrogothic Service." *Historia* 27 (1978):604–612.

———. "The Last Years of Theodoric." *Historia* 32 (1983):106–120.

Moosbrugger-Leu, Rudolf. "Die Alamannen und Franken." In *Ur- und frühgeschichtliche Archäologie der Schweiz*, vol. 6, ed. W. Drack, pp. 39–52. Basel, 1979.

Morosi, R. "I *saiones*, speciali agenti di polizia presso i Goti." *Athenaeum* 59 (1981):150–65.

Moss, H. St. L. B. *The Birth of the Middle Ages*. Oxford, 1935.

Mossé, Fernand. "Bibliographia Gotica, A Bibliography of Writings on the Gothic Language to the End of 1949." *Mediaeval Studies* 12 (1950):237–320. First supplement, corrections, and additions to the middle of 1953, 15 (1953): 169–83).

Musset, Lucien. *The Germanic Invasions: The Making of Europe, A.D. 400–600.* Translated by Edward James and Columba James. University Park, Pennsylvania, 1975.

Nagy, T. "The Last Century of Pannonia in the Judgement of a New Monograph." *Acta Antiqua* 19 (1971):299–345.

———. "Reoccupation of Pannonia from the Huns in 427 (Did Jordanes Use the Chronicon of Marcellinus Comes at the Writing of the Getica?)" *Acta Antiqua* 15 (1967):159–86.

Nasturel, Petre S. "Les Actes de saint Sabas le Goth." *Revue de études sud-est européenes* 7 (1969):175–85.

Nehlsen, Hermann. *Sklavenrecht zwischen Antike und Mittelalter: Germanisches und römisches Recht in den germanischen Rechtsaufzeichnungen*, vol. 1: Ostgoten *Westgoten, Franken, Langobarden.* Gottingen Studien zur Rechtsgeschichte, no. 7. Gottingen, 1972.

Nenquin, Jacques A. *La Nécropole de Furfooz.* Brugge, 1953.

Nestor, I. "Les Données archéologiques et le problème de la formation du peuple roumain." *Revue Roumaine d'histoire* 3 (1964):383–420.

———. "La Fin du monde ancien et les 'Barbares,'" *VIII*[e] *Congrès international des sciences historiques.* Moscow, 1970.

Nischer, E. "The Army Reforms of Diocletian and Constantine and Their Modifications up to the Time of the Notitia Dignitatum." *Journal of Roman Studies* 13 (1923):1–55.

Odobesco, Alexandru. *Opera.* Vol. 4, *Le Trésor de Petrossa*, 1899–1900, with update and discussion "Studii arheologice," by Radu Harhoiu and Gh. Diaconu. Bucharest, 1976.

O'Donnell, James J. *Cassiodorus.* Berkeley, 1979.

———. "Liberius the Patrician." *Traditio* 37 (1981):31–72.

Okulicz, Lucja, and Okulicz, Jerzy. "The La Tène and the Roman Periods in Northern Masovia and in the Southern Mazurian Area in the Light of New Discoveries." *Archaeologia Polona* 4 (1962):286–94.

Oost, Stewart I. *Galla Placidia Augusta.* Chicago, 1968.

Opitz, S. *Südgermanische Runeninschriften im älteren Futhark aus der Merowingerzeit.* Kirchgarten, 1977.

Orlandis, José. *Historia de España: La España Visigótica.* Madrid, 1977.

Ostrogorsky, Georg. *Geschichte des byzantinischen Staates.* 3d. ed. Handbuch der Altertumswissenschaft, pt. 12, vol. 1, pt. 2. Munich, 1963.

Overbeck, Mechtild. *Untersuchungen zum afrikanischen Senatsadel in der Spätantike.* Kallmünz, 1973.

Oxenstierna, E. *Die Urheimat der Goten.* Leipzig, 1945.

Palanque, J. R. "St. Jerome and the Barbarians." In *A Monument to Saint Jerome*, ed. F. X. Murphy, pp. 171–200. New York, 1952.

Parducz, Mihály. "Der gotische Fund von Csongrád." *Dolgozatok* 14 (1938): 124–38.

Parker, H. M. D. *A History of the Roman World, A.D. 138–337.* 2d ed. London, 1958.

Parnicki-Pudełko, Stefan. "Les Recherches archéologiques polonaises à *Novae* (Bulgarie) en 1978." *Latomus* 39 (1980):891–97.

Pašalić, Esad. "Die Wirtschaftsbeziehungen zwischen dem Hinterland der Adria und dem römischen Limes an der Donau." *Quintus Congressus Internationalis Limitis Romani Studiosorum*, 1961 (Zagreb, 1963):167–75.

Patsch, K. *Die Völkerwanderung an der unteren Donau in der Zeit von Diocletian bis Heraclius*. Vienna, 1928.

Paunier, D. "Un Refuge du Bas-Empire au Mont-Musiège (Haute-Savoie)." *Museum Helveticum* 35 (1978):295–306.

Pavan, Massimiliano. *La Politica Gotica di Teodosio nella Pubblicisticà del suo Tempo*. Rome, 1964.

Pepe, Gabriele. *Le Moyen Âge barbare en Italie*. Translated by Jean Gonnet. Paris, 1956.

Percival, John. *The Roman Villa: A Historical Introduction*. Berkeley, 1976.

———. "Seigneurial Aspects of the Late Roman Estate Management." *English Historical Review* 84 (1969):449–73.

Petrescu-Dîmbovita, Mircea. "Die wichtigsten Ergebnisse der archäologischen Forschung über den Zeitraum vom 3.–10. Jh. östlich der Karpaten." *Dacoromania* 1 (1973):162–73.

Petrikovits, Harald von. "Germania (Romana)." *Reallexikon für Antike und Christentum* 10 (1978):548–654.

Pfeilschifter, Georg. *Der Ostgotenkönig Theoderich der Grosse und die katholische Kirche*. Kirchengeschichtliche Studien. ser. 3, no. 2. Münster, 1896.

Phillpotts, Bertha S. *Kindred and Clan in the Middle Ages and After: A Study on the Sociology of the Teutonic Races*. Cambridge, 1913.

Piétri, C. "Le Sénat, le peuple chrétien et les partis du cirque à Rome sous le pape Symmaque (498–514)." *Mélanges d'archéologie et d'histoire* 78 (1966):123–39.

Pietz, Wilhelm M. *Dionysius Exiguus-Studien*. Berlin, 1960.

Piotrowicz, Ludwik. "Goci i Gepidowie nad dolna wisla i ich wedrówka ku morzu Czarnemu i Dacji." *Przeglad Zachodni, Miesiecznik* 5/6 (1951):60–76.

Pleiner, R. "Experimental Smelting of Steel in Early Medieval Furnaces." *Památky Arch*. 60 (1969):458–87.

Póczy, Klára Sz. *Städte in Pannonien*. Budapest, 1976.

Polaschek, E. "Peucini." *R-E* 19 (1938):1391–92.

Pömer, Karl, ed. *Severin zwischen Römerzeit und Völkerwanderung*. Linz, 1982.

Pontieri, Ernesto. *Le Invasioni barbariche e l'Italia del V a VI secolo*. Naples, 1959–60.

Poole, Reginald L. *Chronicles and Annals: A Brief Outline of Their Origin and Growth*. Oxford, 1926.

Popescu, Emilian. "Das Problem der Kontinuität in Rumänien im Lichte der epigraphischen Entdeckungen." *Dacoromania* 1 (1973):69–77.

Post, Paul. "Der kupferne Spangenhelm: Ein Beitrag zur Stilgeschichte der Völkerwanderungszeit auf waffentechnischer Grundlage." *Bericht der römischen-germanischen Kommission* 34 (1951–53):115–50.

Powell, T. G. E. *The Celts*. London, 1958.

Preda, Constantin. "The Byzantine Coins—an Expression of the Relations between the Empire and the Populations North of the Danube in the Sixth–Thirteenth Centuries." In *Relations between the Autochthonous Populations and the Migratory Populations on the Territory of Romania*, ed. M. Constantinescu, pp. 219–33. Bucharest, 1975.

Preda, Constantin, and Simon, G. "Le Trésor de monnaies romaines impériales découvert à Isaccea (distr. de Tulcea) et l'attaque des Goths sous le règne de Gallien." *Peuce* 2 (1971):167–78.

Protase, Dumitru. "Considérations sur la continuité des Daco-Romains en Dacie post–aurelienne, à la lumière des recherches archéologiques et numismatiques." *Dacia* 8 (1964):177–93.

Przewoźna, D. "Osafa i cmentarzysko z okresu rzymskiego w Słopanowie, pow. Szamotuly." *Fontes Archaeologici Posnanienses* 5 (1954):60–140.

Rappaport, B. *Die Einfälle der Goten in das römische Reich bis auf Constantin.* Leipzig, 1899.

Rasi, Piero. "Ancora sulla paternità del c.d. 'Edictum Theodorici.'" *Annali di storia del diritto* 5/6 (1961–62):113–36.

———. "Sulla paternità di c.d. Edictum Theodorici regis." *Archivio giuridico* 145 (sixth series, vol. 14) (1953):105–162.

Reinecke, P. "Aus der russischen archäologischen Litteratur." *Mainzer Zeitschrift* 1 (1906):42–50.

Reiss, Edmund. "The Fall of Boethius and the Fiction of the *Consolatio Philosophiae.*" *Classical Journal* 77 (1981):37–47.

Remennikov, A. M. *Borba plemen Severnogo Prichenomoria s Rimom v III veke n.e.* Moscow, 1954.

Revillout, Charles-Jules. *L'Arianisme des peuples germaniques.* Ph.D. thesis. Paris, 1850.

Richards, Jeffrey. *The Popes and the Papacy in the Early Middle Ages, 476–752.* London, 1979.

Riché, Pierre. *Education and Culture in the Barbarian West, Sixth through Eighth Centuries.* Translated from 3d French ed. by J. J. Contreni. Columbia, South Carolina, 1976.

Richmond, Ian A. *The City Wall of Imperial Rome.* Oxford, 1930.

Riépnikoff, N. "Quelques cimetières du pays des Goths de Crimée." *Bull. de la com. impériale archéol.* 19 (1906):1–80.

Rostovtzeff, M. *Iranians and Greeks in South Russia.* Oxford, 1922.

Rougé, J. "Quelques aspects de la navigation en Méditerranée au Ve siècle et dans la première moitié du VIe siècle." *Cahiers d'histoire* 6 (1961):129–54.

Rowell, Henry T. *Ammianus Marcellinus: Soldier-Historian of the Late Roman Empire.* Semple Lectures. University of Cincinnati, 1964.

Rubin, Zeev. "The Conversion of the Visigoths to Christianity." *Museum Helveticum* 38 (1981):34–54.

Ruggini, L. Cracco. *Economia e società nell "Italia annonaria." Rapporti fra agricultura e commercio dal IV al VI secolo d.C.* Milan, 1961.

———. "Vicende rurali dell'Italia antica dall'età tetrarchica ai Longobardi." *Rivista storica Italiana* 76 (1964):261–86.

Rungg, Josef. *Ortsnamen der Goten, Römer, Franken in Rätien, Noricum, besonders Tirol.* Innsbruck, 1963.

Runkel, F. *Die Schlacht bei Adrianopel.* Berlin, 1903.

Russell, J. C. "That Earlier Plague." *Demography* 5 (1968):174–84.

Rusu, M. "Pontische Gürtelschnallen mit Adlerkopf (VI–VIII Jh. n.C.)." *Dacia* 3 (1959):485–523.

Sahlins, Marshall D. *Tribesmen.* Englewood Cliffs, New Jersey, 1968.

Salamon, Á., and Barkóczi, L. "Bestattungen von Csákvár aus dem Ende des 4. und dem Anfang des 5. Jahrhunderts." *Alba Regia* 11 (1970):35–80.

Salamon, Á., and Lengyel, I. "Kinship Interrelations in a Fifth-Century 'Pannonian' Cemetery: An Archaeological and Palaeobiological Sketch of the Population Fragment Buried in the Mözs Cemetery, Hungary." *World Archaeology* 12 (1980):93–104.

Salamon, Agnes, and Sós, Agnes A. "Pannonia-Fifth to Ninth Centuries." In

The Archaeology of Roman Pannonia, ed. A. Lengyel and G. Radan, pp. 397–426. Lexington, Kentucky, Budapest, 1980.

Salamon, Maciej. "The Chronology of Gothic Incursions into Asia Minor." *Eos* 59 (1971):109–39.

Salin, B. *Die altgermanische Thierornamentik*. Stockholm, 1904.

Salin, E. "Le Forgeron du haut moyen-âge, ses ancêtres, sa descendance." *Archaeologia* 14 (1967):78–81.

Salin, E., and France-Lanord, A. *Le Fer à l'époque mérovingienne*. Vol. 2 of *Rhin et Orient*. Paris, 1943.

Santos Yanguas, Narciso. *Los Pueblos Germanicos en la Segunda Mitad del Siglo IV. D.C.* Oviedo, 1976.

Sarnowski, Tadeusz. "La destruction des *principia* à Novae vers 316/317 de notre ère. Révolte militaire ou invasion Gothe?" *Archaeologia Polona* 30 (1979):119–28.

Sartorius, G. *Versuch über die Regierung der Ostgothen während ihrer Herrschaft in Italien*. Hamburg, 1811.

Šašel, Jaroslav. "Alpes Juliane." *Arheološki Vestnik* 22 (1970–71):33–44.

———. "Antiqui Barbari: Zur Besiedlungsgeschichte Ostnoricums und Pannoniens im 5. und 6. Jahrhundert nach den Schriftquellen." In *Von der Spätantike zum frühen Mittelalter*, ed. J. Werner and E. Ewig, pp. 125–39. Sigmaringen, 1979.

———. *Claustra Alpium Iuliarum*. Pt. 1, *Fontes*. Ljubljana, 1971.

———. "The Struggle between Magnentius and Constantius II for Italy and Illyricum." *Ziva Antika* 21 (1971):205–16.

Scardigli, Piergiuseppe. *Die Goten. Sprache und Kultur*. Munich, 1973.

Scavone, Daniel C. "Zosimus and His Historical Models." *Greek, Roman and Byzantine Studies* 11 (1970):57–67.

Schäferdiek, Knut. "Der germanische Arianismus: Erwägungen zum geschichtlichen Verständnis." *Miscellanea historiae ecclesiasticae* 3 (1970):71–83.

Schaffran, E. "Zur Nordgrenze des ostgotischen Reiches in Kärnten." *Österreichisches archäologisches Institut in Wien. Jahreshefte* (Beiblatt) 42 (1955):111–30.

Schindler, R. *Die Besiedlungsgeschichte der Goten und Gepiden im unteren Weichselraum auf Grund der Tongefässe*. Quellenschriften zur ostdeutschen Vör- und Frühgeschichte, no. 6. Leipzig, 1940.

Schlesinger, Walter. "Das Heerkönigtum." In *Das Königtum, seine geistigen und rechtlichen Grundlagen*. Vorträge und Forschungen, vol. 3, ed. Th. Mayer, pp. 105–141. Lindau, Konstanz, 1956.

———. "Herrschaft und Gefolgschaft in der germanisch-deutschen Verfassungsgeschichte." *Historische Zeitschrift* 176 (1953):225–75.

Schlette, Friedrich. *Germanen zwischen Thorsberg und Ravenna*. 3d ed. Leipzig, 1977.

Schmidt, B. "Theoderich der Grosse und die damaszierten Schwerter der Thüringer." *Ausgrabungen und Funde* 14 (1969):38–40.

Schmidt, Ludwig. "Die Comites Gothorum." *Mitteilungen des österreichischen Instituts für Geschichtsforschung* 40 (1925):127–34.

———. *Geschichte der deutschen Stämme bis zum Ausgang der Völkerwanderung. Die Ostgermanen*. 2d. rev. ed. Munich, 1941. Reprint 1969.

Schneider-Schnekenburger, G. *Churrätien im Frühmittelalter auf Grund der archäologischen Funde*. Münchner Beitrage Vor- u. Frühgeschichte, no. 26. Munich, 1980.

Schönberger, H. "The Roman Frontier in Germany: an Archaeological Survey," *Journal of Roman Studies*, 59 (1969):144–97.

Schönfeld, M. *Wörterbuch der altgermanischen Personen—und Völkernamen*. Heidelberg, 1911.

Schramm, P. E. *Herrschaftszeichen und Staatssymbolik*. Schriften der MGH, vol. 13, no. 1. Stuttgart, 1954.

Schroff, Helmut. *Claudians Gedicht vom Gotenkrieg*. Berlin, 1927.

Schukin, M. B. "Current Aspects of the Gothic Problem and the Cherniakhovo Culture." *Arkheologicheskifi sbornik* 18 (1977):79–91; English summary pp. 129–30.

———. "Das Problem der Černjachov-Kultur in der sowjetischen archäologischen Literatur." *Zeitschrift für Archäologie* 9 (1975):25–41.

Schwartz, Jacques. "Le Limes selon l'Histoire Auguste." *Bonner Historia-Augusta-Colloquium*, 1968–69, Antiquitas, ser. 4, no. 7, pp. 233–38. Bonn, 1970.

Seeck, Otto. *Geschichte des Untergangs der antiken Welt*. Vol. 1, 4th ed., 1921; vols. 2–6, 2d ed., 1920–22. Reprint Stuttgart, 1966.

Seeck, Otto, and Veith, G. "Die Schlacht am Frigidus." *Klio* 13 (1913):451–67.

Service, Elman Rogers. *Primitive Social Organization: An Evolutionary Perspective*. 2d ed. New York, 1971.

Seyfarth, Wolfgang. "Nomadenvölker an den Grenzen des spätrömischen Reiches: Beobachtungen des Ammianus Marcellinus über Hunnen und Sarazenen." *Das Verhältnis von Bodenbauern und Viehzüchtern in historischer Sicht*, Deutsche Akademie der Wissenschaften zu Berlin, Institut für Orientforschung, vol. 69, pp. 207–213. Berlin, 1969.

Sinnigen, William G. "Comites Consistoriani in Ostrogothic Italy." *Classica et Mediaevalia* 24 (1963):158–65.

———. "Administrative Shifts of Competence under Theoderic." *Traditio* 21 (1965):456–67.

Sjövold, T. "The Iron Age Settlements of Arctic Norway. A Study in the Expansion of European Iron Age Culture within the Arctic Circle." Pt. 1, "Early Iron Age: Roman and Migration Periods." *Tromsö Museums Skrifter*, vol. 10, pt. 1 (1962).

Skjelsvik, E. "The Stone Circles and Related Monuments of Norway." *Tirada a parte de la Cronica del IV Congresso Internacional de Ciencas Prehistoricas y Protohistoricas*, pp. 579–83. Madrid, 1954 (Zaragoza, 1956).

Slabe, Marijan. "La Nécropole de la période de la migration des peuples à Dravlje" [in Slovène with French summary]. *Arheološki Vestnik* 21–22 (1970–71):141–50.

Sophokles, E. A. *Greek Lexicon of the Roman and Byzantine Periods*. Cambridge, Mass., 1887. Reprint. New York, 1957.

Soproni, Sándor. *Der spätrömische Limes zwischen Esztergom und Szentendre*. Budapest, 1978.

Souter, Alexander. *A Glossary of Later Latin to 600* A.D. Oxford, 1949.

Spicer, Edward H. "Acculturation." *International Encyclopedia of the Social Sciences* 1 (1968):21–27.

Sprandel, Rolf. "Dux und Comes in der Merovingerzeit." *Zeitschrift der Savigny-Stiftung für Rechtsgeschichte, Germ. Abt.* 74 (1957):41–84.

———. "La production du fer au moyen âge." *Annales, Économies, Sociétés, Civilisations* 24 (1969):305–321.

———. "Struktur und Geschichte des merovingischen Adels." *Historische Zeitschrift* 193 (1961):33–71.

Stauffenberg, Alexander Schenk Graf von. *Macht und Geist: Vorträge und Abhandlungen zur alte Geschichte*. Munich, 1972.

Stefan, Friedrich. *Die Münzstätte Sirmium unter den Ostgoten und Gepiden: Ein*

Beitrag zur Geschichte des germanischen Münzwesens in der Zeit der Völkerwanderung. Halle, 1925.

Stefan, G. "Une Tombe de l'époque des migrations à Aldeni (Dep. de Buzau)." *Dacia* 7–8 (1941):217–21.

Stehlin, Karl. *Die spätrömischen Wachttürmen am Rhein von Basel bis zum Bodensee*. Schriften zur Ur- und Frühgeschichte der Schweiz, no. 10. Basel, 1957.

Stein, Ernst. *Histoire du Bas-Empire*. Vol. 2, *De la disparition de l'empire d'occident à la mort de Justinien (476–565)*, ed. J. R. Palanque. Bruges, 1950.

Stenberger, M. *Valhagar: A Migration Period Settlement on Gotland, Sveden*. Copenhagan, 1955.

Stevens, C. E. *Sidonius Apollinaris and His Age* (Oxford, 1933).

Stjernquist, Berta. *Simris: On Cultural Connections of Scania in the Roman Iron Age*. Acta Archaeologica Lundensia, series in 4°, no. 2. Lund, 1955.

Streitberg, Wilhelm August. *Die gotische Bibel*. Heidelberg, 1908. Reprint 1965.

Stroheker, Karl F. *Germanentum und Spätantike*. Zürich, Stuttgart, 1965.

———. *Der senatorische Adel im spätantiken Gallien*. Tübingen, 1948.

Sturms, E. "Das Problem der ethnischen Deutung der kaiserzeitlichen Gräberfelder in der Ukraine (mit einer Karte)." *Zeitschrift für Ostforschung* 2 (1953): 424–32.

Suceveanu, Al. "Observations sur la stratigraphie des cités de la Dobrogea aux IIe–IVe siècle à la lumière des fouilles d'Histria." *Dacia*, n.s. 13 (1969):327–65.

Sulimirski, Tadeusz. *The Sarmatians*. London, 1970.

Sundwall, Johannes. *Abhandlungen zur Geschichte des ausgehenden Römertums*. Suemen Tiedeseura, Oversikt av Finska vetenskaps—societetens förhandlingar, vol. 60. Helsinki, 1919. Reprint. New York, 1975.

Svennung, Josef Gusten Algot. *Jordanes und Scandia: Kritisch-exegetische Studien*. Acta Soc. Litt. Hum. Upsal., vol. 44, no. 2 A. Stockholm, 1967.

Syme, Ronald. *Emperors and Biography: Studies in the Historia Augusta*. Oxford, 1971.

———. *The Historia Augusta: A Call of Clarity*. Antiquitas, ser. 4, no. 8. Bonn, 1971.

Symonovich, E. A. "Toward the Question of the Scythian Affiliation of the Cherniakhov Culture." *Soviet Anthropology and Archaeology* 1, pt. 3 (1963):17–24.

Täckholm, U. "Aetius and the Battle of the Catalaunian Fields." *Opuscula Romana* 7 (1969):259–76.

Taylor, J. J. "The Early Papacy at Work: Gelasius I." *Journal of Religious History* 8 (1974–75):317–32.

Teja, R. "Invasions de Godos en Asia Menor antes y depués de Adrianopolis (375–382)." *Hispania Antiqua* 1 (1971):169–77.

Teodor, Dan Gheorghe. *The East Carpathian Area of Romania in the V–XI Centuries* A.D. British Archaeological Reports, supplementary series, no. 81. Oxford, 1980.

The Theodosian Code and Novels and the Sirmondian Constitutions. Translated by Clyde Pharr. Princeton, N.J., 1952. Reprint. New York, 1969.

Thibault, Fabien. "L'Impôt direct dans les royaumes des Ostrogoths, des Wisigoths et des Burgundes." *Nouvelle revue historique de droit français et étranger* 25 (1901):698–728, 26 (1902):32–48.

Thomas, B. *Römische Villen in Pannonien. Beiträge zur pannonischen Siedlungsgeschichte*. Budapest, 1964.

Thompson, E. A. "Christianity and the Northern Barbarians." In *The Conflict between Paganism and Christianity in the Fourth Century*, ed. A. D. Momigliano, pp. 56–78. Oxford, 1963.

———. "Constantine, Constantius II, and the Lower Danube Frontier." *Hermes* 84 (1956):372–81.

———. "The Conversion of the Visigoths to Catholicism." *Nottingham Medieval Studies* 4 (1960):4–35.

———. *The Early Germans.* Oxford, 1965.

———. "The End of Roman Spain." *Nottingham Medieval Studies.* Pt. 1, "Hydatius, Settlement of Sueves," 20 (1976):3–28; pt. 2, "The Suevic Ascendancy," 21 (1977):3–31; pt. 3, "The Visigothic Conquest," 22 (1978):3–22; pt. 4, "Conclusion and Appendices," 23 (1979):1–21.

———. *The Goths in Spain.* Oxford, 1969.

———. *The Historical Work of Ammianus.* Cambridge, 1947.

———. *A History of Attila and the Huns.* Oxford, 1948.

———. "Olympiodorus of Thebes." *Classical Quarterly* 38 (1944):43–52.

———. Review of *Die Auswanderung der Goten aus Schweden* by Curt Weibull. *Journal of Roman Studies* 50 (1960):288.

———. *Romans and Barbarians: The Decline of the Western Empire.* Madison, Wisconsin, 1982.

———. "The Settlement of the Barbarians in Southern Gaul." *Journal of Roman Studies* 46 (1956):65–76.

———. "The Visigoths from Fritigern to Euric." *Historia* 12 (1963):105–126.

———. *The Visigoths in the Time of Ulfila.* Oxford, 1966.

Thompson, Margaret. *The Athenian Agora.* Vol. 2, *Coins.* Princeton, 1954.

Thomsen, Rudi. *The Italic Regions from Augustus to the Lombard Invasion.* Classica et Mediaevalia, Dissertationes, no. 4. Copenhagen, 1947.

Todd, Malcolm. *Everyday Life of the Barbarians: Goths, Franks, and Vandals.* Putnam, NY., 1972.

Todorov, Yanko. *Le grandi strade romane in Bulgaria.* Istituto di Studi Romani, Quaderni dell'Impero, ser. 2, vol. 16, Le grandi strade del mondo romano. Rome, 1937.

Tolkin, Ch. "The Battle of the Goths and the Huns." *Saga—Book of the Viking Society* 14 (1953–57):141–63.

Tóth, Endre. "Zur Geschichte des nordpannonischen Raumes im 5. und 6. Jahrhundert." In *Die Völker an der mittleren und unteren Donau im 5. und 6. Jahrhundert,* ed. H. Wolfram and F. Daim, pp. 93–100. Vienna, 1980.

Toynbee, Jocelyn M. C. *Roman Medallions.* Numismatic Studies, no. 5. New York, 1944.

Tudor, Dimitru. "Preuves archéologiques attestant la continuité de la domination romaine au nord du Danube après l'abandon de la Dacie sous Aurélian (IIIe–Ve siècles)." *Dacoromania* 1 (1973):149–61.

———. *Sucidava, une cité daco-romaine et byzantine en Dacie.* Collection Latomus, no. 80. Brussels, 1965.

Turney-High, Harry H. *Primitive War: Its Practice and Concepts.* 2d ed. Columbia, South Carolina, 1971.

Udalcova, Zinaida V. "La Campagne de Narses et l'écrasement de Totila." *Corsi di Cultura sull'arte ravennate e bizantina* 18 (1971):557–64.

Udalcova, Zinaida V., and Goutnova, E. V. "La Genèse du féodalisme dans les pays d'Europe." *XIII Congrès international des sciences historiques.* Moscow, 1970.

Ulbert, Thilo, ed. *Ad Pirum (Hrusica): Spätrömische Passbefestigung in den julischen Alpen.* Münchner Beiträge zur Vor- und Frühgeschichte, no. 31. Munich, 1981.

Ulbert, Thilo. "Zur Siedlungskontinuität im südöstlichen Alpenraum (vom 2. bis 6. Jahrhundert n. Chr.). Dargestellt am Beispiel von Vranje (ehem. Untersteiermark)." In *Von der Spätantike zum frühen Mittelalter*, ed. J. Werner and E. Ewig, pp. 141–57. Sigmaringen, 1979.

Utsenko, S. L., and D'iaknov, I. M. "Social Stratification of Ancient Society." *13th International Congress of Historians*. Moscow, 1970.

Vágó, Esyter B., and Bóna, István. *Die Gräberfelder von Intercisa*. Vol. 1: *Der spätrömische Südostfriedhof*. Budapest, 1976.

Valentin, L. Chanoine. *Saint Prosper de l'Aquitaine: Étude sur la littérature latine ecclésiastique au cinquième siècle en Gaule*. Toulouse, 1900.

Várady, László. *Das letzte Jahrhundert Pannoniens, 376–476*. Amsterdam, 1969.

Vasiliev, A. A. *The Goths in Crimea*. Cambridge, Mass., 1936.

Velkov, V. "Ein Beitrag zum Aufenthalt des Kaisers Theodosius I in der Provinz Skythien im Jahr 386 im Lichte neuer Erkenntnisse." *Eunomia* 5 (1961):49–62.

———. *Roman Cities in Bulgaria: Collected Studies*. Amsterdam, 1980.

Vercauteren, F. "La Ruine des villes de la Gaule." *Brussels université libre. Institute de philologie et d'histoire orientales. Annuaire* 2 (1934):955–63.

Vernadsky, George. "The Eurasian Nomads and Their Impact on Medieval Europe." *Studi Medievali*, ser. 3, vol. 4, pt. 2 (1963):401–34.

Vinskí, Zdenko. "Die völkerwanderungszeitliche Nekropole in Kranj und der Reihengräberfelder Horizont des 6. Jahrhunderts im westlichen Jugoslawien." *Actes du VIIIe congrès international des sciences préhistoriques et protohistoriques*, pp. 253–65. Belgrade, 1971.

———. "Kranj et l'horizon de necropoles en rangées du VIe S. en Yougoslavie occidentale" [in Slovene with French summary]. *Acta Archaeologica. Arheološki Vestnik. Académie Slovène* 21–22 (1970–71):151–52.

———. "Zikadenschmuck aus Jugoslawien." *Jahrbuch des römisch-germanischen Zentralmuseums Mainz* 4 (1957):136–60.

Vismara, Giulio. *Edictum Theoderici*. Ius Romanum Medii Aevi, pars 1, 2b, aa, α. Milan, 1967.

———. "El 'Edictum Theodorici.'" In *Estudios visogóticos* (Rome, Madrid, 1956), pt. 1, pp. 49–89. Cuadernos del Instituto Juridico Español, vol. 5.

———. "Romani e Goti di fronte al diritto nel Regno Ostrogoto." *Settimane di Studio* 3 (1955):409–63.

Vogel F. "Chronologische Untersuchungen zu Ennodius." *Neues Archiv der Gesellschaft für ältere deutsche Geschichtskunde* 23 (1898):53–74.

Vogt, Joseph. *Kulturwelt und Barbaren: Zum Menschheitsbild der spätantiken Gesellschaft*. Abhandl. der Akad. der Wiss. in Mainz, Geistes- und Sozial-Wissen. Klasse, 1967, no. 1.

Vries, J. de. *Altgermanische Religionsgeschichte*. 2d ed. Berlin, 1956.

———. "Das Königtum bei den Germanen." *Saeculum* 7 (1956):289–309.

Vučkovič-Todorovič, D. "Recherches récentes sur le Limes Danubien en Servie." *Quintus Congressus Internationalis Limitis Romani Studiosorum* 1961 (Zagreb, 1963):183–94.

Vulpe, Radu. *Le Vallum de la Moldavie inférieure et le "mur" d'Athanaric*. The Hague, 1957.

———. "Les *valla* de la Valachie, de la Basse-Moldavie et du Boudjak." *Actes du IXe congrès international d'études sur les frontières romaines*, Mamia, Sept. 1972, ed. D. M. Pippidi, pp. 267–76. Bucharest, Cologne, Vienna, 1974.

Vyver, A. van der. "Cassiodore et son oeuvre." *Speculum* 6 (1931):244–92.

Wagner, Norbert. *Getica: Untersuchungen zum Leben des Jordanes und zur frühen Geschichte der Goten*. Berlin, 1967.

Waitz, Georg. *Deutsche Verfassungsgeschichte*. Vol. 1, *Die Verfassung des deutschen Volkes in ältester Zeit*. 2d ed. Berlin, 1880.

Wallace-Hadrill, J. M. *Early Germanic Kingship in England and on the Continent.* Oxford, 1971.

Walter, Christopher. "Raising on a Shield in Byzantine Iconography." *Revue des études byzantines* 33 (1975):133–75.

Wasowicz, A. *Olbia pontique et son territoire.* Ann. Litt. de l'Univ. de Besançon, no. 168. Paris, 1975.

Weibull, Curt. *Die Auswanderung der Goten aus Schweden.* Göteborgs kungl. vetenskapsoch vitthetssamhälles. Handlingar, 6 följden, ser. A, vol. 6, no. 5. Göteborg, 1958.

Wells, C. M. *The German Policy of Augustus: An Examination of the Archaeological Evidence.* Oxford, 1972.

Wenskus, R. "Amaler." In *Reallexikon der Germanischen Altertumskunde* 1 (1973): 224–71.

Wenskus, Reinhard. *Stammesbildung und Verfassung: das Werden der frühmittelalterlichen gentes.* 2d ed. Cologne, 1977.

Werner, Joachim. "Die archäologischen Zeugnisse der Goten in Südrussland, Ungarn, Italien und Spanien." *Settimane di Studio* 3 (1956):127–30.

———. *Beiträge zur Archäologie des Attila-Reiches.* Bayerische Akademie der Wissenschaften, philosophisch-historische Klasse, Abhandlungen, n.s. 38ª–40. Munich, 1956.

———. "Fernhandel und Naturalwirtschaft im östlichen Merowingerreich nach archäologischen und numismatischen Zeugnissen." *Bericht der römisch-germanischen Kommission* 42 (1961):307–346.

———. "Der goldene Armring des Frankenkönigs Childerich und die germanischen Handgelenkringe der jüngeren Kaiserzeit. Mit einem Anhang von L. Pauli." *Frühmittelalterliche Studien* 14 (1980):1–49.

———. "Der Grabfund von Taurapilis Rayon Utna (Litauen) und die Verbindung der Balten zum Reich Theoderichs." *Archäologische Beiträge zur Chronologie der Völkerwanderungszeit*, Antiquitas, ser. 3, no. 20, pp. 87–92. Bonn, 1977.

———. "Kriegergräber aus der ersten Hälfte des 5. Jahrhunderts zwischen Schelde und Weser." *Bonner Jahrbücher* 157 (1958):372–413.

———. *Die Langobarden in Pannonien: Beiträge zur Kenntnis der langobardischen Bodenfunde vor 568.* Bayerische Akad. d. Wissenschaften, phil.-hist. Klasse, Abh., n.s. 55a. Munich, 1962.

———. "Neue Analyse des Childerichgrabes von Tournai." *Rheinische Vierteljahrsblätter* 35 (1971):43–46.

———. "Ostgotische Bügelfibeln aus bajuwarischen Reihengräbern." *Bayerische Vorgeschichtsblätter* 26 (1961):68–75.

———. "Eine ostgotische Prunkschnalle von Köln-Severinstor (Studien zur Sammlung Diergardt II)." *Kölner Jahrbuch für Vor- und Frühgeschichte* 3 (1958): 55–61.

———. "Studien zu Grabfunden des V. Jahrhunderts aus der Slowakei und der Karpatenukraine." *Slovenská Archeologia* 7 (1959):422–38.

———. "Zu den auf Oland und Gotland gefundenen byzantinischen Goldmünzen." *Fornvännen* 44 (1949):257–86.

———. "Zur Entstehung der Reihengräberzivilisation: ein Beitrag zur Methode der frühgeschichtlichen Archäologie." *Archaeologica Geographica* 1 (1950):23–32. Reprinted in F. Petri, ed., *Siedlung, Sprache und Bevölkerungsstruktur im Frankenreich* (Darmstadt, 1973), pp. 285–325, with update to 1972.

———. "Zur Herkunft der frühmittelalterlichen Spangenhelme." *Prähistorische Zeitschrift* 34–35 (1949–50):178–93.

———. "Zur Herkunft und Zeitstellung der Hemmorer Eimer und der Eimer mit gewellter Kannelure." *Bonner Jahrbücher* 140/141 (1936):395–410.

Werner, Joachim, and Ewig, E., eds. *Von der Spätantike zum frühen Mittelalter: Aktuelle Probleme in historischer und archäologischer Sicht*. Vorträge und Forschungen, vol. 25. Sigmaringen, 1979.

Wes, M. A. *Das Ende des Kaisertums im Westen des römischen Reichs*. Archeologische Studien van het Nederlands Historisch Instituut te Rome, no. 3. The Hague, 1967.

Wheeler, Mortimer. *Rome beyond the Imperial Frontiers*. London, 1954.

Wilkes, John J. *Dalmatia*. London, 1969.

Wiseman, James. *Stobi: A Guide to the Excavations*. Belgrade, 1973.

Wołagiewicz, Ryszard. "Der Zufluss römischer Importe in das Gebiet nördlich der mittleren Donau in der älteren Kaiserzeit." *Zeitschrift für Archäologie* 4 (1970):222–49.

Wolfram, Herwig. *Geschichte der Goten: Von den Anfängen bis zur Mitte des sechsten Jahrhunderts. Entwurf einer historischen Ethnographie*. 2d ed. Munich, 1980.

———. "Gotisches Königtum und römisches Kaisertum von Theodosius dem Grossen bis Justinian I." *Frühmittelalterliche Studien* 13 (1979):1–28.

———. "Gotische Studien." *Mitteilungen des Instituts fur österreichische Geschichtsforschung*. Pt. 1, "Das Richertum Athanarichs," 83 (1975):1–32; pt. 2, "Die terwingische Stammesverfassung und das Bibelgotische (I)," 83 (1975):289–324; pt. 3, "Die terwingische Stammesverfassung und das Bibelgotische (II)," 84 (1976):239–61.

———. "Die Schlacht von Adrianopel." In *Veröffentlichungen der Kommission für Frühmittelalterforschung*, vol. 1, Sonderabdruck aus dem Anzeiger der philosophisch-historische Klasse der österreichischen Akademie der Wissenschaften, no. 114, pp. 227–50. Vienna, 1977.

Wolfram, Herwig, and Daim, Falko. *Die Völker an der mittleren und unteren Donau im 5. und 6. Jahrhundert: Berichte des Symposions der Kommission für Frühmittelalterforschung, 24–27 October, 1978*. Veröff. d. Komm. f. Frühmittelalterforschung, ser. 4, Denkschriften, vol. 145. Vienna, 1980.

Woloch, G. Michael. "A Survey of Scholarship on Ostrogothic Italy (A.D. 498–552)." *Classical Folia* 25 (1971):320–56.

Wozniak, Frank E. "East Rome, Ravenna, and Western Illyricum: 454–536 A.D." *Historia* 30 (1981):351–82.

Wrede, Ferdinand. *Über die Sprache der Ostgoten in Italien*. Quellen und Forschungen zur Sprach- und Kulturgeschichte der germanischen Völker, vol. 68. Strassburg, 1891.

Wroth, W. *Catalogue of the Coins of the Vandals, Ostrogoths, and Lombards and of the Emperors of Thessalonica, Nicaea, and Trebizond in the British Museum*. London, 1911.

Yü, Ying-shih. *Trade and Expansion in Han China: A Study in the Structure of Sino-Barbarian Economic Relations*. Berkeley, 1967.

Zaharia, E. M., and Zaharia, N. "Les Nécropoles des IVe–Ve siècles de Botoşani-Dealul (Cărămidărieé)." *Dacia* 19 (1975):201–226.

Zecchini, Giuseppe. "I 'gesta de Xysti purgatione' e le fazioni aristocratiche a Roma alla metà del V secolo." *Revista di storia della Chiesa in Italia* 34 (1980): 60–74.

Zeiller, Jacques. "Étude sur l'arianisme en Italie à l'époque ostrogotique et à l'époque lombarde." *Mélanges d'archéologie et d'histoire publiés par l'école française de Rome* 25 (1905):127–46.

———. *Les Origines chrétiennes dans les provinces danubiennes de l'empire romain.* Studia Historica, no. 48. Paris, 1918. Reprint. Rome, 1967.

Zeiss, H. "Die Donaugermanen und ihr Verhältnis zur römischen Kultur nach der Vita Severini." *Ostbayerische Grenzmarken* 17 (1928):9–13.

———. "Zur ethnischen Deutung frühmittelalterlicher Funde." *Germania* 14 (1930):11–24.

———. "Die Nordgrenze des Ostgotenreiches." *Germania* 12 (1928):25–34.

Ziegler, A. K. "Pope Gelasius I and His Teachings on the Relation of Church and State." *Catholic Historical Review* 27 (1941–42):412–37.

Zimmerman, Franz Xaver. "Der Grabstein der ostgotischen Königstocher Amalafrida Theodenanda in Genazzano bei Rom." In *Festschrift für Rudolf Egger*, vol. 2, pp. 330–54. Klagenfurt, 1953.

Zimmermann, Odo John. *The Late Latin Vocabulary of the Variae of Cassiodorus.* Washington, D.C. 1944.

Zink, Georges. *Les Légendes héroiques de Dietrich et d'Ermrich dans les littératures germaniques.* Lyons and Paris, 1950.

Zwikker, W. *Studien zur Markussäule.* Archeologisch-historische bijdragen, no. 8. Amsterdam, 1941.

INDEX